PRACTICAL
BUSINESS
PSYCHOLOGY

THIRD EDITION

DONALD A. LAIRD, Ph.D., Sc.D.

ELEANOR LAIRD

GREGG PUBLISHING DIVISION

McGraw-Hill Book Company, Inc.

NEW YORK · CHICAGO · DALLAS · CORTE MADERA, CALIF.
TORONTO · LONDON

PRACTICAL BUSINESS PSYCHOLOGY, *Third Edition*

5 6 7 8 9 0 QB-61 9 8 7 6 5 4

Library of Congress Catalog Card No. 60-9848

PUBLISHED BY GREGG PUBLISHING DIVISION
McGraw-Hill Book Company, Inc.
Printed in the United States of America

Preface

Practical Business Psychology, Third Edition, adheres faithfully to the original objective of the first edition published in 1951. It strives to give the reader a summary of modern psychology that is interesting and readable in a form that can be readily applied to help him become a more efficient worker and a more effective leader.

Because the book has become widely used for business training, both in schools and within industry, most of the changes in the present revision have been in details that will make it an easier book to teach, and also more adapted to self-instruction or home study.

Most of the material about the technical methods used by psychologists has been dropped. The book is now aimed directly toward orienting the reader to the human problems he will encounter and the personal adjustments he will likely need to make to get ahead and be happy in modern business life. In a sense, this is a "success book," but with a difference—how to organize your life for a career in business by applying some research findings about human nature in business life.

This book emphasizes principles, or rules, which the employee or employer can put to practical use, whether on an assembly-line job or at the big desk in the front office. The examples and applications deal mostly with white-collar work and with large firms where the majority of people are employed. Both the "why" and the "how to" are considered.

To make it easier to grasp and apply the principles, there has been a major revision in the aids for teaching and studying the book. For instance, some thirty chartoons and other visual aids have been added. Most of these give a concise summary of pertinent research findings, without burdening the reader with details about the research methods and design. Review questions, "The Gist of the Chapter," have been added to guide home study and also to help class recitations.

There has been some rearrangement of sections to make fuller use of the "spiral treatment" by which topics are developed in easy-to-comprehend steps. This spiral treatment also provides an automatic review, which should make it easier to remember the basic points.

More attention has been given to projects, "Things to Do," and these should supply the teacher with additional demonstration material. Some of the projects can be adapted for role-playing demonstrations.

The "Problems to Discuss" have been increased in number and made more pointed. For most of the problems, as with those in business life, there is no "one best answer." There are, instead, "several good answers," depending on many factors in the situation. This true-to-life quality adds to the usefulness of the problems for stimulating group discussion. The problems have been considered extremely useful for giving readers some "skull practice" in making use of psychology in situations they are likely to face later in business life.

Some instructors prepared objective examinations for the previous edition. Most of these questions can be used with the present edition. Any bona fide instructor can obtain more information about these tests by writing to the authors in care of the publisher.

As with the preceding editions, business teachers and industrial trainers have given us useful and highly appreciated assistance in deciding what to put into the book. For this revision, we give a hearty thank-you for suggestions we solicited from: Sherwood D. Burgess, Oakland, Calif.; Edward E. Byers, Boston, Mass.; Melvin Davidson, Buffalo, N.Y.; Walter E. Kamprath, Minneapolis, Minn.; Don E. Matthews, Salt Lake City, Utah; Louise B. Miller, Bangor, Maine; Morris S. Pierson, Spokane, Wash.; Roberta H. Rucker, Dallas, Tex.; and Dean Sweetland, Spartanburg, S. C.

Thanks are also given to the psychologists and sociologists for checking the accuracy of the chartoons, which are simplifications of some of their research findings.

Donald A. Laird
Eleanor C. Laird

Contents

part 1

Personal Efficiency

PERSONAL EFFICIENCY is the topic of the chapters in Part 1 of this book. Here are some practical questions that will help you anticipate some of the aspects of personal efficiency to be discussed. One of the answers given to each question is better than the others. Check the one you think is the best. After reading all the chapters in Part 1, change any of the answers you wish.

1. *The best way to increase personal efficiency is to:*
   ___ Take work home nights.
   ___ Find and then use efficient methods.
   ___ Work faster.
   ___ Be ambitious.

2. *The best method the boss can use to make his workers more efficient is to:*
   ___ See that their equipment is modern.
   ___ Tell them they have to produce more.
   ___ Remove hindrances, irritations, and frustrations.
   ___ Promise a bonus if they do better.

3. *The best procedure to make people willing to use more efficient methods is to:*
   ___ Explain how superior the new method is.
   ___ Discipline them if they do not use the new method.
   ___ Make them ashamed of the inefficient method they have been using.
   ___ Get them to help plan the more efficient method.

4. *The best way to improve one's social efficiency is to:*
   ___ Read the society news regularly.
   ___ Wear the latest style of clothes.
   ___ Make the other person feel at ease and appreciated.
   ___ Let others know how important we are.

5. *Efficient concentration on work is best attained by:*
   ___ Working where there are no distractions.
   ___ Writing everything down.
   ___ Having confidence in your ability to concentrate.
   ___ Reprimanding people who interrupt you.

6. *Efficiency in reading is helped most by:*
   ___ Reading for the meaning.
   ___ Pronouncing the words carefully.
   ___ Reading in spare moments.
   ___ Watching for misprints.

7. *Efficiency in remembering is increased most when we:*
   ___ Use a "memory system."
   ___ Ask someone to remind us.
   ___ Tie a string on a finger.
   ___ Try to remember.

8. *A job is learned most efficiently by:*
   ___ Watching an expert work on it.
   ___ Wanting to learn.
   ___ Thinking you have done poorly.
   ___ Noticing others' mistakes.

9. *The day's efficiency is helped most if the work is organized so that:*
   ___ Hard and easy tasks are alternated.
   ___ You will win a contest.
   ___ You don't have to correct errors.
   ___ You can work steadily without stopping.

10. *The best way to save a worker's energy is to:*
    ___ Make sure he goes to bed early.
    ___ Teach him how to work loose-and-easy.
    ___ Give him free vitamin capsules.
    ___ Have him work with his back to the light.

11. *The best way to judge a person's aptitude for a particular job is to:*
    ___ Decide whether he looks intelligent.
    ___ Detect his weak points.
    ___ Analyze what the job takes and what the applicant has.
    ___ Go by his letters of recommendation.

12. *The best method for keeping workers from stalling at work is to:*
    ___ Broadcast music in the workplace.
    ___ Discharge a shirker at once.
    ___ Supervise them closely every minute.
    ___ Get the work group to co-operate in setting a quota.

1 ■ PSYCHOLOGY IN BUSINESS LIFE AND EFFICIENCY

_ _ _ _ _ _ _ _ _ _ _ _ _ _

WHAT THIS CHAPTER IS ABOUT

1. _People are important in business and psychology_
2. _Groups are important to people_
3. _Books can be important to people in business_
4. _The importance of efficiency for every-body_
5. _Opportunities for greater efficiency_
6. _Gains in productivity_
7. _How the boss estimates personal efficiency_
8. _What efficiency means in muscle work_
9. _Hidden inputs that lower efficiency_
10. _Psychological efficiency_

> Read this before you read the chapter.

1 ■ People Are Important in Business and Psychology

Sometimes a boss says, "People are more important than anything." That is the way business and psychology look upon people, because both depend on and deal with people.

It takes more than desks, ledgers, machines, and materials to make a business. People are needed to make it a going concern—people working together, not necessarily in the same building, but pulling together so that the organization runs efficiently and can continue in business. But, sometimes "people are funny" and do not pull together, or they fail to pull their full share of the load.

Modern psychology is useful for the person in business because it deals with why people do what they do, think as they do, and feel as they do; with their abilities, motives, disappointments, ambitions, queer streaks. Modern psychology helps people to acquire skill, work more efficiently, fit into a work group, remember details, have a personality that is easy to get along with, use their senses, and do creative thinking.

In the early days of business, many guesses had to be made about the human element. Today, however, there is a large body of well-established information that can be used to eliminate some of—but not all—the guess-work.

_4_ ■

Early in this century, psychology was just starting to become scientific. Now it is so scientific that in a typical year some ten thousand research reports are published, of which probably around five hundred have some significance for business people.

Industrial, or business, psychology was under way, as a specialized field by 1920. Business psychology has grown steadily as a specialty and has increased in practical value, so that today it has a significant role in business operation and in training for business careers.

2 ■ Groups Are Important to People

A closely related field is *industrial sociology,* which analyzes the ways in which the human nature of individuals is modified by the groups they belong to and are exposed to. This specialty, which blends into industrial psychology, was beginning to develop by 1930. It had a slow start, because it took time to develop scientific methods for gathering sound information about the influence of groups. Within the last decade, however, industrial sociology has zoomed ahead; and there is now a wide recognition of the practical value of understanding group relationships if a business is to be operated efficiently.

Absenteeism can be used as an example. Absenteeism lowers efficiency, and most companies value the employee who is regularly on the job. Recent records indicate that, when workers feel accepted by their work group, they are less likely to take time off; working with the group is more satisfying to them than staying away from work. The chartoon shows how group *cohesiveness*—liking to stick together—influenced the absences of men workers in the offices of a large electric power company.

The first of more than 100 *chartoons* in this book appears on page 6. Each chartoon gives a visual summary of a practical finding in some recent research. Each usually carries a message that the worker, or employer, should take seriously. The message of each chartoon is statistically significant, which means that it is not likely to be due to chance and is likely to hold true for similar people under similar conditions.

The chartoons should be studied in a different way than the text is read:

1. Take time to read all the lettering on each chartoon and to understand the meaning of the bars, curves, etc.

2. Think about how its message is related to the text; some of the chartoons are not discussed in the text.

3. Recall some situations with which you are acquainted that are similar to those briefly described in the chartoon.

4. Do some creative thinking by figuring how the message, or messages, in the chartoon could be applied in your own business life.

Men saying "Our group better than others at sticking together":

62%

21%

LOW absence offices   HIGH absence offices

Data from research by Drs. Floyd C. Mann and Howard Baumgartel at the University of Michigan

Less absenteeism when the office workers were a cohesive group having "togetherness."

This chartoon shows that the workers in the offices with low absence rates usually felt that the office group hit it off well together. Only about one-third as many of the men in the high-absence offices felt that their work groups had that "togetherness."

The trend of most research in industrial sociology and *group dynamics* indicates that what the average person calls "human nature" is in large part actually social nature. Consequently, a considerable shift is necessary from the old-fashioned way of understanding why people do what they do. Human nature, formerly considered largely inborn, is now looked upon as partly inborn and partly the result of the individual's life-and-group experiences. That is a more encouraging point of view, because it implies that something practical can be done to modify, improve, or adapt human nature to changing circumstances.

In the preceding sentence, the quotation marks have been omitted around the phrase human nature, because from now on you will always—

we hope—have in mind the scientific view that human nature is pliable, the result of inherited capacities and functions that have been developed— or twisted, as the case may be—by our associations with other people.

3 ■ Books Can Be Important to People in Business

It is useful for the individual worker, and for the employer, to have as sound as possible a knowledge about human forces and social forces in business. This is especially true because there are special forces in business.

Sometimes people say, "A business life is a great life—if you don't weaken!" There is a great deal of truth in that. Business life by its very nature is considerably different from home life or school life. Three of the broader differences are that business life (1) has to be efficient, (2) has to be competitive, and (3) also has to show a profit. In chapters 6, 10, and 16 we shall look into more details of the way human and social forces make business life almost a different kind of life.

It seems highly desirable and practical for the person in business to understand these forces and to co-operate with the best of them. Otherwise he may blunder and not make successful adaptations to business life. Those who do not weaken and who get ahead in business, may, of course, adapt on a trial-and-error basis—the "School of Hard Knocks" way. But we feel certain there is a better way.

This book, for instance, is based on the proposition that adaptation to business life will be easier, quicker, and more successful when one has studied about these forces that mold—or stress—human nature in business life.

4 ■ The Importance of Efficiency for Everybody

Everybody has a stake in the efficiency of a business. Efficiently operated businesses can supply their customers with better products or services at lowered costs. The standard of living is affected. It is easier to pay taxes. Jobs are steadier, and there may be more leisure hours for employees each week.

Modern executives are forever asking "How're we doing?" Is production going up? Costs going down? Less absenteeism? Sales up? Workers satisfied? Collections better? Less scrap, waste, and accidents? These are some of the batting averages that the executives use as bases for decisions about the firm's efficiencies.

Keeping an eye everlastingly on indicators of efficiency is necessary if a business is to be managed so that it operates at a profit. Otherwise, it may survive no longer than the seven-year average life of businesses. There is competition, you know. (Dun & Bradstreet reports 10,000 to 20,000 business failures in ordinary years.)

The successful business person is almost always efficiency-minded through and through, whether he is the boss or not. He keeps a close eye on the efficiency of the business, on his own personal efficiency, and the personal efficiency of those working with him. Competition forces this, whether he likes it or not.

Periodic reviews of individual efficiency. Two or three times a year the supervisors and executives of about half the larger companies report on the efficiency of individual workers. Several days may be spent

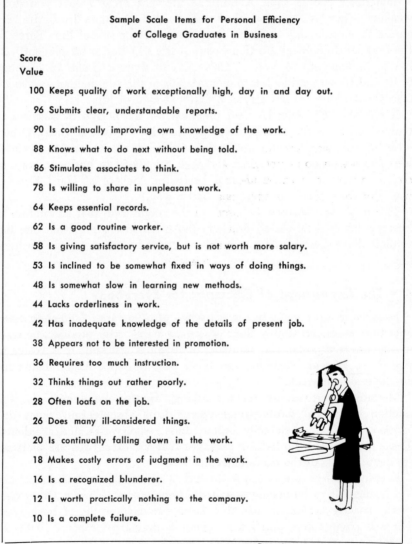

Sample Scale Items for Personal Efficiency
of College Graduates in Business

Score
Value

100 Keeps quality of work exceptionally high, day in and day out.

96 Submits clear, understandable reports.

90 Is continually improving own knowledge of the work.

88 Knows what to do next without being told.

86 Stimulates associates to think.

78 Is willing to share in unpleasant work.

64 Keeps essential records.

62 Is a good routine worker.

58 Is giving satisfactory service, but is not worth more salary.

53 Is inclined to be somewhat fixed in ways of doing things.

48 Is somewhat slow in learning new methods.

44 Lacks orderliness in work.

42 Has inadequate knowledge of the details of present job.

38 Appears not to be interested in promotion.

36 Requires too much instruction.

32 Thinks things out rather poorly.

28 Often loafs on the job.

26 Does many ill-considered things.

20 Is continually falling down in the work.

18 Makes costly errors of judgment in the work.

16 Is a recognized blunderer.

12 Is worth practically nothing to the company.

10 Is a complete failure.

Data from Dr. Richard S. Uhrbrock

in this periodic review of how competent each individual is. Workers are in competition with each other, too.

During this review period, employees usually perk up their good behavior and show much curiosity about their ratings. The boss has this review in the back of his mind all year, of course, and is always watching the work ways and attitudes of the employees. The review period just gives a time to crystallize the preceding few months' impressions.

Various titles are given to these periodic reports of individual efficiency: Merit Rating, Service Review, Progress Rating, Performance Score.

These ratings are made and written into the employees' employment records for several reasons. For one reason, it helps the employee make the most of his own abilities, by letting him know how the boss thinks he is doing. The details of his rating are talked over with him and suggestions worked out which may help him become more valuable to himself and to the company. There will be an example of such a conference in the chapter on "How to Conduct a Personality Interview."

Contracts with labor unions is another reason for these ratings. Many working agreements consider both merit and seniority when promotions are made, or when workers have to be laid off during slack times.

Qualities that are rated. Each company rates personal efficiency according to the qualities that are considered significant for its needs. Factory employees are usually sized up on different qualities than office workers; and salespeople and executives, on still other qualities.

As a rule, the blue-collar workers are rated on the fewest qualities. One electrical company rates them on only two—ability to do the present job and promotional possibilities.

White-collar workers are rated on more qualities. Social characteristics, such as co-operation, talk, appearance are usually included.

Supervisors and executives are generally rated on still more qualities. Winning co-operation, handling people, and reaching business decisions are given more weight in ratings of them.

There is a trend to rate executives' wives, especially when the husband has promotional possibilities. A personable, level-headed wife who has "social sense" is favored for higher executives because they take on more social responsibilities at each step on the way up.

For judging the efficiency of individual office workers, a report of the American Management Association suggests that the following 15 qualities be taken into consideration:

Qualities Desirable in Office Workers

Technical
    1. Accuracy in routine office work
    2. Speed in routine work

3. Planning work in advance
4. Neat and orderly results
5. Knowing general office methods
6. Learning about new methods

Social

7. Appropriate personal appearance
8. Suitable use of language
9. Keeping business secrets
10. Co-operating with other workers
11. Accepting suggestions and criticisms

Personal

12. Getting to work on time
13. Getting work out before deadlines
14. Using suitable initiative
15. Accepting appropriate responsibility

Usually the employee is given a score on each quality. A score of 1 might be given for low or unsatisfactory, with a range up to 5 for high or very satisfactory. Some qualities may be given a heavier score. Keeping business secrets or confidences, for instance, is sometimes counted double for a private secretary, but only once for a person in the typists' pool. By adding together the scores given on the separate qualities, a total "efficiency score" is obtained.

Practical psychology helps get better ratings. One of the most useful applications of business psychology is the aid it gives the individual in knowing (1) how to work efficiently, and (2) how to get along with other workers. Result: higher ratings. Research on the psychology of skill and work, and on group dynamics and human relations, has discovered many principles that the individual can adapt to his own needs.

This research has been going on since the first psychological laboratory was formally organized at the University of Leipzig in 1883, by Dr. Wilhelm Wundt. This work has been steadily expanding ever since. Every university, some businesses, and the armed forces have organizations for psychological research.

Unfortunately, many employers, as well as employees, are not acquainted with these discoveries and consequently do much more blundering than they should.

5 ■ Opportunities for Greater Efficiency

"How are we doing?"

Not as well as we might, probably. That is a human failing.

William James, a medical graduate who became the first professor of psychology at Harvard University in 1889, observed: "Men habitually use only a small part of the powers which they actually possess."

John Wanamaker, who grew up on the wrong side of town beside a brickyard but made himself one of the world's business leaders, said: "Hardly any businessman is half what he might be."

Some of this widespread *in*efficiency is due to neglect—we just don't put on enough steam. But much of this lack of efficiency is also due to poor working methods. How low would efficiency be if typists used the hunt-and-peck method instead of the touch method? That is an obvious illustration of the superiority of some working methods over others.

It is not so obvious, however, that the touch typist will gain more efficiency in the long run if accuracy rather than speed is emphasized from the outset. There will be many similar examples throughout this book of little things that make big differences in efficiency at work.

Is business efficient? The prevailing business philosophy maintains that, no matter how efficient a business is now, it can always become more efficient. There is a never-ending quest for greater efficiency. New laborsaving equipment is installed; and older machines, though still usable, are discarded because they are less efficient than newer models. New methods and systems are continually being tried out, to find better procedures for jobs.

This perpetual quest for more efficiency is one of the factors that make business exciting to those who are "in" on the contemplated improvements. This any secretary knows when the boss asks her to help him select a new-model typewriter, or as the accountant finds when he visits a business show and studies new bookkeeping and calculating machines.

Gains reported by the National Institute of Industrial Psychology. The National Institute of Industrial Psychology was formed in London in 1921. This nonprofit organization has put psychology to work on all sorts of tasks—from heavy work mining coal to light work folding handkerchiefs. The Institute reports that the output on most jobs can be improved 20 to 30 per cent by appropriate methods. On the handkerchief-folding job, output was increased 200 per cent without making any changes in the equipment used.

These great gains were not produced by speeding up. Putting on pressure to work faster is usually exactly the *un*psychological way to go about it. The psychological way is to remove hindrances and irritations, to find easier ways of performing the operations, and to use encouragement rather than scolding.

There is much more to efficiency, as we shall see, than merely increasing output. It is the ratio of input to output that tells the story of efficiency—and of profits.

6 ■ Gains in Productivity

Which do you think counts for more in the efficiency of a business: the efficiency of the machines used? or the efficiency of the workers? This question is somewhat like the chicken-and-the-egg question—which came first?

The great advancements in machines have encouraged some people to jump to the conclusion that the machine determines efficiency. While better machines can increase efficiency, whether they do or not usually depends on the people using them. What good, for instance, is an electric typewriter to a typist who pecks away with only two fingers?

A hosiery mill recently bought some automatic machines that engineers thought were foolproof and "independent of the human element." But after a few weeks of production on them, there was trouble. The company called on the Psychological Corporation for help. This organization was incorporated in 1921 in New York City and now does nearly two million dollars in consulting work annually.

When these psychologists looked into the production troubles of the hosiery mill, they found some two hundred ways in which the operator did influence the production of these "operator-proof" machines. Even the best of engineers apparently cannot eliminate the human element, and it may be costly to imagine that they can.

Year-by-year gains in productivity. Economists compute productivity on the basis of worker-hours rather than machine-hours. Production per worker-hour is the most widely used index of over-all business efficiency. Productivity is figured by dividing the total output by the total man-hours worked to produce that output. Depending on the industry, the output may be totaled in tons, dollar value, items filed, cards punched, checks sorted, or some other measurable unit.

Output per worker-hour has been rising slightly, year after year. From 1899 to 1939 it went up an average of about 3 per cent a year, according to Dr. Solomon Fabricant's computations for the National Bureau of Economic Research.

Another researcher from the same organization, Dr. John W. Kendrick, using a slightly different basis, figured the increase as 2 per cent a year from 1910 to 1950. Whichever way it is figured, American business has apparently been steadily becoming more productive.

How much of this gain is due to the more efficient methods of the workers? how much to improved machines? In some instances the gain is credited primarily to machines. A clear-cut example is that of tractors and other power machinery on farms. They now make it possible for one worker to plant and harvest the crops on a 200-acre farm. During the same period, in contrast, coal miners' productivity steadily went down.

Our nationwide gains in productivity appear to be in large part due to engineers—they design better producing machines. Great gains can still be made by increasing the efficiency that workers themselves use in their work.

The 2 to 3 per cent yearly gains in productivity are small in comparison with the 20 to 30 per cent gains in output produced by the National Institute of Industrial Psychology. The NIIP gains were usually produced without any changes in the machines used. Wonders were worked by improving the human efficiency of the employees.

Company differences in productivity. Do companies that use similar machinery to make similar products differ much from one another in productivity? The United States Bureau of Labor Statistics reported such a comparison for 22 firms that made mining machinery. During a 10-year period one firm increased worker-hour output by 70 per cent, and 10 other firms increased it 5 to 15 per cent. But—one firm dropped more than 20 per cent, and 10 others slipped downward, though not that much. Half of the 22 improved in productivity, half slipped downward.

Who says there isn't a great opportunity to find a more encouraging answer to "How're we doing?" This is a challenge to every person in business. Two-thirds of the manufacturing cost of articles we buy comes from the worker-hours put into them. All the purchasing agent's careful efforts can affect only the one-third of the cost that is due to materials.

7 ■ How the Boss Estimates Personal Efficiency

"That is Miss Wellcombe over by the window. She is one of our most efficient employees." There was a note of pride in the supervisor's voice.

Miss Wellcombe's work output had not been measured. The boss had no figures to prove his impression about her efficiency. Even though the boss may not fill out periodic efficiency reports on each employee, we can be sure that he is still, in some way, keeping tabs on "How's he doing?"

There are many jobs for which there are not tangible output figures. As a consequence, bosses have to size up personal efficiency from indirect details or from the general style of the employee.

Occasionally, the whims or prejudices of the boss influence these judgments. One boss is "dead sure" that a cigarette smoker cannot be efficient. Another underjudges the efficiency of people who belong to a religious denomination he dislikes. Thomas A. Edison would not hire a person whom he saw salting his food before tasting it. And so it goes. It pays to study the boss and find his whims and prejudices.

When such whims do not influence the boss's judgment completely, here are 11 of the more important indirect evidences that lead him to say, "There is one of our most efficient workers."

1. Learns job details quickly. This gives an initial advantage to the employee who had vocational training or experience before starting.
2. Turns out the work without needing close supervision, although the autocratic style of boss may supervise needlessly anyway.

3. Does not give alibis or excuses. One executive has a large dictionary in his office; the name has been painted over and a new title lettered on instead: "Alibis I have heard."
4. Finds ways to do the job better. The democratic style of boss is impressed by this; the autocrat, who wants to do all the thinking, may resent it—so, study the boss.
5. Has general attitude of cheerfulness and co-operativeness.
6. Shows seriousness—horse sense rather than horseplay on the job.

There are other indirect indicators of efficient working that influence the boss's judgment, but some may actually indicate *inefficiency*. Whether the following show efficiency or inefficiency depends on the situation.

7. Has a clear desk or workplace—which may mean he doesn't have enough to do to keep him busy, or that he wastes time being too neat.
8. Takes work home—which may indicate he is inefficient and can't do his share of work during the standard working day, or that the boss is assigning him more than a fair share.
9. Works without apparent effort—which may be because he is stalling on the job, or because he is really efficient.
10. Shows signs of effort—which may mean he is not on top of the job, rather than that he is a hard worker. The efficient worker may be fresh as a daisy at the end of the day.
11. Does not loaf on the job—although occasional letdowns may serve as rest pauses and raise worker efficiency.

The halo effect in estimating personal efficiency. One impression is likely to overpower the person who has not been trained to analyze exactly the details that enter into personal efficiency. This inclination is so prevalent that it has been given the special name of halo effect. Here's how it works:

The supervisor who likes to see people working hard lets that cast a halo over his judgment of the person's other qualities. So, he judges the person who shows great effort as also being one who finds more ways to do the job better, although this particular person may really show little initiative to improve his job methods.

The cost-conscious boss similarly tends to give the economical worker who saves string a better standing on all other qualities.

An outstandingly favorable impression on one quality spills over and makes other qualities seem more favorable. Presumably, the person who has learned to do one thing especially well will be sized up a little more on the plus side in other ways.

A general liking for a person is another strong factor in producing a halo effect. This is illustrated by an experiment that Dr. Milton W. Horowitz made with a group of superior men and women who were leaders in their communities. When the controversial behavior was on the part of a person they liked, it was likely to be approved. But, when similar conduct was that of a disliked person, it was condemned. Psychologists call this the *halo effect*, although it has a close resemblance at times to downright prejudice.

8 ■ What Efficiency Means in Muscle Work

Efficiency does not require working at top speed until collapsing. Rather, it means a reasonable or *optimum amount of work done the easiest and most economical way.* (See the first table in the next chapter.)

The exact meaning of efficiency is the ratio of input to output. This *true efficiency* can be measured for most machines. Consider the automobile engine. For every 100 units of power put into it, the average engine puts out 20 to 25 units of power. Its efficiency thus ranges from 20 to 25 per cent, depending on the design and condition of the engine. Steam engines are less efficient than automobile engines, and diesel engines are more efficient.

How does this compare with human efficiency? The same true efficiency can be used only in a limited way with people. Calories of energy used by the muscles in doing a particular job can be measured, but complicated apparatus is needed.

Human muscles compare favorably with the automobile engine; they have an efficiency of 25 to 30 per cent in the average person. But the athletes' muscle-work efficiency is higher, about 40 per cent. Athletes have higher true efficiency, not because they were born that way, but primarily because of two reasons.

1. Bodily conditioning. Athletes have been in training; so their bodies convert energy into muscle movement with less waste. They have had graduated exercises that harden them, not sedentary work that softens them. Steaks, eggs, fruit, milk—not candy bars and soda pop—have helped condition them. The coach requires the athletes to sleep at night and does not permit them to stay up late or go out on parties.

2. Training in work methods. Coaches have taught athletes energy-saving tricks in the use of their muscles: not to swing the arms wildly when running, as you and I do when hurrying to the bus; to throw with a ballistic rather than a piston stroke; to use rhythm in their actions; to put in the least possible energy to accomplish the work, which increases true efficiency.

Energy input in everyday tasks varies greatly, depending on the method of working. Pushing a heavy load on a smooth surface, for instance, requires less energy input than pulling it.

Walking at the rate of about three miles an hour (about 90 steps a minute) is the most efficient speed for a person of average build. Running and lazy sauntering are both less efficient than the three-mile-an-hour rate—and also more likely to cause a fall or slip. This illustrates the rather general proposition that both the speed-up and the slowdown are likely to be inefficient ways of working. The goal in efficiency is to find the optimum rate; then to follow it except for brief spurts or slowdowns to break the monotony.

Standing, an example of individual differences in efficiency. People differ considerably from one another in their muscle efficiency when doing the same everyday tasks. The chartoon shows the variations in this use of energy when a person is just standing up naturally and doing nothing else. The women were all in sedentary occupations—office workers, teachers, and students.

The average energy increase due to standing was 18 per cent, but one overweight girl used twice this increase to maintain a standing posture.

The differences in efficiency of standing were found to be due largely to differences in posture, not entirely to overweight. The following were found to be significant:

Efficient Standing Posture	Inefficient Standing Posture
Knees pushed back	Knees forward in flexed position
Hips thrown forward	Hips pulled back
Upper back rounded	Upper back flat
Head forward	Head held back
Trunk tilted slightly backward	Trunk tilted forward

Standing up is the chief muscular work in some occupations, such as the salesperson's. Using the most efficient standing posture can lessen fatigue and raise true efficiency in such instances; as will planning the work, so that one can either sit or stand. The shape of shoes and the height of heels should also be considered.

Range of Efficiency in Merely Standing Up

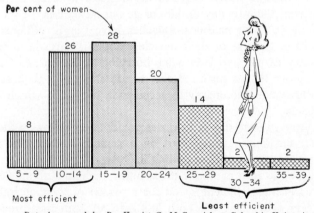

Data from work by Dr. Harriet G. McCormick at Columbia University

Increase in energy used while standing, in per cents.

Force of grip:

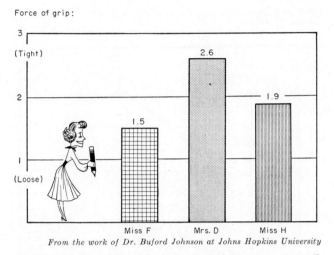

From the work of Dr. Buford Johnson at Johns Hopkins University

How three women differed in the force of their grip on a pencil.

Muscle tenseness as an indicator of efficiency. The energy input can be measured indirectly by gadgets that show how much force the person uses. Typewriters have been modified, for instance, so that the force used on each stroke is shown. With these modified machines, it has been found that poor typists use much more force than do good typists. Also, that more force is used when typing in a noisy place than in a quiet place. More force is used, too, when a person is anxious.

There are individual differences, as in the case of standing. This chartoon shows how three young women differed in the force with which they gripped a pencil while making dots with it. Mrs. D was the least efficient in this work; Miss F was the most efficient in the use of muscular effort to do this work.

Electrical methods are now being used to record the faint currents generated by a muscle when it is used. The more force, the more current is generated. There are only a few laboratories equipped to do this work, but their reports are of basic significance. The measurements are amazingly sensitive—an eyeblink can be recorded. The instruments for making these measurements are called *electromyographs*. The instruments adapted for the measuring of heartbeats are called *electrocardiographs*.

Even reading increases the muscle current, as shown by the curve in the chartoon on page 18. Notice how the muscle tenseness was increased when a radio talk was turned on while the man was reading.

Pulse-rate recovery and muscle efficiency. When we move our muscles, we use up calories of energy stored in the body. The using-up and replenishing affect the heart rate. We all know how our hearts seem to pound after some hard exertion. The heart rate speeds up somewhat

Microvolts of
muscle electricity:

From the work of Dr. R. C. Davis at Indiana University

Tenseness in George W.'s arm and neck while resting, reading, and distracted.

in proportion to the rate at which we are using up energy. (How it speeds up in nervous tension is a topic for a later chapter.)

The Harvard Fatigue Laboratory has found that the promptness with which the heart rate returns toward normal within three minutes after exertion gives a good indication of how much energy was used in the exertion. No apparatus is needed for this testing—the difficulty for the amateur is in locating the pulse.

Here are some records, for example, from men doing rather heavy physical work, as reported by Dr. Lucien Brouha, of du Pont's Haskell Laboratory:

| | **Pulse Rate While Resting Immediately After Work** | | |
	1st minute	2d minute	3d minute
No air conditioning	120	112	109
With air conditioning	112	103	96

Pulse-rate recovery, as this test is called, is useful principally where the work requires enough exertion to speed up the heart. It cannot be applied successfully in most white-collar jobs.

Horsepower replacing muscle power. Much of the heavy work that used to be done by muscle power is now taken over by electricity or compressed air. The Council for Technological Advancement has calculated that the horsepower used per worker was 2 in 1889 and that by

1939 it had increased to 6. Since then, it has probably increased to more than 6 per worker—the electric typewriter, for instance, uses about 1/50 horsepower. As laborsaving machinery has taken over the heavy tasks—and some of the lighter tasks—the measurement of muscle energy and pulse-rate recovery is probably not so important as formerly.

Most office tasks, for instance, do not require any great expenditure of muscle energy or of calorie energy in general. Mental multiplication—multiplying numbers such as 382 times 36 entirely in the head—uses only about 4 calories an hour. Half a peanut supplies that many calories.

We can understand now why industrial physicians try to get white-collar people to take more all-round exercise. The physicians say that sedentary workers do not get enough stimulating exercise to keep their bodies in tiptop working condition. We recall that the athlete gets gradu-ated exercise—going slowly from easy to severe workouts—to get his body in most efficient working condition.

Company recreation programs are to be encouraged as one way of getting general exercise. But white-collar workers, who can benefit most from these, have a tendency not to take part. In one large insurance com-pany, for instance, only about one-third of the girls took part in the organized recreations.

Most sedentary workers would also profit from more walking to and from work, stretching, and bending—regularly, not spasmodically. The exercise should be enough to shake up the body cells a bit, but not necessarily enough to work up a sweat.

Some office managers believe that there is no excuse for office em-ployees becoming tired at work as easily as they do. But white-collar workers do become honest-to-goodness tired. Some of this tiredness is due to the sedentary work making the body sluggish. And some of it is due to hidden inputs other than muscular exertion that go into a job.

9 ∎ Hidden Inputs That Lower Efficiency

Ever hear someone say, "This work seems easy enough, but something about the job gets me down"?

The bodily energy put into a job tells only a part of the story about human efficiency on that job. People put many intangible inputs into their work—discouragement, monotony, dissatisfaction, frustration, irritation, nervous tension, for example.

Consider the salesperson, whose chief energy input goes into standing and walking. But there is an added input from frustration when he keenly wants a commission, but the prospect will not buy. There may be more hidden input of aroused hostility and resentment if the sales manager calls him down for not making the quota and still more hidden input from striving to be agreeable to unreasonable customers.

Similar hidden inputs, or strains, can be found in practically every occupation. There is not much use shopping around for a job that will be free from stresses. Apparently, we just have to train ourselves to be personally efficient, come what may.

These stresses—hindrances, irritations, frustrations—are the special province of the business psychologist. To see for ourselves how important these hidden inputs are, both to the employer and to the employee, we shall briefly look over some typical findings that illustrate various sources of stress.

As an example of the hidden input of psychosomatic ailments as related to the boss, we shall look into the story of Patrick O. next. (*Psychosomatic* simply means bodily ailments that are produced by mental stress of some kind.)

This mechanic developed headaches and arm and shoulder pains when he was thirty-one, after he went to work for an autocratic boss whom he resented. The chart on the left shows how Patrick O.'s neck muscles remained continuously tensed even when he tried to relax away from work. The chart on the right shows how this tenseness was eliminated after 20 days' treatment to change his attitudes toward the boss. Some medication was given at first to ease some of the physical conditions this tenseness had produced. While resentment toward an autocratic boss can be changed to more constructive attitudes, it often requires the help of a specialist. (We will learn more about headaches in the chapter on nervous tension.)

Feelings of failure and discouragement are also stressful. Dr. Sherwin J. Klein demonstrated this with measurements of the microvolts of muscular effort of 60 men business students doing light physical work. For the experiment, half the students were given the impression that they were

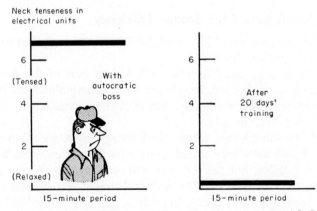

Resentment toward boss caused muscle tenseness in Patrick O.

doing poorly at the work, while the others were given the impression that they were successful. Study this comparison of their average records:

	Success Implied	Failure Implied
Arm tenseness while doing the work	595 microvolts	801 microvolts
Arm tenseness while relaxing immediately after the work	23	51

The "failure" group not only was more tense while doing the work but also was unable to let down as much and relax after completing the same task.

Social factors—not society functions, but social get-along-able-ness within the members of a work group—are also possible sources of stress. These social factors have either been becoming more important in recent generations, or business leaders are becoming more aware of the social influence of the work group over individual lives and efficiency. Social factors apply even to husky men working in a tractor factory, as the following records reported by the Survey Research Center illustrate:

	Men Who Felt They Were NOT Accepted by Their Work Group	Men Who Felt They Were Really a Part of Their Work Group
Reported high satisfaction with the company	30%	45%

The difficulty of work, even light work, is also a factor. Although mental work uses only infinitesimal amounts of energy, it does become tiring as people tense their muscles excessively while doing headwork. Experiments by Drs. William A. Shaw and L. H. Kline, at the University of Pennsylvania, provide a clear-cut example:

	Arm Tenseness, in Microvolts
Working easy problems	12.7
Working medium difficult problems	14.9
Working most difficult problems	17.2

Such hidden factors are probably of more importance in efficiency than is ordinarily realized. Many of the spectacular production gains that psychologists have brought about are the result of reducing such stresses on the workers—not a speed-up, not changes in the machinery, but improvements in the human climate.

"How'm I doing to remove or get along with unavoidable stresses?"

10 ▪ Psychological Efficiency

A hidden input—the psychological overhead—may be caused by work conditions, home conditions, social conditions, in all sorts of combinations. It may also be complicated by hostile attitudes that are brought to the job from home or school.

This psychological overhead may be increased by personal ambitions—wanting to become a vice-president of the firm in six months or to own that solid gold Cadillac next week. Aspirations that are too high lead to frustrations that make life tense—driving but inefficient.

In addition, there are social strains from an occasional annoying fellow employee. And even the best of bosses has days when he can be irritating without trying. By expecting such stresses in advance, we usually feel less strain when we do run head on into them.

As we think over such hidden inputs, it becomes evident that more than muscle energy needs to be considered in sizing up the input that goes into human efficiency. From the psychological approach, efficiency means *using abilities in ways that bring optimum results with least human waste and strain.* It includes more than job know-how. It includes such things as not being irritated by other workers—and also not irritating them.

That is a practical operating concept that can be applied by the individual to himself or by the manager to a department or an entire company. An increasing number of managers are applying it and watching productivity rise as they take steps that cut down human strain and stalling.

Efficiency does not depend on a special method or two or on some new machine. It is *determined by the total situation.* Machines, methods, people, attitudes—all are interrelated in setting the level of productivity. An example of a favorable total situation was given by Dr. Robert G. Neel, of the University of Kansas City, to a session of the American Psychological Association considering industrial psychology. Doctor Neel's comments were based on a thorough study of 2,000 production workers in a firm making heavy machinery. He reported:

"The picture of the average high producer is one of an individual over thirty years of age, who has had some previous experience with the company. An individual who likes the kind of work he does, and likes the over-all aspects of his job situation. He is a member of a work group that is attracted to each other. His foreman and the people above his foreman stress productivity, but do so without applying undue pressure. At the same time, they are more concerned with the individual employee and are more skilled in human relations."

With this as a background, let's look now at some other aspects of efficiency, especially at ways it is measured.

The Gist of the Chapter

At the beginning of the chapter you were asked to read "What this chapter is about." That was to give you a *preview* which would help you get a *mental set* for absorbing the chapter. Such a preview, thoughtfully made, usually helps one remember more of what is read and also to get more meaning out of it. Read "What this chapter is about" thoughtfully for each succeeding chapter. It will usually help your thoughtfulness if the sentences are changed into questions while you are reading, such as: "Why are people important in business and psychology?"

At the end of each chapter there will be a list of review questions. These are to guide you as you refresh your remembrance of what you have just read and to help you clarify the meanings. A review after reading is especially effective for helping to remember the points and facts.

In answering a review question, simply tell yourself the gist of it *in your own words*. If necessary, turn back and skim through the section again.

It will help you remember, as well as make the meaning more personal and sharp, if you actually talk—or whisper—to yourself while answering each question.

1. Why is it useful for the person in business to study about human nature?
2. How old is business psychology, and what does it do?
3. How do merit-rating scales help people and also help efficiency?
4. How many and what qualities are considered desirable for an office worker?
5. What are the direct and the indirect evidences by which an employer judges an individual employee's efficiency?
6. Can there be "bad" halos?
7. What are the differences between rating-scale efficiency, true efficiency, and psychological efficiency?
8. Why do most sedentary workers need more muscular exertion to be efficient? which kind of efficiency?
9. Why are they called hidden inputs, and what is their significance in business life and efficiency? examples?
10. What are some social, or group, factors that lead to business efficiency? to individual efficiency? What can business do about these? what can the individual?

Things to Do and Problems to Discuss

1. Some newspapers, and a few magazines, have "psychology columns." Report on some of the items these columns have that might be applied in business life.

2. Oswald J. wants to take a course in business psychology and would like to have his employer pay the tuition for the course. What points could

Oswald use to convince his boss that it would be a good investment for the firm?

3. Look over the advertisements in some trade journals or business magazines, and report on those that emphasize improving efficiency by using better machines and equipment and on those that emphasize hidden inputs that lower efficiency.

4. Look through some general business, or management, magazines and report on their articles that deal with the human aspect of business.

5. Why should blue-collar workers be rated on fewer qualities than white-collar workers?

6. Find out about and compare the work of such associations as the National Office Management Association, The Society for the Advancement of Management, American Management Association, National Association of Cost Accountants, etc. What emphasis do they place on efficiency? The local Chamber of Commerce can give you the names of any local members or branches of these organizations. You would likely find it useful to talk with some members, or local officers, in getting this information.

7. Find out what local firms use merit-rating scales or other ratings. The firm's personnel manager might like to tell you about these ratings and give you copies for use in class.

8. Work out some recommendations for sedentary workers to keep them in better physical condition. A teacher of physical education, physician, or athletic coach could give you help in this study.

9. Compare an old typewriter, or other business machine, with a recent model, and show ways in which it might influence efficiency.

10. Find out about Dun & Bradstreet and report on them. Their own local representative, a bank, or a credit manager could give you this information. How does Dun & Bradstreet's work affect people in business life?

11. Talk with some young person who has taken his, or her, first job in business a few months ago. In what ways did this person find business life different from, say, school life?

12. Effie K. decided to flatter her boss, in hopes he would give her a higher efficiency rating. What can you say for and against her doing this?

13. Think of some married men whom you know who have executive positions. Describe some of their wives' characteristics that may have been helpful in their husbands' climb up the ladder.

14. Look up in a recent book on sociology and report on what is meant by a cohesive group.

15. You read in Friday's paper that the son of a fellow employee had been killed in an automobile crash. Should you telephone condolences? send a written note? a printed card of sympathy? make a personal visit to the family? What should you do in case the employee works near your desk? what in case he works in a different department but is still a speaking acquaintance?

2 ■ DOING "AN HONEST DAY'S WORK"

_ _ _ _ _ _ _ _ _ _ _ _ _ _

WHAT THIS CHAPTER IS ABOUT

1. *Per cent of capacity as an index of efficiency*
2. *Unused personal talents and job simplification*
3. *Quota efficiency*
4. *Stereotyped efficiency*
5. *Resistance to changes*
6. *Restricted efficiency*
7. *Cures for stalling*

> Think about these
> as if they were
> questions.

1 ■ Per Cent of Capacity as an Index of Efficiency

How much can a person do?

Business often figures the efficiency of a job or a department or an entire company by the per cent of capacity that is being used. Thus, a duplicating machine could produce 7,200 copies an hour if it ran at full speed. If a worker turned out only 3,600 copies an hour, the efficiency would be 50 per cent of capacity.

This does not take into account any muscular efficiency that may go into the job. In the case of the duplicator, an electric motor does the steady grinding. The operator's muscular effort is mostly for standing, with a little walking and lifting of paper. This effort could be cut down, of course, by using a stool of adjustable height, so that he could either sit or stand while tending the machine.

And this 50 per cent of capacity does not take into account any lowering of human efficiency from the noise of the machine. This noise might affect the efficiency of other workers if the machine were out in an open office, where its noise bounced into the ears of other workers.

Such a percentage of possible, or of capacity, is plainly not a measure of true efficiency. It is a convenient index that can be watched from week to week to see how adequately a business is using its mechanical facilities.

The percentage of possible tells more about what a machine or a company might do than it does about how much a worker can do.

Tempered standards of what is possible. The percentage of possible for individual jobs is usually calculated, in the larger companies, by specialized staff departments. These staff people figure what is reasonably possible to produce in different tasks. These departments are variously called Methods, Time, Standards, or Planning.

They make involved calculations that allow time for repairing or oiling a machine, for worker fatigue, for shortages of materials, and for other necessary stoppages. These allowances give a tempered figure for the maximum possible, which is usually more encouraging to the worker. On that duplicating machine, although the theoretical capacity is 7,200 copies an hour, it would be shaved to, say, 5,900 by such allowances.

The larger offices, especially insurance and mail-order firms, have such

THE OPTIMAL WORK LEVEL
—as determined by physiologists

How to Tell How Hard You Are Working and How Long You Can Safely Keep It Up

How hard	Pulse rate per minute	Breathing per minute	Calories used per minute	Work examples (Numeral shows cal/min.)	How long you can safely keep it up
Light work 1. Mild	Under 100	14 or less	1 to 4	Typing 1½, clerical 1½, cooking 1 to 2, ironing 2, light assembly 2, washing windows 3, driving truck 4	Indefinitely
2. Moderate	Under 120	15 or less	5 to 8	Scrubbing on knees 5, assembling 25-lb. parts 5, hand printing 5, shoveling 9-lb. load 8	8 hours daily on job
Heavy work * 3. *Optimal*	Under 140	16 or less	9 to 10	Walking 5 mi. per hr. 10, hand riveting 10, blacksmithing 10	8 hours daily for a few weeks
4. Strenuous	Under 160	20 or less	11 to 12	Shoveling 14-lb. load 11, rowing boat 3 mi. per hr. 11	4 hours, two or three times a week, if special training
Severe work 5. Maximal	Under 180	25 or less	13 to 15	College football 13, hard stair climbing 14	1 or 2 hours, on scattered occasions
6. Exhausting	180 and up	30 and up	16 and up	Shoveling wet snow, 23-lb. load 18, crew rowing 19 to 30	Few minutes only, on rare occasions

* *Work at Optimal Level uses approximately half the capacity the average adult has for physical work and should not deplete the energy of an adult who is in good condition.*
Adapted from research of Dr. J. Gordon Wells and colleagues in the U.S. Air Force School of Aviation Medicine.

tempered standards for most of their routine office tasks. The smaller offices seldom have. In the smaller office, the supervisor is likely to make a running guess at what is a fair day's work.

When the boss makes such a rough estimate of what is par, he may make the estimate too high. This is especially the case when the boss is centered on getting out a lot of work. As a result, the workers may form the impression that he is arbitrary and unreasonable in what he expects from them.

What happens in such a situation was shown in one large corporation's home offices. The work was essentially the same in each office. Eleven offices were high producers, and twelve were low producers. All the bosses in the high-producing offices were considered reasonable by the clerks, while only slightly more than half the bosses in the low-producing offices seemed reasonable. The unreasonableness apparently had a negative effect on production.

2 ▪ Unused Personal Talents and Job Simplification

Useful as the percentage of possible is, it usually tells more about the way equipment is being used to advantage than it does about whether human resources are being put to the optimum use. The worker, for example, may be capable of doing more difficult work. There is a loss of personal potential if a young man might be doing accounting instead of running the duplicator even at 7,199 an hour.

There has been a tendency in business to simplify jobs, partly to speed up the learning rate for a new job. One consequence of this work simplification is that many jobs make use of only a fraction of the workers' capacities. And these simplified jobs generally produce more worker dissatisfaction than comparable jobs that have greater variety. Dr. Nancy C. Morse has reported the following relationship between the variety of tasks on a job and satisfaction with the job. This is for white-collar workers in the same company.

	Clerks Saying They Had High Satisfaction with What They Did on Their Jobs
On jobs having variety	41%
On jobs lacking variety	8%

Job simplification has been most marked in mass-production assembly-line operations. The effect of this on blue-collar workers' interest in their work is shown by the following chartoon, which deals with an ultra-modern automobile factory. These workers all received about the same wages. But one-third of them did only one operation that took about two minutes to do—such as using the same tool on the same part over and over again as the conveyor line passed their stations. Another third did two to five operations, and the remaining third did five or more.

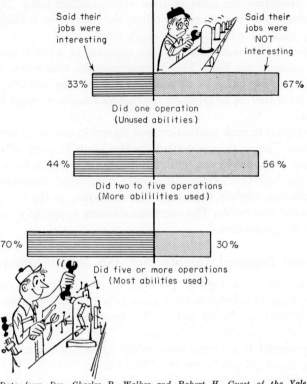

Said their
jobs were
interesting

Said their
jobs were
NOT
interesting

33% | 67%

Did one operation
(Unused abilities)

44% | 56%

Did two to five operations
(More abililities used)

70% | 30%

Did five or more operations
(Most abilities used)

Data from Drs. Charles R. Walker and Robert H. Guest of the Yale
Institute of Human Relations

**More interest in the job when the assemblers had more things
to do.**

This chartoon pictures clearly how more interesting the jobs were
as they made more demands upon the workers' capacities. Unused talents
thus cut into efficiency in indirect ways.

Many surveys have shown that workers on skilled jobs have the most
satisfaction from their work. Qualifying for a skilled job is apparently
good insurance for the individual, over and above any increased earnings
he may receive.

Unused talents are a loss of human efficiency, regardless of how high
the productivity may be. Some personnel departments search for hidden
talent among their workers and upgrade employees to work that will use
their more valuable abilities. That is something supervisors are trained
to look for, too, as they talk over merit ratings individually with each
worker. That can really boost human efficiency.

The "How'm I doing?" question needs to include "How'm I doing with
the capacities I have?"

3 ▪ *Quota Efficiency*

When we hear of an efficiency that goes over 100 per cent—or even comes close to it—we can be sure it is not a true efficiency, but an efficiency computed from some arbitrary base. Quota efficiency is an example.

Companies or departments often set quotas that they hope to reach by a certain time. These quotas are used (1) as a rough indication of efficiency, and (2) as goals to provide incentives for more effective work.

In sales work, particularly, life is just one quota after another. Growth-minded firms, also, are likely to emphasize quotas that represent goals they want to reach soon to help them grow larger faster.

Quotas may backfire. Quota efficiency makes no attempt to gauge the input. As a matter of fact, quotas are commonly used to get workers to put in more input. Quotas can be useful for this, but an unreasonably high quota may lower efficiency (and output) by the discouragement touched off.

A southern garment plant's experience shows this. The story is related by Dr. John R. P. French, Jr. The workers, in order to make them work harder, were told that the quota was 180 dozen a day. But the quota, set by careful time studies, was actually only 140 dozen. In their discouragement, the girls turned out less than 100 dozen.

On the psychologist's recommendation, the supervisor told a few girls secretly that the real quota was only 140. These girls perked up interest immediately and lost the feeling of strain. This convinced the supervisor that the psychologists might be right; and all the girls were told the correct quota.

Output jumped at once to 120 dozen! Equally important, the girls' attitudes changed. The work seemed easier for them. Discouragement evaporated, and they began to feel successful. Their personal efficiency was increased much more than the output figures showed.

Unreasonable quotas, like unreasonable bosses, can be sources of stress that add to the hidden input of a job.

Personal quotas. Individuals as well as departments often set quotas for themselves. One person sets a personal quota to take an evening course, another to learn new words. These personal quotas are often hazy—to learn some new words, for instance. Quotas are more effective when they are made definite—a new word a day.

Time budgeting is a form of personal quota setting. Many executives budget so many hours for checking with department heads, so many for community work, so many for personal conferences with workers, and so on. These time quotas make people more systematic in their use of time. And they also prod them not to neglect some tasks that might be overlooked if they were not given a time quota.

A committee of students and faculty of the University of Chicago recommended the following time quotas to assure a well-rounded development and to avoid becoming top-heavy from specializing in one field.

	Hours per Week
Serious reading	4
Dances and social affairs	2
(5 hours maximum)	
Lectures, concerts, art	3
Movies, shows, games	3
(6 hours maximum)	
Religion and welfare	2

"Getting enough time to do things" may mean that the time for each activity has not been put on a quota basis. It may also mean that one has too many irons in the fire. Much time can be spent to no useful purpose if there is no quota to prod one.

More motivation when the individual sets his quota. People who work toward goals, or quotas, usually make better use of their capacities as well as of their time. Goal-motivated behavior, as it is called, helps people to get things done. A goal generally has most motivating power when the individual has set it for himself, and least effect when the goal is set by someone else for him, such as a parent or an employer. That is one reason why progressive employers are now including the workers themselves in conferences where quotas are set.

An example is a large electric utility having some ten thousand employees. Management was worried because the first-level supervisors showed little interest in the cost side of efficiency. It was found that the most effective way to make the supervisors cost-conscious was to let them take part in the financial discussions in which their department budgets were set up. Then they were motivated to meet their own budgets, not the budgets that someone higher up had imposed on them.

Levels of aspiration in setting quotas. The person who has no quotas is obviously badly off so far as his efficiency goes. He has a low level of aspiration or shifting aspirations that may be gone with the wind by tomorrow. "He lacks ambition" may mean that he has not set any quotas for himself but is just drifting along.

But a person with a high level of aspiration may be badly off, too, though in a different way. He may have too much enterprise, scattered all over town. An overly ambitious person is likely to be under the strain of a goal, or quota, that is set too high and too soon—you remember, vice-president in six months, and that solid gold Cadillac, or the biggest diamond in town, or to finish a course in half the time, or to marry into royalty. Reasonable goals stimulate people, but wishfully high goals produce stress that can make life and work a nightmare.

An ingenious experiment by Dr. Saul S. Leshner shows how the level of only temporary aspirations may be reflected in the tenseness of the individual. High school graduates worked puzzles in their heads while the tenseness of their arms was measured electrically. After some experience with these puzzles, the people were asked to set a goal for working the next puzzles. Half of the people were told to make it a reasonable and *realistic goal* they had a good chance to reach. The other half were asked to set a goal they would like to reach—a *wishful goal* for them.

The people who set the wishful goals were more tense as soon as they set the goals, even though they were still resting and had not been given a puzzle to solve. The people with the wishful goals were more tense while doing the otherwise identical work and more tense while relaxing after the work. We shall come back to this in the chapter on nervous tension.

In daily life either of two things is likely to happen when goals are unrealistically high. For one, the person comes to *feel frustrated*—as the girls in the garment factory did—and gives up. From then on the person who has surrendered may play safe and not expect much of himself—his push and self-confidence dwindle.

The other thing likely to happen is high-pressure, frantic effort, to reach the goal—push enough for several people. That is what happened in the arm tenseness of most of the people who set even temporary, though wishful, goals for the puzzles. Business people with more per-

Courtesy Connecticut Mutual Life Insurance Company

It is sometimes desirable to say "No" to others as well as to oneself in order to keep goals realistic.

manent high levels of aspiration drive themselves to earn more and more—and get ulcers or other psychosomatic ailments thrown in for their extra efforts.

Quotas can be extremely useful stimulants when they are realistic quotas. But, like stimulating drugs, they should be used in moderation. Tempered.

"How'm I doing to reach some quotas I have set for myself? And how realistic are the quotas?"

4 ■ Stereotyped Efficiency

A *stereotyped action* is one that is repeated pretty much without variation. Stereotyped efficiency means doing the same old things in the same old ways with no change or improvement in method—becoming habit-bound.

If human beings are creatures of habit, this is especially true of their working habits. We tend to do jobs pretty much as we did them the first few times they were tackled. Frozen work habits keep many from being the efficient workers they might be. Vocational teachers and job trainers often have tough problems getting people to replace the stereotyped, amateurish ways they used when they started working with more professional and efficient methods.

Stereotyped efficiency, as you have probably guessed, means low efficiency—not merely working at a slow pace, but using inefficient, round-about methods.

There are several reasons why the answer to "How'm I doing?" is likely to be, "In the same old stereotyped way."

Poor transition from play years to work years. A person's initial work period is usually part time, doing odd jobs, after school or during vacations. There is seldom any serious vocational purpose—no special quota or goal. The work is "just to have something to do" or to get some extra spending money—no thought of efficiency; merely puttering at work. Initial work experiences are thus likely to start people in habits of low-gear work—comparable to doing multiplications incorrectly just to do something to keep occupied.

These slack work methods are difficult to shake off when serious life-work begins. That is a factor that causes many shifts in jobs during the first trials at full-time adult work. Beginning workers often have to try several different jobs before they graduate from play work to pay work. In the chapters on the development of personality and on emotional maturity, we shall go into more detail about the adjustments that usually have to be made in the transition from odd-job work habits to professional work methods.

Periods of unavoidable inefficiency. Periods of unavoidable inefficiency are also looked upon as causes of stereotyping at a low level.
Work habits, like water, seem to run downhill at the first opportunity.

It works this way: The worker has been out for illness and returns
to the office while still a bit dragged down. The first few days back on
the job he takes it easier than usual—and has good chances of becoming
stereotyped at this lower level. It might have been wiser if he had not
returned to work until fully recovered, so that he would not have babied
his work habits.

Periods of overtime work have been found to produce similar lowering
effects. As a result of the longer hours, work ways become less efficient
than usual. And, when the overtime is past, many people do not run
uphill to their former standards.

Efficiency may also become stereotyped at a low standard when the
company provides employment the year around. There are some slack
seasons when workers are kept on, but they do little more than putter at
their work and later find it difficult to get going again under full steam
when business picks up.

A similar stereotyping hazard exists in many small offices where there
may be really busy periods only a few times during the week. "Easy
work" may be a worker's worst friend.

Salespeople also tend to become stereotyped when selling is easy. During periods when demand is strong, the salesman may become just an
order taker. When business conditions change and it is necessary to
get out and really sell, he finds his sales skill has deteriorated. Then the
sales manager has to start some sales training as a refresher to pump
habits up to more efficient levels.

It is useful to bear in mind that whatever the cause of the temporary
low level, it is likely to become the new standard unless something is
done intentionally to take up the slack.

Stresses as a cause of stereotyping. Stress is not as obvious a cause
and is probably more widespread than is generally realized. We had a
glimpse of how it operates when we were talking about unreasonable
quotas. One reaction to stresses is to give up, to play safe and not try.

Another reaction to stress that has been investigated is the tendency
to become rigid in one's ways and thinking—keeping in the same old
ruts. This is a close relative of playing safe. The mental rigidity from
stress cuts down the flow of ideas.

This was demonstrated in an experiment in which Dr. Emory L. Cowen
gave high school graduates a series of mental problems to solve. The
problems could all be solved by the same trick, once the people caught
on. After they had become used to solving with that procedure, then
they were given problems that seemed similar, but which could not be

solved in the same old way. The people who had mental rigidity would still try to use the same old ways and were much slower to solve the new problems. Here is what was found:

	Relative Time to Solve the New Problems
People not placed under stress	25
People under mild stress from failure to solve difficult problems	63
People under strong stress from brusque treatment and belittling them	111

Those records indicate that stress made it more difficult (more rigidity) to find the new way. This also suggests how brusque treatment, or bawlings out, may bring out mental rigidity that stereotypes workers.

5 ■ Resistance to Changes

Resistance to changes is related to stereotyping, both as a cause and as an effect. Stress, especially from the way the worker is handled, may make it worse. But the majority of people are not inclined to try out innovations. They feel safer with familiar methods and think new ones might be risky. This applies not only to work methods but also to foods, ideas, clothes, amusements, and so on.

Physicians say, for instance, that it does not matter whether we eat pie as the first course or as the last course of a meal. But how would you take to the idea of starting your meals with the dessert and eating the courses backward? Our eating habits, like most of our ways, have become stereotyped; and we are a bit rigid toward making any changes.

When improvements produce no improvement. Often when air conditioning or more efficient machines are installed, the boss can discover no benefits. Work comes out at the same old rate. Sometimes laziness or resistance to change is blamed, when the real culprit is stereotyping—perhaps complicated by stress effects if the boss is an old ramrod.

The General Electric Company increased the lighting for key-punch operators by seven times. Theoretically, there should have been an increase in output. But output remained the same during the next month—stereotyped efficiency.

After about two months in the better lighted room, output slowly began to climb. The climb was irregular; some weeks there were slumps back to older levels.

It was a year and a half before the full benefits of the improved working conditions showed up. By that time stereotyping had been overcome, so that errors were down 69 per cent and output was up 58 per cent.

That is the way it goes after most improvements in working conditions or methods. For the first few weeks—or months—there seems to be no benefit. It takes several months, as a rule, before the old stereotyping fades away and higher ceilings are reached. It may be foolhardy to condemn an improvement too soon—wait until people have had a chance to break through their old ceilings.

The dead hand of stereotyping has a special challenge to the person who has ability and ambition. Some record of his "How'm I doing?" helps him spot his stereotyping. If he is not doing better, it may be because habit is holding him back. Hosts of people are stereotyped without realizing it, because they haven't tried to figure out how they are doing in comparison with a month ago. Or how they might do the work more efficiently.

6 ▪ Restricted Efficiency

Restricted efficiency is not a cheering topic, but we should be acquainted with it. As in the case of stereotyping, it represents lowered efficiency. But restricted efficiency is intentional, while stereotyping is not.

An end result of both is lowered productivity. Another is the effect upon our standards of living, because both keep the costs of manufacturing higher. Still another result is the pressure that managers naturally put on in hopes of overcoming the stalling—but often nothing comes from this but more stress and a tug of war that no one wins.

Deliberate restriction of efficiency prevails in approximately half of factory work groups. It is not so common among white-collar groups, though a few office people do try to shirk their way up.

This intentional stalling occurs the world over, although different terms are used to describe it: stretching it out, making the job last, the slowdown, gold-bricking, hanging it out, ca' canny, soldiering, spreading the work.

It is usually an entire department, or crew, that stalls—the code of many work groups. More about this aspect in a moment.

How much pride workers have in the productivity of their group gives a rough indication of their attitude toward stalling. Low pride in productivity reflects an atmosphere that approves of restricting output. The chartoon on page 36 pictures how white-collar and blue-collar groups have—or don't have—pride in the productivity of their work groups.

The attitude toward restricted efficiency is also shown by workers' feelings toward others who are high producers. Dr. Nancy C. Morse has summarized the following data, for semiskilled office clerks (girls).

Attitude Toward the High Producers

Admiration	Neutral	Resentment
25%	31%	44%

Causes of stalling. Some of this restricted efficiency is based on poor logic. Workers reason superficially that, if they hold down output, they

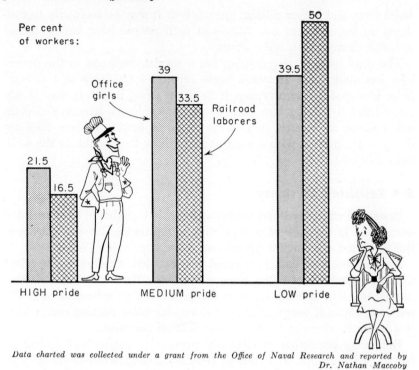

Per cent
of workers:

Office
girls

Railroad
laborers

21.5

16.5

39

33.5

39.5

50

HIGH pride   MEDIUM pride   LOW pride

Data charted was collected under a grant from the Office of Naval Research and reported by Dr. Nathan Maccoby

How much pride they had in the productivity of their work group.

will make the job last longer. But economists point out that restriction hurts those who stall as well as the innocent customers; the cost of goods is kept higher and the market limited. Restricting efficiency thus may actually make fewer jobs. Coal is an example. When low productivity made the price of coal go up, customers turned to fuel oils and gas, with the result that there were fewer jobs for coal miners.

The predominant reasons for stalling, however, are tied in with group conflicts and hostility feelings. The stalling usually springs from feelings of resentment toward supervisors and managers.

Stalling is most marked when the supervisor is a bossy, autocratic person who barks orders and does all the planning himself. It is usually least when the supervisor is of the democratic style and handles workers so that they feel they are part of the business and are not being belittled by the management.

Stalling is almost always an expression of the work group's feeling that they must hold together in self-protection, or self-defense. The group hits upon what it considers a "fair day's work." This quota is lower than what could easily be possible. But the group makes life miserable for the conscientious worker who goes above this low standard.

Group forces in stalling. The work group enforces the low ceiling it considers a fair day's work. Sometimes the group enforces it by direct pressure—reminding the conscientious employee that he will wear himself out and had better slow down. Among blue-collar workers, physical threats may be used.

Subtle social pressure is almost always used. The diligent worker is ignored—a sort of boycott. He is given a snide nickname and "included out" of the group at lunch hour, department gossip is kept from him, and his wife may be snubbed by the wives of others in his work group.

If he persists in turning out more than the group sanctions, his machine may be tampered with and defective pieces put in his output when his back is turned. Hazardous practical jokes are played, too, with the conscientious worker the scapegoat. Gossip is started about him.

Such group pressures have a powerful influence on most individuals. People are extremely sensitive to what others in the work group say or think, and usually—though not always—follow along with the group.

An instance in which girls worked in teams of three making checker-

Experiment by Dr. Stanley Schachter, at the University of Minnesota, supported by the Carnegie Corporation

The boss said, "Speed up." Other workers said, "Slow down"—so they slowed down.

boards illustrates this. The group pressure used was about the slightest possible, merely casual remarks that one girl had been secretly asked to make at certain times during the work spell.

The work spell was divided into three periods. During the first period no comments were made about the rate of working, although the boss had told the girls that speed was important when they were put on the job. At the start of the second and third periods the "undercover agent" made a slowdown comment such as is shown on the chartoon on page 37.

This single casual comment reduced output 20 per cent during the third period. The casual remark of a fellow worker had more effect than the explicit instructions of the boss.

We should emphasize that the group influence can be in the other direction—for higher efficiency—though it seldom is. In a variation of the checkerboard work, the secret conspirator was instructed to make one speed-up comment at the start of each of the last two periods. "Can't you hurry things a bit?" and "Can you step on it?" were typical. These casual speed-up messages increased output 50 per cent in the second period and 96 per cent in the third.

The group can give efficiency, but usually the group takes efficiency away.

Feelings of guilt and rationalization. Though stalling may be approved on a particular job, it is nevertheless a source of stress on some of the workers taking part in it. A feeling of guilt is usually touched off when they start stalling. This feeling may be numbed a bit by the group's approval of restriction. The voice of the group seems to drown out the still, small voice of conscience. Some folks try to feel very self-righteous about their restriction, to push out the feeling of guilt. That is why stallers commonly say: "The company is making too much money, anyway." "The boss has it coming to him." "I'm making work for some other person who needs a job."

Rationalization is the technical term for such pseudological self-defenses for questionable conduct. Financier J. P. Morgan had rationalization in mind when he said, "A man always has two reasons for doing anything—a 'good reason' and the real reason."

A rationalization has also been called an alibi, which the person may come to believe. Rationalizations tend to keep stalling going rather than curing it.

7 ■ Cures for Stalling

Piece rate, a bonus, profit sharing, and other incentive methods of payment have been tried with the idea of breaking stalling. Quotas and production drives and prize contests are also used. Sometimes these measures produce results; sometimes they do not. Whether the incentives work or not seems to depend on (1) the human climate of the firm, and (2) the style of the bosses—democratic or autocratic. In general, the incentive will work when the bosses are on the democratic side, but not when they incline in the autocratic direction.

Threats are sometimes tried as a way to break the stalling. The threat may be of individual discharge or demotion, or of closing down the plant and moving to another city. Threats, as you may suspect by now, almost invariably make the situation worse. This is shown by the following data about railroad laborers, as reported by Dr. Daniel Katz and colleagues.

	Per Cent of Men Who Said Boss Threatened Them
High-producing gangs	39
Low-producing gangs	58

The various incentives and threats do not, of course, get at the bottom of the situation. Because the work group sanctions and enforces stalling, we now realize that the surest way to overcome restricted efficiency is to upgrade the attitudes of the group. But the code of the group cannot be changed by a pep talk, lectures on economics, or a bulletin-board announcement. It is a slow process that requires patience and democratic skills on the part of the supervisor or manager.

Steps by which the group attitudes can be upgraded are summarized under this chartoon, which deals with blue-collar workers.

The Trained Leaders Had More Success Getting Workers to Accept the Improved Work Method

Trained Leaders—
1. *Presented the problem, but not a proposed solution.*
2. *Got each man to suggest a solution.*
3. *Let each man air his views, without arguing with him.*
4. *Answered questions, or referred to someone else in the work group.*
5. *Were tolerant of criticisms, without talking back.*
6. *Kept them talking with each other on the problem, until they were ready to reach a group decision.*

From work by Dr. Norman R. F. Maier

Complete or partial acceptance:

95%

50%

TRAINED leaders

UNtrained leaders

The boss usually feels responsible for the efficiency of his department. The rank-and-file worker seldom does—"Why should I wear myself out for something the boss will take the credit for!" There is ordinarily a great difference between the employee and the employer in this motivation for being efficient. But when a spirit of teamwork is built up, and credit and responsibility shared, the workers come to feel more involved in wanting their work to be efficient rather than restricted.

Some amazing transformations in attitudes and efficiency have been made when work groups came to realize they counted for something more than hands.

For personal efficiency, the individual thus needs to understand the work group and become adept in getting along with its members. It takes more than job know-how to enable a person to have all-round efficiency. In the following chapter, we shall take up the three major objectives to keep in mind to round out one's personal efficiency.

— — — — — — — — — — — — — — — — — — — —

The Gist of the Chapter

To get a better mastery of the chapter, recite the answers to these questions to yourself. Look back in the text, if necessary, to refresh your recollection of the details.

1. Who usually determines the per cent of capacity, and how is it done?
2. What are the advantages and disadvantages of job simplification?
3. How can quotas be made most effective in increasing efficiency?
4. Tell about the Optimal Work Level.
5. What are the causes and consequences of stereotyping?
6. Do many people resist changes, and why? How does this affect their efficiency?
7. How does stalling cause a *dishonest* day's work?
8. Why is stalling worse in some jobs than in others?
9. How have people been made more eager to accept new work methods?

Things to Do and Problems to Discuss

These will help you make more practical use of the material.

1. Observe people working at such jobs as elevator operator, soda-fountain clerk, traffic policeman, librarian, bus driver, cigar- or news-stand attendant, etc., and make note of the variety of tasks they have to do. Which jobs have the most variety, which the most sameness from hour to hour?
2. Talk with a man who does time-study work for a large firm. Find out what he does, and how he can detect a worker's stalling.

3. Observe some people working in a public place, such as a soda or lunch counter. What points can you look for to give some basis for rating their efficiency? How do the human relations seem to be between the workers? with their boss? with their customers? Assume that you have been hired as a consultant to advise the management, and prepare a report of your observations and recommendations.

4. Discuss factors other than the greater variety in their work that could make skilled workers more satisfied with their jobs.

5. In the southern garment plant mentioned, what might have been the effect if the girls had been told the quota was only 130 instead of the actual 140?

6. Discuss some ways an employee should budget his off-the-job time. Should it be different for a blue-collar than for a white-collar worker?

7. Recall some part-time jobs you had when you were younger. What were some inefficient practices you followed then? Discuss how these same practices would be a handicap on a regular full-time job.

8. What reasons could account for less stalling among white-collar employees?

9. Discuss the ethics and long-range effects of stalling.

10. Some people believe that legal provisions for job security and unemployment insurance make many workers lose interest in being efficient. Give the evidence you can think of on both sides of this question.

11. Oswald J.'s boss has suddenly been called out of town, and Oswald has been given temporary charge of the crew. The men take advantage of his inexperience by stalling. Recommend methods he could use to get the crew back into high-gear work again. There may be suggestions in the last chartoon.

12. If people can do the rather heavy physical work of the Optimal Level without depleting their energy, why do so many people get tired out at much lighter work?

13. What things might a boss do to interest his workers to become more efficient?

14. What are some inefficient ways you have?

15. Does efficiency mean working at top speed all the time?

16. Effie K. said, "The company is making lots of money—why should I work myself to death for them?" What might cause that attitude? What effect is it likely to have on her work and her future?

3 ■ BALANCING PERSONAL EFFICIENCY

_ _ _ _ _ _ _ _ _ _ _ _ _ _ _ _

WHAT THIS CHAPTER IS ABOUT

1. *Self-efficiency, group-efficiency, and things-efficiency*
2. *Taylor and one-sided efficiency*
3. *Practical psychology to balance it*
4. *Franklin and self-efficiency*
5. *Job enlargement and life enrichment*
6. *Washington and social efficiency*
7. *Social efficiency in modern business*
8. *"The Lonely Crowd"*
9. *Jefferson and efficiency with things*

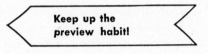

Keep up the preview habit!

1 ■ Self-efficiency, Group-efficiency, and Things-efficiency

Psychological efficiency, we recall, means using our abilities in order to bring optimum results with least waste and strain.

Since each of us is built a bit differently from everyone else, has a slightly different background and slant on life, and has picked up standards from different groups, there is probably no one best way that fits everyone. We have to find the most efficient balance for ourselves. Then apply it on the job and off the job as well.

To become efficiency-minded, one must keep three aspects in view as general objectives. Like the old story of the three-legged stool, it takes all three aspects to balance one's efficiency. These general objectives are:

Self-efficiency: Self-development, so that the percentage of the possible and the level of aspiration are matched
Group-efficiency: Human relations, teamwork, and social efficiency
Things-efficiency: Work methods that save effort and time

These aspects have not been numbered 1, 2, 3, because that might give the impression that number one was the most important. All three aspects are important, but the relative importance of each will vary with the situation.

When a person is training for a new job, things-efficiency may be more important for the time being. When he is starting work on an actual job, then group-efficiency rises in importance. And, after he is getting along on the new job, more emphasis may need to be given to self-efficiency in order to qualify for the climb up the ladder.

Self and group are primarily a matter of applying psychology. Things require a mixture of psychology, common sense, and industrial engineering.

The things are easiest to be efficient with, because they are tangible and can be observed without any abstract thinking. Arranging price sheets for handiest collation is a tangible. Moving desks around to make the flow of work more efficient is another tangible.

But there are also intangibles to consider when desks are moved around. The girl whose desk used to be at a window may find herself facing a corner and may mope at her work because that change makes her feel discriminated against. Another who had the telephone on her desk may lose that token of prestige as tangible desks are moved around. Feeling discriminated against, or that one's prestige is lowered, is an intangible, but mighty important for a person's all-round efficiency. Just as good will is an intangible but a valued business asset.

The self and group objectives in personal efficiency deal with such intangibles. And it usually takes time before a person "catches on" to the meaning and significance of such intangibles. That is a reason why the first practical work on office and factory efficiency was mostly with tangible things.

The big new advances in efficiency are now being made in applying the intangibles of self and group. Today's executives have to work with intangibles perhaps more than with tangibles, as we shall see shortly when we quote some leaders.

Balanced Personal Efficiency

FRANKLIN
Self-development

WASHINGTON
Getting along
with others

JEFFERSON
Efficient
Work methods

2 ■ Taylor and One-Sided Efficiency

In most companies most of the efficiency-mindedness is directed toward the tangible things—a one-legged stool that is wobbly and at times treacherous to use. Automatic machines, conveyors, stop watches, systems, methods, and other paraphernalia of the efficiency expert have produced such one-sided wonders that the unbalanced efficiency they caused has been generally overlooked.

The pioneer who got this work started was Frederick W. Taylor. He made serious beginnings at the time of the Spanish-American War and set a pattern that is still followed throughout business.

Taylor was a young executive, with high aspirations, in a steel company. He paid some attention to self—took night courses in engineering that helped his self-development.

One of his notable accomplishments was made when the steel firm was up against a manpower shortage during the war. Taylor applied scientific methods, as then known, to study the work of loading heavy bars of iron, by muscle power alone, on railroad cars. After some experimentation he concluded that the existing work force could carry more bars of iron if the men took rest pauses at definite intervals during that backbreaking work.

He induced some of the workers to try his new method—he offered them a dollar more a day and flattered them by calling them "high-priced men." Under his new system, a whistle was blown after the men had carried iron for twelve minutes; at this whistle they were to sit down and rest. After three minutes' rest, the tangible whistle was blown again as a signal for the men to pick up their burdens and carry iron. This system increased the amount of iron carried from 12½ to 47 tons a day.

That seeming miracle ushered in the era of rest pauses. But the "high-priced men" didn't take too enthusiastically to it. Whistle blasts were too much like signals for trained seals. The rest pauses weren't their idea, anyway—they were something that had been hatched in the front office by someone with a white collar and a slide rule. The workers had not been given a chance to participate in the planning. Taylor had overlooked the intangible forces in the work group and had won hostility in return for the extra dollar a day. Cartoons lampooned the whistle-blowing efficiency experts.

Another of Taylor's history-making experiments in efficient work methods was in shoveling. After he had concluded that the most efficient, or optimum, load was 22½ pounds, he had the shovels cut to size for various materials. Sand took a small size, ashes a large size, and so on.

"Those are the shovels you use now," he told the much older men who had been shoveling, but inefficiently, all their working lives. So, they had to use the prescribed shovels—but many workers secretly cut an

Courtesy "Banter" of Colgate University

Sad predicament of the efficiency expert who lost his whistle after blowing for the rest period.

inch or two off the shovels. This sabotage, as with most sabotage, was their way of evening things up with an autocratic boss who did not let them take part in planning their own work.

Taylor was right as far as he went, but he didn't go beyond the easily seen and measured tangibles. He had found ways for using muscles that brought better results with less effort—but he had failed to take into account the hidden inputs of injured human dignity and aroused resentment. His group aspects of efficiency were most unscientific by what we know today.

This brings to mind Owen D. Young's comment. He was the farm boy who became chairman of the General Electric Company. "It is not the crook in modern business that we fear, but the honest man who doesn't know what he is doing." Taylor knew only the tangible part of what he was doing. The intangibles he overlooked perpetuated trouble and inefficiency.

3 ■ *Practical Psychology to Balance It*

In Taylor's day, not much was known about practical business psychology, the human intangibles, and the hidden inputs. The "efficiency man" merely followed his impulses in handling people, perhaps polishing up his impulses with some of the tricks of the horse trader.

By the time World War I came around, there was enough new psychological knowledge established for industrial psychology to branch out on its own. That was when the National Institute of Industrial Psychology was founded in London and the Psychological Corporation in New York City. The psychological knowledge that was useful at this time was principally about self: efficient learning, memorizing, and concentrating; the efficient use of muscles and senses; intelligence tests and a few occupational tests; incentives and unconscious motives. Groups were not well understood then.

But, by World War II, group dynamics and human relations had branched out on their own. Today there is a sizable amount of scientific principles that are serviceable for this aspect of practical psychology. And groups seem to have become the central problem in business efficiency. That is why the last three parts of this book are devoted largely to aspects of group dynamics—human relations, personality, and group co-operation.

Frank W. Abrams, a civil engineer who worked up to become chairman of the Standard Oil Company of New Jersey, told young engineers: "In the past decade or two, we have been scrambling to make up for lost time. During the past 35 years—while I have been working in industry—the time that managements have been devoting to problems that have to do with human relations has been vastly increased, until today the manager is apt to spend more hours on such problems than on any others. Perhaps the time that our engineering schools give to studying the stresses and strains of humans should be greatly increased."

Henry Ford II puts it this way: "If we can solve the problems of human relations in industrial production, I believe we can make as much progress toward lower costs during the next ten years as we made during the past quarter century through the development of the machinery of mass production."

Harry A. Bullis, the Iowa bookkeeper who became chairman of General Mills, Inc., sums it up in these words: "During the early years of this century, expansion and production occupied the best business brains. The years between the two world wars were characterized by tremendous emphasis on selling and merchandising. The second half of our century will be marked by inspiring progress in the field of human relations."

Those comments reflect the change that is steadily taking place in the human climate in business. This change is due in large part to new executives with well-rounded training who are taking the places of yesterday's self-made men who were strong on things but weak on groups. This shift is significant for people who are preparing for business today— job know-how has come to include ability to apply some principles of practical psychology in relations with others.

To point up three aspects, or objectives, in this rounding out of know-how, we shall use some famous old Americans. They lived and earned enduring reputations long before Taylor or modern psychology were born. But each, in a sound way that was ahead of his times, was a good practical psychologist. Although each was well-rounded, we shall use them to pinpoint three different goals that should be included in the personal quotas of the business person. This should make the intangibles become more tangible in your thinking.

Benjamin Franklin, George Washington, and Thomas Jefferson are our stars for the next sections. They were efficiency-minded, though too well-rounded to be called "efficiency experts."

4 ■ Franklin and Self-efficiency

Efficiency has been described as a state of mind. An inclination to look for and try out better ways—no stereotyping.

Franklin showed this state of mind as a twelve-year-old. He was helping his father salt down a barrel of meat for the large family. "It would save time," the boy suggested, "if you said Grace over the barrel now and didn't have to do it at each meal." Suggestion not accepted. As a nineteen-year-old, his efficiency was about things. He was cocksure and saw no need to improve himself. At this time he was argumentative and overbearing; an annoyance to others. But a helpful Quaker called his attention to the value of intangibles: "Thee has won an argument, but lost a friend."

That set Franklin back on his heels. Not a chap to be stereotyped, he undertook to develop himself out of his conceit and annoying habits. To check his impulses to make irritating comments, for instance, he would instead say something that might build friendships. "I made it a rule to forbear all direct contradiction to the sentiments of others," he wrote later.

For this section, however, we want to look into the plans he made for his self-development between the ears—the self aspect of personal efficiency. He came to realize that his troublemaking arrogance was a false front to cover up his lack of real knowledge. That is a common cause of conceit—to bluff to conceal a weakness.

Instead of pretending to know it all as a way to compensate for the mere two years of schooling he had, Franklin found a better way out. He began to round himself out by acquiring more knowledge—self-development.

He started serious study of the limited supply of books available, but he soon set a higher quota for himself. To get more books, he organized a group of other young men, who pitched in and bought books together for their own library.

He formed the Junto Club, which met for regular discussions. Each member had to participate in their member-centered rather than leader-centered meetings—in this they anticipated the findings of modern group dynamics about the superiority of member-centered meetings. The topics they talked over were serious and were assorted to round out the members: astronomy, currency, natural science, art, government.

Within a few years, Franklin was one of the best informed young men of his day. No more unconscious motive to put on a cocksure false front. He was developing himself between the ears and never stopped. He retired from business at forty-one, one of the rich men of the time. But his retirement was spent in further self-development and in service to his country, not in the idleness of the fireside.

Self-development counts in personal efficiency, partly because it rounds out the person and partly because it is one of the best antidotes for stereotyping and stalling.

How boss and firm promote self-development. Efficiency can be boosted by encouraging employees into a little self-development. This helps even in laborers' jobs where there is slight opportunity for promotion. In gangs of railroad section laborers, a few of the foremen taught the men some railroading that was in addition to their present work. The following pair of figures shows that this little self-development boosted productivity among men who were tamping crossties and leveling rails because they knew more than the absolute essentials of their present jobs.

	Per Cent of Men Who Said That Their Boss Taught Them New Duties
High-producing gangs	39
Low-producing gangs	19

Some executives informally pass along book-club selections and other books for their employees to read. Many of the larger firms provide courses that are not directly related to the work of the company. Other firms pay tuition charges for courses that seem to have little bearing on the job, but which may have beneficial results in the long run as they round out the employees' personal efficiency.

"A strong leader knows that if he develops his associates he will be even stronger," James F. Lincoln, president of the Lincoln Electric Company, told a group of executives.

5 ▪ Job Enlargement and Life Enrichment

One feature of modern business makes self-rounding-out more essential than it was in Franklin's era. As firms increase in size, a large share of jobs is made smaller and repetitive. Job simplification, which was started by Taylor, breaks big jobs into little ones with an aim for efficiency with things.

The job of office clerk used to include, say, six different operations, which gave the clerk some variety and required a little more skill than a single-operation job. But now that job is likely to be divided into six different jobs, one clerk doing just one operation—the trained-seal situation that uses a small per cent of the workers' capacities.

A few companies have taken steps to repair this oversimplification of jobs. J. D. Elliott, supervisor of the customers' billing department of the Detroit Edison Company, reported some experiences with job enlargement at a session of the American Management Association. Job enlargement puts back together some of the operations that had been separated when the quest for one-sided efficiency with things was in vogue—using a larger per cent of the workers' capacities.

In one billing routine, for instance, three typists and a tabulating-machine operator made up the working unit. Under job simplification, the

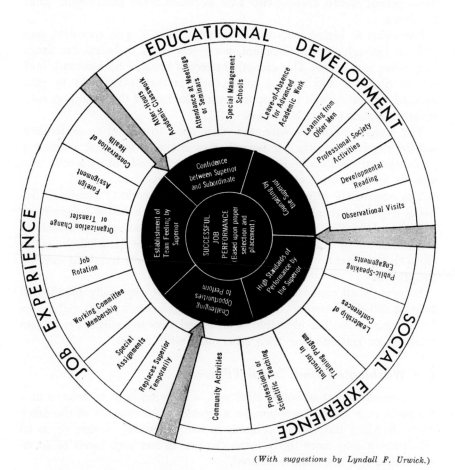

(*With suggestions by Lyndall F. Urwick.*)

Monsanto Chemical Company: methods of developing key employees.

typists typed bills all day long; and a fourth girl operated the machine. It was simple to enlarge this job. Instead of three typists and a machine operator, they used four typists. The typists took turns running the printing machine—more variety and more skill.

Mr. Elliott made a cost survey of comparable operations in 122 electric utility companies. Some of the companies had used job simplification, and others had kept the jobs enlarged. He found that the work was done 40 per cent cheaper on the enriched jobs. This is a thought-provoking demonstration that more than things determine efficiency. Self has to be included in the figuring.

The railroad section bosses who taught the men more about railroading than their immediate jobs required were enriching jobs informally. The humdrum work on the section became more meaningful.

Life enrichment. The big return to the individual in his quest for self-development is life enrichment. Life becomes more meaningful, more satisfying.

Promotion to higher responsibilities often hinges upon rounding oneself out through self-development, not solely upon technical excellence in running a machine. The executive needs a broader background, both for his decisions and for the social contacts that increase as he goes upward. Quotas for self-development can take care of this rounding out—realistic quotas, not wishful ones.

The junior executive's wife, too, may need to set up some realistic self-development quotas for herself. Her husband may not become a major executive unless he is backed up on the home front by a wife who also fits into executive circles. She is his social assistant.

The executive's private secretary, who is his working assistant, also needs more of this self-enlargement than do the girls in the typing pool.

But Andrew Carnegie cannily noted, "You cannot push anyone up the ladder unless he is willing to climb himself." He speckled the country with free libraries to give help to those who were trying to develop themselves.

Soon we shall come to some chapters that are especially planned to help in self-development: Reading, Memory, Learning. But right now let us look at another objective of balanced personal efficiency; human relations, or getting along with others and with groups.

6 ■ Washington and Social Efficiency

The smallest part of social efficiency is knowing how to behave at a tea party or a formal reception, in a swanky restaurant, or at the office party. Reading the society columns is not necessarily a sign of social efficiency—it may more likely mean the person has high levels of social aspirations that are a bit frustrated.

Social efficiency takes in the broad field of human relations—getting along with fellow workers as well as the casual contacts with the bus driver or the blind woman at the newsstand.

Getting along with groups, too—with groups that follow different religions, belong to other lodges, are of various occupational levels, and have other hobbies and recreations. The world is crisscrossed with people who are organized in formal groups as well as in—the larger number—informal groups without officers or written constitutions. A labor union or a camera club is a formal group. Cliques and most office groups are informally organized. These groups usually pull in different directions, which does not help the general harmony. The person with efficient human relations gets them to pull together more for him.

George Washington's story can highlight this aspect of efficiency. He was not so all-round efficiency-minded as Franklin. Washington did not give much attention to self-development or study and little to efficiency with things. But, when he was fifteen, he took a big step in the quest for social efficiency and kept on stepping in that direction. This quest probably changed the history of our country.

This aspect of personal efficiency may have interested him because he was chided about his homeliness and hot temper. Good human relations might make up for these handicaps, he probably thought.

His mother told him, "Your nose is growing up before the rest of you." It was a big nose, always. Feet, too—shoes size 13. Face pitted with smallpox scars and embroidered with freckles. That was the shy fifteen-year-old who felt conspicuous and inferior when around others.

He might have overcompensated by belittling others or have withdrawn inside his shell and stayed in the corner. Instead, at fifteen, he made a direct attack to build good human relations on something besides the handsome looks and wealth that he lacked.

The young backwoodsman sharpened a quill pen and wrote in a notebook some guides he was going to follow. He worked out his own rules of practical social psychology. Here are some of them, in his own picturesque wording that reminds us of a prayer book.

> Jog not the desk on which another reads or writes; lean not on anyone.
> Show not yourself glad at the misfortune of another, though he were your enemy.
> When a man does all he can, though it succeeds not well, blame not him that did it.
> Break no jests that are sharp-biting, and if you deliver anything witty, abstain from laughing thereat yourself.
> Be not hasty to believe reports to the disparagement of any.
> Gaze not on the blemishes of others, and ask not how they came.

The full list of his fifty-seven rules is given in *The Technique of Personal Analysis*, starting at page 17. (Your public library probably has a copy.)

Washington carried that book of self-made rules with him for years. It was a secret treasure he carefully preserved and followed. Several Virginia belles rejected him as a suitor—he was so homely and without property. They might have felt differently had they known what that secret treasure was going to help him achieve through getting others to follow him.

His level of aspiration was moderate. Not grasping or driving. He would not accept a salary as President. He did not push himself but was pulled forward by others. The offices sought the man whose book of rules won honors that only other individuals and groups can give. He could get better teamwork and co-operation than many of his contemporaries who were better educated and more capable, but who could not measure up to him in human relations.

Washington's boyhood analysis gave him a you-point of view that dominated his relations with others. This is a large ingredient in what is popularly called personality. As first President, he was ill at ease in his duties of entertaining visiting nobility. But his you-point enabled him to make the other fellow feel at ease and appreciated. *How the other fellow feels is the important point in human relations.*

7 ■ Social Efficiency in Modern Business

In seventeen offices in the eastern headquarters of one of our largest firms, the work was practically identical. But these offices varied in their productivity and also in the supervisors' attitudes about human relations. About half the supervisors considered human relations an important part of their jobs. The following breakdown, reported by Dr. Daniel Katz, shows how this human-relations attitude was related to higher productivity.

	Per Cent of Supervisors Who Thought Human Relations Important
High-producing offices	83
Low-producing offices	30

Records such as those are one reason why progressive firms are now training their supervisors in human-relations methods. The right training can be highly effective, as is shown by studies Dr. Irving Lorge has made for the United States Air Force. In one project with 400 officers, the following gains were made as a result of training.

	Quality of Decisions on Human-Relations Problems
Before training	13
After training	24

Washington, at fifteen, had discovered the hazards of even mild criticism. In his notebook he wrote: "Being to advise, or reprehend any one, consider whether it ought to be in public or in private, presently or at some other time, and in what terms to do it; and in reproving show no signs of choler, but do it with sweetness and mildness." Criticizing others is something supervisors often have to do; Washington's guide can be helpful when these occasions arise.

Over-all efficiency is also influenced by the way the people in a work group "hit it off together." How great this influence can be is shown by a construction contractor's records. His firm was building identical rows of houses in a new suburb. On some rows, the union carpenters and bricklayers were teamed together on the usual random basis; but, on other rows, the workers were teamed on the basis of their mutual liking.

Sociometric methods. Sociometric methods were used to arrange these mutually attracted work teams. Each worker gave, in confidence, the names of other workers he would most like to work with. The psychologists used these choices to arrange teams in which John not only preferred Henry as a working mate but Henry also preferred John—two-way, mutual attraction.

The chartoon shows lowering in labor cost for those rows of houses that were built by the sociometric teams. There were pleasant human relations between these workers, without anyone having to make much effort to get along with the others. There were also marked savings in materials used. The net result was that these sociometric groups pro-

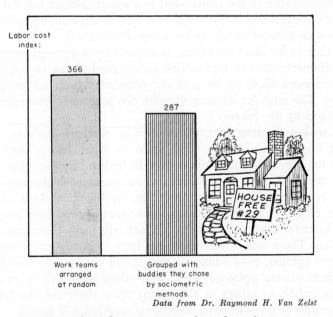

When the workers chose teammates themselves, the contractor got every twenty-ninth house free.

duced so much more and saved enough materials, so that the contractor got every twenty-ninth house free. In addition, absenteeism and labor turnover were significantly reduced.

This shows dramatically the business value of good working relations among the workers. But we must remember that only natural groupings, or cliques, were used. The individual workers had made no special effort themselves to improve their human relations, as Washington did.

8 ■ "The Lonely Crowd"

Social efficiency has probably counted since the Garden of Eden. But there is evidence that it counts more than ever in our present world. There have been many changes that seem to make human relations the number-one problem of the twentieth century, as Edward Bernays expressed it.

An account of these changing forces, and how they have affected the typical American, has been given by Dr. David Riesman in his book, *The Lonely Crowd* (Yale University Press). The increase in population, the switch to city life, higher living standards, and larger business units are some of the forces that have put people under more stress in their social relations—not like Washington's time, when most people lived in rural sections and were self-employed. (Today, only about 18 per cent of the gainfully employed are their own bosses.)

As a result of these changes, to state it in extreme fashion, people tend to feel buried alive in the crowd—lost in a sea of familiar but not friendly faces on the street and in the workplace. This swallowing up by the crowd leads people to want keenly to be accepted by others.

Wanting to be liked by others is apparently a stronger motive than it was formerly. It was wealth that determined status in Taylor's day; now it is more likely to be personal popularity built on good human relations. The wish for keeping up with the Joneses is weakening, while being liked by the Joneses is rising.

This makes it easier to understand why workers—such as the girls making checkerboards—responded more to what fellow workers said than to the boss's orders. Workers want to be liked by the other workers. If they are liked, then they do not feel so lonesome in the crowd.

At a recent meeting of the American Psychological Association, Dr. Bertram H. Raven reported an experiment that showed how people even distort facts in order to hold opinions that will make them popular with the group. There was distortion of the facts to justify going along with the group opinion, even when the people did not have to tell the group what their private opinions were. But, when they had to make their opinions public to others in the group, they stretched the facts to a much greater degree—in other words, rationalized still more.

They feel less lonely when they think as the crowd does. So, they hold

Data from Drs. Daniel Katz and Robert L. Kahn

Half felt accepted, the others felt more or less lonely in their work crowd.

together to turn out only as much as the group feels the boss deserves. Standards of thinking as well as standards of living are greatly influenced by group forces.

Do many workers feel they are left out of the work crowd? This cartoon shows what was found among a tractor plant's blue-collar workers. This firm has a progressive personnel department that tries to keep the men from being swallowed up.

Do you wonder how many of those who did not feel completely accepted had tried to follow Washington's example? Or did they think it was entirely up to the personnel department to solve the problem of human relations by making sociometric groupings, so that their social efficiency—and happiness—would not require their own efforts?

The verdict of business leaders. In Section 3 we listened to what such leaders as Frank W. Abrams, Henry Ford II, and Harry A. Bullis had to say about the changing human climate in business. They spoke from a company point of view. Now let's hear some other leaders about the individual you-point in human relations.

Every businessman needs to learn how to get along with others, both as individuals and as groups. Some of that knowledge can come only through experience, but much of it can be taught.—John L. McCaffrey, the Ohio boy who became president of the International Harvester Company.

In almost every business relationship the human touch counts. Business at rock bottom is essentially a human undertaking, run by and for human beings.—Sir Henri Deterding, bookkeeper who organized worldwide oil companies.

Men are judged to a large degree by their ability to work with other men.—Robert F. Black, the truck salesman who became president of the White Motor Company.

The last two parts of this book are devoted to ways for removing hindrances and irritations that otherwise make the crowd lonely.

9 ■ Jefferson and Efficiency with Things

Efficiency with things scarcely needs to be given separate emphasis. It is easy to presume that a shiny, new gadget, which is tangible, means new efficiency. It is this obvious aspect of efficiency that has been used most and that people are inclined at first thought to imagine is all there is to efficiency.

Shy, sandy-haired Thomas Jefferson knew there was more to work than mechanical efficiency. He watched his self-development, and his relations with others, too. But he was mechanically inclined and enjoyed tinkering and planning things. When he went to the White House, he took along his own set of tools for spare-moment tinkering.

It was not until his second year in college, however, that he began to get efficiency-minded. This shift in his thinking helped his transition from play years to work years.

One of his first steps in efficiency was to put time to work for him. He laid out a daily time quota for various activities and followed it. Later in life, the long-time foreman of his plantation said he had seen Jefferson sitting unoccupied only twice—once when he had a toothache, the other time when he had an attack of neuralgia. "Mr. Jefferson was the most industrious person I ever saw in my life," said the admiring foreman.

To use odd moments during the slow travel of those days, Jefferson had a Philadelphia carpenter build a traveling writing desk that Jefferson himself designed. He could hold this desk on his lap or place it on a stand and could tilt the adjustable top to a convenient angle and take writing materials—including sand for blotting—from the drawer at the side. He wrote the Declaration of Independence on this desk.

Answering letters was a major task for him as he rose in influence.

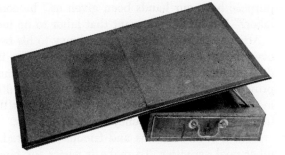

Portable writing desk that Jefferson had built to increase his working efficiency.

Courtesy of the Smithsonian Institution, Washington

There were no typewriters or carbon paper. But the polygraph had just been invented, and Jefferson eagerly used it to make copies of his outgoing letters. The polygraph had a series of pens connected by levers, so that when one pen was moved the others moved in a similar route. The writer simply fastened a sheet of paper under each pen, and as he wrote with the master pen, copies in his own handwriting were made simultaneously. Jefferson invented some improvements to boost the efficiency of this polygraph.

He was enthusiastic about the polygraph as an aid to personal efficiency and promoted its use. Sometimes he sent friends the copy rather than the original letter, to demonstrate its usefulness.

Our decimal system of currency was also promoted by him. It seemed to him more efficient than the pounds, shillings, and pence that had been in use in the colonies.

The mass system of production, which had just been devised by Eli Whitney for making army muskets, was also promoted arduously by Jefferson. Some of the 1,267 letters he answered in longhand in one year as a private citizen deal with the superior efficiency of this new production method.

He made time studies long before Taylor's day. When building his mansion at Monticello, he timed the work when one-wheeled and when two-wheeled barrows were used to transport materials. He found the two-wheeled more efficient.

Pedometers had just been invented—they hung on one's belt and measured the distance walked. Always interested in innovations, he used these instruments to find the most efficient walking speed and decided it was 4 miles an hour. Metabolism studies have shown that for the average person it is 3 miles an hour. Jefferson's rangy leg length may have made the 4-mile speed more suited to him; there are, of course, individual differences and not one way that is the optimum for everybody.

Fatigue study also intrigued him—work with least effort. He was not a lazy man; he preferred to build his own fires rather than have a servant do it. He planted thousands of trees with his own hands. "For what purpose have our hands been given us," he commented once, "if not for labor?" But he did not want that labor to be inefficient. For instance:

After he retired from the presidency to his beloved Monticello, he was overwhelmed with visits from admirers. The isolated mountaintop was difficult to reach, and there were no nearby motels. Jefferson hospitably provided food and lodging for as many as fifty guests at a time—and most of them unexpected guests with horses that also had to be cared for. This was social efficiency under handicaps.

Such a swarm of fans and friends distracted his letter answering and other goal activities. To make it easier for him to concentrate, he built a poplar forest a short distance from the main mansion. He would go there at regular hours each day—still following a time quota, as in his sophomore year—to keep caught up with his goals without being interrupted or distracted.

Nothing high pressure or driving about Jefferson, a relaxed worker, a steady worker, efficiency-minded, as he progressed toward realistic goals.

"How is my efficiency?" is really three questions in one. It breaks down into:
"How efficiently am I developing myself?"
"How'm I doing in efficiency with people?"
"How's my efficiency in working with things?"

— — — — — — — — — — — — — — — — — — — —

The Gist of the Chapter

1. What are three general objectives to keep in mind in balancing one's efficiency? How does the relative importance of these vary with circumstances?

2. Which of the general objectives is usually the most difficult to apply? Why?

3. What were the good points and bad points of Taylor's methods?

4. How is balancing one's efficiency affected by changes that have been and are taking place in the human climate of business?

5. Which objective was illustrated by Franklin's story, and how did he work toward it?

6. What are some things businesses do to help the self-development of their employees?

7. Which objective was illustrated by Washington's story, and how did he work toward it?

8. What are some differences between formal groups and informal groups?

9. What are sociometric methods, and how are they used?

10. What does "The Lonely Crowd" suggest about the way human conditions have been changing?

11. Which objective was illustrated by Jefferson's story, and how did he work toward it?

Things to Do and Problems to Discuss

1. Find out what some firms in your locality do to help the self-development of their employees, and report on it. Or, work out a plan that some firm could adopt for helping that self-development.

2. Observe some workers and report to what extent their methods and attitudes confirm the quotation from William James in Section 5 of the first chapter.

3. Give a report on someone you know who has failed in business, or has lost his job. How could his failure be attributed to his neglect of some aspect of his efficiency?

4. Interview some executives to find out and report on how much of their working time they estimate is spent on problems relating to things; how much, relating to people? Which do they find easier to deal with?

5. Discuss whether the desire to develop oneself is inborn or acquired. What difference would it make to management? to the individual?

6. Describe situations you have observed that might make employees feel their dignity was injured; also some situations that might lead them to feel they were respected as individuals.

7. Discuss why a person's desire to be popular with others might motivate him to follow the crowd and stall on the job.

8. Discuss whether or not it would be a good policy to place people from the same neighborhood on jobs where they could work together.

9. Would it be a good policy in seeking new employees to ask present employees to suggest to their friends that they apply for work?

10. Jefferson was eager to use new machines, but many workers resist changes of that sort. Discuss how this difference could be accounted for.

11. Discuss Taylor's findings about shovel size and how it jibes with the information in Chapter 2 on The Optimal Work Level.

12. Consider some simple jobs you have observed, such as elevator operator, cigar-stand clerk, and discuss what could be done to enlarge them.

13. Give some examples you have observed of people who bluff to conceal a weakness.

14. Which would be the better job for twenty-two-year-old Oswald J. (a) high pay with a firm that left it up to the employees to sink or swim, or (b) average pay with a firm that assisted in self-development? in case of a middle-aged employee?

15. Effie K. believes in "doing others before they do you." For good social efficiency, however, which is the better way (a) to do to others as you would like to have them do to you, or (b) to do to others as they want you to do?

16. Just to see how good your incidental observation is: on which paper money have you seen the picture of Franklin? of Washington? of Jefferson?

4 ■ RAPID READING,
WORD POWER,
AND EASY SEEING

WHAT THIS CHAPTER IS ABOUT

1. *The cash value of reading*
2. *Read for meaning*
3. *Steps to gain reading speed*
4. *Reading habits for special uses*
5. *When and how to skim a page*
6. *Building word power*
7. *Primary mental abilities in word power*
8. *Legibility in reports and writing*
9. *Lighting for reading and working*
10. *Are your eyes right?*
11. *Right-eyed or left-eyed?*
12. *Eye hygiene and exercises*

< **Get the Mental Set.** <

1 ■ The Cash Value of Reading

Before Morris Fishbein entered medical school, he took a course in shorthand to speed note taking. He was a brilliant student, who added to his brilliance by adopting efficient working methods. Speedy reading was one of his accomplishments. His colleagues report that he could read an entire paragraph at one glance, and sometimes a page in two glances. When he was a young doctor, the American Medical Association appointed him editor of their weekly journal, a post he held for more than thirty years. To keep himself busy, he started other medical journals. When he retired, the association had to appoint four people to do the work this speedy reader had been doing!

Money-making ideas, promotions, fun, and a complete education can be gained from reading.

Thomas Edison did not have many years of schooling, but his wide reading made him well educated. His deafness made it easy for him to concentrate on reading. In his laboratory, he built up one of the best scientific libraries of his time.

"When I want to discover something," he said, "I begin by reading up everything that has been done along that line in the past—that's what all those books in the library are for. I use these books to prevent waste of time and money, by not doing again the things that have already been done or tried out by others. I generally recommend only those books that are written by men who actually describe things plainly, simply, and by analogy with things everybody knows."

Case Institute of Technology found that engineers average three hours a day of on-the-job reading. If they could read faster, the time released could be used otherwise.

Our fast-moving world requires more and more serious reading if we hope to keep up with it. There are more than thirty magazines published in the field of advertising alone and another ten on salesmanship. There are thirty more on business and office methods, seven on women's clothing, and nineteen on textiles. The plumber has more than thirty magazines dealing with his trade, as does the motor-truck operator.

Books galore, too. Nearly ten thousand new books are published in the United States each year. Some years, more than that also are published in England.

Then there are all the memos, reports, and instructions within a firm to read, as Case Institute of Technology found.

Yet reading is a recent accomplishment. A hundred years ago, not half the people in the country could read. Those who could read usually had been taught by methods that made their reading inefficient. They read too slowly and did not gain enough of the sense from their reading.

Most adults today do not read so well as a well-taught seventh-grade pupil of a modern school—less than 200 words a minute. An efficient reader can cover more than 700 words a minute, and he can glean more sense from it than the slow reader.

Many firms are now giving their executives courses to train them to read more rapidly. The top twenty-one executives in a plant of the Monsanto Chemical Company illustrate the benefits. Here is what Dr. Cecil J. Mullins reported about the executives' improvement.

	Words Read a Minute
Before training	257
After 43 hours' training	811
One year after close of the training	537

This greater reading speed cut in half the time these executives needed to spend on their essential reading each day. It meant an annual saving of $40,000 in executive time that could be used for duties other than reading.

How can well-educated adults, who have been reading since they were six, be taught to double their reading speed? Haven't their many years of practice made them as perfect as they can be? They have had years

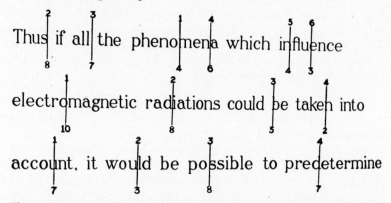

The eye pauses are shown by vertical marks. The numerals at the top of the vertical marks show the order in which eye pauses were made. The other numerals show how long the eye paused, in 30ths of seconds. This reader got off to a poor start by beginning in the middle of the first line and so had to jump back to the first word. But that was the only regressive movement he made. His eye paused 5 times a line. The average pause was not quite ⅕ second for him to catch the meaning.

of practice, true enough, but wrong practice. It is that way with practice in many things—the wrong kind of practice.

2 ▪ Read for Meaning

Eyes and mind co-operate in reading—the eyes to see, the mind to understand. The aim in reading is to grasp the meaning quickly and easily. So, *look for the meaning,* not for the spelling. Reading and spelling are two separate arts.

Here are three lines, each of which can be read with equal ease.

p r h w
auto single
The apple is big and red

The first line is meaningless. The second line is two unrelated words, totaling ten letters. The third line is six related words that make sense, but it is nineteen letters long. Nineteen letters that make sense can be read as easily as only four that have no meaning. That is one secret of speedy reading. *Read for meaning.*

Do you realize that you are blind much of the time while reading? Watch your eyes move while you look in a mirror. You cannot see them while they move, for the eyes are as good as blind while in motion. This is why police are trained to read license numbers of moving automobiles with a quick glance, rather than try to follow the moving license plate. The same principle applies for inspecting products on a moving conveyor or typewriter carriage.

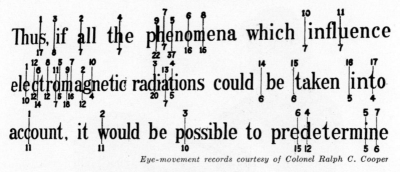

Eye-movement records courtesy of Colonel Ralph C. Cooper

An Inefficient Reader

This man had 12 pauses a line, and 9 regressive movements in the 3 lines. Notice that he must have spelled out "electromagnetic." His average pause was a little more than ⅓ second to catch the meaning—or was it to spell the words out?

When you are reading a line of print, the eye jumps from one place to another along the line. It does not move steadily. It jumps and pauses. It is only during the pauses (called *fixations*) that the eye sees. During the jumps, everything is blurred.

A poor reader has a dozen fixations along a line. An efficient reader has only half as many of these stop-to-get-the-sense pauses.

The poor reader looks at each letter to catch the word. The efficient reader senses the word from *a quick look at its general form.* The poor reader pauses longer at each fixation.

The very poor reader not only tries to see each letter but also spells out each one. Spelling is not reading. Read with the head, not the lips. The brain is quicker than the lips.

The old saying about "slow but sure" is not true for reading. Rapid readers get more sense from their reading. When a slow reader's speed is increased by training and the right practice, he learns more from his reading.

3 ■ Steps to Gain Reading Speed

Several gadgets have been invented to train people to read better. Some of these are exposure devices, similar to a camera shutter. They flash a phrase for a fraction of a second. Short phrases are flashed first, to train the person to *read an entire phrase at a glance.*

Another instrument holds a book page, over which a curtain is drawn steadily, a line at a time. This forces the person to read quickly or miss the line entirely. It *sets a pace* that makes the reader speed up to keep up with the curtain.

Reading can be improved without using apparatus. After all, the es-

Courtesy Science Research Associates, Chicago

The reading accelerator. The moving curtain lowers down the page, forcing people to "put on the gas" and read faster. The speed at which the shutter descends can be adjusted to speed up the pace of reading as more skill is gained.

sential apparatus is your own head and eyes. Use them according to the following rules until good, speedy reading becomes a habit.

Read phrases, not words. Notice more words during each eye pause. Concentrate directly on words, not on letters.

Look at the upper half of words, not at the lower half.

Look at the beginning of words. Skip the endings of English words.

Keep eyes moving from left to right. Eliminate backward moves. Get it the first time, so that you do not have to look backward.

Push yourself to catch the meaning. Read a newspaper line in two eye pauses. For a book-width line, strive to cover it in four or five pauses.

Keep lips and tongue motionless. Control any tendency to spell or pronounce words. Avoid "inner speech," too. If you read less than 350 words a minute, you are probably saying the sounds in some way. Reading seldom becomes silent reading until the rate is 400 words a minute or faster.

Keep alert to catch meanings faster. Try to read five words faster each succeeding day for a month, by catching the meanings of increasingly longer phrases. Look for the ideas, don't expect them to hit you on the head. Reading with the radio turned on slows speed and lowers comprehension.

Keep at it until faster reading is a habit. Reach the goal of reading 400 or more words a minute.

4 ▪ Reading Habits for Special Uses

The typist needs rapid-reading-for-sense for her personal reading but needs reading-for-spelling in her work. Proofreaders need the same two sets of reading methods. Students must read textbooks differently from favorite magazines.

Chart reading also requires different habits from prose reading. Studies by Dr. Francis P. Robinson, at Ohio State University, indicate that blueprint reading may require still different reading skills.

While the individual needs an assortment of reading habits, most emphasis should be given to speedy comprehension as the basic habit. The following reading rates should be minimum goals for self-development.

	Words a Minute
Study	200
Serious books	250
Serious magazines	300
Fiction	400
Telephone directory, signs, advertisements, newspapers	2,000

5 ▪ When and How to Skim a Page

The ultraspeedy method of reading is skimming, or scanning. This is the way to read most newspapers. Hit the high spots in headlines, with an occasional fixation on an entire first paragraph in a single glance. The skimming method also should be used when hunting for a date, a name, an address, an idea, or a price quotation.

Use a diagonal sweeping glance downward across a page when skimming. With practice, one can soon scan five or six lines of type in a single brief pause of the eye.

It has not been proved that practice in skimming helps reading speed otherwise. But skimming is a habit worth having when one is hunting information in correspondence, files, or books. When looking up a word in the dictionary, for example, skim down the column until the word you are looking for hits you in the eye.

Skimming is also a helpful preliminary for studying. Skim through the chapter first, noticing key phrases, pictures, and charts, to obtain a general view of what is ahead. This takes only three or four minutes but makes the thorough reading easier and more meaningful. That is why this book has the section "What this chapter is about" at the beginning of each chapter.

After skimming through an assignment or a trade-journal article to find your bearings, settle down to read for ideas—but read rapidly. It helps to underline key words with a soft pencil.

6 ▪ Building Word Power

Strange words throw a roadblock across the path of rapid reading. The serious reader needs to pause at a new word long enough to (1) try to figure the meaning, or (2) look it up in a dictionary and perhaps pencil the meaning right on the margin of the page, then (3) say it aloud to get the pronunciation. After pronouncing the word, go back to rapid silent reading for ideas.

Anyone aiming for executive work needs especially to develop a good vocabulary, partly because he must keep up necessary reading to stay abreast of the field, partly because the executive's principal tools are words. The executive needs a two-way vocabulary. He must understand the meanings of big words himself, and he must translate meanings into little words in passing on the idea or instructions to workers. Take in big words. Give out little ones.

Little words are important in sales work, too. One paint manufacturer lost sales because his house paint was advertised as "for exterior use." Many persons did not know whether exterior meant inside the house or outside. Sales jumped as soon as the paint description was changed to "especially for outside use."

John Wanamaker kept a daily list of new words that he looked up every evening. Some evenings he would continue to read the dictionary

Vocabulary
score:

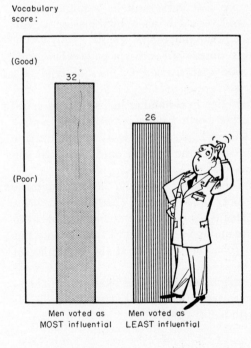

(Good)

32

26

(Poor)

Men voted as
MOST influential

Men voted as
LEAST influential

A good vocabulary made them more influential.

Data from Major Norman E. Green

as if it were a mystery story. He started this habit when ten years old and kept it up for more than sixty years.

Some people have to try harder than others to build a vocabulary. This is due to differences that seem to be largely inborn. Women, as a rule, excel in the ability to learn to use words. This is one of the few sex differences that really seems to be inborn. Often, a secretary can write a better letter than the one her boss dictates.

7 ■ Primary Mental Abilities in Word Power

Experiments on *primary mental abilities* (usually abbreviated *PMA*) have shown that people have more or less inborn specialized word powers. *PMA* are discovered by mathematical methods of *factor analysis*. Facts uncovered by factor analysis have revolutionized the knowledge of human abilities.

Factor analysis makes it possible to find the lowest common denominators of mental powers. Each primary mental ability, segregated by factor analysis, is virtually independent of all other mental abilities and is a basic factor. This is similar to such chemical discoveries as that water is not an element but is made from hydrogen and oxygen. Factor analysis splits the atom of the mind.

Here are primary mental abilities that are related to vocabulary building.

Word fluency is the ability to think of the right word. How many given names, such as Mary and Frank, can you think of in one minute that begin with the letter *L?* That is a sample test of word fluency. This ability to think of the right word is independent of the size of your vocabulary. It is useful in solving crossword puzzles and prevents hemming and hawing in dictation. Good talkers need good word fluency.

Talking fluency may in turn be made up of two factors: word fluency plus *idea fluency*. When a person hems and haws to find the right word, he may not know the word or he may have run out of ideas.

Word meaning is another PMA, distinct from fluency. It is the ability to understand words heard or read. It matures rather late in life and is one reason why it is difficult to understand intangibles until late in the teens or after. Word meaning is important for understanding directions and learning foreign languages.

Émile Zola was a prolific French writer with good word and idea fluency. But his PMA for word meaning was so weak that he could not learn foreign languages.

Versatility is another PMA that relates to the turnover or rate of using words. The chatterbox who talks a mile a minute but keeps saying the same thing in different ways has a high versatility. He is likely to waste words in letters or telegrams.

Although the PMA are largely inborn, they can still be improved somewhat by intelligent effort.

You will get acquainted with other primary mental abilities in the next chapter.

8 ■ Legibility in Reports and Writing

Legibility means easy to read. In printing, legibility is influenced by the size of type. Newspaper type is too small for easy reading. Type a size larger than you see in most books has the best legibility, and that size is used in most advertising booklets. Elite typewriter type is not so easily read as pica.

The length of lines also influences ease of reading. Newspaper line length is easier to read than book length. A typewritten line across an 8½-by-11 inch letterhead is too long; a sheet 5¼ by 8½ inches, the so-called half size, allows for a more legible length of line. Most professional advertisements use short line lengths.

White space between the lines adds ease to reading. Solid type with no extra white space between the lines is difficult to read. A double-spaced typewritten letter is much easier to read than a single-spaced letter. Extra spacing between paragraphs also adds to reading ease.

Styles of type vary greatly in legibility. In general, the style of type that most people have become accustomed to is the most legible to them—stereotyping in our perceptions. But Old English, script, gothic, and italic types are harder to read than everyday roman. Words printed entirely in capitals are difficult to read and should be used very sparingly.

Occasionally, someone favors an unusual style of type, aiming to be distinctive. While a peculiar style may be suitable for a trade-mark, it is risky to use for advertisements or letters if it is not easy to read. An unusual style of handwriting is sometimes cultivated to be distinctive, but the most legible handwriting, as with printing, is a style that looks like everyone else's.

The color of paper and ink also influences ease of reading. No combination has yet been invented that beats a good black ink on soft white paper. Glossy paper causes irritating glare. Colored paper lessens the contrast between paper and type and makes reading more difficult. If colored paper must be used, the type size or the spacing between lines should be increased.

Newspapers and telephone directories are tiring to the eyes partly because they have small type and also because the paper is grayish. A fresh ribbon and fresh carbon paper add legibility to typewriting by keeping the printing black rather than gray.

9 ■ Lighting for Reading and Working

Eyes will adapt themselves to unfavorable conditions and can be used well enough for a time. Lincoln studied law by the flickering light from a fireplace, but that was not easy for his eyes. Poor lighting makes one put more input into work. As eye fatigue increases, there is an increase in involuntary blinking.

There is a loss in visual acuity when the eyes are used continuously for close work. The loss of acuity is most under poor lighting, as shown here.

Loss of Acuity

After three hours of reading in:	
Good daylight	6%
Totally indirect electric light	9%
Semi-indirect electric light	72%
Direct (gooseneck) electric light	81%

Here are eight rules for better reading and working light.

1. Light-colored walls, window shades, and furnishings, even light-colored clothes are helpful.
2. Keep windows and light fixtures washed. Walls need occasional washing, too.
3. Have many small lights evenly scattered rather than a few high-powered ones.
4. Eliminate glaring or shiny spots.
5. Have no light bulbs visible to the eyes.
6. Allow 2½ watts a square foot for general lighting.
7. Have supplementary local lights for tasks requiring close eye work.
8. When in doubt, turn the lights on. Save eyes rather than electricity.

A word of caution is in order about the brass-shaded or green-shaded lamps that many students and some office and machine workers turn on directly over their work. These produce direct, local light. The rest of the room may be dim or dark, but the small area under the light is bright. Such local direct lighting is undesirable, though it may be necessary for diemakers, yellow pages of telephone directories, sewing, and watch repairing.

Local lighting produces great variation in the brightness of the area you look at. The center of a large magazine may be as much as 50 per cent brighter than the edges when local direct light is used for reading. As the eye jumps and jerks across the page, it moves from bright to darker spots—about as hygienic as a light flickering off and on.

Human eyes developed before the age of artificial light. For hundreds of centuries, mankind could do nothing but rest when darkness fell.

Courtesy Cities Service Co.

Shadowless, glare-free lighting, which is of a relatively uniform intensity throughout the room, makes this an easy office in which to use one's eyes. The air conditioning makes it a more comfortable place in which to work. The noncluttered desk tops indicate good working habits.

People worked outside, in full daylight. Eyes work best in daylight, which is many times brighter than the best-lighted office. The artificial lighting under which people read and use their eyes should duplicate the shadowless conditions of daylight.

10 ■ Are Your Eyes Right?

There are many differences between people in the accuracy with which their eyes see. Some people are born with oval faces, some with round faces. Likewise, some have eyeballs that are slightly too long from front to back, others are too short for easy seeing. In some people, the lens that focuses light is out of true and causes blurring in spots.

These individual differences produce problems in reading and seeing when fine work or safety is involved. At age twenty, about one person out of four needs glasses to compensate for these differences. And about half the fifty-year-olds need glasses. More men than women have eye defects that reduce efficiency.

Nearsightedness. The nearsighted person has to hold objects so close to the eyes that he seems to be reading with the end of his nose. Nearsightedness means that the eyeball is too long from front to back, making it diffi-

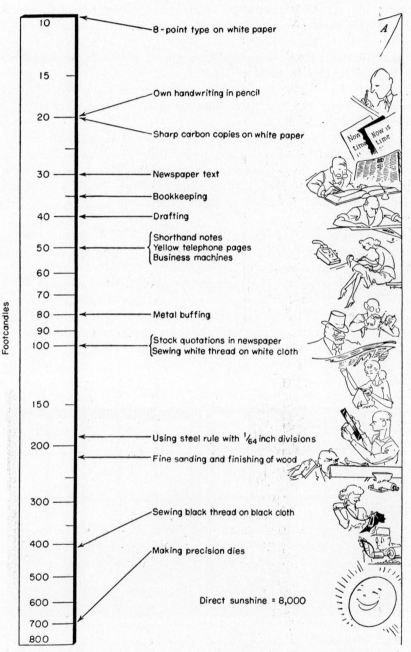

Footcandles of lighting to give equal visibility for the tasks indicated.

cult to see distant objects. These eyes see objects best near to them. A high percentage of brainy people are nearsighted. Nearsightedness usually shows up in early school years, steadily becoming worse until about age twenty-five.

Because it is difficult for nearsighted young people to see distant objects, they acquire the habit of doing a great deal of reading. They cannot play ball and other games, as things a dozen feet away may become hazy. Close eye work is not desirable for nearsightedness, and excessive reading of fine print may make it worse.

Nearsighted people should drive automobiles at slow speeds, as they do not see well far ahead. Some nearsighted people win undeserved reputations for snobbishness because they pass friends on the street without recognizing them—lowering their social efficiency. People who are only slightly nearsighted are likely to stand too close to others when talking with them.

Glasses with concave lenses, which usually look thick, make seeing easy for the nearsighted. The lenses may need to be changed once or twice a year until around age thirty.

Farsightedness. Farsighted people can read street names two blocks away but may knock over a glass of water that is under the elbow, because near objects are indistinct. Farsightedness is due to short eyeballs. People who were nearsighted in youth may become farsighted later. After about age fifty, almost everyone is somewhat farsighted. This is the time when some executives decide to write with heavy crayon pencils, so that they can see what they write.

Photographs here and on the three following pages courtesy Bausch & Lomb Optical Co.

What the nearsighted person sees when looking out the window. The window frame and objects on the ledge are focused, but the buildings across the quadrangle are blurred.

This is how it looks to the farsighted person. Distant objects are clear, but the objects on the window ledge are hazy.

An office manager who stressed neatness became annoyed because the middle-aged janitor was leaving streaks on windows, dusty spots on desks, and scatterings of dirt on the floor. Yet the man seemed conscientious, for the office manager had seen him pick up small bits of paper from the floor. When he noticed that the janitor also was knocking articles over when dusting, it dawned on him that the man's eyes were changing, as most eyes do in middle life. Glasses quickly corrected the situation.

Some clumsiness and inaccuracy among older people is due to the fuzziness of objects close to them. Glasses with proper convex lenses correct for individual differences.

When you are demonstrating merchandise, or showing how to do a job, it is a mistake to assume that the other person can see best at the same distance you can see. Avoid this by putting the merchandise in the other person's hands, suggesting that he hold it where he can see best. When teaching someone a job, ask the learner to stand where he can see best. Because many people are slightly farsighted, yet do not wear glasses, it is always wise to keep at arm's length when talking with others. If the other person wears thick-lensed glasses, then it may be all right to stand closer. Don't make yourself look like a blur, or cause the other person eyestrain.

Astigmatism. In astigmatism (eh-*stig*-ma-tizm), there are blurred zones in the field of vision. This is due to a slight imperfection or flat spot in the eye lens. When a person with astigmatism looks at a wheel, some of the spokes are indistinct and others are sharp. The same axis is hazy when an astigmatic person is trying to read, of course. A person may have astigmatism and nearsightedness or farsightedness at the same time.

Heredity seems to play some part in causing near- and far-sightedness, but not in causing astigmatism. Overuse of eyes or use under poor seeing conditions will make any of these conditions worse. Glasses that are

The person with astigmatism sees this. Everything, both far and near, has an up-and-down blurring. In some forms of astigmatism, the blurring is from side to side, which makes seeing just as difficult.

properly fitted will not weaken the eyes in the least. There are no exercises that will take the place of glasses, though from time to time health fads pretend so. There are exercises that benefit seeing, which are revealed later; but they do not take the place of glasses that correct for individual differences in the size of eyeballs and shape of lenses.

Night blindness. Night blindness is inability to see at night or in dim light. It is a rather rare visual peculiarity that may have considerable business significance. In some instances, night-blind people have serviceable vision only on bright days or under intense light. It is unsafe for them to be working or on the street after dusk. Sometimes vitamin A will remedy this condition, but glasses are of no benefit.

Cross-eye. Cross-eye occurs when the two eyes do not look at the same object. Many persons are slightly cross-eyed, but do not know it. The eyes often deviate slightly inward, but not enough to be visible to others, though enough to make seeing troublesome. Or the two eyes may deviate slightly outward. With other persons, one eye may look a bit higher than the other. These conditions are due to lack of balance in the muscles that move the eyes.

Poor tracking of the eyes is a disadvantage in business, as it causes eyestrain, and also makes it difficult to *perceive distance* or depth. When both eyes do not look squarely at the same object, a person often is as good as blind in one eye. Usable sensations from both eyes are essential to perceive depth. One-eyed people have difficulty knowing when to start turning an automobile around a corner or reaching for an object at a distance.

Many firms, to protect themselves under workmen's compensation laws, give routine eye tests upon employment. Other firms use visual examinations to select employees for work that requires close eye use. A few

Test for astigmatism. Hold a piece of paper in front of the left eye, and look at these disks with the right eye. If one disk is blacker than the others, the right eye has astigmatism. Now try the other eye.

It takes two good eyes to judge distance. Try the test shown here. Lay a pencil so that it sticks over the edge of your desk. Now close one eye tightly, either eye. Then try to touch the tip of the pencil with the tip of your finger, keeping one eye closed all the while. If the pencil had been a punch press, you might have lost your finger!

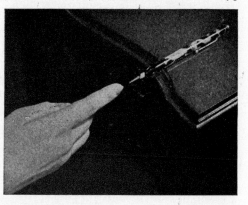

give tests every year, without charge, and furnish glasses at cost to any employee needing them.

Business has a practical interest in improving eyesight. It helps accuracy, production, and safety. It also increases the general well-being of the individual. Poor vision causes tiredness, headache, twitching eyelids, and at times reddening of the whites of eyes.

After high school age is reached, it is wise to have an eye examination at least once a year, whether or not you wear glasses. Change of vision takes place so gradually that you become used to the condition and do not realize that you are using extra effort to see, even to see poorly. Be sure to select a doctor who knows how to test for convergence. This is the term for tracking, or co-ordinated movement, of the eyes.

11 ■ Right-Eyed or Left-Eyed?

Most people depend more on one eye than on the other, some being right-eyed, others left-eyed. This condition can be compared to right- or left-handedness.

There are tests to determine which is the more favored eye. Trial-and-error tests can be made by the individual to decide whether material being copied should be placed on the right or left side of the typewriter for easier seeing.

A better test can be made by looking at an object on the opposite side of a large room through the *big end* of a short megaphone. (Make one from a file folder.) Hold the big end tight to your face, so that both eyes are included, and look through the small end at the distant object. Now close your right eye. If the object disappeared, you were looking at it with your right eye. If you can still see it with the right eye closed, then you are favoring your left eye when looking at objects. You may favor your left hand and your right eye.

Although not related to "eyedness," there is the practical question of the best angle at which material being copied on the typewriter should be held. Dr. Vance T. Littlejohn, head of the department of business administration at the Woman's College of the University of North Carolina, discovered most fatigue when the copy was flat on the desk. There was least fatigue when the copy was held so that the middle was at a right angle to the line of vision. The middle of the copy is at a right angle to the eye when the copy is supported at an angle of 41 degrees to the desk top.

12 ■ Eye Hygiene and Exercises

Every half hour or so, the eye worker should rest his eyes by looking into the distance or to the other side of the room. Closing the eyes for a few moments is restful—but don't let the boss think you are asleep on the job.

Alternate your fine and coarse eye work. If work has to be done closer than about a foot from your eyes, use a magnifying lens or special glasses— or give the job to a nearsighted person.

A good eye exercise after close work is to rotate them. Move them slowly around a big imaginary circle. Move them to the right, then left, up, then down. These exercises help strengthen the muscles, which may weaken and cause poor convergence, or mild cross-eye.

Excessive use of tobacco is hard on eyes. Movies are about as hard on eyes as the same amount of time spent in close reading. Reading on buses or trains is hard on eyes, due to vibration and bouncing. Limit such reading to skimming newspaper headlines.

Seeing out of the corner of the eye is especially sensitive to motion. The less motion in the field of vision, the better for eyes.

To match colors or to see forms, look squarely at the objects.

Blonds need to watch light more than brunets, since the eyes of blonds are often more irritated by bright light. Blonds are more likely to need dark glasses in direct sunshine or on the water.

Direct sunlight is too bright for reading.

Put nothing in your eyes but a weak solution of boric acid.

When you get something in your eye, go to the first-aid room or to a physician.

A stye is a tiny boil on the eyelid, painful but not serious if it is treated as a boil should be. Keep fingers away from it, and let the first-aid room or a physician take care of it.

Scaly eyelids may be due to nutritional deficiencies. Don't buy ointments for this condition yourself, but report to first aid or a physician.

Circles under the eyes are due to thin skin, which allows the dark blood in the veins to show through. The circles may mean lack of sleep, lack of exercise to keep circulation stimulated, or poor general health.

An inadequate diet may cause temporary discomfort in reading. This is usually because the eyes need vitamin A. Butter and fat meats are good sources of this. Fresh vegetables, except potatoes, are fair sources.

The most common causes of inefficient reading, however, are a limited vocabulary and reading just to kill time.

A limited vocabulary hampers reading, as arithmetic is hampered if you do not know the multiplication tables.

Reading just to kill time is comparable to working arithmetic incorrectly for the fun of it. Reading to kill time forms habits of dawdling and slow reading. Don't bury yourself in the newspaper and spend the evening with it. Finish it with judicious skimming in five minutes.

One of the oldest languages in the world, and the first to be printed, was Chinese. In one of their centuries-old classics, *Sweet Dream Shadows,* the philosopher Chang Ch'Ao wrote:

> Reading books in one's youth is like peeping at the moon through a crevice. Reading books in middle age is like looking at the moon in one's courtyard. And reading books in old age is like playing the moon on an open terrace. This is because the depth of benefits of reading varies in proportion to the depth of one's own experience.

The Gist of the Chapter

1. Tell why reading is important in modern business.
2. How do the eyes move during reading?
3. What are eight steps for gaining speed in reading?
4. When should skimming and underlining be done?
5. Why do executives need a two-way vocabulary?
6. What is meant by Primary Mental Abilities?
7. What is the difference between word fluency, meaning, and versatility?
8. What things influence legibility?
9. Give eight rules for good lighting.
10. Describe the most common eye defects and their consequences in business life.
11. What should a person do to keep his eyes in good seeing condition?

Things to Do and Problems to Discuss

1. Arrange with an engineer of your local electric lighting company to give a demonstration of good and bad points about lighting.
2. Arrange with some paint firm to have a colorist give a demonstration of ways color can be used to advantage in offices and factories.
3. Find out what your local schools try to do to help pupils who have reading disabilities, and how they do it. Make a report.

4. Arrange with a typographer or an advertising lay-out man to give a demonstration of factors that influence legibility in letterheads and booklets.

5. Arrange with some specialist or an industrial nurse to give a demonstration of how common eye defects can be detected.

6. Effie K. said she gave up reading because it interfered with her gum-chewing. What does that indicate about her method of reading?

7. Discuss how reading can help a person balance his personal efficiency. Consider the time budget suggested by the University of Chicago, which was given in Section 3 of Chapter 2.

8. Secretly observe some adults who are reading comic books. Discuss signs you noted of inefficient reading habits they have.

9. Analyze your workplace for distractions that might draw your attention from what you are reading or doing. How could these visual distractions be reduced?

10. The workers in Oswald J.'s office collected 5 cents when anyone used a word incorrectly. The money was used for an office party, the boss doubling the money collected by the fines. What can be said for and against such a plan?

11. Analyze some office or workplace and make recommendations for improving the lighting in it.

12. Watch different people at work and report what you see that suggests some of them need glasses, or should have their old glasses changed.

13. What are the professional differences between an optician, an optometrist, an optimist, and an oculist?

14. Analyze how the scales and dials on some machines could be made more legible.

15. In what ways could eye defects or inadequate lighting add to the hidden inputs which were outlined in Chapter 1?

5 ■ MORE EFFICIENT REMEMBERING

— — — — — — — — — — —

WHAT THIS CHAPTER IS ABOUT

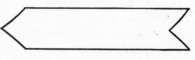

1 ■ Where Is Memory Located?

In ancient Greece, before there were town clerks and county recorders to keep records of transactions, the busiest man in town was the professional "Rememberer." He was paid to remember details of contracts and the sale of property. Some people have exceptional memory powers, which are likely inborn. Women, on the average, have slightly better memory power than men.

You cannot increase the number of your brain cells, but you can improve your memory. There is no nerve or special corner of the brain that is used exclusively for memory. *Memory* is a term used to label the way facts can be impressed, retained, and later recalled. Memory is an activity, not a brain storeroom. All kinds of nerve and brain cells take part in it.

Memory, intelligence, thinking, and the other terms are just convenient ways to segregate different aspects of mental life for study. This is similar to talk about the hardness, torque resistance, elasticity, and other properties of a piece of steel.

Your thinking will be sharper if you bear in mind that those terms do not describe concrete objects, but powers and properties. Strictly speaking, for instance, we do not have *a* memory; what we have is the *power* of remembering. Don't look for a pigeonhole location for memory in the brain, any more than you would expect elasticity to be located in the upper left corner of a steel bar. We can see how remembering works, but we cannot see it. Intangibles, again.

It is much the same situation with such a concept as "break-even point" for costs, sales, and profits. The break-even point is not a piece of machinery, like a duplicating machine, nor a definite place, like the top drawer. It is a function, and an important one. Memory, too, is a function. To be precise, we should speak of memoriz*ing*, not memory; of concentrat*ing*, not concentration; of acting intelligent*ly*, rather than of intelligence.

Phrenologists made the mistake of thinking that a function or property was a concrete thing, which must be located under a certain bump. One might as well ask the architect to build a room for storing the break-even point.

2 ■ Try to Remember More

When William Howard Taft was Secretary of War, he cultivated his ability to remember names and faces. On an inspection tour of the Panama Canal, he amazed everyone with his memory of local officials' puzzling names. He did this by repeating the name to himself and linking it with some distinctive quality of the person's appearance. He tried to remember and, consequently, did remember.

But, when he became President, he neglected this effort and so lost some of his influence over people. Newspaper correspondents, who saw him almost daily, cooled off toward him when he did not remember them. Taft's memory powers were as good as ever, but he was neglecting to use them; less per cent of possible.

George Calvin Carter, formerly Dun & Bradstreet's representative in New Hampshire and Vermont, was with the firm more than a half century. His memory for confidential details of the businesses in those states gave him the reputation of being the best-informed businessman of that section. His system was simplicity itself, and sound psychology.

"I have no special system," he said. "I have just had a good memory and have always made it a point to keep it exercised. If something is not worth remembering, I dismiss it immediately. If it is worth while, I think about it momentarily in a serious way. My only system is to see that every fact I think may be used again is properly impressed." For one hobby, he remembered the height of every factory smokestack in his states. In a few paragraphs, you will learn how this was done.

When you remember something without trying, it is *incidental mem-*

ory, a hit-or-miss variety. People forget most of what they read in newspapers because they read with no special intention of remembering.

A telephone number, used only once, is quickly forgotten for the same reason.

Intentional memory is much more serviceable. Simply trying to remember a telephone number, or a person's name, makes you remember it 50 to 100 per cent better. Intending to remember takes only a little longer, but makes memories last a great deal longer.

People who complain about "poor memories" are usually neglecting to try to remember. *Be confident that you can remember better. Then TRY to remember.*

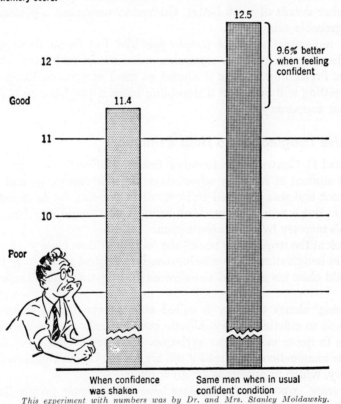

Memorized Better When They Felt Confident

Memory score:

12.5

} 9.6% better when feeling confident

12

Good 11.4

11

10

Poor

When confidence was shaken

Same men when in usual confident condition

This experiment with numbers was by Dr. and Mrs. Stanley Moldawsky.

Memorizing long numbers similar to telephone numbers was tested in 16 men. Later in the test their confidence was shaken by telling them there was something peculiar about their memory. Many other tests confirm these results which show how feeling confident helps one use one's abilities.

3 ▪ Make Remembering Pleasant

John Locke pointed out years ago that pleasant experiences tend to be better remembered. Attitude is important in remembering. Attitude includes not only confidence and intention to remember but also pleasantness. The executive remembers a golf date but forgets to adjust a complaint. Since people tend to forget unpleasant things, it is wise to do unpleasant tasks right away before they slip from mind. It also makes your job more enjoyable.

"If you break down almost any job, you will find a large per cent of it is disagreeable work," comments Austin Ingleheart, who worked up to become chairman of General Foods Corporation. "I have never had a disagreeable job in my life, but I have had to do a lot of disagreeable things."

When the boss or teacher makes work pleasant, workers and students remember details of work better. Customers remember a pleasant store and agreeable salespeople.

You remember names of people you like, but forget those you dislike; therefore, in order to remember more names and faces, like more people. Pretending a liking is almost as good as genuine liking.

Forgetting will be less of a stumbling block if you have an attitude of pleasant expectancy.

4 ▪ Use Imagination to Help Remember

Russell H. Conwell, who founded Temple University, said that he was a poor student in his early school days. For one reason, he had a sense of humor and was whipped eight times in one day for laughing at the teacher. But a new teacher, Miss Salina Cole, taught the farm boy to help his memory by using imagination.

"Look at the word in the book," she told him, "then close your eyes and see it in imagination." The mischievous boy became so adept at this that he could close his eyes and visualize an entire paragraph, then an entire page.

"Seeing" things this way is called *eidetic* (eye-*det*-ik) imagery, and gives rise to eidetic memory. Eidetic memory makes it possible for some people to quote many pages verbatim. Such people just "see" the page in their imaginations, and read it off. Sir Arthur Conan Doyle had eidetic memory, which improved as he grew older.

"Hearing" words in imagination also helps. Some people "hear" in imagination easier than they can "see" in imagination. If you can both "hear" and "see," it helps that much better.

While riding on a bus or train, recall in imagination the people you have met during the day. "See" their faces, and "hear" their names. Practice "hearing" their voices so that you will recognize them on the telephone. Since many people have a distinctive footstep, listen for that, and practice "hearing" each kind of step.

When studying a book or job-instruction sheets, close your eyes for a moment, and "see" the items that should be remembered. If you cannot "hear" them, then whisper them to yourself.

5 ▪ The Best Times to Refresh Memories

Hermann Ebbinghaus (EB-ing-*hous*) was a well-to-do young man with a sense of humor. His merchant father let him go to the university, where the boy became interested in history. After graduating, Hermann thought it would be fun to keep right on learning things; so, he worked for a doctor's degree at the University of Bonn (pronounced *bun*), near his home town. His doctoral thesis was on unconscious mental processes. He had deserted history for the study of mental activities.

Ebbinghaus proceeded to live a life of independent study, to the pride of his merchant father. His reading started the ideas in his methodical head spinning faster. "Why not apply psychophysical methods to the higher mental processes?" he asked himself. "Perhaps we could measure memory by finding the number of times we have to repeat something before we remember it. Maybe we could measure forgetting by testing how well we can recall something a week after memorizing it. Or, by the savings in the number of repetitions, to rememorize a poem a month later. I think perhaps we can, *nicht wahr!*"

Perhapses may have dominated his cautious thinking, but not his action. Ebbinghaus did not dillydally; he started things. So, this independent young man, with no university or laboratory position, invented the famous *nonsense syllables* to test how memory works. These nonsense words, such as *zat, boh, sik,* had no meaning; so would not be associated with meanings and could be used to test "pure" memory. He invented more than two thousand nonsense syllables. (He must have had good word fluency.)

Using these meaningless words and the methods of *repetition, recall,* and *savings,* he buried himself in experiments on human memorizing and forgetting. In 1885, when he was thirty-five, this self-taught psychologist published his book on memory. The book is still a classic, still being sold.

Ebbinghaus found that *forgetting takes a nose dive at first,* then slows down, as the chart on page 84 shows. Forgetting is fastest when meaningless material has been memorized. Usually, more is forgotten the first half day after memorizing than is forgotten all the next month.

This law of forgetting has many important applications. The time to review a lesson or a job-instruction sheet, for instance, is the first day after studying it. Early review offsets the rapid initial forgetting and pushes the curve of what you remember higher. Advertisers apply this law as they schedule advertisements for a new product. They run advertisements in rapid-fire sequence early in the campaign; then schedule them farther apart as people become more familiar with the new name or product.

How You Forget

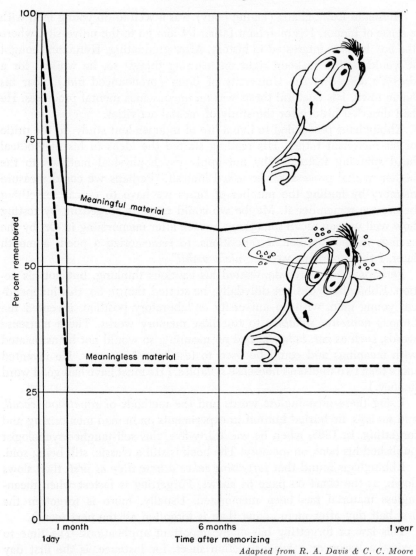

Adapted from R. A. Davis & C. C. Moore

Memories stick longer when the meaning of the memorized item is clear. Strive to understand and to make the other person understand clearly.

The same application is practiced in this book. The material is presented so that there will be an automatic review. When a new word or concept is introduced, you may have noticed, it is soon mentioned again on later pages. This should hammer it into your memory, by giving a little *overlearning* at the outset. Then, in a later section of the book, you will notice old terms and names appearing again. This is done to refresh your memory and offset some inevitable forgetting unless memory is refreshed.

Because *meaningful memories last better,* human-interest and self-interest examples have been sprinkled throughout, for they are remembered better. There has been extra effort even to make the charts interesting.

This planned repetition to strengthen your memory should help you gain more from the book. If you read it at the rate of about fifteen to twenty pages a day, these built-in refreshers will keep brightening up your fading memories and boost them back to useful levels.

6 ▪ How to Reduce Interference in Memories

Give your memory a better chance by not trying to remember too many things at the same time. Give things a chance to "soak in."

Retroactive inhibition. Retroactive inhibition (in-hi-*bish*-un) makes fresh memories wipe out older ones. Newer memories interfere with slightly older ones before the older ones have gelled. The student who studies business law for an hour and then business organization the next hour will have his memory for law inhibited by the organization studies. The memories are too similar; they interfere with each other and get mixed up.

A person who remembers names and faces well enough ordinarily may find his memories of them blurred when he meets several dozen new people. The first dozen would be remembered easily if the second dozen did not interfere. When getting acquainted with workers on a new job, don't try to get acquainted with everybody all at once. Learn two or three new names the first hour, and keep on at that rate.

Alternate widely unlike subjects when studying, to lessen retroactive inhibition. Try to have a distinct change in subject matter about every hour while studying.

Dr. William C. Gorgas, who eradicated yellow fever in Cuba, and was chief sanitary officer during the building of the Panama Canal, read three books on three different subjects at once. After studying one subject for an hour, he would turn to another that would not produce interfering memories. But he always had difficulty spelling.

A good way to avoid retroactive inhibition is to alternate intense study with short periods of complete rest or with longer periods of activity in which memorizing is not involved. Study an hour; then write letters for an hour.

A subject studied just before bedtime is better remembered. This is because there are some eight hours with no interfering work to erase the new memories.

Take memorizing by easy stages, but memorize rapidly while you are at it. Don't weaken memories by crowding too many at once. Cramming for examinations is inefficient because of this mixing up and erasing.

7 ■ Alcohol, Coffee, and Remembering

Alcohol makes a person feel that he is smarter and able to think more quickly than usual. But his listeners may think he is just sillier than usual. Measurements show that mental powers almost invariably are impaired by even slight amounts of alcohol. Of all mental functions, memory is affected most unfavorably by alcohol.

Heavy users of alcohol may develop an interesting memory disease known as Korsakoff's psychosis (*kor*-sa-koffs si-*ko*-sis). These people become unable to remember what they did two minutes before. Old events, of twenty years ago, will be remembered; but memory for immediate events is practically nonexistent. They cover gaps in immediate memory by glib and incessant talking—word versatility.

John Barrymore, the famous actor and matinee idol, had this ailment; and during his last few years on the stage he could not remember his parts. He walked around the stage, glibly making up dialogue and clowning to the delight of audiences. They were unaware that they were having a demonstration of memory disease.

Coffee, in moderate amounts, appears to help memory, though it may interfere with a student's sleep if he drinks an unaccustomed amount to help his evening study. Tea and chocolate drinks contain similar drugs that give memory a slight boost. Cola drinks also contain it, in about the same strength as coffee. A small amount helps memory, but larger amounts seem to produce effects similar to retroactive inhibition.

8 ■ False Memories, Liars, and Rumors

"It was just after James came to work last summer."

"No, I'm sure it was before then."

So starts another endless argument because memories tend to become twisted. It pays to keep a diary or some dated record of events that may have later significance. Many executives dictate memos that summarize every interview and conference, which are filed for possible future use.

Retroactive falsification is unintentional inaccuracy or mixing up in memories. Everyone is a partial liar as a consequence. Memories usually cover the high spots; many details are missing. When trying to recall the details, a person is apt to be misled by retroactive falsification.

Numbers involved are usually exaggerated. The salesman "recollects" that the Amazon Corporation bought 200 of his widgets five years ago— but it was only 15. These memory distortions are more apt to involve matters in which there is self-interest. Salesmen particularly have to guard against this inclination, lest they earn the reputation of being liars. It is usually safest deliberately to understate what you remember.

The memories of some old people are mostly retroactive falsifications. They cannot remember what they ate for breakfast—similar to Korsakoff's psychosis, but due to old age rather than to alcohol. So, they draw on their imaginations to describe the meal they might have had, as if it were fact.

The tendency to confuse imagination with memory is called *confabulation*. Women workers sometimes confabulate wild stories about their employers making ungentlemanly advances to them. Many workers confabulate alibis to explain their failure to follow orders.

The gossip, or rumormonger, is usually a confabulator. His motive may be spite or too much curiosity about the personal affairs of others or feelings of guilt that he wants to shift to others. These motives make retroactive falsification worse. And, as the story is passed along the grapevine, retroactive falsification keeps changing it. Details are added to the original story, numbers are magnified, and soon all resemblance to fact is lost. As examples, recall rumors you have heard about a company's profits, the number of people laid off, or the story about the unpopular boss's wife leaving him when she only went out of town to nurse a sick sister.

Then there are a few people, lacking consciences, who tell whoppers more easily than an honest person tells the truth. These are *pathological liars*. Such a person has a sick mind, but he can make endless trouble starting rumors or misleading customers.

Some promoters and swindlers distort their memories so often they begin to believe their own statements. The pathological liar does not try to tell a consistent story, but the swindler does and carries the blueprints to prove his story. Some high-pressure salesmen incline in this direction; it is wise to weed out these confabulators.

Since normal memories of past experiences usually are lacking in detail, the person who supplies many details may be suspected of some confabulation. When a sportsman says the fish weighed four pounds, believe him. But if he adds a number of details that are supposed to convince you that he is not lying—look out.

Lawyers take advantage of this to trip up witnesses in cross-examination. They like to lead a witness into relating details; then they come

How time makes people bigger liars

Per cent of error in describing a scene

20

15

10

5

Immediately after seeing | After 5 days | After 15 days | After 45 days

From experiments by Dr. K. M. Dallenbach

When describing a scene that was shown to a group, each person insisted as "the gospel truth" that he saw many things not in the scene. Retroactive falsification increased their misreports and made them more unreliable gossips as time elapsed.

back with some of these details, hoping to show up the witness as a liar. Parents can be easily trapped by questions about the ages at which their children walked or talked. These were momentous events at the time; but as parents do not try to refresh their memories, most of them cannot recall the exact age truthfully three years afterward.

Avoid the all-too-human tendency to fill in possible details, to magnify numbers, to distort in other ways. Say quickly, "I'm not sure" or "I'll have to hunt it up" or "You're expecting too much of my memory." Don't jump off the deep end and try to pull up something that might be as you remembered it. For example, keep a written record of where you worked, the dates, pay, work done, and similar details for use when you apply for a job. Don't get your story mixed when applying for work. 'Tis better to start a new job with the repute of a slow memory than of a fast memory for things that are not true.

You will be less likely to become involved in a pointless argument, too, if you do not supply too many details—and if you let the details the other fellow gives pass without either challenging or believing them. That was one of Washington's rules.

When a lawyer asks whether you have ever told a lie, there is only one answer you can give honestly, as retroactive falsification makes everyone an unintentional liar at times. Answer such a question: "Yes, I've lied, but not under oath" or "I have told untruths, but not on important things."

9 ▪ When Not to Remember

Memory improves with use. That is the well-established *law of use*.

Apparently opposed to this law of use is the fact of retroactive inhibition. Paradoxically, one can remember better by remembering less. It is this way.

You have to go to the dentist on the fifteenth or have to attend a business conference on the seventeenth. Make a memo of these in your pocket date book and on your desk calendar; then forget them. Or you may have errands to do this afternoon. Don't try to keep them in the front of your mind all day. Let your pocket memo book do this remembering for you.

Use judgment in what you try to remember. There's no use remembering a telephone number you may never call again, or the entire bus or train schedule, but do try to remember the part you use. There's no point trying to remember every face you see, but do try to remember customers and associates. It is foolish to try to remember everything in the newspaper, but do remember news of lasting importance or that has a bearing on your business or profession. Memorize rapidly the things that count, and let the rest become incidental memories.

Intend to remember more than you probably have in the past, but don't clutter up your head trying to remember everything. A flypaper memory to which everything sticks is not efficient—it's a freak of nature.

But do remember to look at your memos and calendar.

10 ▪ Make Recall Easier by Recalling

Impressing a thing on the mind is only the start of memory. Being able to recall it when wanted makes the memory cycle complete and useful. The best way to develop recall is to recall—the law of use again.

Thus, the second time you see Mr. Smith, mention his name aloud, and think of his hobbies or of where he lives or of interests he expressed when you talked with him before. Every time you see him, mention his name and recall some of the things about him. You'll find it easier each succeeding time, and your use of his name will make you more popular with him.

Exercise recall of facts that you have just learned by talking them over with someone. Talk them over with yourself if no one else is interested. Exercise recall on technical points in your work by talking them over with others in the same firm. But avoid such business talk with persons who are not in the same company. Be careful not to give away company secrets in such talks.

Recall can be practiced without talking. Thinking about something—"hearing" and "seeing" in imagination—is almost as good as talking. Many people put their odd moments to work by using them to recall in imagination.

11 ▪ How to Tie Memories Together

Do you recall what you read a few pages back about George C. Carter, the Dun & Bradstreet man who remembers the height of smokestacks? He remembers them by tying them in with the height of Bunker Hill Monument. Every good Yankee knows that this monument is 221 feet high. Mr. Carter makes the remembering of chimney heights easy by noting that the left chimney of the Public Service Company generating plant is the same height as the monument; the right chimney, 2 feet higher.

It helps strengthen memory by associating new facts with ones already memorized in ways like those just demonstrated. Don't merely repeat the new name or fact, but think how it is related to something you already know. This is using *association*.

You already know John Brown well. He has a booming voice and is in women's-wear. You have just met Frank Brown, who has a squeaky voice and is in men's-wear. Their last names are similar, but the *association of contrasts* helps you remember both more efficiently.

Association of similars makes it easy to recall the outline shape of Italy, the boot. *Association by contiguity* makes it easier to remember things that happened together.

A stenographer had difficulty reading some of her shorthand notes. To help herself, she went into the boss's office and sat down as if she were taking dictation. With pencil in hand, she went through the motions of taking down the letter. When she reached the puzzling portion, the meaning came automatically.

It thus helps recall if you go back to the original setting or attitude. When you have difficulty recalling someone's name, think back to where you met him, visualizing the setting entirely by thought. Don't say to yourself, "Why don't I recall his name!" Instead, ask yourself, "Where did I meet him?"

12 ▪ The Prime-and-Wait Method of Recalling

Ever have a name on the tip of your tongue and yet be unable to recall it? When that happens again, don't try to recall it. Do something else for a few minutes, and the name may pop into your head. The initial effort to recall primes the mind, and subconscious activities go to work to pry up the dim memory.

Students find the priming method helpful on examinations. They read over the list of questions before trying to answer any. Then they answer the ones of which they are most confident. Meanwhile, deeper mental activities (subconscious) are working on the questions that were more difficult. By the time the easy ones are answered, answers to some of the difficult ones will pop into consciousness.

This prime-and-wait method is useful when you are trying to locate a letter that might have been filed under one of several classifications. Instead of tearing the file cabinet apart looking for it, think about where it might have been filed, then do some other work. The work done while you are waiting should not require too much concentration. Ten minutes or so later, go back to the file cabinet and resume the hunt. There are good chances that you will put your hand on it the first thing after priming and waiting.

When trying to recall something that is elusive, don't push yourself too hard too long. Push hard for a short time to prime. Then wait.

13 ▪ Specialized Memories and PMA

Some people have difficulty remembering dates, others have difficulty with geography, others with foreign words. A memory that is poor for some subjects does not mean a generally poor memory. One memory power may be high, another low, without reflecting on a person's mentality.

This specialization in memory is due in part to interests.. The office manager remembers the price of office machines but not the dates of famous discoveries in which he has little interest. He could remember the dates if he became as interested in them as he is in office equipment.

Associative memory. Associative memory, or rote memory, is the PMA that is used mostly in memorizing the multiplication tables, foreign vocabularies, and such.

Memory for details. Memory for details is a variety of incidental memory in most instances. It helps the typist to notice that one letter on a letterhead is slightly battered. Or helps a man to recognize his own hat among a dozen much like it in the cloakroom or his own automobile from another of the same make. It makes it possible for an automobile mechanic to notice that a machine part does not look like a genuine factory-made part. It helps the cashier spot forged signatures or counterfeit money.

Quick memory for small details is a quick memory for fine details and about objects seen or studied only briefly. The repairman needs it to tell at a glance whether the new bolt is the same size as the one just removed. Merchandise buyers need it to help them evaluate goods they are purchasing for a retail store. They should note immediately and remember little details that the customer may not discover for a month.

Visual memory. Visual memory, which is the power of remembering visual patterns, helps a person who is studying shorthand or blueprints. People who have strong visual memories will remember the charts from a book. This visual memory is closely related to quick memory for small details. They may turn out to be the same.

Memory for spoken instructions. Memory for spoken instructions is needed when a person has to keep in mind several things concerning the instructions for doing a job.

Other primary or specialized memory factors are likely to be discovered. At the present time, however, we can be certain of only those just described.

14 ▪ Helping the Other Person to Remember

Advertisers hammer their points and trade names into memory by (1) making the advertisement interesting, and (2) repeating and repeating it.

Repetition is the stand-by of conventional teaching. Listen to this job-training instructor: "This is a micrometer. We shall first study the micrometer. I am holding a micrometer in my hand. This word I am writing on the blackboard spells micrometer. You will use a micrometer to inspect diameters. The micrometer measures in thousandths of an inch. What is the name of the instrument I am holding?"

That may sound very elementary and simple, but it gives a picture of the methods that have proved most successful from the training of mechanics to the teaching of foreign languages, or even atomic energy.

Such repetition gives rote memory. There is much repetition in good teaching and in a good textbook.

Memory was strengthened still more when the job instructor asked the learners to repeat the name, micrometer. When the salesclerk repeats a new customer's name four times, it is remembered twice as well; the use of the name also flatters the customer. The supervisor helps the employee remember spoken instructions by asking the employee to repeat them.

It helps memory to *hear the new word before its meaning is given.* That job instructor did not start by saying: "We shall now learn how to measure one thousandth of an inch." He wisely made their minds sit up and take notice by using the new word first.

When a person is learning a foreign vocabulary, new words should be given before their meanings.

This is an application of the general law that *first impressions are lasting impressions.* The first impression you make on the personnel interviewer, or on your prospective boss, is apt to be lasting. The first part of a book is remembered best. The last part is remembered better than the middle, perhaps because there is less retroactive inhibition at work on the last part.

Emphasis by dramatizing to a sales-training class how to sell related items. These two "customers" came to buy flashlights for a summer camp. The girl on the left was sold just that. Related items were suggested to the girl on the right. Dramatizing helps sales students remember to make related sales.

Courtesy Macy's New York

Emphasis helps memory. Advertisers use large type or color for emphasis. The strange new word also gives emphasis. The job instructor gives emphasis by tapping the margin release of the machine he is talking about. Some job trainers emphasize by using a ruler to tap the beginner's hand when he starts to do the wrong thing. The salesman who is trying to remember customers' names puts a little vocal emphasis on the new name every time he says it. He emphasizes sales points to be remembered by making a demonstration or by dramatizing the product in some way.

15 ■ The Best Age for Remembering

Paderewski played the piano with one finger when he was three; at four, he could use all his fingers. His childhood music, however, did not forecast his future as the world's foremost pianist. He had only a few piano lessons, and they bored him completely.

But two important things happened when he was fifteen. A new music teacher aroused his interest in music; and, for the first time, he began to remember music. His new teacher, by arousing his interest, doubtless helped his musical memory. But there was something else. This was the natural growth in memory power, which all people have.

Memory power gradually grows through childhood until about the first year of high school. From about fifteen to fifty, it is at the peak. After age fifty, it drops slightly, perhaps from carelessness. But some people let it drop right after graduation from school, from lack of use.

The private secretary and associates of an older executive may find it wise to refresh the older person's memories by tactfully giving cues, such as: "Mr. Brown, who used to be with the Chamber of Commerce, is here to see you. He is a very fat man, now with the ABC Advertising Agency. Mr. Brown was on the Community Chest Committee with you several years ago."

The chief weakness of memory in later decades of life is for recent impressions. The older executive may slip on new names and faces, but don't let this fool you; he still may have a tenacious memory for details of his business or profession. Older persons have to exert effort to keep recent memories fresh.

Younger persons, on the other hand, need to form habits of really using their memories, and using them in right ways. Memory powers for both young and old are kept in best working order by:

Having confidence that you can remember
Deliberately trying to remember
Understanding clearly
Tying in with older memories
Making mental pictures and sounds
Not overcrowding memory
Using recall often
Making remembering pleasant and interesting

You will see in the next chapter how these, and other principles, can be applied to make learning of all kinds more efficient.

— — — — — — — — — — — — — — — — — — — —

The Gist of the Chapter

1. What is meant by "remembering" that is different from having "a memory"?

2. What is the difference between incidental and intentional remembering? Which is the more useful?

3. How can imagination be used to help one remember?

4. What did Hermann Ebbinghaus learn about remembering? Where? When? How?

5. Explain applications of the laws of forgetting.

6. What does retroactive inhibition do, and how can it be made less of a handicap?

7. What errors of remembering should you guard against when on the witness stand? How?

8. What are the effects of alcohol, coffee, and old age on remembering?

9. Give examples of the law of use as applied to remembering.

10. When and how should the prime-and-wait method be used?

11. What are the PMA of remembering?

12. Give eight guides, or principles, for more efficient remembering.

Things to Do and Problems to Discuss

1. Pass around a short business letter, or invoice, so that each person can read it once. After everyone has read it, ask them to write answers to your questions about what they read; such as: name of firm, date of letter, to whom addressed, name of person who signed it, his position, subject of letter. After they have written answers, find out which individuals had made an attempt to try to remember the letter when they read it. Did those who tried to remember have more correct answers? What does this demonstrate about the need to try to remember business communications when they are read?

2. Interview some executives and other business people to find out what they have observed about business blunders that were caused by not remembering. Report on these, adding your suggestions of how the forgetting might have been avoided.

3. Invite one person to leave the room for a few moments. While he (or she) is gone, ask one person to describe the clothes worn by the person who is now outside. Then ask another to correct or add to that description. After several have described how they remember the clothes, bring "the victim" back into the room so that all can see how poorly they remembered the details. What could account for all their errors?

4. Talk with some successful salesmen, such as insurance, real estate, or automobiles, and find out what helps they use for remembering names and faces.

5. When writing an important letter, what could you do to make more certain the person reading it would remember the significant details?

6. You are sending Effie K. out of the building on two important errands. How could you give her instructions so that she will more likely remember all the details of both errands?

7. Analyze the part remembering plays in (a) balancing personal efficiency, and (b) building a vocabulary.

8. Some business people have the habit of starting each day by briefly reviewing (that is, recalling) some business happenings of the preceding day. What can be said for or against this? What happenings should be reviewed?

9. Think of someone you know who exaggerates. Discuss whether this is due to a poor memory or to something else. What effect does it have on his efficiency and value as a worker?

10. Report on some rumor or gossip you have heard. How much truth was in it? What is your guess as to why it started? How was it spread? Did people believe it when they first heard it?

11. Discuss reasons for having instructions in writing; for making notes of telephone conversations at the time they are received; for making notes of lectures and serious reading. Should the notes be reviewed? When?

12. What are some details we should not trust to remembering, but instead should write on a desk memo or in a pocket memo?

13. Discuss how family worries, or being in love, might make it difficult to remember things.

14. Oswald J. is leaning back in his chair, giving instructions to a worker whose attention seems to wander from what Oswald is telling him. How could Oswald get him to concentrate on the instructions and try to remember them?

15. You are a retail salesperson and want to build up a following of regular customers. Describe some subtle strategies you could use to make certain they remembered your name and appearance.

16. In the chapter on reading, we learned that people who read for meanings are the most rapid readers. In the present chapter, we learned that people remember more when they try to get and try to remember meanings. Discuss the connection between those two facts.

17. In this book, why is it useful to have "What this chapter is about" at the start, and "The gist of the chapter" at the end? How could you apply that in (a) business reports, and (b) longer business letters?

6 ■ EFFICIENT LEARNING
AND VOCATIONAL TRAINING

_____

WHAT THIS CHAPTER IS ABOUT

1. *Wanting to learn is basic*
2. *How to unlearn errors*
3. *Strive for accuracy*
4. *Learn from an expert teacher*
5. *Learning curves*
6. *How to break through the plateau*
7. *Learn the job as it is*
8. *Learning one job may not help on another*
9. *Learn by easy stages, without overcrowding*
10. *Make it a game by keeping score on yourself*
11. *Give it a final push*
12. *What to learn for highest success*
13. *Learn from the layer above you*
14. *Things to learn about the organization*
15. *Learn to solve business problems*

1 ▪ Wanting to Learn Is Basic

Landing a job is often easier than holding on to it.

Max Thorek, for instance, came from Czechoslovakia to Chicago. His constant companion, a violin, brought him work with a "gypsy" band. To resemble a gypsy, he grew a fierce black mustache, although he was only eighteen. He did well enough as an imitation gypsy, but he wanted to become a surgeon.

The next spring he tucked the violin under his arm and called on the director of the university band. In America, the director told him, violins are not used in bands. But they did need a snare drummer who would be paid half the tuition charges.

"Only half tuition? Wouldn't an extra-good drummer be worth full tuition?"

The band needed a drummer desperately; so, the director phoned the University of Chicago president and won permission to give an exceptional drummer full tuition.

This exceptional drummer hurried to a pawnshop and bought the first snare drum he had ever touched. He settled down in a tenement to learn drumming during the hot summer. Neighbors complained, and he was hailed into police court. Judge Sabath let Thorek off when he promised to practice in the cellar.

Then came the first rehearsal of the band that autumn. Thorek now had to prove that he was an exceptional drummer. He drummed in a self-conscious daze until the music for Meyerbeer's *Coronation March* was passed around, a real test for any drummer. The youth lost color as he looked at the mounting series of bravado rolls he would have to play.

After one try at the march, the director rushed to the telephone and talked with President Harper. "That new drummer is a wonder," he exulted; "he certainly deserves full tuition."

Thorek had taught himself drumming, with a little help from the gypsy drummer, and was on his way to become a great surgeon. He learned to operate so skillfully that, when his right hand was injured by the awkwardness of another surgeon, he prevented its amputation by operating on it himself with his left hand.

Doctor Thorek's progress as a drummer was exceptional because he wanted to learn. He had to master the drum to attend medical school. This wanting to learn is a prime requisite for efficient learning. *Intense effort speeds learning.*

Mere repetition produces only *rote learning*, the poorest way to learn. Rote learning is seldom useful, since there is no understanding with it. An example is the way some three-year-old children are taught to count but are unable to use numbers. Unless a thing is understood, it is rote learning.

Industrial training directors have a tough problem making some employees want to learn. Graduates of engineering or other special schools sometimes imagine they have already learned everything, and may have to be humiliated into wanting to catch on to job details. Some apparently cruel treatment of new workers is an effort to shock the self-satisfied into wanting to learn. The know-it-alls can expect some jolts.

Learning takes place in the nervous system, not in the hands. That is one reason we learn best when we try to learn.

Memory is closely related to learning. But learning includes many more things than conscious memory. Memory and learning follow many of the same laws. Trying to remember helps us remember, and trying to learn helps us learn. Lack of confidence harms memorizing and also harms learning.

Memory helps us to recall past experiences. Learning is broader, dealing with the modification of behavior by past experiences. Learning is modification, change, improvement. Memory is the impression, retention, and recall of things from the past. Memory is involved in learning, which is why in this book you have studied memory before learning.

2 ■ How to Unlearn Errors

Learning often is held back by some persistent minor error. You may have an impulse to turn a knob in the wrong direction, spell a word incorrectly, hit the wrong key. One of the best ways to eliminate these inaccuracies is by *negative conditioning.*

Strange as it may seem, many errors can be uprooted by deliberately repeating the error until you become fed up with doing it the wrong way. The secret in this negative conditioning is to give the error unpleasant associations. It would seem silly, except for the fact that it has always worked.

This unusual method was devised by Dr. Knight Dunlap, who was annoyed because he often typed "hte" when he intended to type "the." To break himself of this, he typed an entire page the wrong way. After typing a few lines, he was thoroughly aggravated with this inaccuracy. The last half of the page was punishment.

By doing the incorrect thing (1) *to the point of self-punishment,* and (2) *with the mental set that it was being done wrong,* he broke the habit right on the spot.

This negative conditioning method can be applied to get rid of, or weaken, many pesky little habits. In one instance, college students who bit their fingernails tried it. They stood in front of their bathroom mirrors and watched themselves go through the motions of biting their nails. While doing this, they kept saying "This is what I am supposed *not* to do." They did that, off and on, for three months. When checked on ten months later, about half of them no longer had the nail-biting habit. This was recently reported by Dr. Max Smith, of the College of the City of New York.

Ordinarily, it is best to focus attention on the right way. But when the wrong way does get started, it can be conquered by Doctor Dunlap's method of repeating the wrong way intentionally to the point of punishment. It really works *if* you have the mental set that it is incorrect. Unpleasant experience causes the unlearning.

Pleasant experiences can be repeated to the point that they become unpleasant, too. Eating too much candy is one example.

3 ■ Strive for Accuracy

Know-how is picked up more quickly when accuracy is emphasized from the outset. Work for accuracy, not speed, to gain most speed in the long run. Then you will have less to unlearn. In a typewriting experiment, for instance, one group of beginners was told to emphasize accuracy and another group to emphasize speed. After four months, the speed group typed 38 words a minute. The accuracy group typed 45

Accuracy brings speed

Data from Dr. G. C. Meyers

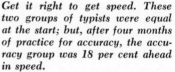

Get it right to get speed. These two groups of typists were equal at the start; but, after four months of practice for accuracy, the accuracy group was 18 per cent ahead in speed.

words—working for accuracy made them 18 per cent faster. The accuracy group also had only half as many errors.

The more difficult or complicated the work, the more it helps if the learner watches for accuracy. In some simple tasks, such as packing candy in a box, emphasis on accuracy does not help much. But for most tasks, the learner should stress accuracy to learn faster.

4 ■ Learn from an Expert Teacher

Young Thorek had the gypsy drummer give him pointers on drumming. It helps a beginner start right to have an expert open his bag of tricks, though many experts are weak in show-how. They can do, but not show. Even when the expert is a "born teacher" and can show how, it is better for the learner to spend more time trying and doing than watching others. A green salesman can learn a little by watching a skilled salesman, but he will learn better by trying some selling himself. Watch the expert— but not too long. Watch a bit; then do it yourself.

When you are watching to gain pointers, stand beside the instructor. Surgical interns used to stand opposite the surgeon at the operating table; but they saw things backward, like mirror writing. Now the intern stands beside the surgeon so that he can see things done in their true relationships. Watch the expert's hands, not his face—unless you are studying acting.

The expert who is not a "born teacher" is likely to show off rather than show how. His manner says, "See how good I am." He should say to the beginner, "See how much better you are getting!" Experts often have I-strain, but a good instructor uses the you-point. The expert is often discouraging, without intending to be, because he seems so much more skilled than the slow beginner. These are some of the reasons why modern business is making less use of expert workmen and more use of expert teachers to break in new employees.

The expert trainer follows six steps when helping employees catch on to their jobs.

a. He tells the why first.
b. He has the beginner explain the why.
c. He then shows how briefly.
d. He lets the beginner try it.
e. He encourages the beginner.
f. He motivates him to improve.

But there can also be *expert beginners.*

a. They learn why before starting.
b. They watch to see how.
c. They try it to get the feel-how.
d. They keep trying for accuracy.
e. They want to improve.
f. They believe they can improve.

The wise learner sticks to one instructor until he gains a good amount of skill. Different experts teach different methods. Shifting from one teacher to another causes confusion.

The best teacher of all is the effort to learn and to understand why. Tackle new work confidently. It is possible to learn anything until honest effort has proved otherwise.

5 ■ *Learning Curves*

Learning curves were discovered by Dr. William L. Bryan in studies of people who were mastering the telegraph code. His findings, a landmark in the foundations for applied psychology, were published in 1897. This was just nine years after the young psychologist had started the psychological laboratory at Indiana University. (Later he was president of the university for thirty-five years.)

Dr. Bryan was the first to find:

a. Learning does not progress smoothly—it has ups and downs; there are good days and poor days.
b. Learning is rapid during the first few practice periods; then it slows down as the ultimate skill is approached.

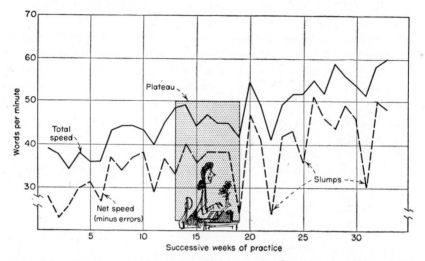

Learning curve of an average *typist. The separation between the solid and the dotted lines indicates the errors. Note that there is more variation from week to week in errors than in total speed. One plateau is marked by the shaded area. You can find others in this curve. Note the slumps when the typist is coming out of each plateau. These usually are due to a slight change in method, which takes fresh practice to master. Note especially the higher level after each plateau. Now compare this with the learning curve for a superior typist.*

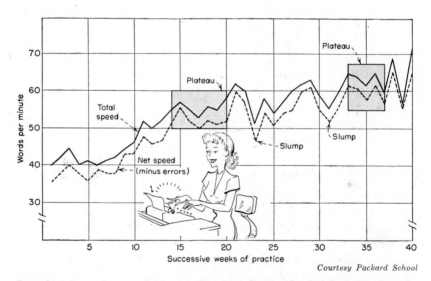

Courtesy Packard School

Learning curve of a superior *typist. She started out only slightly faster than the average typist, but she emphasized accuracy as shown by her better net speed. This superior typist also kept on practicing longer. The second plateau on this curve came during the month after the average typist quit practicing, but this month of extra practice helped the superior typist reach 70 words a minute.*

c. There is a plateau (*platt-o*) in learning, a time when the learner does not seem to improve; he may actually slump downward.

The learning curves of two typewriting students are reproduced on the opposite page. Study these two sets of curves for some time before going ahead with the next section.

6 ■ How to Break Through the Plateau

Businesses and individuals run into periods of apparent stagnation, standstill periods when they seem to be getting nowhere rapidly.

When Paderewski was twenty-five, and already a well-known concert pianist, he was on a plateau of no progress. He bogged down in his usual practice methods. The practice sheets were thrown out the window; and he started over again, practicing elementary finger exercises and scales. This different kind of practice corrected his errors and enabled him to break through the plateau and emerge with higher skill than before.

It takes more than mere repetition or rote practice to change an amateur into a professional. The professional has not only practiced for accuracy but has also improved his methods so as to rise above his plateaus. Just working on a job in the same old routine way does not master it.

When a person is beginning to typewrite, for instance, he spells out words letter by letter and finger by finger. This puts a ceiling on speed; and, within a few weeks, a plateau of no progress is hit. As the serious learner keeps practicing on this plateau, he begins to type words as a unit, not as single letters. The more frequently used words become typing units first—*t-h-e* becomes *the*, *a-n-d* becomes *and*. It is not greater finger speed but the larger working units that leave this first plateau behind.

A plateau in learning anything usually means that the limit has been reached for the present method of work. It does not help to try to work faster. Look for slight changes in method. Consult an expert or a teacher. Watch others for suggestions. Or improvise some change. One student broke through a typing plateau simply by moving two inches farther away from the typewriter. Little things like that blast away a big plateau!

To break through a standstill:

Keep confident and encouraged.
Analyze for better methods.
Keep on keeping on.

Keep on to avoid slumping backward from a plateau. As Paderewski commented: "If I miss one day's practice, I notice it. If I miss two days', the critics notice it. If I miss three days', the public notices it."

Too many learners imagine they have reached their ceilings at the first plateau and quit trying too soon. Those who let themselves slip are working for a booby prize. Willis Whitney, the research director who led

General Electric Company scientists to many discoveries, often told them: "You get there just about the last thing before giving up."

Keep encouraged. And keep at it. A plateau in progress should be a station where you figure how to break through.

7 ▪ Learn the Job as It Is

A job is a *sequence* of related activities.

If one simple part of a job is learned, then another simple part, the second, is likely to set back the learning of the first. That, as you know, is retroactive inhibition, or the interference of the new with the old. A slump is to be expected when a new part is tacked on.

This is interestingly shown by a Chinese graduate student who learned English grammar and spelling well and could write beautiful letters in her own handwriting. Then she got a typewriter and methodically learned the touch system. But there was an instant interference between her new-English habits and her new-typewriting habits. The English she wrote in longhand was perfect, that in her typewritten compositions and letters was filled with errors. Her typewriting was accurate, but not her English on the typewriter until she had practiced that sequence for half a year.

A task is done differently when it is part of a sequence than when it is done by itself. Many new co-ordinations and timings have to be learned when two things are combined. Learning to drive an automobile in a classroom dummy car has to be learned over again in a real car in real traffic. Most of such make-believe practice on parts of a job is inefficient except for (1) a feeling of confidence it may give, and (2) the strengthening of muscles used in the work.

In a football game, there are about two seconds for a drop kick. One inexperienced coach wanted his men to be perfect at drop kicks; so, he foolishly let them practice a four-second kick. In an actual game, the players blew up and fumbled when they had to drop-kick twice as speedily as they had practiced.

Learning public speaking is another example of the value of learning the job as it is, as a real thing, not as make-believe parts. You can practice a speech in the solitude of your room or shout a speech in the woods. But, as soon as a crowd is faced, there is a different situation; and the solitary practice gives little help.

Selling is a good example of the value of learning the sequence of activities. It is not much help to practice knocking on doors, then to practice opening and shutting the display case, then to practice the sales talk to an empty chair. Instead, practice the entire sequence on your friends, on homemakers, on anyone. You are not apt to make a sale to the first few prospects; but you will have the best kind of practice, going through the job as a real job.

It is not unusual to put the worst foot forward when applying for a job, because that is something in which people have little practice. Especially when it is the first job, the applicant is apt to be ill at ease and give an unfavorable impression. The best cure for the situation is to practice applying for work. Make the application under actual employment-office conditions.

8 ■ Learning One Job May Not Help on Another

There is *not much transfer of training* from one kind of work to another that looks similar. Learning to operate a printing press gives little advantage when trying to run an office duplicating machine. Practice in mechanical drawing does not improve handwriting.

A student may be neat in bookkeeping because the instructor insisted on it, but sadly lacking in neatness of personal appearance. And the boss who hires a girl because she has a neat appearance may get one who is an untidy worker. Such qualities as neatness, accuracy, honesty, and promptness do not become generalized, unless they are continually kept in view as all-round desirable qualities in all activities.

There is only a little transfer of training. For instance, skill with a ten-key office machine is of some help when using a similar keyboard on another machine. In most jobs, however, there is not much transfer. Most jobs are different in the skills they require, although they may seem alike on the surface. When the stenographer becomes a private secretary, for instance, her skill in typing and shorthand will be transferred to the new work. But she has a hundred and more additional tasks to learn. The average secretary does more than 130 different things in the course of a few weeks.

Wade right in to learn the complete job. Unless life and limb are at stake, tackle it as a real job for most efficient learning. You will have fewer plateaus if you do not dillydally with small bits. But give the bits that prove difficult, such as multiplying by 7 and 9, a little extra practice. Give extra practice to strengthen the little fingers in typewriting.

And also give extra attention to making accuracy, promptness, dependability, and trustworthiness general characteristics.

9 ■ Learn by Easy Stages, Without Overcrowding

Spare-time learners are often the best learners. Their learning is helped by the fact that they want to learn. But they also are helped because circumstances force them to *take learning by easy stages*. People who try to learn too much in too short a time may end up with an overcrowded dyspepsia of learning.

Overcrowded study or practice produces fatigue and boredom, which interfere with learning. You cannot gain wisdom quickly, but you can gain it steadily. Follow the principle of moderation, and avoid crowded learning. Try hard when you try—but give it time to soak in between tries.

Instead of practicing for two solid hours, practice one hour; then take a short breather before continuing. Such *spaced practice* is better than continuous practice. Long practice periods can be used safely only after considerable skill has been acquired.

The most efficient distribution of practice varies with the kind of material being learned as well as with the stage of progress. Each person has to find the best spacing of practice that fits him and his task. Follow these two guides to space your learning periods.

1. Each practice period should be long enough for warming up and for reaching the peak of skill already attained.
2. The practice should be halted when fatigue, boredom, errors, or slowness appear.

When an athlete practices too long without spacing he "goes stale." An important part of the work of an instructor is to space practice periods so that the learner is pushed, but not to the point that he goes stale. After a certain period of study, the more you study the less you learn. Take it by easy stages in the beginning then lengthen practice periods steadily as skill is increased.

10 ■ Make It a Game by Keeping Score on Yourself

Learning is more efficient when it is fun; inefficient, when it is drudgery. That is why learning often is done better in a group where it becomes something of a game or contest. Practice periods can be made longer safely if the person is excited about learning. The clever teacher, coach,

Making learning fun. Employees open a before-work training session by singing an appropriate parody on a popular song. Even that old solemn face, the section chief wearing the oversized chrysanthemum, is put in a good humor. Articles used in the training demonstration are on the table.

Courtesy Macy's New York

or job trainer knows how to arouse the learner's interest to the point of actual excitement. An ambitious person lets his ambition provide the excitement.

Keeping score on yourself gives a game spirit if you are learning alone. People usually make good progress learning a sport, such as golf or bowling, because the scores keep tab on "how'm I doing." Scorekeeping is easy for some kinds of learning, such as typing speed, for the scores can be charted week after week in order to show the learning curve.

Sometimes a numerical score is not possible, but there are other ways to keep a line on your progress. If you are trying to improve your handwriting, for instance, keep samples of your penmanship each Saturday morning, pasting them side by side to observe the improvement. Don't guess at your progress if it is possible to figure a way to keep a week-by-week record.

11 ■ Give It a Final Push

There is rapid progress the first few days of learning; then it tapers off. After six months of practice, it may take another month to make as much gain as was made the first week. Sometimes this is called *diminishing returns*. While the weekly gain may diminish, it is still a gain that brings perfection closer. As the gains slow down, the time has come to get excited over even a slight gain. The jack-of-all-trades stops practice when the gains become small; as a result, he never becomes master of any trade.

Just enough practice to learn is not enough. The extra practice after you believe that something is learned makes learning more permanent and a job easier to perform. This is called *overlearning*. The expert is the man or woman who has overlearned.

Bus and taxi drivers can weave their vehicles through traffic with breath-taking skill because they have overlearned. Their careenings may frighten bystanders, but these overpracticed drivers have the world's best accident records.

Job details that are not routinely used over and over can be practiced to advantage during slack times until they, too, are overlearned.

When Raymond L. Ditmars was sixteen, his job did not give him enough practice to overlearn shorthand. So he practiced it in church, taking down the sermon.

Keep your learning useful by rehearsing it in spare moments. Keep it growing by expanding your reading, your observation, and your thinking. Give it a final push—and keep on pushing.

You are what you have learned. What you have let slip is what you used to be.

12 ▪ *What to Learn for Highest Success*

Motor learning. The simplest learning is that of muscle control, as learning to walk, swim, or throw a ball, and also some simple factory operations. This motor learning, as it is called, is about all an idiot can learn. But a high degree of motor skill can be learned, as with the baseball pitcher.

Sensorimotor learning. Sensorimotor learning requires co-operation of muscles and senses. Learning to play a musical instrument or to type-write and many factory jobs are mostly sensorimotor learning.

Ideomotor learning. Ideomotor learning combines higher thought processes with muscular actions. Learning shorthand, bookkeeping, or to speak a foreign language are examples.

Ideational learning. Ideational learning is the highest type. Muscles are not appreciably concerned. This learning is in the realm of ideas and includes intangibles and learning to handle people.

This classification from muscular to ideational learning is convenient but somewhat artificial. In daily life, learning is usually a mixture of several levels.

The level of learning for one job also may vary during the different stages of learning that particular job. Laying bricks can be mostly a muscular task, in which case we have merely a mechanical bricklayer assigned to rough work. After the muscular parts of bricklaying are learned, ideational learning can be added. That is what Frank B. Gilbreth did when he learned to lay bricks with one-third the conventional number of motions.

The motor or mechanical parts of a job are likely to be learned first, then the sensory and ideational aspects. When these higher aspects are neglected, the learner remains a mechanical worker—who may be wondering why he doesn't get ahead.

For individual advancement, strive to learn not only the motions of a job but also the notions. Salary schedules run parallel to learning levels. Jobs that call mostly for motor learning have lowest pay scales, except for a few professional athletes. Sensorimotor jobs pay a little higher; ideomotor, still higher. Ideational jobs pay the highest. History remembers chiefly those who were strong in ideational learning. Socrates is the only stonecutter of his day whom the world remembers now.

It is easier to land a job, and your value on a job is increased, if you have learned enough variety not to be a narrow specialist. The man who has learned both acetylene and electric welding has doubled his job chances. The woman who knows both shorthand and typewriting has increased her job chances and job value. Learning more than one skill is good job insurance.

13 ■ *Learn from the Layer above You*

The right associates can help you master more than just your own job. Get acquainted with office workers and executives who hold jobs above you. Observe their work and the way they do it. Ask questions. Find out the "whys." Do not expect them to become chummy with you, but some will help you; and you will win favorable attention. If one rebuffs you, it reflects on that person not on you. Try another until you find an executive who realizes that an important part of executive work is training understudies. As a rule, you will find that a college graduate shows most interest in ambitious workers.

Off the job, too, associate a bit more with people who can teach you something.

Charles H. Percy had the president of Bell & Howell Company guide his program of plus-learning. And at twenty-nine, Percy became the youngest president of any major company in America. His family had fallen on hard times; and he started college with his life savings of $150, waiting on table for his board. Then he obtained part-time work with Bell & Howell to help his finances—and advice from the company president to guide his studies. As a result of this advice, Percy took courses in advanced accounting, statistics, corporation law, and labor problems, training he might not have considered but for associating with the layer above him.

Learning becomes an acute problem with every promotion. You may be a bigger shot after promotion, but you are a beginner on a new job at the same time. If plus-learning has not prepared you for the new job in advance, you must scurry around to make good. James B. Conant, for instance, had devoted his life to chemistry; but at the age of forty, he was unexpectedly elected president of Harvard. Thereupon, he quit reading his beloved chemical journals and studied the history of universities in order to learn his new job. His promotion came unexpectedly, and he had to bone up after advancement. Usually, it is the other way: those who have boned up win advancement.

The bigger the job, the more plus-learning helps. When learning stops, you stop.

14 ■ *Things to Learn about the Organization*

People have to condition themselves to each new job or location. This is conditioned-response learning, not athletic conditioning. Some old methods have to be dropped and new ones added. Some former ways of thinking also have to be changed.

After moving into a new house, it takes about six weeks before you grow used to it and begin to feel at home. It takes that long for the average person to change his previous notions of home. A few people cannot change their ideas; so they never feel at home in any house except the one where they were born—rigidity, again. The new house is a reality and requires a change of ideas and habits to match that reality. This process of making mental images match reality is called *adjustment*.

Adjustment has to be made on a new job. The average person can expect about six weeks to pass before he begins to feel at home on the job. It will take longer if a person was with another company for many years. Expect the new job to seem strange the first few days, but also notice that it continues to seem "more natural" every day.

Many well-qualified people stub their toes and fail to make progress on a job because they neglect to learn the ins and outs and the ups and downs of the organization. You must learn the way around an organization just as you would around the building. Some rules and regulations, for instance, are unwritten customs. These can be followed without any loss of individuality.

Some organizations use given names, familiarly; and others prefer the dignified "Mister" or "Miss." Keep your eyes open, and do as others do in such folkways. They may seem minor; but, if you overlook them, others will say, "So-and-so does not seem to fit into our organization" or "He is a good enough worker but does not seem to be our type." It takes more than job skill to fit into an organization. Learn your way around in it.

Watch for factions. They exist in every company. A few firms are riddled by scheming factions.

Your boss and fellow workers. Study your boss, just as he is sizing up you. Learn his soft spots. He may be "ga-ga" about fishing, his grandchildren, his travel experiences, or whatnot. He probably has hard spots, too. He may be pernickety about accuracy, promptness, personal appearance, and working right up until the bell rings. The boss is a big part of any job, and the bottleneck for promotion. Study him, and act accordingly.

Fellow workers also have tender spots. Watch for their individualities, so that you will be able to get along well with them. You cannot change them, but you can humor them. These differences in personality make work interesting, and their neglect can be the start of a dead-end job if you let your sociometric rating go down.

New work routines. A new vocabulary has to be learned on each job. Companies develop their own lingo. What one firm calls a yellow second sheet, another calls railroad paper. One firm calls it onionskin, another calls it flimsies. Sometimes sub-rosa vocabularies are developed, as in the case of an office supervisor who was perpetually battling against typists who made strikeovers. In this firm, they were called "Miss Crocketts," after the supervisor who hated strikeovers.

On the more formal side, there are many details you will need to know to fit into an organization. For example:

Whom should you notify by telephone when you are unable to go to work?

When you change your address, whom should you notify?

Where should you send a news item if there is a company newspaper?

Where can you cash a check in the building?

Can you borrow money from the company?

How do you request new equipment or repairs?

Where should you report in case of an accident?

Can you use the company telephone for personal calls?

Can you buy at a discount through the company?

Who grants wage increases?

How can you get insurance through the firm?

Can you receive medical advice?

Can some officer give you legal advice?

How can you use the company library?

Where do you report a lost or found article?

Whom should you tell if you figure out a better way of doing a job?

Who should be informed if you lose your pay check?

What should you do if you see indications of dishonesty?

How should you go about trying to get a job for a friend?

Who can help you on a tax problem?

How could you arrange to take an advanced course?

How do you arrange for friends to visit the company?

Learning such ins and outs about a company is almost like getting acquainted with a foreign country. Get well acquainted with the corner of the business world in which you work, and don't expect it to be just like other corners.

15 ■ Learn to Solve Business Problems

About four hundred thousand new businesses are started each year in the United States. Half of them are out of business within seven years. A significant reason for that large mortality is that the persons who started the businesses had not learned to think about, and to solve, business problems. This is illustrated by the following incident.

A mechanical engineer, an accountant, a salesman, and a corporation lawyer met in a war plant where they had temporary employment. Each was a capable man in his specialty. Evenings they made plans for a business of their own, which they started when the war was over.

The first year after the war, the former salesman was president of the new firm. Business was good, as it was for all businesses in that period; and the four partners felt successful. The second year, the new business slowed down; so the accountant tried his luck as president. The little firm's condition kept getting worse, however. Then the lawyer was made president so he could liquidate the business. This once-booming little firm now consists of the engineer and an assistant, who run a small machine and repair shop.

These four men were technicians employed by a business concern. They imagined that this work made them businessmen, but they remained technicians. The four of them together knew about all there was to be known about business details. But they could not run a business because they had neglected to study the co-ordination and balance of activities within a company. They had everything—except business sense.

When the salesman partner was president, he had a big sales force and spent large sums for advertising, though it was a time when anything could be sold without effort. About the time they had used up their capital in this needless expense, they really needed sales effort. So, the accountant was made chief; he devoted most of his thinking to collecting slow accounts when there should have been increased sales effort. None of the partners could view the business as a whole and plan a proper balance of company activities.

Promotions at the executive level almost always are made on the ability to solve business problems, not on skill in some technical process. Technical skills help to get the first few jobs. From then on, business sense, or judgment, counts more. One incorrect executive decision can bankrupt a company.

Learn to think about more than your job—about the business world into which it must fit. Think ahead about problems that might arise; then they will be less of a problem if they do arise. Practice thinking about big problems that involve several departments and not just one job.

The craftsman thinks about one job. The businessman has to think of the relationships between all jobs, the public, competitors, sources of supplies, and the government. The businessman has to know a great deal, most of all he must know how to solve practical business problems.

A survey by the *Harvard Business Review* showed that executives who had the best positions did the most nonfiction reading. The weaker executives did little serious reading. Leading and reading go hand in hand. Reading to keep up with the world and your vocation is one way to keep the habit of learning. Read one or two trade journals regularly and a couple of new books in your field each year. Then there is less chance of your becoming a stereotyped has-been.

Attend meetings of trade and professional associations.

Go to other meetings that will keep you in step with modern thought.

Visit trade shows and get acquainted with new machines and methods.

Find out what competitors are doing.

Take an occasional course in adult education in some subject utterly unrelated to your work.

Gradually learn more difficult material.

Associate with people who are learners.

Keep your curiosity working.

Look forward to changes and new ideas. You cannot stop them any-way—so why not be among the first to know about new developments?

Most of the employees of the du Pont Company are working at jobs and processes that did not exist twenty-five years ago. The world moves, and rapidly. It is wise to push yourself to keep moving ahead with it.

— — — — — — — — — — — — — — — — — —

The Gist of the Chapter

1. Why is rote learning seldom useful?

2. What are the likenesses, and the differences, between remembering and learning?

3. Explain negative conditioning, what it does, and how.

4. On which kind of tasks is it most useful to emphasize accuracy when learning them?

5. What are the characteristics of an "expert beginner"?

6. Tell what learning plateaus are and how they can be broken through.

7. Tell about transfer of training.

8. When and why is spaced practice an advantage? overlearning?

9. Describe the four levels of learning and the relative usefulness of each.

10. What should one look for when learning about the organization?

11. How can one learn about business problems?

Things to Do and Problems to Discuss

1. Interview some people who have been at least ten years on their jobs. Find out the changes they say have taken place, and report on the new things they had to learn. Were there more new things to learn on unskilled or on skilled jobs? Did the people who had to learn more new things seem to be the more satisfied with their jobs?

2. Talk with someone from the personnel or training department of a firm. Find out how long it takes to train employees for different jobs and how much it costs.

3. Interview the owner of a filling station, or restaurant, or drugstore to learn what some of his business problems are as distinguished from job problems.

4. Effie K. has the annoying habit of smacking her lips much of the time. Apparently she does not realize she does this. How could you (a) tactfully call her attention to this bad habit, (b) lead her to want to break it, and (c) use negative conditioning to break it?

5. Many new employees, after some blunder, say "I didn't suppose I was

to learn that." How can a new employee know what he is supposed to learn about the job?

6. Look back over your own vocational preparation, and report on the things that stimulated you to exert yourself hardest to learn.

7. Imagine that your boss has asked you to teach the owner's only son how to do your work. The young fellow does not seem to be interested in learning. What things could you do to get him more interested in mastering the work?

8. Many jobs have been simplified, so that they will be easier to learn. Check back in earlier chapters and report on some disadvantages of job simplification.

9. Oswald J.'s firm has fire drills at regular times, so that work will be disrupted as little as possible. Oswald wants to have the fire drills at unexpected times, to give better training in case of actual fire. What reasons could he give to support his proposal?

10. The chartoon in Chapter 1 gave Dr. Richard Uhrbrock's scoring for items affecting personal efficiency in business. Analyze those 23 items, looking especially for ways learning and vocational training could improve the scores.

11. Consider some job you know, and also the one next above it in line of promotion. Upon being promoted, what new things will have to be learned?

12. Why do high school students usually try harder to learn from an athletic coach than from a classroom teacher?

13. You work in the purchasing office of a firm that has secret processes. A new employee is eager to learn from you what the materials are used for. You begin to wonder (a) if he is an eager worker who should be encouraged, or (b) if he is a spy trying to get secrets for a competitor. How could you find out which he is? What should you say to your boss about it?

14. Experienced workers often resist having to learn new job methods. Discuss why in the light of information given in earlier chapters. Also discuss how resistance to change can be lessened.

15. Suppose your firm transferred you to a branch in some foreign country. Although the details of your work would be the same, what new things would you have to learn in addition to some acquaintance with the language?

7 ■ WAYS TO PLAN
AND ORGANIZE WORK

_ _ _ _ _ _ _ _ _ _ _ _

WHAT THIS CHAPTER IS ABOUT

1. *Unscramble your work*
2. *Group similar tasks*
3. *Change tasks about every two hours*
4. *Alternate hard with easy tasks*
5. *Start with the hard or disliked part*
6. *Plan stopping places*
7. *Get the benefits of goal gradients*
8. *Value of subgoals*
9. *Applied in public speaking and conferences*
10. *Effect of unfinished work*
11. *Pre-position to cut down searching time*

1 ■ Unscramble Your Work

Lena specialized in traffic-rate work. She was clever with figures, skilled with a slide rule, and the most efficient traffic-rate clerk the firm had found. As word of her computing abilities spread, more and more people made use of her skill. They would interrupt her at any moment to ask for help.

She was becoming irritable, getting behind in her work, and losing confidence. The office manager grew uneasy about her—perhaps she was not having enough sleep or was troubled by secret worries. He asked the company nurse to talk with Lena to find what was troubling her.

The cause of Lena's decline, of course, was the interruptions. She would be part way through a computation when the phone would interrupt her; so she would have to start from scratch again. These interruptions were a help to others, but a handicap and irritation to Lena. Her job had become a scramble.

So her job was unscrambled. A typist whose work did not require intense concentration was detailed to the adjoining desk. The typist served as buffer, answering the telephone and serving as information clerk to protect Lena from distractions.

Interruptions can be made partial if we give only one corner of our minds to the interruption. When checking a ledger page, for instance, we should keep a finger at the point where we were interrupted. This makes it easier to resume where we left off and also reminds the inter-rupter to be brief. If we are called away from our work, we should make a brief note, to "prime" ourselves when we return; we shouldn't leave it all to memory.

Think more about what you are doing and less about the interruption.

Chronic interrupters are pests. When you really have to interrupt some-one, wait until the other person is at a break in his work or shows signs of fluctuation in his attention. Wait until he looks up, changes his position, turns a page, answers the telephone. Or save your interruption for the start or the end of the work period.

A needless or poorly timed interruption is a crime against personal efficiency. It makes the interrupter as popular as poison ivy. The private secretary helps the executive's efficiency by saving interruptions until the psychological moment to present them.

But once someone interrupts you, *settle the matter right then*. Other-wise, your chain of thought will be interrupted again. General George C. Marshall, as Chief of Staff, avoided the same interruption a second time by a sign on his office door: "Once you open this door, *walk in*, no matter what is going on inside."

Self-interruptions can be avoided by sticking to the present task until it is completed or until you are definitely tired and need a change. Don't interrupt your work to make a telephone call. Instead, make a memo about the call and continue your work without that interruption. Don't interrupt

Courtesy Connecticut Mutual Life Insurance Company

Many jobs are a series of explosions until some details and decision making are delegated.

yourself to go for supplies or to do anything else you just happened to think of. Make memos instead. Then do all the errands at some break in your work.

Many jobs are a scramble and are done on a catch-as-catch-can basis until they are planned and organized. The private secretary's job is a good example of the possibility of tasks becoming mixed up. Surveys show that secretaries have some 871 different duties. The fewest found for any one secretary was 15, the highest 479. The average secretary has 132 different tasks, ranging from routine typing to such irregular tasks as paying the boss's traffic fine and buying his family birthday presents.

Here are several psychological principles to follow to change a scrambled job into a well-organized job.

2 ■ Group Similar Tasks

Group similar tasks so that specialized work can be done in one sitting. The "Do it now" slogan violates this principle. If there is enough of a particular duty to keep you busy for an hour, do it now; otherwise wait for similar work to accumulate into an hour's work.

The secretary, for instance, should accumulate dictation until there is about an hour's typing. Then do the typing at one sitting. After the typing is done, proofread it all. It is a work scramble to type one letter, then proofread it, have it signed, then fold and insert, and then start the next. Stick to one kind of task until a stopping place is reached. Folding and inserting letters require little concentration and can be done for relaxation when fatigue or interruptions have lowered efficiency for the tasks that require alertness.

3 ■ Change Tasks about Every Two Hours

Change tasks about every two hours. This lessens boredom and fatigue. After a couple of hours at the same task, workers can truthfully say, "I'm not tired, but I am tired of *this!*" This is particularly true of work that is brought along in a steady flow. Repetitive work gives high mechanical efficiency but makes workers inefficient after an hour or so. The endless supply of work makes the job seem harder and causes unrest. Humans work best when there is a change of task every hour or two.

A subordinate rule is: Change the tempo if you cannot change the task. Work a bit faster, or a bit slower, for a few minutes.

When the tempo is determined by a conveyor that moves on unchangingly, a change of task still can be provided. Some factories allow workers to swap jobs every couple of hours. In a laundry, for instance, girls feed the mangle one hour, then switch to folding the next hour. When it is not possible to switch jobs, some benefits of change can be had by working for a while sitting down.

Both extremes are inefficient. Lack of change is bad. Too frequent change is also bad. The rate of change depends on the nature of the work and has to be determined by experience.

4 ▪ Alternate Hard with Easy Tasks

Hard and easy tasks should be alternated. When the task has to be the same all day long, with no easy parts to sandwich in, a change of pace will help. Set a fast pace the first hour, then take it easier the next. Always make the first hour a brisk one.

Music is sometimes used for pacing, to alternate brisk and leisurely gaits. A half hour of two-steps is followed by a half hour of silence; then a half hour of waltzes is followed by another period of silence. Continuous music, or the same type of music, is not so helpful as brief spells that set a change of pace.

The old-time "efficiency engineer" or "systems expert" failed to take into consideration this human need for changing pace. He tried to keep workers at top pace all the time, which cannot be done. Change of pace is supplied in this book by sprinkling easier sections among the more difficult ones.

A rest pause, combined with a coffee break, plus a pleasant visit with working friends, adds to the satisfaction and efficiency of most workers. Note the trim appearance of these secretaries and that one is "ready for active duty" with her shorthand book in hand, in case she is called for dictation. Being "ready for active duty" is one aspect of organizing work.

5 ∎ Start with the Hard or Disliked Part

Start with the difficult or disliked task. A homemaker who hates to make beds should make them first, thereby reducing the feeling of drudgery. Get the difficult part out of the way first, so that it is not hanging over your head, haunting you.

There is one exception to this rule. The learner should start with the easier parts of a job, for the feeling of confidence it will give him. Tackle the job as it is, of course; but tackle the easier part at the beginning.

6 ∎ Plan Stopping Places

Work should be planned so that there are definite stopping places where we can feel that something has been accomplished. Stopping places are needed particularly in routine repetitive work. The demoralized feeling when household goods are moved into a new house is an example of what happens when work is piled up in a heap with no stopping place in sight.

When a big pile of work is doled out at one time, it causes jitters. Workers complain that management has started a speed-up when a foreman distributes by the barrelful parts to be assembled. There are fewer complaints, and work is actually speeded up, when only a basketful of parts is given at a time. People like the security of steady employment, but they cannot do their best work when they have an unending stream of work staring them in the face.

Workers always *want to feel they are making headway.* The mechanical savings accomplished by the conveyor have been paid for many times over in the cost of labor unrest it sometimes causes. The conveyor and assembly line are here to stay. So is unrest, until conveyor work is organized so that people feel they are making headway. The conveyor has the merit of grouping similar tasks together. From then on, it has mostly demerits, though clever management can change these into merits.

Organize and plan work so that you think more about what has been accomplished than about what remains to be done. In one sales office, envelopes were being addressed by hand to telephone subscribers across the country. This was unskilled temporary work, and high wages were paid. Yet only a few girls stayed on the job more than two or three days. The boss was a slave driver, they said on quitting. Investigation showed that each girl was given a thick telephone directory and a stack of several thousand envelopes each morning.

To change the system so that it would provide stopping points, the telephone directories were cut apart. Each girl was given one sheet (two pages) at a time. This broke the work into smaller chunks, which gave a feeling of headway as each small batch was finished. The girls no longer quit after a couple of days, and the output increased despite the time lost walking for supplies.

The individual can make better progress if he sets himself definite goals that are close at hand. For example, a person may resolve to improve his vocabulary but never does, because that is a vague goal. But, if he makes the goal definite—to learn and to use three new words a day—progress results, because he can see results each day. Definite goals give "will power."

Now let's take up some other unexpected benefits that definite goals or stopping points give.

7 ▪ Get the Benefits of Goal Gradients

Do you gallop through work a little faster just before quitting bell? Yes? Then your *goal gradient* is in good order. The goal gradient is the stimulating effect experienced when nearing a goal.

When you are waiting for a telephone call, do you sometimes imagine the phone ringing? That's your goal gradient at work again. It gives an expectant frame of mind.

You may never see your goal gradient, but it is apparent in almost everything you do. Sometimes, it shows up plainest when it is missing. Supervisors sometimes complain that workers are shirking when, in fact, the manager is shirking goal gradients.

The Imperial Works, for instance, had a lot of rush business. The manager thought it would be good strategy if, just before quitting time each afternoon, a few big bins were wheeled in loaded with the next day's supply of work. That should keep the workers on their toes, he calculated —but he calculated wrongly.

Some workers had puzzling headaches the next morning. A few went fishing. Output slumped. The manager was defying goal gradients when he ended the day with the threat of hard work the next day. He had taken away the home stretch. It is an old practice to keep work piled ahead in the hope that it will overcome stereotyping (remember that?) and stalling. But human nature is such that this tactic produces exactly the opposite results.

People are more efficient when they are working toward goals. But a goal that is unreasonably high, or too distant in the future, may be a hoodoo rather than an incentive. People work best when they feel they have a fighting chance to succeed.

8 ▪ Value of Subgoals

Many minor goals that can be reached during the day's activities help personal efficiency. When work is properly organized, there is a spontaneous spurt to finish the forenoon's quota during the half hour before

Courtesy Procter & Gamble Co.

A goal-gradient effect may be obtained by having an hour-by-hour record of production posted so that everyone can see it.

lunch. There is a stronger spurt the half hour before quitting time in the afternoon. Most production curves show slumps during the closing half hour—indicating that the work has not been properly organized.

This is a continuation of the idea of having many home stretches, but it is worth extra emphasis. Ambitious individuals, driving bosses, and conscientious homemakers make the inefficient blunder of biting off too big chunks for a half-day quota. Plan goals so that there is a definite stopping place at noon and again at the end of the day. Better yet, have subgoals you can reach about every hour.

Long automobile trips can be made less fatiguing by planning not just the total mileage for a day but also numerous subgoals to anticipate. Instead of looking 350 miles ahead, look 35 miles ahead to the next county seat. These subgoals will help realize your expectations sooner and more often and make the long trip seem easier.

It is astonishing how little things can be goal gradients. In the monotonous job of thinning sugar beets, yellow flags were used to give goal gradients. The flags were stuck in every 100 feet along the rows. Production increased 32 per cent. The workers weeded from flag to flag, reaching many of these subgoals during the day.

Another example is the executive who wanted to cut down on smoking. He rationed himself to one cigarette after he had finished the morning's dictation, another after he had checked departmental reports, and cigarettes at other natural stopping places in his work. He was astounded how much quicker he finished his detail work and attributed it to less nicotine. While less smoking may have helped, there were also strong goal-gradient effects as each budgeted cigarette served to mark off a subgoal. His day had been organized by budgeting cigarettes so that they gave him several home stretches.

Dividing these chapters into convenient study sections gives many subgoals in reading this book. (One teacher suggested that the sections should be the right length to read during a television commercial!)

9 ■ *Applied in Public Speaking and Conferences*

"He had me convinced after fifteen minutes—but he lost me by talking too long." The goal-gradient effect in a talk is the climax. When the climax is reached, it is time to stop talking and sit down.

Skilled speakers quit talking while listeners are still intensely interested, or after a telling point has been made. To continue after either of those goal gradients is reached is as much of a mistake as the manager's dragging in the unfinished work at quitting time. The effective speaker stops before the listeners' goal has been passed. He ends early, with a bang. He avoids tapering off to nothingness.

When one is conducting conferences, it is not wise to adjourn them entirely by the clock. A meeting is more effective if it is adjourned right on the heels of some high spot in the discussion or as soon as a decision has been reached. The decision gives the conference a new goal gradient, and dragging in something else to fill in the time is out of step with the goal effect.

It also helps, when one is conducting meetings or giving talks, to get the listeners actively involved. This builds up their goal gradients. They can be involved by asking them questions that make them think themselves into the meeting. Familiar, everyday examples make them feel that they are part of the talk. This has been described as talking *with* them, not *at* them.

It has been estimated that a class listening to a teacher, an employee listening to his boss, or an audience listening to a lecture has serious lapses of attention about every seven minutes. The expert public speaker jerks attention back by telling a story, making a demonstration, or doing something unusual about every five minutes. Interest, action, or noise will renew attention. Interest is best, action next best, and noise last. Bear that in mind when you plan an oral report to a group, or when you give job instructions to someone.

There often are breaks in dictation, due to fluctuating attention. If too long a gap occurs, it may help if the stenographer, without being asked, reads back the last dictated paragraph.

Courtesy Johnson & Johnson

Keeping a conference on the beam. This group of supervisors in conference-leadership training is given practice on how to use a blackboard and posters to recapture attention after it fluctuates and so keep the discussion on the main track.

In sales work, fluctuation of a prospect's attention must be watched closely. The attention may be won back by lowering the voice and talking in a confidential tone. Or give the prospect something to handle. Or ask a question that will catch his attention.

A well-modulated voice helps to hold attention, a monotone loses it.

Breaking sentences—into brief phrases—helps recapture fluctuations—and goes naturally *with*—changes in voice volume. This paragraph—has been broken into phrases—to show you *how* easily it is done. You should pause—only a second—between phrases. If you pause longer—your talk will drag.

The *with* and *how* in the preceding paragraph are emphasized to demonstrate the strategy of pausing on a word, or at a point, that will arouse curiosity and cause the prospect to listen more intently for what follows.

The person who is active, who moves around slightly, can hold attention better. Gesture and move more than you may have been doing. Lively people win and hold attention.

Looking the other person in the face also helps to hold his attention. A salesman looks the customer in the face and talks to him, not to the merchandise. When presenting new ideas, look at the person, not at the blueprint. Skilled public speakers find it easier to "hold an audience" if they look at and talk to first one member of the audience and then another.

Here is another secret—about the writing of this book. Dry-as-dust facts have been salted and peppered with human-interest examples. These are inserted, not only to make the points clearer, but also to jerk attention back about the time it might go off woolgathering.

10 ■ Effect of Unfinished Work

Workers are irritated if they are pulled off a job before they have finished. Unless it is an emergency, the wise boss asks the worker to fit other work in when he can. (An emergency may mean the boss himself has done some poor planning.)

Some "unreasonable actions" of workers are caused by the irritation of interruptions before they finish their present work. One automobile company had a sit-down strike in the paint department because inspectors interrupted the painters to have them touch up imperfections. This was a two-way blunder: calling attention to mistakes and interrupting other work. The trouble was simply solved. A touch-up expert was assigned to each inspector. The expert repaired the blemishes, and the regular painters were not taken from their goal-motivated work.

Interrupted work is unfinished work. Needless telephone calls, long visits, unnecessary requests for help—all produce annoyance rather than efficiency. So does much pointless small talk that scatters in all directions. So does keeping a person waiting on the telephone; call back later when the information is located.

Time-consuming people were a pet annoyance to Herbert Spencer, the philosopher, economist, and psychologist who lived in a world of deep thoughts. He avoided the time-wasting chatter at his boardinghouse by wearing ear pads at the meal table so that he could keep his goal in mind without being distracted. That was bad manners, very bad; but he was genius enough to get by with such behavior. The point is not to do as he did, but to keep in mind not to distract others or waste their time— don't cause people to want to wear ear pads when you are around them.

Make it a rule to stick to business during business hours. When it is necessary to interrupt, do it at psychological moments—about which you will learn later.

If interruptions do not annoy you, then I am afraid you are not goal-motivated in your work.

11 ■ Pre-position to Cut Down Searching Time

The new salesman had looked promising—but prospects lost interest while he hunted for order blanks. He had memorized the canned sales talk, and answers to all possible objections were on the tip of his tongue. But he always had trouble finding the order blank. The golden moment for closing the sale slipped away as he fumbled through his brief case.

Searching time is a symptom of inefficient work habits. The efficient person has figured out the most convenient location for each work tool and always keeps his tools where they belong.

Employment interviewers sometimes ask an applicant for a match or a pencil. This is a rough-and-ready test to see whether an applicant knows where things are or has to play hide-and-seek in his pockets. Although a popular test, this tells nothing about a man's other work habits.

Pre-positioning keeps the tool in a position so that it is ready for use as soon as it is picked up. No fumbling to get the right hold after picking it up. That salesman, for instance, now heads all his order blanks in the same direction. They are so placed in the brief case that he can pull one out and place it in front of the customer without missing a sales point. It is not pre-positioning when the shears are placed so that they are picked up by the point.

The kitchen is a good place to observe how pre-positioning can help efficiency. It takes the average homemaker 1,516 steps to do work that could be done with only 131 steps if the kitchen utensils were organized efficiently. Take saucepans, for instance. They are usually hidden in a drawer, often far from the spot where they are used. Keep saucepans pre-positioned beside the faucet and the can opener, where they are used first, thus saving an extra step. Frying pans, too, should be in plain sight, hanging beside the gas stove, to pick up and use without an extra step.

A new-type desk that saves searching time, backtracking, stretching, and floor space.

Duplicate equipment is often a good investment if it reduces searching time. In the home have a dust mop and other cleaning equipment on each floor of the house. In the office have pencil sharpeners, dictionaries, and other office aids centrally located, and more than one in a large room. These are economies in searching time.

Efficient workers keep regularly used articles pre-positioned—like a fireman's boots—and thus cut down searching time by a systematic arrangement of tools and equipment.

— — — — — — — — — — — — — — — — — — — —

The Gist of the Chapter

1. How do interruptions make a scramble of a job?
2. Why is it sometimes a mistake to "Do it now"?
3. Why should tasks, or the tempo of work, be changed from time to time?
4. How is music used to pace tasks?
5. What are some good ways to deal with the hard or disliked parts of a job?
6. What can be done to give the person a feeling that he is making headway toward getting the job finished?
7. Explain what the goal-gradient effect is, and how to get it.
8. What are some points to follow to make a conference more effective?
9. Why should we be careful about interrupting people who are at work?
10. What is pre-positioning, and how is it applied?

Things to Do and Problems to Discuss

1. Talk with some successful executives, or their secretaries, to find out how the executives organize their many tasks. Report on how they apply some of the principles given in this chapter.
2. When people move into a new home, getting settled is usually a wearisome matter because it is a job scramble. Work out a plan for moving, so that the scramble would be taken out of getting settled. Or, do the same for moving a small office into a new building.
3. Observe some workers at work. Report how many chances they overlook for organizing their tasks.
4. Analyze a filling station, and report how it could make more use of pre-positioning.
5. Draw on material from earlier chapters to discuss the advantages of having the workers affected assist the staff specialists in planning and organizing a job.
6. What safety factors should be kept in mind when organizing work?

7. Discuss the differences between job simplification and unscrambling a job.

8. What study materials can a student keep pre-positioned? How?

9. How can a student organize his study periods so that he has some "home stretches"?

10. Effie K. likes to telephone a friend every hour or so for a short visit. Considering the material in this chapter, do those visits help her efficiency? Do they lower it?

11. Refresh yourself on what was studied earlier about quota efficiency, and show how subgoals and stopping places could best be planned.

12. Professional job trainers like to use the S-O-S method: a series of successes. They believe that the beginner who succeeds is more likely to keep trying. Discuss the merits of that in the light of this chapter.

13. Study the electric-light switches and hot-and-cold water faucets in several homes and business buildings. Most building codes require a certain pre-positioning of these, such as the "On" position of a switch being up. What points made in this chapter are illustrated by the standard arrangement of switches and faucets? Can you suggest ways in which their arrangement could be improved?

14. How may the coffee break work out as a stopping place?

15. Several of the points for efficient remembering are parallel to the points 'n this chapter. Report on those that are similar.

8 ■ THE EFFICIENT USE OF MUSCLES

WHAT THIS CHAPTER IS ABOUT

1. *Cut down backtracking*
2. *Cut down muscular tenseness*
3. *The right amount of tenseness*
4. *The relaxed approach to work*
5. *Work "loosy"*
6. *Curving movements preferred*
7. *Keep the eyes away from the hands*
8. *Aim; then move*

1 ■ Cut Down Backtracking

The table showing "The Optimal Work Level" in Chapter 2 indicates that white-collar jobs do not use enough energy to make people tired. Yet sedentary workers do become tired out. Sometimes they feel tired because the work strikes them as boresome, or because they are anxious about making good, or because they are frustrated by interruptions.

This feeling of tiredness, when one really has energy to spare, may also be due to an inefficient use of muscles, as when a person uses tiring ways to do work that should not be tiring. This applies to homes as well as to business.

Did you ever wonder how many miles each year a homemaker walks when making a bed? She does a great deal of backtracking. Yet nurses and sleeping-car porters are trained to make a bed standing on just one side of it, without backtracking to the other side.

A trip that might be avoided is backtracking. The usual method of table setting is a good illustration of too much backtracking. The cloth is brought in and spread. Then a trip is made to fetch the silver. Then other trips for this and that. Those trips back with empty hands are wasteful. By using a tray to carry supplies, the average table can be set with only a couple of trips.

Storing things near where they will be used also cuts down backtracking. In the average kitchen, pre-positioned saucepans can be picked up, filled, used, served, washed, and hung back in pre-position with a total of only three steps.

Backtracking also can be cut down by planning work in a sequence, so that one thing leads naturally to the next, without requiring fresh starts. A Vermont farmer who had formerly walked $3\frac{1}{4}$ miles daily doing his chores reduced the amount of walking to $1\frac{1}{4}$ miles by planning the work to cut backtracking and long moves.

When a stenographer needs a supply of letterheads, she can cut down backtracking if she collects on the same trip a fresh stock of other supplies that may be needed soon.

The outside salesman cuts down backtracking by arranging his calls in a sequence that will use least time and least gasoline or shoe leather. When his calls are some distance apart, he sometimes telephones to see whether the prospect is at home, or in the office, before making a long trip.

The inside salesman can lessen backtracking, too. One retail shoe chain found that the average salesman went through 167 operations selling a pair of shoes. Many of these operations were backtracking—double-crossing themselves. They made extra trips to the stock room, for instance, to fetch the other shoe of a pair. And they walked back to the stock room empty-handed, when they could have carried back the shoes the customer did not want. Altogether 96 of the 167 operations could be eliminated, and most of those eliminated were backtracking.

Interruptions often cause backtracking. The secretary who is looking up a telephone number when the telephone rings should find the number and write it down before answering the call.

There is one operation, however, in which backtracking is the efficient way. It is writing your signature. Write it all, then backtrack to put in the dots and cross the "t's." But with about everything else, keep headed ahead to push ahead of your job.

Searching and backtracking have been found to be prime causes of inefficiency in as everyday an activity as housework. Investigators at Wayne University spent a year studying how a group of housewives did their housework. It was found that in preparing a meal the typical housekeeper walked nearly 500 steps, stooped a dozen times, and reached up nearly 50 times. But, by planning the work so that it could be done more efficiently, it was also found that around 75 per cent of that customary walking, bending, and lifting could be avoided.

You can find more details about the application of efficiency principles to housework in our book, *Increasing Personal Efficiency*.

2 ■ Cut Down Muscular Tenseness

"Wanna see me write my name?" asked the seven-year-old, as she laid her writing tablet on the visitor's knee and proudly showed off her new accomplishment.

It was real work for her. She worked all over, as beginners do. She twisted her face, one eye half-shut and tongue pushed between the lips. Her toes dug into the carpet while she squeezed the pencil so firmly the tips of her fingers turned white.

The inefficient worker is often like that little girl. He uses many more muscles than are needed. He uses the essential ones so forcefully that he breaks tools and is awkward. The extra tension is more wearing than the work, for he is as tense as an unsprung mousetrap.

"Hard workers" may be inefficient workers if much of their exertion is waste energy. Excessive effort makes nervous impulses spread and stimulate too many muscles. For personal efficiency, the stimulation should be of the fewest muscles possible. Tensing muscles that are not needed or using needed muscles with excess force are poor work habits.

Only a few ounces of pressure are needed on typewriter keys; yet many typists strike as if they wanted to hammer the machine to pieces. The hunt-and-peck typist, who has trouble finding the letters, bangs too hard because she is uncertain. People who are not sure of themselves try to make up for lack of sureness by putting too much energy into a job.

But experienced typists also often put unnecessary muscle tenseness into their work. This is illustrated on the chartoon that indicates that the typists felt tired in their necks, scalps, shoulders, and eyes. Their fingers, which were doing the productive work furiously, did not feel tired.

You have perhaps seen typists pause after an hour or so of work and move their heads around, swing arms, rub shoulders. That is a good way to get rid of the tiredness in the muscles that have been held tense, and held tense needlessly. One advantage of stopping places (preceding chapter) is that a person can move around. The moving gives the muscles an internal massage that usually relieves the tired feeling or actual pain that sometimes occurs.

People whose work taxes the limits of their abilities also have tension from uncertainty of themselves. It keeps them keyed up on the job. Persons who are really trained and qualified for their work should not have excessive tension, but some of them do.

Dr. Elizabeth Duffy has found that individuals vary widely in the tenseness with which they work. In writing, some persons grasp the pen twice as firmly as others. Doctor Duffy's experiments show that some persons maintain an intense tenseness in all their activities, for months at a time.

Job instructors can do much to prevent working tenseness by starting beginners with relaxed attitudes. This was shown by the experience of a firm that established radio-tube factories in two different cities. Instructors from the home factory trained the inexperienced girls. The girls in the Lancadelphia branch quickly caught on to their new work, and liked it. But the girls in the duplicate plant, at Wilkesville, had trouble learning. Many of them quit within a week because they said the work

How Tired the Typists Felt During the Day's Work

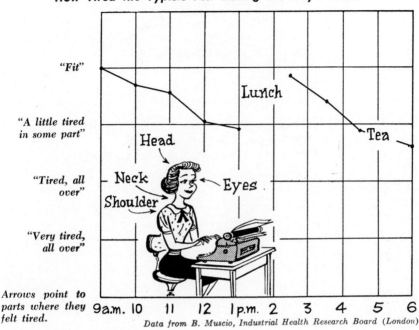

Arrows point to parts where they felt tired.

Data from B. Muscio, Industrial Health Research Board (London)

was "too strainful." Employment tests indicated that the Wilkesville girls were just as capable of learning the work as the Lancadelphia girls.

Investigation showed that the instructors at Wilkesville were at fault. Their chief was a bear for perfect work and no spoilage. His job instructors, therefore, warned the girls about the difficulties of the work and the need to avoid breakage. Those instructions started them on the job filled with ideas of trouble and self-doubt. Their tensed attitudes made the work difficult, and after a week of it the girls were in the "punk" of condition.

It's a good plan to keep relaxed when starting a new job. If you are an old-timer, help beginners keep relaxed.

3 ▪ The Right Amount of Tenseness

Experiments have shown that a slight physical tension helps concentration; not enough tension to cause physical fatigue, but enough to keep you alert. When driving an automobile late at night, even if fatigued, you can keep more alert and avoid accidents if you merely grip the steering wheel harder than usual.

Sit *up* to think, don't slump down. Sit forward. Shoulders up and back. Eyes on work. Hold the pencil as if it is part of you. Relax the legs, but

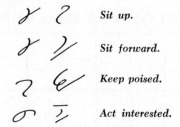

Sit up.

Sit forward.

Keep poised.

Act interested.

keep trunk and head under working control. Act expectant—like a dog that is eagerly waiting for someone to throw a ball.

A stenographer who had to take technical dictation from a monotonous researcher was embarrassed because she yawned while he dictated. His dictation was putting her to sleep. To prevent this, she wrote reminders in advance, at the top of each page of her notebook. They cured her spells of yawning and wavering concentration.

Each person has to learn by experience how *little* general tension he requires to keep alert, and he should not exceed that amount. A little tension is desirable; otherwise, one is on the flabby side. The flabby person goes through life limp. He sinks into a chair, instead of sitting on it. He walks as if he were tied together with rubber bands and might fall apart before he gets there.

The tense person, and many have this failing, goes through life stiffly, moving as if he were trying to tear himself apart. The tensed person sits as though someone had put a tack on his chair. He walks by jerks and bumps into things—including accidents. He drives his automobile fast and fights traffic. He smokes cigarettes in a chain without much enjoyment. You have to be relaxed to keep a pipe lighted.

If you are graceful in walking and working, you are probably neither flabby nor tensed.

4 ■ The Relaxed Approach to Work

De-tensing before starting an activity is helpful. Ruth St. Denis, for example, was a tensed, clumsy girl on a New Jersey farm. Part of her tenseness was due to worry over her father and the difficulty her mother had taking in boarders to make ends meet.

Ruth ran away from school and was anything but poised and graceful. Yet she became a famous dancer. Part of her secret was the half hour of concentrated relaxation that she took before each dance performance. She would put on her make-up and costume early; then meditate alone for thirty minutes, so that she could go on the stage poised, lithe, and graceful.

Paderewski, the world's greatest pianist, practiced making his entrance to the stage piano before each recital, counting the steps to the instrument. Then, twenty minutes before the recital, he locked himself in the dressing room, with the lights out, and relaxed with eyes shut. When the time came for entrance, he was led to the wings, his eyes still shut. Counting the steps, still with his eyes shut, he walked to the piano.

A calm, careful approach to work helps efficiency. The high-speed worker may be a tensed worker, and his speed may be self-defeating. Like the young father who enlarged the hole in the nipple of the baby's bottle to speed up the feeding time; the baby choked. The efficient person is seldom in a rush unless there is an emergency, and he usually takes emergencies in stride. One night, G. F. Swift, the Chicago meat packer, was awakened to be told that the plant was burning down. "The firemen will do all they can without me to help them," he replied. "I'll take care of the rest when I get up in the morning."

Unhurried thoroughness gives greatest speed and accomplishment in the long run—not time-killing dawdling, but steady and accurate application. And it does not cause high blood pressure, ulcers, or nervous indigestion, which we will take up later. Occasional bursts of speed to break monotony are approved, but not even a machine works efficiently at continual top speed.

The efficient person makes effort invisible. Signs of effort are signs of waste effort. The office that is a helter-skelter of activity is an inefficient place. The workers probably are afraid either of the boss or of their own abilities. The illusion of working hard is often just running around in circles, backtracking, and searching in a tense condition.

5 ▪ Work "Loosy"

No, "loosy" is not a misprint. It is a good word, *loosy*—from *loose* and *easy*. Athletic trainers invented this term to describe the ideal condition for muscles.

Loosy muscles are lithe and graceful. Loosy muscles waltz. Work is easier for loosy people.

Tense muscles jerk and jig. Tense people grab things. Tense people make themselves muscle-bound and their work harder.

There are easily understood reasons why loose and easy muscles work best. It is simple: something has to give when you move. Take the arm, for example. The muscles are arranged in opposed pairs. There are flexor muscles, which contract when you pull the hand toward the chest; and, on the opposite side of the arm bones, there are extensor muscles, which pull the hand away.

When you move in any direction, half the muscles contract, and the opposed muscles should relax. If they do not relax, they have to be stretched by brute force—which is not being loosy. Unless the muscles on one side of a joint relax, there is a tug of war, and energy is spent doing nothing. Contracting all muscles produces a spasm, not work.

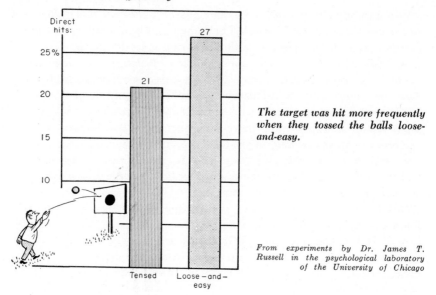

The target was hit more frequently when they tossed the balls loose-and-easy.

From experiments by Dr. James T. Russell in the psychological laboratory of the University of Chicago

The time to relax the half of muscles that will be elongated is at the start of a movement. Otherwise, it is like trying to drive an automobile with the brakes set. Pull on half the muscles; let go on the others.

6 ■ Curving Movements Preferred

Although a straight line is the shortest distance, it is not the most efficient way to move. Muscles and joints are put together so that curved movements are easier. Try drawing a straight line from the top left corner of a sheet of paper to the lower right corner. That is work, and the line is not straight after all. Now draw an arc or gently curving line between the same two corners. Easy. And a pretty line.

Curving motions are easier to make and also are made more gracefully. The awkward person jabs his cigarette straight into the ash tray and jerks his hand back in a straight line. The graceful person swings the cigarette in a gentle arc. Does Yehudi Menuhin jerk the bow up to his violin and seesaw back and forth in jerks? He'd be just a fiddler if he did.

Keep the joints flexible, not stiff-armed like a scarecrow. Swing the arms from the shoulders and a little at the elbows when walking. This helps keep your center of gravity in balance. Don't overswing, as in the goose step, but do swing to avoid a stiff walk.

When shaking hands, keep the shoulder and elbow flexible. Offer your hand in a graceful curve. Don't poke it out in a beeline, or overcurve it, as if trying to dodge, but do move it in an arc.

It is natural to move in arcs. When a person is lost in a forest, he walks in circles, although he thinks that he is going straight. Self-consciousness makes a person move unnaturally in a straight line; so do hurry and tenseness.

Studies of floor mopping show that the quickest and easiest way is to stand with the feet well apart and swing the mop from right to left, about three inches in front of the feet. The conventional method of pushing the mop straight ahead, then jerking it back, is less efficient.

Vacuum cleaners cannot be swung from right to left, but experiments have shown they can be used more efficiently if they are "looped" at the end of each stroke. Usually, they are pushed forward, then pulled back sharply in a series of V-shaped zigzags. There is a definite start and stop for each stroke. But, by making the change of direction a curving U-shaped loop at the end of each stroke, zigzagging is avoided. The looping is easier and 15 per cent quicker than the zigzagging.

Spencerian, Palmer, or any cursive handwriting are designed to fit this natural swing.

7 ■ Keep the Eyes Away from the Hands

Work is also done more efficiently and gracefully when you do not watch hands or feet. Hands have eyes of their own—millions of them—which are much better guides than the eyes in the head. There are special sensory nerves in muscles, tendons, and joints, which guide movements.

As a rule, you are not conscious of sensations from muscles, tendons, and joints; but they are steadily at work—unless you let the eyes in the head interfere with them.

Very few persons lack some of these movement senses, just as some are color-blind or deaf. There was a young mother, for instance, who could not safely carry her baby in her arms. She had to look at her arms to know their position. But with 999 out of 1,000 people, these movement senses are acute enough to guide muscles better than eyes can. A big step in efficiency is made when you wean yourself from watching your hands at work. Get the *feel* of the work, not how the hands look. Consider all the things blind persons do with just the movement senses to guide them.

Some plateaus that beginners experience in typewriting and similar skills are caused by the time it takes to acquire confidence in movement senses as a guide rather than eyes.

When you watch your hands, there is a tendency to move them in a straight line, the shortest distance to the eye. Also, it is tiring for the eyes to watch moving objects. "Keep your eye on the ball, not on your hands," is the advice given to all golfers. It is good advice for personal efficiency in all muscular skills.

8 ▪ *Aim; Then Move*

Use muscles as if they were darts: aim, then toss. This aiming, then tossing, produces a *ballistic* movement—the way bullets are aimed, then fired with a burst of energy, and allowed to follow their course.

A fisherman casts his trout line with a ballistic movement. The cat's paw moves ballistically to catch an insect in flight.

The dub piano player plays with a piston movement, pushing the fingers all the way down on the keys. The skilled pianist keeps fingers poised above the keys and merely aims and then trips. He does not look to see which finger is being tripped. That is the difference between a light touch and a heavy hand on the piano.

The amateur carpenter uses the piston method, as he follows down with all his strength the entire distance of the hammer blow—and misses the nail. The professional raises his hammer, aims, gives it a quick start downward, and, from then on, uses his movement senses to guide the hammer. He watches the nail, not the hammer. He puts force on the movement's start, not on the finish.

Ballistic movements have their force at the start, and the hands have a free ride the rest of the way. They are light-handed movements, more accurate and less tiring.

Try it yourself. Take a magazine page, or a typewritten sheet of paper, and put dots in all the *o*'s. Use a forceful piston movement all the way until the pencil hits the paper. Then try it with a ballistic movement. Hold the pencil lightly, aim, then give a quick start, and let the pencil bounce back ready for the next dot. Lots more fun the ballistic way, isn't it?

When you use ballistic movements, you work with a bounce by catching natural swings on the rebound. Using the rebound puts rhythm into repetitive work.

A long ballistic movement is less tiring than a short piston stroke that does the same work.

Some plateaus in learning typewriting are broken through when a ballistic tap is substituted for a piston push on the keys.

There are a few activities in which ballistic movements cannot be used. A screw driver cannot be used ballistically, but it can be used loosy. A paintbrush can be used with safety only semiballistically; otherwise, paint will be speckled all over the place. A calculating-machine crank and other levers that have greater resistance at the end of the stroke can be used only semiballistically. But, whenever you can, make your movements ballistic.

Aim; then trip. Tap; don't push.

Use a loosy, curving motion without watching your hands.

Organize your tasks so that you do about an hour of similar work at one time. And plan the stimulation of many subgoals throughout the day.

———————————————————————————

The Gist of the Chapter

1. What is backtracking, and how does it lower efficiency?
2. Give four general reasons why people get tired at work that should not be tiring.
3. How is unnecessary muscle tenseness shown in working methods?
4. What are some causes of needless tenseness?
5. How can a person determine what is the right amount of tenseness?
6. How does one "work loosy"?
7. Give some examples of the superiority of curving movements.
8. Why is it not necessary to watch the hands as much as beginners do? What are the advantages of not watching them?
9. What is a ballistic movement, and how is it performed?

Things to Do and Problems to Discuss

1. Get some ping-pong balls and toss them into a wastebasket, standing about 10 feet from the basket. (a) Toss them ballistically and then with a piston movement. (b) Toss them "loosy," then tensed. Which ways give you the better score?
2. Observe a short-order cook or soda-fountain clerk, and notice which parts of their work they do ballistically; which "loosy"; which curving.
3. Try carrying a glass filled with water (a) looking at the glass while you walk, and (b) looking where you are heading for rather than at the glass. Why did you spill less water the one way?
4. Study some signatures on actual business letters. Can you make good guesses about whether the person was tensed or relaxed when writing the signature?
5. Refresh yourself on earlier chapters, and discuss some factors in the work environment which might make it difficult for people to have a relaxed approach to work—interruptions, for instance. What other factors?
6. Effie K.'s low work efficiency may be due to her slouchy, inattentive posture. Make recommendations for her, drawing also upon the information about the standing posture given in an earlier chapter.
7. Consider some job and work out a plan for organizing it to cut down backtracking, searching time, and deciding time.
8. Some people are said to have "tensed voices," others "relaxed voices." Listen to strangers talking and see if you can detect such differences. Do these

voice differences seem to have a bearing on their general attitude of tenseness or relaxing?

9. Is a person with a high level of aspiration more likely to be a tense worker?

10. Should you watch your hand when writing?

11. Oswald J. is breaking in a new employee, who is obviously bothered by beginner's tenseness. What could Oswald do to make the beginner more relaxed and "loosy"?

12. Analyze some long business letters, and look for backtracking (repetition) in them. Figure some way to calculate the cost of that backtracking.

13. Would sedentary workers become less tired if they had more exercise?

14. Why does "just sitting" make people feel tired?

15. Why do other people often become tensed when in the presence of a tensed person? What significance does this have in business?

9 ■ GETTING THE RIGHT JOB

_ _ _ _ _ _ _ _ _ _ _ _ _ _ _ _ _ _ _ _

WHAT THIS CHAPTER IS ABOUT

1. *How large are differences in ability?*
2. *The normal distribution of abilities*
3. *Experts are much like other people*
4. *Job analysis and specification*
5. *The primary office functions—POF*
6. *A profile of ability*
7. *Primary vocational interests—PVI*
8. *Primary personal interests—PPI*
9. *Using your unfulfilled interests*
10. *How to size up applicants*
11. *How to make the best impression when being sized up*
12. *How to get more salary*

1 ■ How Large Are Differences in Ability?

"That young Thomas boy is clever with tools. We need an extra mechanic; so I'll hire him to help us make clocks." It was that easy for Eli Terry to find "who could do what" in the old days when businesses were small and the owner knew almost everybody in the neighborhood. The employer knew which young men had a "natural bent" for work with tools and which for work with books or figures—and also those bent on loafing or starting arguments with other workers.

Nowadays, however, workers to be selected usually are strangers, and only a few minutes are available to size up a job applicant. This quick sizing up of a stranger's fitness for a specific job can be more accurate if one knows some of the ins and outs of human capacities and skills.

How great are differences in abilities? Some people are called "quick as a cat," others "as slow as molasses in January." Sometimes a supervisor says, "John is ten times the worker Fred is." Such figures of speech make individual differences seem greater than they are.

In bodily characteristics, such as *height*, the tallest and shortest persons on the street have a ratio of about 1.25 to 1 in height. (This does not include any circus giants or dwarfs who happen to be on the street.) People seldom differ from one another by more than 25 per cent in bodily measurements. This is not a great difference, although it can be important when the best height for a typist's chair or an assembler's bench is being determined.

Individual differences in muscular control are greater than for bodily measurements. The fastest person moves about twice as speedily as the slowest, which is about the difference between the speediest and slowest typists who apply for their first jobs. In many factory production departments, the best worker turns out twice the work of some others, even when there is a piece-rate plan of payment.

The differences are still greater when mental factors enter the performance. People vary from 2.5 to 1, for instance, in the length of numbers they can remember.

In *intelligence,* or general mental horsepower, people vary in a ratio of about 3 to 1. That is about the ratio in brain power between the brightest executive in the firm and the dullest worker on the simplest job.

When it comes to learning difficult material, such as advanced accounting, the difference between best and poorest is a little more than 3 to 1.

John, therefore, cannot be ten times better than Fred, although Fred may take three times longer to learn the job or may turn out only one-third as much work as John. But that is enough difference to change a profit into a loss.

2 ■ The Normal Distribution of Abilities

Can people be separated into "fast" and "slow"? While some people move with twice the speed of others, most people are neither fast nor slow, but in between. The chart, "Reaction Times of 1,000 Machinists," shows measurements of French machinists. Some took only $125/1000$ second to move when they were given the signal, and others took $245/1000$ second. But notice from the chart that half of these machinists took only from $165/1000$ to $185/1000$ second—the large in-between group.

The average person is located in this big in-between group. The percentages taper rapidly from this average group toward each extreme in speed.

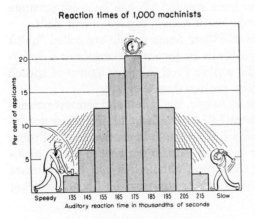

Reaction times of 1,000 machinists

Per cent of applicants

Speedy 135 145 155 165 175 185 195 205 215 Slow
Auditory reaction time in thousandths of seconds

These experienced machinists were applying for work. Their personal equations for speed of movement when a signal is heard are distributed in a bell-shaped curve. What bearing might these differences in reaction time have on output? on accidents?

This tapering off, which leaves only a few people at each extreme, is a feature of all human qualities, whether height, intelligence, co-operativeness, neatness, musical ability, or whatnot. When an unselected group of people is charted on any ability, the chart is bell-shaped, which indicates a normal distribution of abilities.

This normal distribution makes it impossible to separate people into clear-cut types or classes. It would be necessary, for instance, to measure some 3,500 machinists to locate 100 whose reaction times were as fast as $^{135}\!/_{1000}$ second. While the goal is to employ the most capable workers, a compromise has to be made with the normal distribution. To find many from an extreme end of the distribution is like looking for a needle in a haystack.

Are the differences inborn or acquired? Differences among people are not eliminated by practice or training. Practice sometimes increases the differences. The person who was speedy at the start is apt to improve more than the one who was slow at the start. The new worker who is best on the job the first day is most likely to be best after a year, unless he becomes too self-satisfied and lets himself slump. Practice helps people improve but does not shift the normal distribution greatly.

The chart, "Individual Differences in Ability to Read Business Material," shows how training and experience do not eliminate the normal distribution. This type of reading is an ability that profits more from training than did the simple reaction time of the French mechanics. Beginning students, for instance, do not average so well as professional accountants. This is partly because some beginners are low in the aptitude required to understand such terms as inventory reserves, depreciation allowances, and funded debt. It is also partly because beginners have not yet been trained to be familiar with business vocabularies and thinking.

But there is still a normal distribution among the professional account-

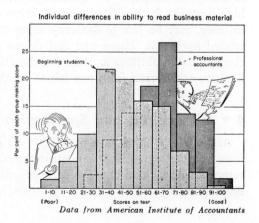

The distribution of ability to read business material also follows the bell-shaped pattern. The 275 professional accountants average higher than the 5,328 beginning students of accounting. But many students are higher in this ability than some of the professionals. Which students will have to study harder to become professionals?

Individual differences in ability to read business material

Per cent of each group making score

Beginning students

Professional accountants

1-10   11-20   21-30   31-40   41-50   51-60   61-70   71-80   81-90   91-100
(Poor)   Scores on test   (Good)

Data from American Institute of Accountants

ants of long experience. They average higher than the beginners, of course; but even experience and the elimination of the less capable have not altered the normal distribution much. It is still a "normalish" distribution, merely shifted toward the higher end of the scale.

3 ▪ Experts Are Much Like Other People

Do experts have abilities others lack? No. As we would suspect from the normal distribution curve, the expert merely has more of the aptitude than most other people have. Even the idiot has some intelligence, and your senator may have three times as much. We are *all alike in the kinds of abilities* we have, but we *differ in the amounts of each ability.* You have some musical memory, though it may be small; whereas Toscanini could remember the score of an entire opera with his eyes shut.

To find the right job, or the right worker for a job, we do not ask, "Does he have the ability?" but "How much of the needed ability does he have?"

Are experts likely to be shortchanged in other abilities? Experts are no more shortchanged than the rest of us who are not experts. It is not true that, if a person is outstanding in one ability, he must be weak in some other to "make up" for it. The person who is superior in one ability is likely to be superior in most (but not all) other abilities. And the mediocre person in one line is likely to be mediocre in most other abilities.

Consider the many-sided activities in which Benjamin Franklin and Thomas Jefferson were successful, as examples of the all-roundedness of abilities that experts usually have. Consider the neighborhood tinkerer who does lots of things, but none of them well, as an example of the mediocre.

Each person does have ups and downs in abilities, his strong and weak abilities. Geniuses are no more an exception to this rule than are the feeble-minded. These little ups and downs are of importance, however, in the specialization of occupations in modern industry. The person with high dexterity for handling a screw driver on an assembly operation, for instance, may be low in dexterity using tweezers when transferred to a related operation. These ups and downs in what would appear to be closely related abilities account for the failure of some employees when they are transferred from one job to another.

4 ▪ Job Analysis and Specification

Ralph is employed as a machinist; all he does is grind rough edges from iron castings. Edgar is also employed as a machinist, but he uses a complicated machine to make parts according to blueprint specifications. Ralph and Edgar have the same job title, but much different abilities are needed for the two jobs. When one is hiring a person, or taking a job, it is more important to know the exact nature of the work than the title given the job.

Job analysis. Job analysis is a study of each operation needed to do a certain job. It includes something about the essential abilities, experience, and training needed to do the job.

Job specification. Job specification can be made after the job analysis

WORKER CHARACTERISTICS REQUIRED

Job Title . . . .

Indicate: H for high ability needed
A for average ability needed
L for low ability needed
O when not needed for this job

1. Work rapidly for long periods
2. Strength of hands
3. Strength of arms
4. Strength of back
5. Strength of legs
6. Dexterity of fingers
7. Dexterity of hands and arms
8. Dexterity of foot and leg
9. Eye-hand co-ordination
10. Foot-hand-eye co-ordination
11. Co-ordination of both hands
12. Estimate size of objects
13. Estimate quantity of objects
14. Perceive form of objects
15. Estimate speed of moving objects
16. Keenness of vision
17. Keenness of hearing
18. Sense of smell
19. Sense of taste
20. Touch discrimination
21. Muscular discrimination
22. Memory for details (things)
23. Memory for abstract ideas
24. Memory for oral directions
25. Memory for written directions
26. Arithmetic computation
27. Intelligence
28. Adaptability
29. Ability to make decisions
30. Ability to plan
31. Initiative
32. Understanding mechanical devices
33. Attention to many items
34. Oral expression
35. Skill in written expression
36. Tact in dealing with people
37. Memory of names and persons
38. Personal appearance
39. Concentration amidst distractions
40. Emotional stability
41. Work under hazardous conditions
42. Estimate quality of objects
43. Unpleasant physical conditions
44. Color discrimination
45. Ability to meet and deal with people
46. Height
47. Weight

and with the job analysis as a guide. The table lists 47 characteristics that the United States Employment Service considers when it is making a job specification. Many state and company offices follow this list of characteristics. These characteristics are based more on common sense than on profound psychology; yet they are very helpful for sizing up a person—or oneself—for a definite job. (You will find more detailed analyses of primary human abilities in *Sizing Up People* by Laird.)

5 ■ The Primary Office Functions—POF

There are several ways of arriving at the qualifications needed for a job. In Chapter 1 we listed 15 characteristics that are recommended for use in making merit ratings of office workers. Another way is to make an analysis of people who have been successful at a job. In analyzing successful secretaries, Drs. W. W. Charters and I. B. Whitley found the following traits mentioned most often by the executives with whom the secretaries worked:

	Per Cent
Accuracy	86
Responsibleness	82
Dependability	75
Intelligence	75
Courtesy	71
Initiative	71
Tact	68
Pleasantness	64
Appearance	64

Another approach is the use of factor-analysis methods, similar to those used to discover the primary mental abilities (PMA). There are some 139 different clerical operations in offices. But factor analysis has found they can be reduced to eight basic operations, or lowest common denominators. This is the list as reported by Dr. Leon L. Thomas, of Dunlap & Associates, Inc:

Primary Office Functions (POF)

Typing
Listing and compiling
Communicating
Planning and supervising
Filing
Handling stock
Routine clerical operations
Calculating

6 ■ A Profile of Ability

Psychological analysis adds to skill in finding the right person for the job, as can be seen by studying the profile of Samuel Q. He had been in personnel work and was doing well enough. But he did not enjoy the clerical and computing details of that job and was not able to use his strong sales drive.

Samuel Q. resigned his personnel job to become a life insurance salesman and went "like a house afire" in his new occupation. His insurance earnings, entirely on a commission basis, are five times his personnel salary. Equally important, he enjoys his new work and is much happier,

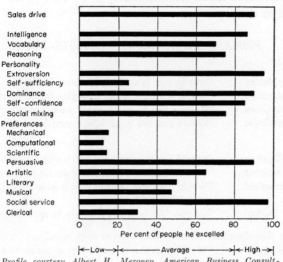

Profile of Samuel Q.

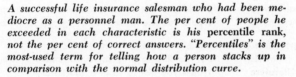

Profile courtesy Albert H. Meroney, American Business Consultants, Inc., Chicago

A successful life insurance salesman who had been mediocre as a personnel man. The per cent of people he exceeded in each characteristic is his **percentile rank,** *not the per cent of correct answers. "Percentiles" is the most-used term for telling how a person stacks up in comparison with the normal distribution curve.*

though the personnel work did give him the satisfaction of doing a worthwhile social service—but so does selling insurance.

Study the characteristics charted on the "Profile of Samuel Q.," to become familiar with some of the human qualities that vocational psychologists find essential for placing the right man in his right job.

Notice, also, that Samuel Q. has those ups and downs that were memtioned at the close of Section 3.

7 ■ Primary Vocational Interests—PVI

Primary interests, similar to the PMA and POF, have recently been discovered by factor analysis. The following summaries of primary interests are based on the work of Dr. J. P. Guilford and colleagues at the University of Southern California.

Some of the "ingredients" that enter into these primary interests are given beneath each primary interest, with an illustrative question. A "Yes" answer to the question indicates a leaning toward the interest. The ingredient listed first contributes a little more to the primary interest than the second ingredient, and so on down the list of ingredients. The questions are not a test, but are added to help make the meanings clear. The illustrative questions can be answered more easily by men.

Women readers can think of some man they know who would likely give a "Yes" answer to each question.

PRIMARY VOCATIONAL INTERESTS—PVI

Mechanical

Manipulating	"Would you like to run a turret lathe?"
Constructing	"Would you like to cut and glue things together?"
Precision	"Do you like to make exact measurements?"
Cleanliness	"Would you like a job where your hands get dirty?"

Scientific

Investigating	"Would you like to help a scientist do research?"
Theorizing	"Would you like to figure how the moon causes tides?"
Mathematical	"Would you like to study how electronic computing machines work?"
Logical	"Do you like to look for errors in reasoning?"

Social Welfare (See the needs of others and want to help them.)

Welfare of others	"Would you like to work with a group to help the unemployed?"
Communicating	"Would you like to write a booklet explaining traffic laws?"
Personal service	"Would you like to serve as personal secretary or aide?"
Civic-minded	"Would you like to work with a group to get out the vote?"

Aesthetic Expression (Participating, not as a spectator.)

Music	"Do you like to play some instrument or sing?"
Literature	"Would you like to write a short story?"
Drama	"Would you enjoy taking part in a play?"
Graphic arts	"Do you like to plan a furniture arrangement?"

Clerical

Computing	"Would you like to figure out a payroll?"
Clerical	"Would you like to look for letters in a file cabinet?"
Mathematical	"Do you like to study algebra and geometry?"
Administrating	"Would you like to supervise a branch office?"

Business (Working in a commercial atmosphere with others.)

Administrating	"Would you enjoy managing a business office?"
Selling	"Would you like to work as a salesman on a commission basis?"
Contacting	"Would you like to contact firms to start a trade association?"
Communicating	"Would you like to write a letter to a newspaper explaining the trade association?"

8 ▪ *Primary Personal Interests—PPI*

The PVI are useful in indicating the general type of work—scientific, business, etc.—an individual is likely to do best provided, of course, that he has the abilities required. The PVI bring out what a prospective employer wants to know about an applicant.

The PPI, in contrast, are concerned more with activities that are personally satisfying to the individual himself. They supplement the PVI by showing what the person is likely to want from the job in order to be happy in it.

The vocational and personal interests are interrelated in actual life, and employers should give more attention to the personal interests than they usually do. As an example: an applicant may have high business interest (PVI), but he may also have a high interest in outdoor working (PPI) and would presumably be more satisfied with a business job that was outdoors—as with a contractor—than "cooped up indoors."

PRIMARY PERSONAL INTERESTS—PPI

Wanting Adventure

Exploring	"Would you like to explore a cave?"
Risk-taking	"Would you like to drive in an automobile race?"
Outdoor life	"Would you like a job that is mostly outdoors?"
Nature	"Would you like to be in a forest of giant trees?"

Aesthetic Appreciation (As spectator, not creating.)

Literature	"Would you like to browse in a library?"
Graphic arts	"Would you like to make a collection of drawings?"
Drama	"Would you like to watch a dramatic group rehearse?"
Music	"Would you like to attend a series of symphony concerts?"

Conforming (With an ethical emphasis.)

Conscience	"Would you feel uneasy about getting a raise you did not merit?"
Custom	"Do you believe in 'When in Rome do as the Romans do'?"
Competing	"Do you work best where competition is keenest?"
Discipline	"Do you think stricter parents would lessen juvenile crime?"

Wanting Diversion (Escape from routine.)

Playfulness	"Do you like to play with pets?"
Romanticism	"Do you like to read about movie stars?"
Athletics	"Do you enjoy active sports and exercise?"
Problem-solving	"Do you like to work crossword puzzles?"

Wishful Thinking (Substitute satisfactions and indirect outlets.)

Comical situations	"Do you like to watch circus clowns?"
Daydreaming	"Do you like to think how it would feel to be a hero?"
Indirect hostility	"Do you enjoy hearing the boss call down a person you dislike?"
Amusement flight	"Do you want more time for fun and amusement?"

Wanting Attention

Recognition	"Would you like to have a business named after you?"
Social status	"Do you like to be seen talking to important persons?"
Exhibitionism	"Do you like to do unusual things so people notice you?"
Assurance	"Are you uneasy if you don't know how you stand with others?"

Resisting Restrictions (Wanting freedom in personal work and habits.)

Individualism	"Are there too many straight-laced people who spoil your fun?"
Unsystematic	"Do you dislike following a fixed schedule?"
Disorderly	"Do you feel that some people are just too orderly?"
Independence	"Do you want to work for yourself rather than for somebody else?"

Outdoor Working

Agriculture	"Would you like to tend a vegetable garden?"
Open spaces	"Do you think a forest ranger has an interesting life?"
Constructing	"Do you like to build things?"
Manipulating	"Would you enjoy painting garden furniture?"

Physical Push

Stamina	"Can you work long hours without feeling tired?"
Self-reliance	"Do you make weighty personal decisions without asking for help?"
Aspiration	"Do you expect to earn more than most people your age by ten years from now?"
Persistence	"Can you plug at a job even when the end is not in sight?"

Aggression (Expressing hostility.)

Direct	"Do you let a person know you dislike it when he edges ahead of you in a line?"
Coercive	"Do you like to make others correct their mistakes?"
Indirect	"Do you like to see the villain made a fool of and punished?"

The following PPI are not as general as the ones previously listed.

Realistic Thinking (Dealing with intangibles and concepts.)

Mathematical	"Do you like to work complicated mathematical problems?"
Logical	"Do you like to figure out things by rules of logic?"
Organizing	"Do you like to plan things for the sake of efficiency?"
Problem-solving	"Do you like to plan strategy for a game or business deal?"

Cultural Interest (Broadly informed citizen.)

Civics	"Would you like to be on a group to improve the parks?"
Communicating	"Would you like to write letters telling about a charity?"
Literature	"Do you like to read best-selling books?"
Social science	"Do you like to read about the causes of poverty?"

Orderliness

Surroundings	"Would it embarrass you to be seen with your workplace cluttered?"
Personal	"Do you keep everything in its place?"
Seriousness	"Do you think too many people waste time joking at work?"
Cleanliness	"Do you dislike work that involves grease, dirt, or paint?"

Sociability (Akin to what is called extroversion.)

Making friends	"Do you enjoy being friends with all kinds of people?"
Initiative	"Do you often get up a party without waiting for someone else to?"

| Affection | "Are close friendships extremely important to you?" |
| Personal service | "Do you like to help a person find where to buy some article he wants?" |

Physical Fitness

Activity	"Do you like to take physical exercise?"
Dominance	"Would you like to tell people what to do in an emergency?"
Healing	"Would you like to try to cure mentally disturbed people?"
Recognition	"Would you like to be recognized as an expert in something?"

Precision

Exactness	"Would you like to inspect jewels for small defects?"
Science	"Would you like to work with scientific instruments?"
Detail	"Would you like to adjust the alignment of a typewriter?"
Computing	"Do you enjoy adding up a long column of figures?"

Wanting Variety

Adventure	"Do you want to change your place of living frequently?"
Travel	"Would you like to travel to have some new experiences?"
Personal service	"Would you like to be a companion to some old person?"
Risk-taking	"Do you like thrilling, dangerous activity?"

Wanting Sympathetic Environment

Assurance	"Do you want to feel others know how hard you are trying?"
Approval	"Are you bothered when others do not encourage you?"
Comfort	"Do you dislike being in the rain?"
Controlling others	"Do you like to persuade others to agree with you on how a job should be done?"

Ambition (Social and professional advancement.)

Aspiration level	"Do you expect to be better off than most people your age ten years from now?"
Responsibility	"Do you like to make plans for others?"
Recognition	"Do you want others to realize you are successful?"
Social status	"Do you like to belong to groups of higher status people?"

Social Initiative (Competitive, but socially minded.)

Initiating	"Do you like to lead groups of people?"
Competing	"Do you like to surpass others?"
Gregariousness	"Would you like to be a member of many clubs?"
Tempo	"Do you usually get where you are going in a hurry, even when there is plenty of time?"

These primary vocational and personal interests are undoubtedly of basic importance in the matching of jobs and people. When the interests match what the job needs, the person would be naturally motivated to work with a will. In addition, the person whose job uses all his predominant interests should get much more satisfaction from his work.

These PVI and PPI merit reviewing. They will be referred to in several later chapters. Your review will be more interesting and practical, if you write beside the name of each interest the name, or initials, of someone you know whom you size up as being high in that interest. Is his work such that he can use that interest in it?

Since he was a small boy, John Jones, Jr., has wanted to be a forest ranger. But his father has been so wrapped up in building a business that he has never asked his son what he wanted to do with his life.

Courtesy Connecticut Mutual Life Insurance Co.

9 ■ Using Your Unfulfilled Interests

People usually have a larger number of strong interests than today's jobs call for.

It is relatively easy to find a job for which a person's interests qualify him. But it is more difficult to find a job that provides opportunities for him to follow all his strong interests in his work. There might be a job calling for only five primary interests, for example; but the young man on the job has a dozen interests he is keen to exercise. Five from twelve leaves seven leftover interests that are not satisfied by his workday activities.

Modern business and factory methods tend to limit the chances for following one's full range of strong interests. Most work is now indoors, giving fewer chances to follow an interest in outdoor activity. Mass production of the same product (designed by someone else) has cut down the opportunities for aesthetic expression in the work itself. Simplifying jobs and reducing them to routine procedures means that many workers are unable to follow some of their strong PPI in their work.

The leftover interests cause feelings of frustration and dissatisfaction. Some people shift from one job to another, hoping to find one where the leftovers will be used. These people may not be consciously aware of what makes them restless, but the frustrated interests can be a factor.

Sometimes the job-shifter is lucky and finds a job that matches his interests better. As a rule, more of one's interests will be satisfied when a job requires more skilled work or gives the variety and recognition that comes with promotion. Just switching jobs is not so effective as preparing for a job that can use more interests.

Afterhour outlets for the leftover interests are extremely useful. Some firms have hobby and activity clubs that give outlets for interests that may be stifled on the jobs. Most communities also have many activities that can give exercise for one's PPI that are not used in the daily work. It is probably good mental hygiene for a person to take part in such activities to round out his satisfaction from life and work.

A prime minister, for instance, has work that calls for a variety of interests. But it does not give a chance for his aesthetic expression. He takes up oil painting as a hobby to fill this gap.

A self-employed pharmacist uses a variety of interests in his profession, but his interest in outdoor work is left over. He organizes a local fish-and-game club. Others whose PPI for outdoor work is unfulfilled take up hiking, go on camping trips, or become "sundowners" as they putter around their homes and land on the fringe of the city.

His social-welfare interests were strong and left over for the owner of a small office-supply business. He became active in a local social-service organization as an avocation. Now he is so much wrapped up in the welfare work that his wife has to run the business.

A bookkeeper had a strong interest in adventure, which he could not find in the ledgers. He found he could satisfy this interest, and other leftover interests, by helping out in Boy Scout work.

A young typist in an attorney's one-girl office had a strong leftover interest in sociability. After several months of increasing frustration, she accidentally ran across a hobby group that gave her an outlet for sociability as well as for her cultural interest.

Under modern business conditions, most workers—of all levels—need some off-the-job activities to take care of unfulfilled interests. Suitable afterhour outlets can be a very real help in rounding out life and adjusting to the job.

10 ■ How to Size Up Applicants

The employment interview is used universally to size up a prospective employee. In smaller firms, the owner himself does the interviewing, usually on a by-guess and by-gosh basis. Some proprietors imagine they can "see right through people," but to be safe usually make the offer of employment on a trial basis.

In about half the larger firms, applicants are given a series of psychological tests to find their percentile standing in qualities that personnel research has shown are needed for a certain job. These may be called personnel tests, placement tests, classification tests, or occupational tests. About four million job applicants are tested each year. Wise applicants give preference to the firm that uses tests, for tests greatly increase the chances of getting work in which the applicant will be both happy and proficient.

But tests are seldom the sole reason why an applicant is hired or passed over. The interviewer may decide that there is something undesirable about the applicant, and reject him despite a favorable showing on tested aptitudes. The interview is a critical part of employment, even when placement tests are used.

The interviewer can size up applicants most successfully if he will study and then always bear in mind all the following suggestions.

Establish rapport at the outset. Rapport (ra-*port*), as applied here, is a harmonious condition in which the person being interviewed has an attitude of trust and confidence toward the interviewer. A fishy-eyed interviewer with a gruff manner defeats himself, since he loses rapport and makes applicants keep on guard. The applicant may be offered a cigarette or extended little courtesies that make him feel welcome. The interview may be just routine to the interviewer; but it is a high spot in the life of the applicant, who may remember it for years.

Make the interview conversational. Don't fire questions point-blank. An interview has been called a conversation with a purpose. Asking rapid-fire questions is dingdonging, not interviewing, and it misses much information. A conversation helps rapport; cross-examining destroys it.

The aim of the interview is to direct conversation so that clues are developed which show the kind of person the candidate is. Here is an example.

> INTERVIEWER. "Come right in. Rainy morning, isn't it? Was it inconvenient for you to get here in the drizzle?" (He might have asked point-blank where the applicant lived and about transportation facilities for getting to work.)
>
> APPLICANT. "Very convenient, since we live in the Highland addition and the bus comes within a block of your office."
>
> INTERVIEWER. "Highland is a pleasant place to live." (A statement to further rapport and to encourage the applicant to continue talking.)
>
> APPLICANT. "We like it very much. We are making payments on a new home there, much better than when we rented an apartment."
>
> INTERVIEWER. "That's fine. Many people in Highland find an automobile convenient." (He is probing with this bit of conversation.)
>
> APPLICANT. "We considered that, but thought it better to put the money into larger payments on our house and into a night course I am taking. Anyway, we have several friends with cars who invite us for picnics and such; so we don't miss an automobile." (What a lot that tells the inter-

viewer: the man is thrifty, has friends, is improving his training, does not worry about keeping up with the Joneses.)

INTERVIEWER. "Yes. I see. Was your wife a city girl, too?"

APPLICANT. "Both of us came from a small town. We met at business school and fell for each other right away. But we waited until I received a promotion before getting married. She worked in the tax office a couple of years after, until I took a job in the auditor's office at the Mercantile Branch. She insisted on being married in the little church in her home town. But we both prefer the city now." (Apparently his wife will be a good influence. The interviewer has also learned something about the family's religion and the applicant's training and experience.)

INTERVIEWER. "I don't know the mercantile people very well, but they have a good reputation." (He is setting a trap for the applicant.)

APPLICANT. "They should have. You know their products, of course. Best in their line. I hated to leave, but they had so many long-service employees ahead of me that promotions would come slowly; so I took the offer from the Commerce Affiliates. The principal of the business school told the commerce people about me. This was a younger firm and seemed to be going places, but they have been short of capital and have not grown—and that's why I am here to talk with you." (The applicant did not knock his former employers and apparently got along well with fellow workers. His principal seems to have a high estimate of the applicant's potentials.)

Keep the conversation on the beam. The interviewer's opening small talk should put the applicant at ease and start the conversation on topics that will uncover pertinent information about his training, background, habits, interests, attitudes, and experience.

The applicant should do at least three-fourths of the talking. Some interviewers like to do most of the talking themselves; as a result, they learn little about the applicant except that he is a patient listener.

The interviewer must be alert to switch his own talk and to get the talk on the beam if the applicant starts with details that are not relevant. The talkative candidate can be brought back on the beam by saying something like this: "You mentioned Moreland High School. What school activities did you take part in?" or "And what did you do on your next job?"

Keeping the conversation going. Show interest in what the applicant says. Give the impression that you are just getting acquainted with him rather than weighing his faults and assets. Avoid the impression that you disapprove of some of his experience or attitudes. Many applicants are uneasy during an interview and find it difficult to talk naturally. The interviewer needs conversational dexterity to draw out the silent applicant so that he talks naturally to his new-found friend.

The interviewer should make frequent use of such conversation-encouraging expressions as: "That sounds interesting." "Tell me more." "Yes—go on."

The conversation will dry up if the interviewer looks out the window, or at an application blank, instead of at the applicant. Don't stare, but do look at the applicant's face as if you were interested. If you are not interested in him, you will miss much when you are sizing him up.

Sell the applicant on the firm. This does not mean telling him fancy stories about promotional opportunities, but by the general atmosphere in the interview room and surrounding the interviewer's manner. You may not make the applicant an employee, but every applicant should be made the firm's friend.

Know your prejudices and allow for them. If you are an engineering graduate, you may be prejudiced against self-taught machinists. If you are a self-taught machinist, you may be biased against graduate engineers. It is human to have prejudices, lots of them. But the good interviewer knows his own prejudices and does not let them lead him astray.

Beware of your first impression and of a general impression. It is equally human to form first impressions and stick to them. The good interviewer disregards his first impressions and looks for details rather than over-all impressions. The conversation in the foregoing interview shows how details can be uncovered and how to note their significance.

Give more weight to the applicant's past than to his appearance. What the applicant has done in the past and the style or attitude in which it was done tell much more about him than his present appearance. He is probably dressed in his best for the interview, anyway. The unskilled interviewer, however, hires mostly on the basis of "he looks good to me."

Estimate percentiles. Refresh yourself on percentiles by studying the profile of Samuel Q. again. Instead of sizing up an applicant as "good" or "poor," estimate where he ranks in comparison with other applicants in the qualities needed for the job. Is his technical training better than that of 15, 50, or 75 per cent of the people on the job? Estimate how many people he would exceed in the other essential characteristics. Think in terms of the normal distribution curve, not of the extremes.

Know why you estimate him as 15 per cent or 75 per cent. If you cannot give yourself at least three reasons for each characteristic you estimate, you are probably just making a guess based on a general or first impression. Avoid the pitfalls of the halo effect.

Pay little attention to the letters of recommendation. Previous employers and teachers will say things they hesitate to put in writing. Telephone to them, and get a quick report on things you want to know. If they stall or hem and haw, it may mean that something unfavorable is being covered up.

Check on claims of job skill. A sizable percentage of job seekers exaggerate their previous pay, experience, and skill. A call on previous employers gives some check on these claims. In addition, it is often desirable to use trade tests, or questions, which will show whether the applicant knows as much about the work as he pretends. Proficiency tests often are used to give an indication of, say, a prospective secretary's skill in typing or shorthand—but they will not tell whether she is even-tempered and courteous.

11 ■ How to Make the Best Impression When Being Sized Up

The applicant has more at stake in an employment interview than the firm. Emory Strachen knew this when he had to leave school and look for a job. He did not want just any old job; so he did not ask any of the merchants who had been his steady newspaper customers. Young Strachen thought wholesalers had bigger businesses than retailers; so he applied to a wholesaler for work.

"I'll try you for a couple of weeks," the wholesaler told him, "and if I like you, the job will be yours."

"No," the fourteen-year-old said, eying him calmly. "To you, I am just another kid looking for a job. But for me, this may be my lifework; so I'll work for you for a month—and, if I like you, I'll tell you whether I want to stay or not."

Emory Strachen became president of the wholesalers and many times mayor of Elmira, New York.

It usually is not safe to talk to a prospective employer as audaciously as Strachen did. But it is always wise to bear in mind that to the applicant the interview may be the difference between personal success or failure, landing a job or being out of work. Worst of all, he may land the wrong job, or one with a company that pays well for a couple of years and then lets employees out.

Everyone tries, often in crude ways, to make a good impression in an interview. It is equally important for the applicant to give a true impression, so that he will be placed where he will have a fair chance to succeed. A falsely favorable impression may merely mean failure, and dismissal soon. For self-confidence and later success, it is sometimes better for an applicant to be turned down than to get a job in which he cannot succeed. Applicants should keep their sights set reasonably at the outset and should make honest impressions.

Usually, however, applicants show up poorly when being interviewed. Eagerness to win the job, uncertainty about their real abilities, and the newness of the interview situation combine to make applicants tongue-tied, fidgety, and forgetful, and thus to make weak impressions.

Watch your waiting time. Some interviewers like to keep applicants waiting, partly to "humble them," partly to size up their conduct during the annoyance of waiting. Always carry a magazine or book to read while waiting. It should be something you like to read, but not anything that will give a poor impression of your reading tastes.

If other applicants are waiting, carry on a friendly conversation with someone, if that is easier than reading. Come what may, don't sit like a bump on a log waiting for something to happen. You will be more at ease in the actual interview if you have been occupied profitably while waiting.

Demonstrate in everything connected with the interview that you know how to make profitable use of time. In case you have an appointment for the interview, be right on time, neither late nor early. Play safe by arriving a block from the office a few minutes ahead of time; then walk into the office right on the dot.

Let the interviewer make the first moves. Business favors employees who have initiative, but it is wary of those who are too aggressive. Take the tip for shows of initiative from the interviewer. Let him be the one who first offers to shake hands. As soon as he indicates that he wants to shake hands, shake his hand firmly, briefly, and without hesitation. Smile pleasantly and look into his face while shaking hands. Say: "I am glad of the opportunity to talk with you." Then wait for him to start the conversation as he wants it.

As soon as he motions toward a chair, or asks you to sit down, sit. And thank him as you sit down. Don't rush into his office and slump in a chair without an invitation. Sit alertly; and lean a bit toward the interviewer, as if you were dying to listen to him.

If he offers you a cigarette, accept it with thanks, in case you smoke. Don't pull out one of your own cigarettes uninvited, even if there is an ash tray beside you. Accept the cigarette he offers; don't say you prefer your own brand—that's unflattering to his taste.

Make the interviewer feel important. Make the other person feel important—that is a basic principle in all human relations. It usually is neglected when a person is applying for work, since the applicant is striving primarily to give a good impression of himself.

Use a few flattering phrases to the interviewer, such as "You have had so much more experience than I" or "You are quick to understand."

He may have some photographs or prized knickknacks on his desk. Mention *one* of these flatteringly during the first minute of the interview, but make it brief, for you do not want the conversation to go off the beam.

He may be a conceited interviewer and go off on a "talkathon." If this is the case, it is flattering to listen, even though you may not be interested in his reminiscences or sermon.

Use his name early in the interview, and several times later. You may learn it from the lettering on the door, a name plate on his desk, or by asking in advance at the information desk. If you cannot learn it by these methods, ask him directly at the start of the interview. Always use the title "Mr.," "Mrs.," or "Miss." Don't try to be pally.

Have your educational and work record on the tip of your tongue. Applicants often put the worst foot forward by stumbling as they try to recall dates and places. Memorize the dates you finished school and of various jobs you have held. Mention the exact names of persons for whom you have worked. Tell in brief the nature of the work, not just the name given the job. Give the definite reasons for leaving, even if you were fired; they will find out anyway.

A typewritten sheet on which your education and experience are listed simplifies a job application. This can be left with the interviewer or clipped to the formal application blank. This record can make a more favorable impression if it is bound in an attractive cover and carries the applicant's photograph.

Outside activities should be included in the record—clubs to which you belong and any offices held. Church groups in which the applicant has been active tell the interviewer a great deal. Include school activities, such as student newspaper, athletic teams, or debating.

What answers to give? About a third of job applicants make the error of trying to give answers they think will impress the interviewer. This is a waste of effort. Let your record speak for itself; interviewers are not impressed with bragging or bluffing.

Answer all questions on the application form. The interviewer becomes suspicious when questions are evaded—he thinks bad news is being concealed. Take time to read the application form, and check it over a second time to make certain you have not skipped any information.

Maybe the interviewer will try to trap you into an argument. Just don't argue with him or say anything unfavorable about previous employers or teachers. Boosters are more likely to be hired than knockers.

Photographs and appearance. Photographs tell nothing about an applicant's abilities, but firms often want a photograph as part of an employment record. Photographs are usually required when the application is by mail.

Select the photograph you use with care. Passport photographs or coin-in-the-slot photographs should not be used. Snapshots taken at close range or small studio prints are better.

Use a photograph in which you look pleasant, yet serious. Old photographs may be a liability, especially if they show out-of-date clothes. Glamour poses or playboy pictures are a definite handicap, unless you are applying for a night-club job.

When applying in person, wear appropriate business clothes, not party or vacation clothes. Be neatly dressed even when applying for a greasy job. Observe how business people dress, and imitate their dress, not the drugstore cowboy's or movie queen's. Employers favor conservative dressers. Perhaps they fear the individualistic dresser may have too big a personal equation to fit into the business.

Be in good physical condition. A young executive was recommended to a pharmaceutical manufacturer, who paid his expenses half-way across the country to interview him. The young man was turned down; he made a poor impression because he was not feeling well at the time. Two days later, he had an emergency operation on his appendix. (But the recommendation was vindicated when he became a keyman with a competitor.)

Delay an interview if you are not in good physical condition, even if you have an appointment. Lack of sleep the night before the interview may be as much of a disadvantage as an attack of appendicitis. A cup of coffee or tea a few minutes before the interview may pep you up a little.

During the actual interview, keep relaxed, yet alert. Relaxing is easier if you hold something familiar in your hand, such as the book or magazine you were reading during the waiting time.

12 ■ How to Get More Salary

Bargain discreetly with the interviewer. After your appearance, manner, and previous record have made a favorable impression, there is still the hurdle of getting together on salary and other details.

The initial salary is not too important on the first job. The pay you do not get at the start will be made up later as you make good. A beginner can seldom be demanding about pay. After age thirty, however, it is good policy to ask for plenty.

The interviewer is likely to offer you less at first than he will pay, especially in the small firm. Larger firms may have definite starting rates, with little leeway for the interviewer to increase the offer. In either case, they respect the applicant who gently bargains for more.

If asked point-blank what salary you want, answer obliquely by turning the question back to the interviewer. Ask him, "What do you usually pay?" or say, "With your experience, what figure would you suggest?" Use strategy to lead the other person to mention a figure first, but he will seldom mention first the highest pay he would give. Aim high, and let him know it.

Should the offer he makes be disappointing, don't bluntly reject it. Keep the door open. Tell him you want time to think it over, or something in that vein. Let him know, also, that it is not what you expected. The surest way to have an offer raised is to receive a better offer from another firm, but don't raffle yourself off blindly to the highest bidder.

You want to know more about the job than the salary. You are interested in the working hours and vacation arrangements, of course, but don't emphasize these interests. The interviewer wants to hire a worker, not a vacationer.

You want to know whether the job is a blind alley or leads somewhere. Ask what work you could be promoted to. Ask how long before promotion may be expected. Discount the stories about promotion a bit, for he is apt to exaggerate to make the job attractive.

You want a full account of the job duties, also. The job title may not tell you that the "private secretary" also acts as baby sitter when the boss's wife parks the children in the office while she is shopping.

Ending the interview. Whether accepted or not, end the interview with a burst of glory. When you see it is over, stand up without being invited to leave, and extend your hand without waiting for an invitation. Thank him, and smile while you look into his face. Under some conditions, it is wise to say you will check back in a couple of weeks to see what has developed.

Leave while the leaving is good, and without dillydallying.

A cheerful, confident departure that shows initiative has caused many interviewers to revise their estimates upward.

--- --- --- --- --- --- --- --- --- --- --- --- --- --- --- --- ---

The Gist of the Chapter

1. How great are the differences between people in various classes of abilities?

2. Tell about the normal distribution curve.

3. What does this chapter tell about experts?

4. What is the difference between a job analysis and a job specification?

5. What are profiles of ability, and why are they usually shown in percentile ranks?

6. Tell what is meant by PMA, POF, PVI, and PPI.

7. What is the problem of unfulfilled interests, and how can it be made less of a problem?

8. List twelve points an employment interviewer should follow.

9. List seven points the applicant should watch before, during, and after the interview.

10. How may the salary offer be increased?

Things to Do and Problems to Discuss

1. Make a job analysis of some jobs with which you are familiar, using the U.S.E.S. list given in Section 4.

2. Ask the personnel department of a large firm to give you some of their job analyses. Study these and report on them.

3. Consider some occupation with which you are familiar, and prepare a

list of trade questions that would reveal whether an applicant was bluffing or actually knew the work well.

4. Have a friend play the role of employment interviewer and interview you for the job you have in mind. Then shift roles, you being the interviewer and asking the questions of your friend. Note the different perspective it gives you to ask the employer's questions yourself.

5. Look over the details of the PVI and PPI, and decide which ones might be strong in the boy who wanted to be a ranger.

6. In what ways would it be useful for an individual to know his own ability profile? In what ways undesirable? Do the schools or employers in your locality tell individuals what their profiles are?

7. Think of some instances in which knowing another person's PPI has been useful in motivating him to work more efficiently.

8. Discuss what you think are important things an applicant should look for in deciding (a) what kind of work he wants, and (b) the kind of employer he wants.

9. Figure out ways you could find out something about a firm's human climate and the kind of company it is before applying for work.

10. Discuss (a) occupations, and (b) industries that are likely to have an increase in job openings in the future.

11. Go over the list of PVI and PPI and prepare questions that you think would indicate whether a person had primary interests to fit such jobs as: receptionist, laboratory technician, beautician, others.

12. What are some of your leftover interests? Outline a plan for spare-time activities which would give an opportunity to use these leftovers.

13. Check through the list of scale items for personal efficiency in Chapter 1. Which ones would seem to depend on some inborn characteristic? which on acquired characteristics?

14. Should you speak well of your previous employer, though you do not feel that way? Discuss this from the ethical angle, too.

15. You are sizing up two young men for work as bookkeeper. Both are the same age and graduates of the same business school. Peter H. is a stylish dresser, from a prominent family. He lives at home and has an automobile his father gave him. He has ability and has worked for three companies. He left two of the jobs to take vacation trips with his parents. Oswald J. is a plain dresser. He took longer to finish the business courses, because he was working while taking them. Oswald has recently married, and his wife works. They live in a partly furnished apartment. He is still doing part-time bookkeeping for the small firm he was with while taking night courses. Would Peter or Oswald be the better bet for your firm? Why?

part 2

Human Relations and Morale

HUMAN RELATIONS AND MORALE are big things in personal life and business success. The next six chapters will deal with these. As an introduction to Part 2, here are some questions from the correspondence course, "Be a Better Boss!" This course was prepared by the personnel department of the New York Central System, for use with its far-flung supervisors. The copyrighted questions are used with the special permission of the New York Central System.

Answer each question by placing an X in front of the one answer you think is most nearly correct. After reading all the chapters in Part 2, turn back to this page and see what answers you want to change.

1. *What, most of all, is a supervisor's responsibility to the people who work for him?*
   ___ Impress them with the story of his success.
   ___ Help them develop a sense of satisfaction in their work.
   ___ Constantly check up on them.
   ___ Inquire into their personal lives.

2. *What first steps should you take if one of your workers develops a bad work symptom?*
   ___ Suggest that he look for another job.
   ___ Bawl him out and try to make him ashamed of his shortcomings.
   ___ Discuss the matter with your other subordinates.
   ___ Look behind the symptom and try to find its cause and cure.

3. *In trying to understand others, what must be your attitude toward yourself?*
   ___ Know your own weaknesses and make allowances for weakness in others.
   ___ Consider yourself a model for the behavior of other people.
   ___ Adopt the attitude that the boss can't be wrong.
   ___ Don't think about yourself at all.

4. *How should you regard the human trait of hero worship?*
   ___ Hero worship is childish and belongs only in a fairy-tale world.
   ___ Hero worship is not related to leadership.
   ___ The good leader has his own hero and follows him; he, in turn, should be a hero to his subordinates.
   ___ Hero worship is a dangerous psychological pastime.

5. *How should you try to handle the chronic complainer?*
   ___ Tell him the employees have nothing to complain about.
   ___ Try to get to the root of his problem and solve it.
   ___ Always yield to his demands just to keep peace.
   ___ Ignore him completely.

6. *Under what conditions will your people best achieve the goals set for them?*

    __ Under constant pressure.

    __ When encouraged and praised.

    __ Under threats of discharge.

    __ When you let them know that you're the boss.

7. *How should you regard an employee's desire for recognition?*

    __ As a sign of immaturity and should be discouraged.

    __ As unnecessary to recognize people for doing what they're paid to do.

    __ As unrelated to the problem of morale.

    __ As a basic desire to which you must appeal in developing the full capacities of your people.

8. *To what extent is the supervisor responsible for building morale among his employees?*

    __ To the extent that morale depends solely on top management policies.

    __ To the extent that morale is only incidental to getting the work done.

    __ To the extent that emphasis on morale factors makes workers soft.

    __ To the extent that the employee looks to his immediate supervisor for the things he wants; morale building is one of your most important jobs.

9. *When are people most likely to be interested in you?*

    __ When you talk about your personal affairs.

    __ When you are genuinely interested in them.

    __ When you boast of your accomplishments.

    __ When you do others special favors.

10. *How will you deal with the problem of absenteeism?*

    __ Ignore the employee the day he returns.

    __ Always threaten the absentee with dismissal.

    __ Hand out a sharp reprimand within earshot of other workers.

    __ Welcome back the absentee, and show him his importance.

11. *How can you assure that your best workers will continue to produce?*

    __ By belittling their achievements so they won't get big heads.

    __ By just leaving them alone.

    __ By recognizing and rewarding their good work.

    __ By telling them how much they owe to your training.

12. *What should be your attitude toward the worker who is different from average?*

    __ Get rid of him because he doesn't fit into the group.

    __ Recognize his differences and make them work to your advantage.

    __ Try to force him into a mold.

    __ Make fun of him in front of other workers.

10 ■ HUMAN RELATIONS
IN LIFE AND BUSINESS

－－－－－－－－－－－－－－－

WHAT THIS CHAPTER IS ABOUT

1. *Problems growing from interdependence*
2. *Human relations a personal matter*
3. *Human relations begin at home*
4. *Person-centered attitudes needed*
5. *Principle of reciprocal behavior*
6. *You-point, a key approach*
7. *From family sufficiency to modern business*
8. *Congestion and specialization*
9. *People who are hard to get along with*
10. *Levels of human relations*
11. *Morale*

1 ■ Problems Growing from Interdependence

We promised early in this book to tell more about some of the features of modern business life that are quite different from, say, home or school life. An account of Reuben's experiences will be a good start toward making good on this promise.

Reuben did not like the way his father bossed him on the farm, nor the way his mother tried to keep track of his spare-time pleasures. So, shortly after his twenty-first birthday, he left home to work in a small city.

There he earned more money each week than his father had given him each month. No early rising to do morning chores, and on Sunday he could sleep all forenoon. It was good to feel independent. The second week he made a down payment on a portable radio. But the landlady objected when he played it mornings on awakening.

That prompted him to move to another rooming house, closer to work. The new landlady scolded when he forgot to leave his mud-covered rubbers on the porch. The supervisor was beginning to annoy him, too.

Reuben thought things over; and after studying the want ads in the Sunday paper, he went to the big city to work. His new foreman supervised 130 men and was too busy to find fault with the new worker. The men on each side of him ate their lunches together and ignored him. He stood in line to punch the time clock, to board the bus, to buy a movie ticket, to eat in the lunch wagon, and to use the bath in his cheap rooming house.

It was a lonesome life, with nothing to anchor to. He saw thousands of faces, but few familiar ones. He talked with few people; and, when he did, his voice was sharp and he often said the wrong things.

This new independence, about which he had dreamed, was not such a tasty dish. His personal morale began to decline. The thought of going back to the farm occurred to him, but he quickly put it out of mind—he was not going to complicate life any more than necessary.

Poor distraught Reuben failed to realize that his life, like everyone else's, was bound to be complicated by people. He could not get away from them by running from the farm to the small city or from the small city to the big one, for each of us is in partnership with hundreds of others. Our culture is built upon an interdependence of people, which has been steadily tightening over the years. Some of Reuben's primary interests were frustrated.

For centuries, people worked mostly outdoors, with no bosses but themselves. Their work was coarse and did not require accurate use of muscles or fine work with eyes. The work was either solitary or with the immediate family. Now, all that is changed. There has been a slow revolution that requires us to use effort to adapt ourselves to changed conditions. Chief among these changed conditions is the association and interdependence of large groups of people—the lonely crowd.

The problems of human relations are so vital to the individual today that it is worth while to learn how they started, as well as what they are. Many people are bogged down in their human relations without being aware of it.

Although job ability counts—perhaps more than previously for a small share of jobs—today it is essential to get along with people, on all kinds of jobs, if one is to get ahead.

2 ■ *Human Relations a Personal Matter*

Human relations, as we consider it, is simply getting along with other people, keeping their loyalty and good will. Whenever two or more persons are together or work together, problems in human relations arise.

Since businesses emphasize human relations, some people have inferred that human relations is something that pesters corporations only. Yet every individual—hermits excepted—is surrounded by a sea of human-relations problems. Many of life's difficulties are caused by individuals who botch their human relations.

Contacts with others may be brief, but they may be momentous. A

This telephone order taker can watch herself in the small mirror to be sure that she looks pleasant when she is talking to an unseen customer.

surgeon noticed, for instance, that his office patients seemed to be surly and critical. He blamed their bad humor on the humid spell of weather—until he overheard his new typist-receptionist give patients curt orders rather than friendly welcomes.

Brief contacts with strangers over the telephone also may either build or wreck human relationships. When the first telephone exchange was installed, in Boston, men were hired as operators. But the men had a tendency to talk back to impatient customers; so they were replaced by tactful and patient women.

If you had some bad luck, would your associates feel sorry for you, or would they say (behind your back, of course) that it served you right? If you were in a jam, would friends try to help you out of it? Do co-workers volunteer to help you when extra work has to be turned out or something breaks down? When someone is hostile to you, do others rally to your defense?

With good human relations, you are more likely to receive those price-less helps from others. Sometimes you get such help because you have given similar help to others—the principle of reciprocal behavior, to which we will come in a moment.

3 ■ *Human Relations Begin at Home*

The individual's human relations begin in the family. Sometimes these family relationships are rough. Unappreciative parents can strain children's home relationships to the breaking point. That was why Dorothea L. Dix, the prison reformer, ran away from home to live with her more appreciative grandmother.

A nagging wife made home relations so uncomfortable for John Fitch, steamboat inventor, that he left home and family.

School brings problems in human relations, too. Some solve the problems of getting along with cranky teachers by quitting school. Others solve the human-relations problems in school by learning how to get on the good side of a cranky teacher.

There is another strain on human relations when you begin your first job. The boss may be crankier than any teacher. Matthew Vassar, founder of Vassar College, walked out—the easiest way he could figure to solve his clash of temperament with his first boss, a tailor. Later, Vassar took stock of himself and changed his philosophy from running away to "My motto is progress."

There is often an impulse to walk out or talk back when relations with others become unpleasant. That is sometimes the only solution that

Jimmy and Grandpa should respect each other, understand irritating little habits. Different generations have different needs. Acceptance of this fact can make a happier home.

occurs to a young person. Many older people, also, can think of nothing more constructive. This accounts for some of the high rate of turnover among employees. One large electrical corporation, for instance, found that employees who had left school because they had trouble getting along with teachers seldom stayed on the job more than two months. Apparently, these people had the habit of walking out rather than trying to get along. This firm no longer hires applicants who left school because of difficulty with a teacher. After all, it takes two people to make a difficulty.

Evasion, or walking out, seldom solves a problem. And it may start the habit of evading rather than solving.

4 ■ Person-Centered Attitudes Needed

"That turret lathe sounds a bit sick. Get the master mechanic right away. That machine cost too much to let it break down. I'll be back in half an hour to see how she's going."

Late that afternoon, while this same superintendent was studying some

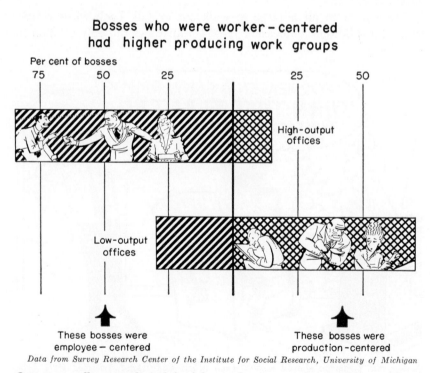

Data from Survey Research Center of the Institute for Social Research, University of Michigan

Output as well as morale is helped by employee-centered supervision, as these records from an insurance office show.

specifications, he was interrupted by Gertrude, a typist, who stood in his office doorway. Her left hand was covered with a blood-stained handkerchief. She had nicked a finger tip on the paper cutter.

"Don't stand there acting like a baby," he barked. "You know where the first-aid room is. Don't be so clumsy next time. Accidents cost money."

That was all the attention he gave Gertrude, but he dropped other work several times to check the condition of that precious lathe. He was machine-centered. He babied the machine but left the frightened typist to her own fate.

People who are centered on machines, profits, or themselves are likely to have difficulties in human relations. Every individual is the center of his own universe, and his likes, interests, and aspirations have to be considered by others. He is part of the workaday world, too.

5 ■ Principle of Reciprocal Behavior

The golden rule is an application of the principle of reciprocal behavior. Aristotle taught a version of that rule—"We should behave to people as we would wish people to behave to us." Reciprocal behavior is an ageless principle.

You get back what you hand out—sometimes with interest added. That is the principle. If you smile, the other person will likely smile. If you complain, he is likely to do the same. If you ignore him, he will ignore you.

Courtesy The Rotarian magazine

6 ■ You-Point, a Key Approach

Listen in on conversations, and you will be amazed to hear how often the word "I" is used. It is the most used word in the language. But for good human relations, "you" should be used more.

It is not as easy to quit using "I" and substitute "you" as you might think. You almost have to turn your thinking upside down to get the habit of making the other person a center.

The executive who says, "I want these letters done by three o'clock" is taking the wrong point of view. His secretary would like her job better if he used the you-point and asked: "You can probably have these done by three o'clock, can't you?" It is still an order from the boss, but what a difference it makes in the attitude of the person who is given the order.

In everyday requests, this you-point should be cultivated. "I want to borrow your knife" should become "Will you lend me your knife?"

When you say the word "you," put a little vocal emphasis on it. Make the "you" a bit louder and sweeter than other words. "*I'm* glad to see you" should be transformed to "It's good to see *you!*"

There is much more to the you-point than just using the word. When buying gifts, for example, we usually buy for the other person something we want ourselves. But the tactful person buys something he knows the other person wants. There was a standing joke in one small company because the owner always gave a chess set to each employee on his fifth anniversary with the company. The owner was wild about chess and imagined the employees were. He lacked a you-point, for chess was the last thing that interested any of them.

In correspondence, the you-point should be developed. "I have heard there is a position for bookkeeper, and I wish . . ." is a self-centered way to apply for a job. It would be better to start: "You are looking for a book-keeper, and you will be interested . . ."

Dolly Madison probably had the best human relations of anyone who has lived in the White House. She was a bubbling Quaker who kept the you-point uppermost, even in letters. Read the opening and closing paragraphs from this letter to her sister, who had just left on her honeymoon.

> Though few are the days passed since you left us, they have been spent in anxious impatience to hear from you. Your letter from Baltimore relieved my mind, and the one from Philadelphia this hour received gives me the greatest pleasure. To trace you and your dear husband in that regretted city, where we have spent our early years, to find that even there you can recollect with affection the solitary being you have left behind, reflects a ray of brightness. . . .
>
> I am delighted with the kind attentions you meet from old acquaintances, and have no doubt but that you will have a grateful welcome in all the places you are destined to visit. Remember me to the McKeans, and

to Sally say a great deal, for I feel a tenderness for her and her husband, independent of circumstances.

Try reading those paragraphs aloud, putting vocal emphasis on each "you."

Two girls from the same office went on a mountain vacation together. Each sent numerous picture post cards to her fellow employees. Blonde Mary wrote: "You enjoy swimming and would love a dip in this sparkling lake." "You could dance forever to the music of this band. Wish you were here." And on a card to her boss, she wrote: "You would probably catch all the big trout in this stream."

Brunette Agnes wrote: "I swim every afternoon, then I lie on the sand. Last night I slept under blankets." "I dance to this band every evening and have met some lovely boys." And on her card to the boss, Agnes wrote: "I miss the office and hope it misses me."

Mary had the you-point. Agnes was afflicted with I-strain.

7 ▪ From Family Sufficiency to Modern Business

The you-point, reciprocal behavior, and person-centered attitudes are more needed now than in the past, because working conditions have changed greatly. Your ability to get along with others will be aided if you understand how these changes have affected human relations.

At the time of the Declaration of Independence, folks' interdependence did not extend much beyond their immediate families. The family was the unit of industry—big families, with seven to ten children.

Most of the food, clothing, soap, even furniture were made by the members of the family. They were kept as busy as a hive of bees and were very dependent on each other. When the family needed something, a member of the family made it or the family did without. There was little ready cash, and there were no installment sales. The family entertained itself at home. So many things had to be made and done at home that the children were trained to work early in life. Every member of the family had useful work to do and felt he was needed.

A few individuals, who had particular abilities, specialized and did work that others found difficult. Many family names originated from a special ability of an ancestor. Such vocational names include: Baker, Butcher, Carpenter, Carver, Clark (clerk), Cooper, Mason, Shoemaker, Smith, and Taylor.

Eli Terry was one who had a special ability. He was a "born mechanic." When he was twenty—while Washington was still President—Terry made his first wooden clock, works and all. It is still keeping good time!

Terry moved to Plymouth, Connecticut, when he was twenty-one and during the winter worked beside the fire making clocks. When the roads dried out in late spring, he loaded the clocks he had made that winter onto a cart and peddled them up and down the countryside. Sometimes, he had to go as far as Pennsylvania before he sold all of them. He had to be a good trader, as well as mechanic, for often there was no money for a clock; so he took hams or homespun woolens in exchange. The reputation of his Yankee clocks spread—young engaged couples thought they were equipped to set up housekeeping if they had a Terry clock and a feather bed.

By the time Thomas Jefferson was inaugurated, selling the clocks was so easy that Terry, then twenty-eight, hired two helpers. One of these was a fourteen-year-old boy, Seth Thomas, who became a skilled cabinetmaker. He built sturdy cases of cherry, maple, and pine for the tall grandfather clocks.

With this expansion, Terry lost some of his independence, and so did the neighbors who worked with him. They worked together in the shed in Plymouth Hollow, from sunup to sundown. The hours did not seem long, since they were working together as friends and neighbors. They still had the family spirit, though it was now an industrial group.

That young Seth Thomas was a go-getter as well as a craftsman. When he was twenty-four, Thomas bought out his boss and put more push into the business. He built a small factory on the western part of the Hollow and soon had twenty men making clocks with him. The twenty were not enough; so he increased production by hiring families around the Hollow to make parts in their homes.

These workers were paid once a year. Payday consisted of settling the employee's charge account at the store Thomas operated.

Seth Thomas clocks were good clocks, and folks were eager to buy them; but they usually did a bit of conventional dickering to try to lower the asking price. The salesman always asked more than he expected to get; so a sale consisted mostly of price haggling. It was not until the time of the Civil War that Wanamaker and Macy started marking prices in plain figures and allowed no haggling.

The story of these clocks illustrates how human-relations problems pyramided with the growth of the country and business. This Seth Thomas story is used here because it is one of the oldest widely known firms that is still doing business at the old location. Seth Thomas had a thriving nationwide business when Chicago was just a swamp of wild onions.

The demand for Thomas clocks increased partly because they were good clocks, partly because of the brass works that were adopted in 1837, and partly because the country was growing. When Thomas bought out Terry in 1810, there were only 7,240,000 people in the United States. Ten years later, the population had grown to 9,639,000, an increase of about one-third in his potential market.

For miles around Plymouth Hollow, families punched out, polished, and fitted parts for Thomas clocks, right in their own kitchens. The shed

RULES & REGULATIONS
To Be Observed By All Persons
Employed In The Factory Of
A M A S A W H I T N E Y

FIRST : The Mill will be put into operation 10 minutes before sunrise at all seasons of the year. The gate will be shut 10 minutes past sunset from the 20th of March to the 20th of September, at 30 minutes past 8 from the 20th of September to the 20th of March. Saturdays at sunset.

SECOND : It will be required of every person employed, that they be in the room in which they are employed, at the time mentioned above for the mill to be in operation.

THIRD : Hands are not allowed to leave the factory in working hours without the consent of their Overseer. If they do, they will be liable to have their time set off.

FOURTH : Anyone who by negligence or misconduct causes damage to the machinery, or impedes the progress of the work, will be liable to make good the damage for the same.

FIFTH : Anyone employed for a certain length of time, will be expected to make up their lost time, if required, before they will be entitled to their pay.

SIXTH : Any person employed for no certain length of time, will be required to give at least 4 weeks notice of their intention to leave (sickness excepted) or forfeit 4 weeks pay, unless by particular agreement.

SEVENTH : Anyone wishing to be absent any length of time, must get permisison of the Overseer.

EIGHTH : All who have leave of absence for any length of time will be expected to return in that time; and, in case they do not return in that time and do not give satisfactory reason, they will be liable to forfeit one week's work or less, if they commence work again. If they do not, they will be considered as one who leaves without giving any notice.

NINTH : Anything tending to impede the progress of manufacturing in working hours, such as unnecessary conversation, reading, eating fruit, &c.&c., must be avoided.

TENTH : While I shall endeavor to employ a judicious Overseer, the help will follow his direction in all cases.

ELEVENTH : No smoking will be allowed in the factory, as it is considered very unsafe, and particularly specified in the Insurance.

TWELFTH : In order to forward the work, job hands will follow the above regulations as well as those otherwise employed.

THIRTEENTH : It is intended that the bell be rung 5 minutes before the gate is hoisted, so that all persons may be ready to start their machines precisely at the time mentioned.

FOURTEENTH : All persons who cause damage to the machinery, break glass out of the windows, &c., will immediately inform the Overseer of the same.

FIFTEENTH : The hands will take breakfast, from the 1st of November to the last of March, before going to work—they will take supper from the 1st of May to the last of August, 30 minutes past 5 o'clock P.M.—from the 20th of September to the 20th of March between sundown and dark—25 minutes will be allowed for breakfast, 30 minutes for dinner, and 25 minutes for supper, and no more from the time the gate is shut till started again.

SIXTEENTH : The hands will leave the Factory so that the doors may be fastened within 10 minutes from the time of leaving off work.

AMASA WHITNEY

Winchendon, Mass. July 5, 1830.

Working conditions and rules are much better today than in the "good old days," as a close reading of these regulations will show. Note the date.

grew into a factory building, and power was drawn from the Naugatuck River. This factory was a group of separate shops. The head of each shop was a contractor, who was given a contract to make certain parts. The contractors dickered with employees over wages and such, which relieved Seth Thomas of some details; but the dickering also produced some ill feeling and discrimination—the start of resentment that was to give rise to restricted efficiency and labor organizations.

The fourteen-year-old lad's problem of getting along with his boss and one fellow worker had become multiplied. He now had a factory full of workers, and a valley full of families, to give him problems in human relations. He could no longer work side by side with them. Many were strangers to him, though they knew him by sight, and all respected Thomas. But those contractors who ran some of the departments—they were the villains in the valley.

And today, with some 180,000,000 people in the United States, sheer size has multiplied our human-relations problems far beyond anything Thomas could have imagined in his day. Plymouth Hollow was renamed Thomaston years ago. A mammoth factory of General Time Instruments Corporation makes Seth Thomas clocks on the site of the original twenty-man factory, but electricity has replaced water power. Clock parts are no longer made in homes. The womenfolk work in the factory building now, and the children play around the town.

Working conditions and hours are vastly better than in the "good old days." Workers do not have to wait a year for their pay, and then take it out in trade at a company store. They are not chiseled down by a department contractor. They have their own athletic teams, magazine, and parties, Employees get hot meals in the cafeteria and have pension and sick-benefit arrangements, two weeks' vacation with pay, bowling alleys, and attractive meeting places for the camera club and other recreational activities.

Each morning, employees come from five, ten, twenty miles away to file past the time clock. In the afternoon, they scatter to their widely separated homes. It used to be just Plymouth Hollow folks. Now they come from surrounding towns and counties. It is no longer neighbor working beside neighbor.

That is the situation now across the country, in most factories and offices. Many employees are practically strangers to one another and have scarcely a speaking acquaintance with the boss. Human-relations problems, of individuals and of business, are more complicated as a result.

8 ■ Congestion and Specialization

The shift from family industry to factory industry is more recent than you may have realized. There has not been time to make full adjustments to the changes. Present-day business and industry are only a generation or two old.

When Seth Thomas went into business for himself, there were no cigarettes, no baseball, no steel, no vertical files or carbon paper, no interchangeable parts. Adhesive postage stamps were yet to be invented —in England in 1839. The first in the United States were used July 1, 1847, in New York City. The speediest transportation was on the Erie Canal, a mile and a half an hour at a cent and a half a mile. The only alarm clocks were family roosters, crowing in dawn's early light. They never needed winding, but they could not be turned off for another cat nap.

Health conditions were poor, and the death rate was high. There was no plumbing, no pasteurizing, no fly screens, no sewers. Vaccination for smallpox had been developed by Edward Jenner in 1790, but people did not "believe in it" and preferred to die early, or be disfigured by the pox like their fathers. Back in Seth Thomas's day, the life expectancy at birth was only 35 years. Today it is 70 years, which poses other problems.

Ready-made "store suits" did not appear until after the Civil War. Contractors who had made uniforms for soldiers during the war converted their businesses to civilian ready-made suits. These store suits usually were better tailored than homemade ones; so the needle trades zoomed ahead. Thus, more people joined the ranks of employees and added the job of getting along with fellow workers and bosses to the job of getting along with members of their families.

The railroad and the telegraph, giving mobility and communication, expanded about the same time as the store-suit industry. These new triumphs of invention widened horizons and at the same time increased interdependence. But it was the automobile and the telephone, around the turn of the century, that brought the biggest changes. More people became foot-loose. Contacts were widened. Places of residence became less permanent. You could pick and choose where to work.

We're on the move! In a typical year about thirty million people move. People move from job to job, also; the average person stays only three and a half years with the same company. You can analyze the PPI that cause this moving.

This mobility broke up family solidarity, as the more ambitious, or more disgruntled, broke away from the family hearth to try their wings elsewhere. Families themselves became mobile, moving as a family from city to city, as employment opportunities shifted. Today, families are so much on the move that in most suburbs few families have been there as long as five years. Many people today cannot figure what is their home town, and children often feel they have nothing to anchor to. As President Eisenhower has said: "Today the business of living is far more complex than it was in my boyhood."

Electric motors and safety devices made the modern elevator possible, which in turn made high buildings practicable. Story was piled on top of story, until office buildings and factories now often contain a small city of workers. City congestion came—and came to stay. More PPI unfulfilled.

As cities grew larger, workers grew smaller, figuratively speaking. The individual all-round workman has become well-nigh extinct. His place has been taken by *integrated groups of specialized workers,* who can turn out more and better work at lower cost. Mass production has been a great cost reducer, but it has increased the problems of human relations. The individual works more and more at less and less, and some are so specialized they work at practically nothing. That is an economic gain, but it has been bought at the price of increased strains on human nature.

"We are apt to overlook the reward which lies in the deep personal satisfaction from doing something worth while," said Frank W. Pierce, a mechanical engineer who changed to personnel work and became president and director of Standard Oil Company of New Jersey. "The worker who merely solders two radio connections hour after hour does not gain that personal satisfaction of creating—but the high school boy who builds a crude radio set that actually works has a great thrill from his accomplishment."

Henry Ford II has observed: "Mass production did not invent the human equation, but did alter it in a number of important respects which we have been slow to take into account. Under mass production large numbers of people flocked to the assembly line, each to perform a highly specialized duty. Mass production produced great concentrations of people. And it produced the difficult problem of specialization, where the individual loses sight of the social usefulness of what he does."

That all-too-human desire to be noticed as an individual is also cramped by congestion and specialization. Individual recognition is difficult when there are several hundred others working in the same plant or building. As a result, many workers feel like forgotten men, lost in a sea of strange faces—lonely in the crowd.

Back in Seth Thomas's time, families averaged seven to ten children. From infancy, each individual had practice in getting along with a group. Give and take and the inevitable compromises of human relations were learned early. Today, when the working world calls for unlimited give and take, families have an average of only one or two children. As a result, the first experience of some individuals in the necessary compromises of personal desires in human relations comes only after they leave home to make their way in the world. They have to learn rather late in life that the world requires partnership and teamwork, not the play of personal whims.

All these changes have made human relations the central problem for most people today. The changes have given some a feeling of futility that is a symptom of poor personal morale.

9 ■ People Who Are Hard to Get Along With

"In business," said president George H. Bucker of the Westinghouse Electric & Manufacturing Company, "we must have patience to bear with things that are not pleasant."

And a saying around the plants of Thompson Products, Inc., is: "The job of management is to get the good out of a man without letting the bad interfere."

Human relations—a 50-cent phrase for getting along with people—is a stumbling stone for those (1) who have not cultivated the knack of getting along with others, and (2) who live or work with people who are hard to get along with.

Reuben was an example of the first group. He did not cultivate the knack, but tried to evade the issue by moving away from his human-relations problems—like the boy who quits school because he does not like his teacher.

Examples of the second group are the employee who likes the job but does not like the boss and the employee who likes the pay but does not like the people with whom he has to work.

It is necessary early in life to realize that about one person in ten will be difficult to get along with all the time and that others will be difficult perhaps one-tenth of the time. These touchy, cantankerous, troublesome people cannot be changed as easily as a troublesome machine can be adjusted. "Telling them off" does not help in the least. You simply have to learn to get along with them. Like the mountaineer with the erratic clock; when the hands pointed to six-thirty, and it struck four, it was ten o'clock.

It is easier to get along with these cantankerous folk if you try to figure why they are that way. Look upon them as interesting specimens of human vagaries, not as personal enemies. You will find this easier to do after you have studied the chapters on personality in this book.

Some people think the fault is theirs when they cross paths with hard-to-get-along-with people, but do not let them undermine your own self-confidence. They do not dislike you—they dislike themselves most of all. Although employment interviewers try not to hire bothersome types, you will still find plenty of "pests" in your working environment.

In sales work, particularly, it is necessary to take people as they are. The salesperson must be pleasant, co-operative, and helpful to all. He may not want some of his customers as neighbors, but he handles all kinds so that they will remain customers.

It takes all kinds of people to make the world. You will always be running into the faultfinding, bossy, critical, suspicious, moody, outspoken, buck-passing, belittling, deceitful, jealous person and others who are a pain in the neck. If such a person really becomes a stumbling stone in your working environment, talk it over with your boss or with someone in the personnel department.

10 ■ Levels of Human Relations

A human-relations problem may be largely *individual,* as getting along with a crotchety neighbor or handling a domineering fellow employee.

It may be the problem of one group getting along with a different group: such as members of one church getting along with members of another church; or of diesinkers getting along with the time-study men. These are called *group relations.*

The problems may be still wider, as when people of different races have to live in the same community and work together. These are problems in *race relations.*

When the relations between nations are involved, they are *international relations.*

Poor human relations may result in family spats and lawsuits to break wills or in neighborhood feuds. They range from these to religious quarrels, labor strife, race riots, and wars. Defective relations are the starting point for all these catastrophes.

"Since wars begin in the minds of men, it is in the minds of men that the defense of peace must be constructed," reads the preamble to the constitution of the United Nations Economic, Scientific, and Cultural Organization, known more familiarly as UNESCO.

11 ■ Morale

Morale in the individual is his zest for living and working—or lack of it. The person with high morale believes in himself, in his future, and in others. He thinks his work is worth doing, and that he is doing a good job at it. High morale helps him to take minor irritations in stride, to work under pressure when necessary without blowing up, to get along with people who want to take more than they give. High morale makes a man unbeatable.

Good personal morale is evidence that the person has adjusted his whims and aspirations to life as it must be lived. He is in harmony with the world around him, and there is harmony in his own little world of mind. He has found how to have happiness, and remembers the happiness rather than the barren moments. He has found off-the-job outlets for his leftover primary interests.

There appears to be a cycle through which a worker's morale swings during his working life. Dr. Nancy C. Morse has found a fall, then rise, of workers' satisfaction, as reported for office clerks. The working conditions and treatment were the same for all these white-collar people in the home office. But the workers went through what can be called an occupational morale cycle.

The new employee tended to have high morale about the new life and opportunity. But after a year this honeymoon bliss was over. After two years the work was becoming humdrum, and enthusiasm was at the low point. Some of this low-ebb morale may be due to a wish to get married after the second year of employment, but the new workers do not yet feel financially able to take the step. We have seen earlier that the average person changes jobs about every three and a half years— when the cycle for occupational morale hits bottom.

Things seem to pick up after five years on the job. Although it is the same old routine, and the pay not much different, things seem rosier. After five or more years the worker has probably shifted some of his aspirations and come to adjust realistically to the situation as it has to be. He decides to put up with what has to be put up with. He has found how to be accepted by the others in the work group and how to get along with the few "characters" who would otherwise be irritating. And he has some pride in his job accomplishments as well as afterhours' hobbies to exercise leftover interests.

A person's morale is a rough index of how well he has solved his human relations. Good morale came easier in the day of the three-person village firm. Today, it has to be worked for. That is why modern business has made an important niche for experts who are trained in psychological methods to ease the strains on human relations. We'll see how they do it in the next few chapters.

— — — — — — — — — — — — — — — — — —

The Gist of the Chapter

1. How can the conflict between independence and interdependence be solved?

2. How does this book define human relations?

3. In what places, in addition to business, are there human-relations problems?

4. Give some examples of person-centered attitudes.

5. Tell how the principle of reciprocal behavior works.

6. Give some examples of the you-point.

7. Explain how the Seth Thomas story illustrates the change from family sufficiency.

8. How do congestion, specialization, and mobility affect human relations?

9. Why is it easier to get along with cantankerous folk if you can understand why they are hard to get along with?

10. Define morale.

11. Describe the usual cycle of morale during a person's working life.

Things to Do and Problems to Discuss

1. Eavesdrop on several conversations, on the bus, in stores, offices, etc. Keep a record by tally marks of each time you hear the word "I," or "you." What do the totals suggest about neglect of the you-point?

2. Check back over the various rating scales earlier in this book, and report on the items that deal with some aspect of human relations.

3. Report on evidences you can find where you live and work that reflect: congestion, mobility, job specialization.

4. Interview some police officials and social-service agencies for information on the possible influence of poor human relations in the family as a cause of juvenile delinquency and street gangs.

5. Effie K. says that human relations is "Just being glad-handed and using lots of soft soap." Discuss.

6. Look back to question 15 at the end of Chapter 3. Relate that to the principle of reciprocal behavior.

7. How could it help one's human relations by making special efforts to remember peoples' names, faces, and interests?

8. Refresh yourself on various hidden inputs, and show how human relations have a bearing on them.

9. Oswald J. has been promoted and now will have to point out errors other employees make. He knows that criticism is hard on human relations, and wants to correct errors without seeming to criticize. Make suggestions he can follow in doing this.

10. In what ways could unfulfilled interests make a person difficult to get along with?

11. Think of two people you know who do not get along with each other. Try to figure out what makes their human relations toward each other so bad.

12. Think of some people you have observed who meet the public and seem to have good human relations, such as bus drivers, traffic police, receptionists. What do they do that gives them good human relations?

13. Talk with some old-timers, and make a report on conditions when they first started work many years ago. Point out ways in which conditions are different at present.

14. You are a chief clerk. The company gives you a 5-pound box of candy at Christmas, but none is given the employees in your department. Discuss whether you should take it home or pass the candy among your workers.

15. Select two people you know fairly well, one of whom has high personal morale, the other low personal morale. Discuss in what ways they show their morale, possible reasons for the difference, and what the person with low morale might do to help himself.

11 ■ THE RISE OF MODERN HUMAN RELATIONS

WHAT THIS CHAPTER IS ABOUT

1 ■ How the Problems Grow

It is increasingly important to study the human equation as an individual's power or circle of acquaintances grows. The little boss needs some knowledge of human relations, the medium-sized boss needs more, and the top boss needs a great deal.

When the proprietor has a small business of a dozen or so employees, his problems in human relations should not be much greater than if he were one of the employees instead of the owner or manager. He knows each employee personally and talks often with each.

After a firm grows to around twenty-five employees, its human-relations problems increase by leaps and bounds. It has been said that human-relations problems increase as the square of the number of employees. When a firm grows from twenty-five to fifty employees, its problems in industrial relations are not doubled but quadrupled. While this exactitude cannot be proved, it does reflect the way that human problems pyramid with the numbers involved.

The critical point may be higher than twenty-five employees if the boss is the "sales type," with a spontaneous interest in people. When the boss is an engineer, with interests that are mostly machinery and materials, the breaking point may be lower than twenty-five. The human-relations problems of this type of boss are likely to increase as the cube of the number of workers.

Weakness in industrial relations is also often multiplied because the proprietor selects subordinate leaders who are cast in the same mold as himself. The autocratic president of a concern of some thirty thousand employees, who was continually in hot water for horse-trading tactics, is a wiry, slightly built man who wears double-breasted coats to make him look broader. Seven of his eight vice-presidents also wore double-breasted coats! Imitation of the big boss did not stop at appearance. The straw bosses, supervisors, department heads, all imitated the methods and ideals of the big boss. When one proprietor said he was looking for someone to fill his shoes, it was observed behind his back that the person who filled the same shoes would have to be mostly heel. The executive who complains about his subordinate bosses may be finding fault with his own shadow.

2 ■ Horse-Trading Methods Made Relations Worse

In the past, many businessmen were horse traders at heart. They depended on crafty methods to get the better of the other fellow, so they spread a cloud over all business.

The horse trader kept employees in the dark about business plans. He figured their ignorance was a good trick to outsmart the other fellow. He did not understand that this cloak of mystery bred rumors and mistrust. His methods encouraged the belief that business was indifferent, impersonal, and full of deceptions.

The horse trader thought people would keep on their toes if the threat of discharge hung over their heads. And then he wondered why his employees were suspicious of each other and concealed poor work or blamed others for it. Of course, he was increasing jealousies and frustrations.

The horse trader thought employees were a commodity, like mechanical dolls, that could be bought. He overemphasized money and overlooked basic human needs, which we all crave and for which we will work harder than for money as we will learn in the next chapter. He liked to shut down the business once in a while, too, so that employees could learn during a long layoff what their jobs meant to them. He wanted to keep jobs scarce, on the theory that scarcity of jobs would keep workers more willing. Workers need to feel that they are needed; but the horse trader wanted them to feel that they were a drug on the market. So, employees began to look to the government to provide stability and security to take the place of the uncertainty the horse trader supplied. Many employees deliberately stretched out their work, to make jobs last longer between layoffs.

The horse trader believed in faultfinding and no praise. He liked to fire and find fault in front of others, for the healthy effect he imagined

How Mild Criticism Harmed Easy Headwork

Seconds to do
one work unit:

Fifty men and women were timed while they translated short sentences into an easy code. From time to time they were given mildly critical remarks. These slight criticisms slowed each one down by 8% on the average; and after the critical comments, they made 55% more errors.

that such measures had. His horse-trading shrewdness made him suspect that an employee who was praised would ask for a raise. His knack for doing the wrong things was and is pathetic. Many of his employees were ungrateful and mean because his methods brought out their worst or warped their best—the principle of reciprocal behavior, again.

3 ■ Profit-Sharing Plans and Fringe Benefits

There is a brighter side to this twilight period of industrial relations. Although all business has had to pay for the poor relations engendered by the horse traders, we should not overlook the few employee-centered firms that flourished during the same period. These firms set up health services, clubhouses, recreational facilities, pension plans. In some cases, these were only gestures, as when a company president gave a community swimming pool, named in his honor, and then set up rules for its use that added to his unpopularity. But some businesses went all out to provide services to increase the standards of health, recreation, and working.

The horse traders called this mollycoddling the workers—playing Santa Claus. Some called it socialistic. Others called it "do-gooding."

World War I brought about a blending of horse trading with do-gooding. Stimulated by the army's successful work with psychological tests and the welfare activities in army camps, personnel departments sprang up like mushrooms. The new employment tests, some thought, would make it possible to place each worker in the right work. Everyone was going to be happy.

Jobs were simplified to be easier, rest pauses adopted, and cafeterias installed. Company newspapers, picnics and parties, athletic teams, and singing societies were organized—just like college activities—in hope that the business would get some college spirit among its workers. Everything seemed rosy. Surveys showed that two-thirds of the employees now found their time at work more interesting than their spare time away from work.

Economists also were heeded, and employees were dealt a hand in the business. Pension plans erupted, employee stock ownership was aided and abetted, thrift plans were encouraged, profit sharing became popular. These were supposed to involve the employees economically in the business and give them economic security.

By the time World War II swept over the horizon, many firms had dropped their profit-sharing plans. Other firms wanted to, but had the bear by the tail and dared not let go. Some firms frankly told employees that money motives had failed to help morale. These share-the-wealth schemes failed because they did not get at the root of human relations. Poor human relations are due almost always to nonfinancial causes. Money is a recent invention. Loyalty does not always go with the pay envelope.

Money incentives aroused suspicion in many employees from the start. "See how much the firm has been holding back on us," some said. "They're doing it just to reduce their income taxes," said others. The more cynical observed, "The company's conscience is bothering it at last." Most employees appreciated the extra cash and added security, but they still hated the way the bosses handled them. All the money in the mint could not buy better human relations for some bosses.

As enthusiasm for profit-sharing plans tapered off, there was a rise in fringe benefits. Fringe benefits have been called "painless profit sharing." A study made for the *Harvard Business Review* indicated that in 1953 the fringe benefits gave the worker about 40 cents in value for each hour worked. Since then they have been rising slowly but steadily from year to year.

Fringe benefits have been spreading. This spread of fringe benefits is partly due to pressure by the unions and partly to the businessman's feeling that the benefit is a way of doing good. It has also been helped along by poor cost accounting: the study just mentioned found that many corporations did not have records of what the fringes were costing them. Managerial ignorance of the costs may be what makes it seem "painless." Here is a list of fringes included in the Harvard survey:

Sick pay	Christmas bonus
Vacation pay	Group life insurance
Holiday pay	Hospitalization insurance
Paid rest periods	Health and accident insurance
Lunch-period pay	Death benefits
Jury-pay allowance	Food-cost subsidy
Voting-pay allowance	Work clothes and shoes
Pay for military service	Separation-pay allowance
Old-age compensation	Pay allowance for union stewards
Unemployment compensation	Athletics, recreation facilities
Pension plans	Community activities

Several other studies have indicated strongly that the generosity of the fringe benefits has no effect on boosting workers' productivity nor on the workers' satisfaction with their jobs. The benefits may be useful to draw workers away from competing employers.

Some things more fundamental than a hatful of fringe benefits appears necessary for good human relations and higher productivity.

4 ■ The New Philosophy of Industrial Relations

There is no gain from having the right man in the right job if he is not handled right. It is the man-to-man relations on the job, between boss and employee, between one employee and other employees, all up and down the line, that make or break human relations. Getting along with workers is not the job of just the industrial-relations department, but of every boss. As modern industrial relations emerged from the partial collapse of horse trading, paternalism, and economic man, leaders realized that the bottlenecks wore white collars.

When the self-taught horse-trading or do-gooding founder retired, his place often was taken by a young man who had been trained to make management his career. A new generation in management was coming on the job. The new generation thought more deeply than in terms of labor supply and demand. Modern psychology had taught them about:

Motives and incentives that people need to feel wanted, appreciated, and understood

Emotional strains and frustrations in business that touch off peculiar mental responses—leftover PPI

Individual differences in ability and personality
Negative streaks and attitudes of hostility
Resentment when workers are handled the wrong way

The new generation decided that it might not be the work or the working conditions but the boss that causes poor industrial relations. Maybe bosses could be made easier to work with.

Dr. Daniel J. Bolanovich has reported the experience of some departments where turnover was high. Other departments, with the same pay and work, but different supervisors, had low turnover. The supervisors who had high labor turnover were hard-headed production men who had taken little notice of the subtle personal element. Training these supervisors in handling employees lowered the turnover.

Formerly, supervisors had been appointed by most businesses because they knew job details and were also aggressive. These are two desirable qualities. But neither tells whether the supervisor is employee-centered and can handle workers without causing ill will and slowing down. The new training in handling people supplies the missing ingredients, for it teaches what makes people tick and how to keep them ticking.

Previously, supervisors had centered their efforts more on their own bosses than on employees. The supervisor tried harder to make a good

"Humanizing" the boss made more employees think the company deserved more than 6 per cent profit.

Data from Drs. Norman R. F. Maier and A. R. Solem

impression on his boss than to establish good relations with his workers. All up and down the line, the tendency was to figure ways of getting along with the boss instead of with subordinates and co-workers. The new philosophy directs attention more toward giving the employee some human satisfactions.

Jobs make more than a living; they can make lives.

5 ■ Empathy to Understand Others

Louise thought her boss was swell in many ways. But there were things . . .

Sometimes, she caught him going through her desk. He had good light in his office, but her desk was so poorly lighted her eyes burned after close work. A couple of days a week, he had many letters to get out late in the afternoon, making her late for the evening meal.

He seemed satisfied with her work but never said anything about it. He had a nasty trick of telling visitors lies and then asking Louise to confirm his misstatements.

So . . . she got a job with a competitor. Her old boss could not understand why she was leaving and offered her more pay. But the economic motive did not work. "Women sure are funny," was his explanation. If he had only known what Louise was thinking!

Empathy (*em*-path-e) is impersonal recognition of what lies behind another person's thoughts and actions. The old saying that "it takes a crook to find a crook" is based on empathy—a crook knows from the inside how crooks plan and think. The best cures of drunkards are made by Alcoholics Anonymous, groups of former alcoholics who know from inner feeling how the alcoholic thinks and feels.

The clever merchandise buyer has empathy. He buys merchandise the customers of his store will want, not what he personally prefers.

The person who has empathy can understand the point of view of others. It is easy to take the you-point when you have empathy.

The social uplifter may feel sympathy for the downtrodden and do things from the goodness of his heart. But often the uplifter's actions might better not be done, for sympathy does not give understanding of what others want or need. *Sympathy* is based on imagining how others feel, but they may not feel the imagined way. Cold-blooded understanding (empathy) is more to be trusted than emotional sympathy.

The agitator may identify himself with the downtrodden and become fighting mad. He then engages in hostile activities that give him satisfaction, but which make everything worse. *Identification*, like sympathy, is emotional. You imagine that your own attitudes are those of the person with whom you identify yourself.

Empathy, in contrast to sympathy and identification, is an intellectual process. Empathy makes it possible for one person to recognize the significance of another's behavior. With empathy, you do not take sides but are as impartial as a referee is supposed to be.

Empathy has been likened to a radar that is tuned to the other person's wave length.

Supervisors and executives need empathy for workers. The boss who really knows how the other person thinks and feels has a high empathic index—"the wisdom of the race." Experience and observation, when analyzed with cold impartiality, help raise the empathic index. So does reading the right things. Even statistics help, when gathered and evaluated with an open mind.

The boss who is humanized has a high empathic index.

Said Owen D. Young: "The man who can put himself in the place of the other man, who can understand the workings of other minds, need never worry about what the future has in store for him."

6 ■ Do Workers Understand Themselves?

Ask employees point-blank what they want, and you will get one-sided information. A worker is careful not to say anything that might prejudice the boss against him, unless he is one of the few who have been waiting for a chance to tell the boss to go to blazes. Communication between worker and boss is almost always with an eye to the impression it will make.

The worker himself, in addition, seldom understands his own attitudes. He does not know about his strong leftover interests. He may feel resentful or helpless but does not understand why. These feelings may be due to home troubles, to the way his parents raised him, or to his work. It has been estimated that at least one-fourth of troubled industrial relations are due to things outside business.

Factors in the working environment may be injuring morale without boss or workers understanding what is contributing to the feeling of frustration. An example was the textile mill where slits were cut in the floor at the ends of the looms so that netting dropped to the next floor as it was woven. This produced an economy in handling materials. But the workers never saw the finished product. The workers complained about a thousand and one things, never mentioning the vanishing netting. Neither workers nor the efficiency engineer had ever heard of a goal gradient. But the disappearing netting took away their last goal gradient and caused the unrest. Not knowing about goal gradients gave the efficiency engineer a low empathic index.

There usually is more behind a grievance or a fed-up feeling with work than the worker realizes. The boss should have the training to see what is behind it.

7 ■ Indirect Morale Surveys and Exit Interviews

Turnover, absences, and tardiness are tangible signs of low employee morale. Within the departments of a firm, there is a wide range in such records. Although pay scales and fringe benefits are the same for all employees, there are still department ups and downs. Morale surveys are used to find the troublemaking factors in supervision or working conditions that cause departmental variations and also affect the general morale level of the entire company.

Some morale surveys are made indirectly, as in the recent General Motors contest for employees on "My Job and Why I Like It." Employees in forty-nine cities submitted 174,000 letters. Dr. Chester E. Evans, consulting psychologist, devised ingenious means for using these letters to compare the morale status of various plants. (See chart below.)

The average letter mentioned 7½ reasons for liking the job. And 48 per cent gave their boss as the reason for liking the job. Picnics, which are the only thing some firms do for their employees, were mentioned by 1.3 per cent.

"Why I Like My Job" Morale Survey

Per cent of 174,000 letters mentioning these 18 general themes

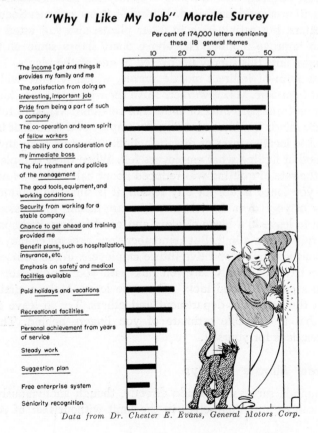

Data from Dr. Chester E. Evans, General Motors Corp.

"Why I Like My Job" Morale Survey

A few points in which Plant No. 48 went
above or below the corporation average

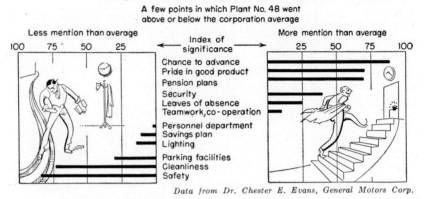

Data from Dr. Chester E. Evans, General Motors Corp.

When the letters from one General Motors plant mentioned safe working conditions more than liking the boss, it was an indirect indication
that something was wrong with the boss. Plants that had few contest
entries were suspect; their workers evidently did not like their jobs, and
an explanation should be found. Desirable items not mentioned in one
plant's letters, but rating high in other plants, also suggested points to
correct to improve morale. The above chart shows some of the weak
and strong points this survey uncovered in one of the plants.

Another form of indirect morale survey, which is more widely used,
is the *exit interview.* When workers leave their jobs, they are interviewed
by someone from personnel or industrial relations. Workers feel free to
speak their minds frankly on leaving the employ of a firm. Exit interviews
are useful to locate causes of dissatisfaction. One steel company adopted
this method of finding what employees felt. When these complaints were
heeded, the rate of quitting was reduced about half within a few months.

When you leave a job, for any reason, it is smart to conduct an exit
interview of your own. Last impressions are lasting impressions, and it
is helpful to leave in a blaze of glory and good feeling. Perhaps you will
feel like quitting in a huff. But remember your present employer will be
asked about you by prospective future employers. Force yourself, if necessary, to have a friendly farewell talk with your immediate boss and
wish him a cordial "Good luck!" when you leave. Make a similar grand
exit with the personnel department and others. Try to leave in such a
fashion that a favorable estimate of you lingers behind. That builds
human relations for yourself.

8 ■ Direct Morale Surveys

Most morale surveys are made directly, though anonymously, so that
workers can express themselves to the limit without fear of retaliation.

Dr. Willard A. Kerr, of the Illinois Institute of Technology, devised an ingenious "tear ballot" for these. An employee can express his general opinions without having to write. He merely tears out an arrowhead at the end of the line that expresses his opinion. (See pages 192-193.)

Special opinions are uncovered by using questionnaire blanks that are planned to get at problems peculiar to a particular firm. Guy B. Arthur, Jr., of Management Evaluation Services, has made extensive use of this method. Usually, workers are given a few days' advance notice that a survey will be made of their opinions. The complete secrecy of their reports is stressed. The blanks, which the employees do not sign, usually start with a few neutral questions, such as "How long have you worked here?" These starter questions are important for breaking the ice.

The total list of questions should be answerable in about fifteen minutes. Employees answer the questions on company time in groups of fifteen to twenty, with someone present to assist if they have difficulty understanding any questions. Morale surveys are not successful when tried by mail; few blanks are returned, which gives an unrepresentative sample of opinion.

In a company that placed emphasis on profit sharing as a morale builder, it was found that less than 20 per cent of the employees understood or favored the arrangement. After an educational campaign, which explained the plan in terms the workers could grasp, a new survey showed that 70 per cent now liked the profit-sharing idea.

Special question surveys are used to help decide contemplated changes. One firm wanted to employ some women on work that formerly had been done only by men. A quickie anonymous survey was made, asking the men concerned for their opinions. This produced some valuable suggestions that management had overlooked, such as the need to provide suitable rest-room facilities, and to get "Old Fritz" to launder his vocabulary.

In this department, the workers' first opinions were equally divided between dislike, like, and indifference. Two women were cautiously put to work there, on a trial basis; two weeks later, two more were added. At the end of a month, another quickie survey showed that this gentle start had changed opinions so that two-thirds of the men liked having women in the same department. (Old Fritz had been "promoted" to another department.)

Without morale surveys of some sort, management is often blind to what is going on right under its nose.

A recent survey of direct morale surveys was reported in *Management Record* by S. Avery Rabue, who had studied the situation in 107 companies. He found that, before the morale surveys were made, in slightly more than half of the firms some or most of the executives had misgivings about doing it. The misgivings about such a survey were mostly the pos-

ANSWER BY TEARING   **Dept.**

The Tear Ballot For Industry, General Opinions

by Willard A. Kerr, Ph.D.

DEAR EMPLOYEE: It is the obligation of each of us in this company to try to improve the happiness and welfare of others. You are one of the large random sample of employees being asked to cooperate in this sincerely constructive scientific survey of opinions. No one will ever try or be able to connect your name with this ballot. You don't sign your name—in fact, you are not even required to expose your handwriting on this new type of opinion ballot! Only a sincere and honest expression of your opinion is requested.

DIRECTIONS: *Check one answer to each question by* **TEARING THE ARROWHEAD**

1. Does the company make you feel that your job is reasonably secure as long as you do good work?
   1. Yes, job seems wholly secure
   2. Usually
   3. About half the time
   4. Rarely
   5. No, job seems very insecure

2. In your opinion, how does this company compare with others in its interest in the welfare of employees?
   1. It's tops, shows more interest than any other
   2. Slightly above average
   3. It is average
   4. Slightly below average
   5. Poor, shows less interest than other plants

3. How does your immediate superior compare with other managers, foremen, or section leaders as to supervisory ability?
   1. Among the best
   2. Slightly above average
   3. Average
   4. Slightly below average
   5. Among the worst

4. Considering your work, are your working conditions comfortable and healthful?
   1. Yes, excellent
   2. Slightly above average
   3. Average for type of work
   4. Slightly below average
   5. No, very bad

5. Are most of the workers around you the kind who will remember you when you pass them on the street?
   1. Yes, they are very friendly
   2. Yes, usually
   3. About half the time
   4. Rarely
   5. No, they are unfriendly

6. Do you think your income is adequate for your living needs?
   1. Yes, enough for enough luxuries
   2. Slightly above average
   3. Just enough for average comfort
   4. Barely enough to get by on
   5. Much less than enough to get along on

Over→

7. Do you feel that you have proper opportunity to present a problem, complaint or suggestion to the management?
    1. Yes, always————————————————————————→
    2. Usually ——————————————————————————→
    3. On occasion ————————————————————————→
    4. Rarely—————————————————————————————→
    5. No, never————————————————————————————→

8. Do you have confidence in the *good intentions of the management?*
    1. Yes, it is sincere————————————————————→
    2. Usually ——————————————————————————→
    3. Half the time ————————————————————————→
    4. Not often ———————————————————————————→
    5. No, it is insincere ——————————————————————→

9. Do you have confidence in the *good sense of the management?*
    1. Yes, it is capable and efficient————————————→
    2. It is usually efficient—————————————————→
    3. Half the time————————————————————————→
    4. It is often inefficient——————————————————→
    5. No, it is stupid and inefficient——————————————→

10. What effect is your experience with the company having upon your personal happiness?
    1. Improves it greatly—————————————————————→
    2. Slightly beneficial——————————————————————→
    3. Little or no effect——————————————————————→
    4. Slightly disturbing——————————————————————→
    5. Extremely harmful—————————————————————→

11. Special problems: Please indicate any or all of the following problems which are really sources of frequent annoyance to you:

NOTE: *We can all imagine problems that don't exist. Just report the facts.*

    1. Inconvenient or undependable transportation————→
    2. Unfairness in promotion policy——————————————→
    3. Lack of time to take care of personal business————→
    4. Lack of attention to employee recreation—————————→
    5. Broken promises on part of supervisors————————→
    6. Family troubles at home—————————————————→
    7. Poor housing conditions or excessive rents—————→

WE SHALL APPRECIATE YOUR PROPERLY TEARING each of the following tabulation items:

12. Your sex:_____ Male ——————————————————————→
    Female—————————————————————————→

13. Your present work:_____ Office ——————————————————→
    Non-Office——————————————————————→

14. Are you a supervisor or foreman?_____ Yes———————————————→
    No————————————————————→

15. Your hours of work (*chiefly*):_____
    Day shift—————————————————————————→
    Swing shift ————————————————————————→
    Night shift ———————————————————————→
    Rotation shift system—————————————————→

16. Your age (*tear nearest*):

    15 20 25 30 35 40 45 50 55 60 65 70 75 80
    ↓ ↓ ↓ ↓ ↓ ↓ ↓ ↓ ↓ ↓ ↓ ↓ ↓ ↓

sibility of starting negative thinking or increasing complaints. But after the direct surveys had been made, here is what was found:

	Per Cent
Surveys did *not* start negative thinking, or increase griping by employees	91
Most employees showed interest in survey	84
Most employees took survey seriously	95
Most employees were frank and honest	98

9 ■ Open-End Questions

In the quickie survey of the department where women were put to work, the most helpful question was "Why?" That was an open-end question that did not limit or suggest a definite answer. Open-end questions are difficult to tabulate—Yes and No answers can be tallied quickly—but are more useful to catch gripes or get suggestions. The "My Job and Why I Like It" contest was open-end. "What other things do you think should be improved in your office?" is an open-end question.

Open-end questions usually uncover many seemingly trivial irritations that should be heeded and corrected before they become big troubles. Human relations depend on many little things, not one big thing.

10 ■ Value of Getting It Off the Chest

Morale surveys help morale even when nothing is done to correct the things complained about. Merely airing the pet peeves makes employees feel relieved. Some companies have been afraid of making a morale survey, for they figured it would start employees looking for things that might be wrong. The fact is that, when there is no chance to get peeves off the chest to the company, employees complain to other workers, neighbors, family, or the gang in a favorite tavern. A morale survey lessens gripes and stops unfavorable word-of-mouth gossip.

As one executive said: "I'm glad to get their complaints, and early, so that we can make things right before trouble starts."

Not so another hard-driving executive, who did not want the next survey anonymous. "Make 'em sign their names," he insisted, "so that I can know who the employees are who don't like the way we run things here." Of course, they never had that next survey. His firm is paying a high price for the survey that was not made.

11 ■ What Is Beneath the Surface?

Workers can report accurately on poor ventilation, slow promotion, a grouchy foreman, and similar complaints. But there are many irritations they cannot explain—such as a missing goal gradient.

People have motives and mental mechanisms of which they are not

Greatest Dissatisfaction

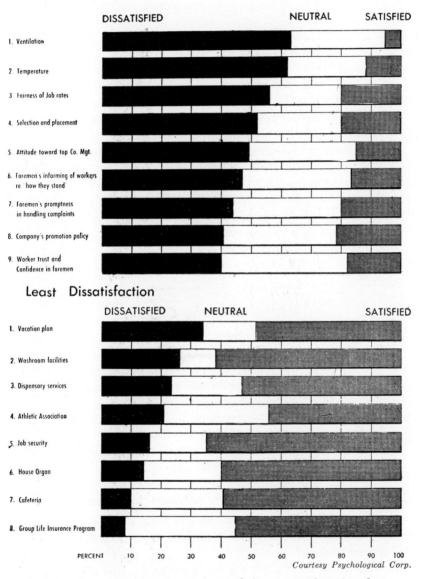

DISSATISFIED   NEUTRAL   SATISFIED

1. Ventilation
2. Temperature
3. Fairness of Job rates
4. Selection and placement
5. Attitude toward top Co. Mgt.
6. Foremen's informing of workers re how they stand
7. Foremen's promptness in handling complaints
8. Company's promotion policy
9. Worker trust and Confidence in foremen

Least Dissatisfaction

DISSATISFIED   NEUTRAL   SATISFIED

1. Vacation plan
2. Washroom facilities
3. Dispensary services
4. Athletic Association
5. Job security
6. House Organ
7. Cafeteria
8. Group Life Insurance Program

PERCENT 10 20 30 40 50 60 70 80 90 100

Courtesy Psychological Corp.

The sore spots and strong spots in morale in one manufacturing plant.

aware. Of some, they are dimly aware but hesitate to admit them. What he-man, for example, likes to admit he craves sympathy when things go wrong? Or that he dislikes his job because the worker beside him is speedier? Or that he is inclined to boss others too much because he is henpecked at home?

Such reasons, concealed beneath the surface of mental life, may mean more in human relations than the peeves of which a person is clearly aware. These hidden reasons are like the electricity that brings a motor to life or the spring that makes a watch tick. These beneath-the-surface forces are desires, motives, wishes, impulses, yearnings, ambitions. The study of these concealed forces is known as *depth psychology*—the deeper parts of mental life where the mainspring is located.

Look beneath the answers and the figures to discover what the irritations mean in terms of motives, aspirations, hopes, prejudices. That requires a good empathic index.

In the next few chapters, you will learn about these deeper forces, about motives that business cannot control, but with which it has to work.

The Gist of the Chapter

1. What effect does size of company have on its human-relations problems?
2. Describe some of the blunders made by the horse-trading type of boss.
3. Compare do-gooding, profit sharing, and fringe benefits.
4. What is the point of view of the new philosophy of industrial relations?
5. Contrast empathy, sympathy, and identification.
6. What are differences between direct and indirect morale surveys?
7. Discuss starter questions, and open-end questions.
8. Explain the usefulness of getting complaints off the chest.
9. What does depth psychology do?

Things to Do and Problems to Discuss

1. Interview employees of various firms to learn what fringe benefits they receive. Try especially to find out whether or not these benefits make them more efficient workers.

2. Try this role playing. Have a friend act as the boss who is giving you an exit interview when you have quit a job. Then reverse the roles, you be the boss who is interviewing a disgruntled worker who has quit the job. What does this experience show you about the way people are likely to act when leaving a job, and about the way they should act?

3. Report on what some large firm, such as a public utility company, is

doing to have better human relations (a) with its employees, and (b) with the general public.

4. Compile a list of morale-survey questions that would be useful to uncover sore spots in a department or a company with which you are familiar.

5. Report on things various bosses or teachers have done which boosted your morale and made you more co-operative toward them.

6. Discuss whether (a) a union steward, or (b) the foreman, is likely to have better empathy for the workers in a department. Would the steward be likely to lose some of his empathy if he were promoted to foreman?

7. Analyze ways in which horse-trading methods would create a human climate that might make workers feel justified in stalling on the job.

8. Refresh yourself on what was reported in earlier chapters about changing work methods. With that background, compare the possible merits of profit sharing with decision sharing.

9. Which would be the better firm to start working with (a) a small one-man company where the owner is considerate and well-liked by the workers, or (b) a large company which has managerial training courses for its supervisors?

10. What could an employee do to improve his, or her, empathy for fellow employees?

11. Oswald J.'s boss told a deliberate lie about the department and turned to Oswald saying, "Isn't that so?" What should Oswald have said or done?

12. A morale survey in one department showed some complaints because of the odor of perspiration from one worker. Discuss how to handle this situation.

13. Effie K. is with a company that has no suggestion system, no provisions for airing grievances, and no union stewards. She wants to register a couple of complaints as well as some ideas for improving departmental efficiency. How should she go about it?

14. In what ways would a worker have a better understanding of himself if he were aware of his PVI, PPI, and leftover interests? Is that depth psychology?

15. Give some examples of how talking over troubles or gripes has changed attitudes by getting it off the chest.

16. Why do employees talk about their complaints to people outside the company? Is it ethical to do so? Is it good human relations?

12 ■ MOTIVATION FOR MORALE AND THE WILL TO WORK

─ ─ ─ ─ ─ ─ ─ ─ ─ ─ ─ ─ ─ ─ ─ ─ ─ ─

WHAT THIS CHAPTER IS ABOUT

1. *The feeling that your work is respected*
2. *Reflexes and biological needs*
3. *Five psychological wants*
4. *The dynamic urges of depth psychology*
5. *The "atom" and the "tree" of motivation*
6. *"Human nature" does change*
7. *Slot machines vs. total situations*
8. *Motives ever present*
9. *Value of pride in work*
10. *Let them know why*
11. *Give them some "secrets"*
12. *What the individual can do*

1 ■ The Feeling That Your Work Is Respected

A Michigan firm had janitor trouble. The janitors had become surly, careless, complaining. Those who did not quit were knee-deep in complaints. The brush handles were too long or too short, the waste cans too heavy, nothing was right. Such a flood of trivial complaints means that something is wrong in human relations. Human problems that the complainers themselves do not understand are often the cause of such gripes.

Analysis of the janitor trouble, by Dr. Irwin A. Berg, showed that the company was doing nothing wrong but that it was neglecting some important human considerations—which is the same as doing the wrong thing. Janitors' work was considered a simpleton's job. Employees looked down on the janitors, gave them ridiculous nicknames and occasionally made their work especially dirty in an outburst of perverted humor.

Each new janitor quickly had his fill of this humble pie and lost all vestiges of pride in his work. The many trifling complaints were attempts to get even for the disparagement heaped on the job. It is often easier to stand pain or poverty than disparagement.

The situation became so ugly that it was discussed at an executive conference, and action was planned to alter the human relations that caused the trouble. A campaign was mapped to show the janitors, and other employees, the worth-whileness of janitors' work and to build respect for them as individuals.

Positive aspects of janitors' work were emphasized in talks with supervisors and in company magazine articles. Everyone was reminded that janitors prevented slips and falls, improved health conditions, protected company equipment. Janitors were trustworthy, since they had access to desks and offices containing valuables and secrets. Examples of an automobile firm that required more than 5,000 janitors and of the 750 needed at Rockefeller Center were cited to show that janitoring was big business.

As evidence of this importance, the job title was changed to "custodian," and the janitors were given coats bearing that word.

These tactics changed employee attitudes. The new title and uniform coats were visible evidences of importance, which helped this change. The custodians became proud of their new status, and their self-respect returned. Complaints melted away, and morale rose, as the work was upgraded in public esteem. *Upgrading is more than promoting a worker; it includes making the job more desirable in social approval.*

Many vexing human relationships can be relieved as simply as that janitor trouble. Whenever there are evidences of strained relationships, an analysis should be made to find the human needs that are being thwarted. People are not disagreeable because they prefer to be, but because some frustrations are making them that way. Discover those frustrations, and correct them. Better yet, *anticipate possible frustrations, and keep them from happening.*

Frustrations are seldom due to hunger or physical discomforts. Shorter working hours or more pay would not have improved the janitors' morale. Like all humans, they wanted things more desired than money, and which money cannot buy. They were being deprived of a basic human need: *a feeling that your work is worth while and respected.*

2 ■ Reflexes and Biological Needs

Let us dig deeper into the nature of human nature to understand why it helped when the janitors were made to feel their work was important.

Reflexes. We humans are put together so that we act in certain ways when certain things happen to us. Much human action can be predicted, especially reflexes.

We have several hundred reflexes, each of us, which are inborn, automatic, and usually beyond voluntary control. We all have the same reflexes, except when some of them become altered by disease. Food in the stomach makes the gastric juice flow reflexly. When an insect or metal chip flies toward an eye, we blink reflexly. (But a seriously feeble-minded person may not!) Breathing is a reflex action, stimulated by the accumulation of carbon dioxide in the lungs.

Reflexes work because there are inborn connections between sense organs, nerves, and muscles. When a sense organ is stimulated the right way, impulses are carried through nerves to the muscles where the response is made. Reflexes scarcely ever can be changed by intention. But in conditioned-reflex learning, a substitute stimulus can become effective in bringing out a reflex action, as when a machine operator blinks automatically at the sound of a chip breaking off. He may blink without knowing he is blinking, and even without being aware that he heard the chip break off. Reflexes are the machinelike parts of human behavior.

Biological needs. In addition to inborn reflexes, everyone also has inborn biological needs, which lead to actions that maintain life and perpetuate the race—hunger, thirst, love, bodily comfort. These biological needs arise from stimulation and response between nerves, ductless glands, and muscles. An internal condition serves as the stimulus in most instances. Vague internal sensations make people want to eat food, drink water, flirt, or turn on the fan to restore the internal equilibrium, or steady state. The need for bodily comfort makes business property on the shady side of the street in temperate zones worth more than that on the sunny side. In Alaska, it is the opposite.

3 ■ Five Psychological Wants

Humans also have psychological wants, which must be satisfied or they will cause trouble. These psychological wants arise from the fact that humans are social creatures who grow up and live and work with other people.

There are five classes of psychological wants that have been generally accepted by scientists who study human motivation. These are basic satisfactions that people want from life and work—the things people work for.

1. *To keep alive.* Reflexes and biological needs are involved in this. We want to eat, sleep, breathe, rest, fall in love, and marry.

2. *To feel safe.* Closely related to the first, but less biological and more psychological. Expressions of this motivating force are often seen in such human characteristics as the desire for insurance, religion, year-round employment, protection from criminals and unfair competition, resistance to innovations.

3. *To be social.* To be accepted by others, so that the crowd seems less lonely. We join clubs and form cliques with our own friends. When others laugh we laugh, too, although we may not have heard the joke. Family life and marriage are part of this strong impetus to be social, not hermits. Productivity can be tied in with this, too, as shown by the contractor who built every twenty-ninth house free when workers were teamed on a sociometric basis.

The want to be social! Don't laugh. This is a tragic moment. Of course she will go to more dances, even look back on this and smile.

Courtesy Connecticut Mutual Life Insurance Co.

4. *To feel respected.* We want to think well of ourselves, and desire others to, also—as with the janitors. We select clothes not merely for bodily comfort (to keep alive) but to give us reassurance and to show our good standing in the community. We buy a more expensive car than we can afford for similar motives. The next chapter, on self-esteem, will go into more detail concerning this want to feel worthy and respected, which is widely frustrated in the business world.

5. *To do work we like.* "The postman's holiday"—taking a walking trip—is an example. The sailors who spend shore leave rowing a boat in Central Park, and with no pretty girl in the boat. The garage mechanic who spends every spare moment tinkering on an old car in his backyard. Pride in workmanship may be due mostly to this want, or it may include some motivation from the basic satisfactions 3 and 4.

In this age of mass production and occupational specialization, not all of us can do exactly the work we should like to; consequently, we seek other outlets. Some find the outlet in hobbies. Others go to ball games and watch somebody else do what they would like to do. As humorist Finley Peter Dunne said: "Wurruk is wurruk if ye're paid to do it, an' it's pleasure if ye pay to be allowed to do it."

Some of those five psychological wants take priority over others at times. Dr. A. H. Maslow has pointed out that the ones listed first usually take precedence over the others in human behavior. Consider the want to keep alive. Go without food for a few days, and your motivation to be social or feel respected will be overwhelmed by an animal-like and selfish struggle for food—as happened in concentration camps.

Another example, closer at home, is how the want to be social takes precedence over the want to feel respected. Workers stall on the job and lower their self-respect in order to satisfy the want to be accepted as one of the crowd, which has higher priority in the system of human motivation.

The want to feel respected takes priority over the want to do work one likes, as shown by the many who do work that only half interests them in order to be on a job that has prestige in the community. Related to this is the fact that placing workers on jobs that fit them best may not count so much in the long run as handling them so that their feelings of personal worth are enhanced.

These wants may be intangible, but they are all powerful. They are thought to spring from two unconscious urges that are still more intangible.

4 ■ The Dynamic Urges of Depth Psychology

Psychoanalysts find the two urges described by Dr. Sigmund Freud sufficient to give an understanding of the deeper motives involved in our psychological wants. These two are:

Life urge, or *libido* (li-*beed*-oh)
Death urge, or *mortido* (mor-*teed*-oh)

Each of these urges is so inclusive that the two of them cover the full range of human motivation. The life urge and death urge are fundamentally opposed to each other. This opposition causes much inner conflict and apparently contradictory behavior. For instance, some things about the boss are likable, but at the same time he is hated for other qualities. Or we want to have our own way, yet wish to retain the friendship of others who want a different way. The following tabulation gives examples of these two many-sided urges and shows how they are also in opposition to each other.

Life Urge (Preservation of race)	Death Urge (Preservation of self)
love	hate
approach others	withdraw from others
co-operation	quarreling
encourage others	discourage others
praise others	find fault with others
elation	depression
creative	destructive
procreation	murder
sympathy	anger
forgiveness	retaliation
eating, sucking	biting, cannibalism
giving	taking

In some individuals, the life urge develops more clearly than the death urge. In other people, the death urge seems to predominate. In Benjamin Franklin, the life urge was stronger; with Hitler, the death urge predominated. In most of us, both opposed tendencies are easily found; and they live a kind of tug-of-war existence.

The libido and mortido are *primitive yearnings*—"the old Adam"—an *unconscious source of motives*. These yearnings are the oldest parts of human nature. They sometimes make it difficult for people to adjust themselves to modern conditions, such as a factory or an office. These urges are looked on as legacies from the distant past of human nature, as dim memories from the childhood of the race.

These urges, combined with biological needs and psychological wants, make people feel they need to do something, though they may not know what that something is. The boss cannot give motives to workers. He has to learn what motives are, then develop situations that more or less satisfy these motives, and restore equilibrium within the individual workers.

5 ■ The "Atom" and the "Tree" of Motivation

The interrelationships between urges, needs, and wants in motivating people may become more tangible if we make some diagrams to visualize these forces.

We might visualize them as an atom. The pent-up energy in the central nucleus would be man's deep urges. These urges could be thought of as giving off invisible rays that influence the activities of the layers surrounding them.

The layer closest to the deep urges would be the biological needs. But the rays from the nucleus would affect the needs. The mortido (death-hostility) is sometimes turned against oneself, for instance, and suicide is attempted.

The five layers surrounding the biological needs would be the psychological wants. These layers should not be sharply separated, because they blend into one another, more like the colors in a rainbow than the layers of an onion. Strong invisible rays from the nucleus and weaker ones from the ring of biological needs would penetrate these outer layers, giving a direction or color to the behavior. If, for example, the mortido is in the ascendant, an individual might like to do work that would give him a chance to show hostility toward others—say, as a traffic cop. But if the libido force were stronger in the outer layer, an individual might like to do work where liking could be shown toward others—say, as a receptionist.

The outer layers of this atom would be loosely attached. They would fall off, or temporarily separate, under stress. Those layers nearer the nucleus stick tighter, reflecting their higher priority in motivation.

The central layers—urges and needs—represent "the old Adam" in

Diagram of the Atom of Motivation

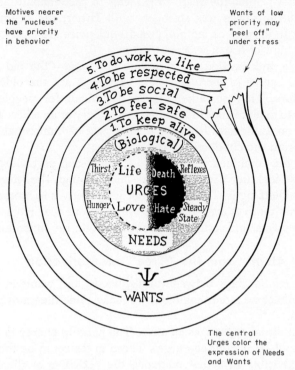

Motives nearer
the "nucleus"
have priority
in behavior

Wants of low
priority may
"peel off"
under stress

5. To do work we like
4. To be respected
3. To be social
2. To feel safe
1. To keep alive
(Biological)

Thirst Life Death Reflexes
URGES
Hunger Love Hate Steady State

NEEDS

ᛘ

WANTS

The central
Urges color the
expression of Needs
and Wants

human nature. The five outer layers represent the results of civilization, which adds the veneer of the Modern Man.

There are other relationships between urges, needs, and wants that can be brought out by visualizing them as making up a Tree of Motivation. The soil that gives the roots nourishment is represented here by the deep urges. Depending on the soil, the roots may take up more love than hostility. Or the roots may be feeding in a balanced soil in which libido and mortido are in equilibrium—neither acid nor alkali soil. Continued frustrations may upset the acid balance in this soil, which in turn causes peculiarities in motivation and behavior. The psychoanalyst or clinical psychologist tries to get this soil into a balanced condition.

The biological needs are represented by the roots, which start the energy-giving substances up the trunk of the tree. The contributions from the roots are blended to produce a balanced sap as a rule. But a long period without food, as we have seen, may disturb this balance, so that food seeking dominates all other behavior and the once perfect gentleman eats like a voracious cave man.

As these energy-giving materials get above ground, they are branched off to the limbs. The psychological wants represented by the limbs thrive on the nourishment that comes up the trunk. But there are also the whims of climate to consider (and perhaps a few injurious insects)—these may frustrate this flow and affect the branches and their fruit.

The climate comes from other people—the human climate of the home or workplace. (The insects, too, are likely to be people.) If the climate

The "Tree of Motivation"—with Samples of Its Fruits

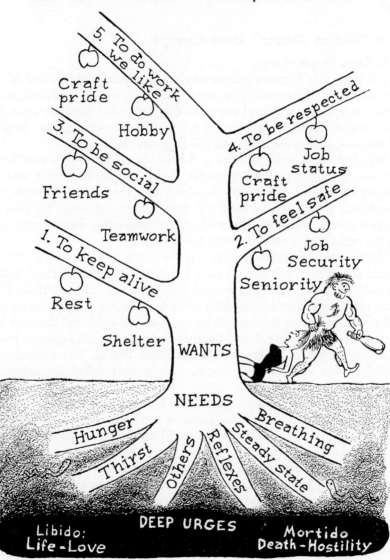

does not give the top branches enough sunlight, the tree becomes half-dead, or dies from the top down. You have heard of people who seemed only half-alive on the job—bodies there but the spirit missing, or they were practicing for a slowdown.

Those Michigan janitors are an illustration of how the death urge (hostility, complaining) takes over when the climate nips the top branches of the tree of motivation. All the psychologists did was to change the situation, so that the climate became more favorable for the top of the tree.

6 ■ "Human Nature" Does Change

Reflexes do not change.

But purposive human conduct involves emotional and intellectual elements that may far overshadow any reflexlike parts. The conditions under which people grow up and live alter the things that are "just natural to do." In most adults, it is difficult to tell what is the unchangeable heritage of the race, except for the broad life urge and death urge.

Social pressure molds motives as it heads mortido or libido in different directions. During prudish Victorian times, people thought it was improper to express life urges. Anything less than four petticoats was immodest. Some libraries seriously debated keeping books by men authors separate from those by women. The suggestion that women work in the same offices with men was horrifying.

There was not similar restraint on the death urges, however. Women might not work in offices with men, but it was all right for them to flock to public hangings. Mothers wanted their little boys to be soldiers. Foremen enforced orders by knocking a workman down. Promotion to foreman was sometimes determined by an all-round fight, and the man who lasted longest became boss. Combat was in the atmosphere; boxing matches were bare-knuckled, with no blows barred. The mentally disordered were chained and beaten. People were jailed for debts and hanged for horse stealing.

Gradually, social pressure shifted the evaluation of the life and death urges. Dueling and heavy-fisted foremen went out of style. Women went into offices and factories. A person could fall in love without feeling he should be ashamed.

Our culture today tries to keep death urges down and gives life urges the right of way. The world-wide trend toward health and social security is an expression of this change. Slum clearance and societies for the prevention of cruelty are another expression. Corporal punishment is outlawed in many schools. We even like to fool ourselves into thinking we are not eating flesh by calling cows beef, pigs pork, and sheep mutton. Some will not eat meat under any name, becoming vegetarians.

7 ■ Slot Machines vs. Total Situations

There are "cents" in incentives—when used with psychological sense. Many incentive systems fail to produce results, for they look on human nature as a slot machine. Drop the coin in the right slot, and out comes the wanted response. We may be that mechanical at the reflex level, but not in the complications of daily life.

We have attitudes and resistances between a stimulus and our response to it. No use giving an automobile more gas when its brakes are set. The miser has his brakes set one way; the spendthrift has his brakes set another way. Social pressure set the brakes one way during Victorian days and today sets them in another way. The brakes in Georgia are not set the same as the brakes in Maine. Coffee does not "taste right" in Georgia, unless it contains a large amount of chicory seasoning; in Maine, people imagine chicory gives coffee a "bad taste." This difference is due to tradition, not climate.

The coin-in-the-slot theory of motivation ignored brakes. It gave more gas—a pep talk, a prize, a bonus, a vacation with pay. But the brakes should be taken off first. The boss may need to be changed, or goal gradients set, not a threat of discharge or promise of bonus, which is the coin idea.

A group of young women in an embroidery factory give an interesting illustration of this. The girls had been on hourly pay rates. The manager concluded they would be stimulated to be more efficient if they were paid instead on a piece-rate basis.

Their production on hourly rates had been 96 dozen a day. Under the new piece rate it promptly fell to 75 dozen a day.

Apparently the opportunity to earn more money was not the right coin-in-the-slot to motivate the girls. Christopher A. Lee reports in the *Human Factor* magazine that second thought uncovered the fallacy in the piece-rate scheme in this situation.

The girls all lived with their parents, and their pay was turned over to the head of the house. Had they been living in a boardinghouse, the situation would have been different.

So the plan was changed to motivate them by something they wanted and could use themselves. The girls were told that, when they finished the day's quota, their job was over for that day and they could play or do what they liked from then on. By the second day, the forewoman was astonished to find the girls had finished 100 dozen by two-thirty and were ready to leave for the day.

People respond to a total situation. Double pay for those janitors would not have changed the critical factors in the total situation. Fifty or more methods of "incentive" payments have been tried and have failed in many firms because they were nickels-in-the-slot, which overlooked the set brakes. The total situation must match the motives of people in the culture in which they live.

This is shown by the fact that there are a few records of businesses where noble experiments, such as religious participation, employees as managers, or extreme profit sharing, have produced amazing results. Usually, these same methods fail when other firms try them. The method produced exceptional results for the originator because it was part of the total situation created by a colorful leader. The owner thought his "system of incentivation" did the trick. But it was the *general atmosphere* his personality spread through the business that produced the results. When he died or retired, the wonderful system usually failed to work any more.

There is always danger when one firm copies an incentive scheme used successfully by others. It probably will not work, unless the general emotional atmosphere also is copied. Human relations depend on a lot of little things, not on one or two coins-in-the-slot.

Before deciding to adopt some incentive, the situation needs to be analyzed to find any brakes that may be set. Then changes can be made that will take the brakes off the good side of human nature while keeping on the seamy side the restraints imposed by our civilization or even by the locality. This involves depth psychology; for example, looking beneath the surface to discover that it was not poor equipment that bothered those janitors. A man who engineers good human relations has the depth-psychology knack of sensing what lies behind complaints or what may give rise to stresses and frustrations, although no complaints are mentioned. Empathy.

Brakes that need to be released vary from firm to firm, depending largely on the style of bossing set by top management. They also vary from locality to locality, depending on cultural evaluations of the community.

8 ■ Motives Ever Present

There is always unfinished business when motives are concerned.

It is different with reflexes, which are an immediate reaction to the stimulus (coin-in-the-slot). As soon as the reflex stimulus is removed, the machine comes to rest—except in rare instances, such as an attack of hiccups, where the response acts as a stimulus for another response. Such circular reflexes require some strong stimulus, like a fright, to break the circle.

Biological needs are intermittent, coming and going as bodily conditions change. Eating allays hunger. As Seneca wrote way back around A.D. 30: "The stomach begs and clamors, and listens to no precepts. And yet it is not an obdurate creditor; for it is dismissed with a small payment if you give it only what you owe and not as much as you can."

Motives, in contrast, are fairly continuous and persist in the dreams of sleep. Motives last. Motivated action is ongoing action.

As the first goal is approached, motives shift somewhat; but they do not dissolve into nothingness. A young woman studied typing to earn money in congenial surroundings, so that she could buy nicer clothes than an older and favored sister. Then she studied shorthand nights to become a private secretary and boost her self-esteem more. Then she set up her own direct-mail service to become her own boss. She expanded this business to send her children to a better school than her sister's children attended. Her motives really did not shift much, when you examine them, since in all these successive goals, the motive was to excel the older sister, of whom she was jealous.

This ongoing nature of motives merits emphasis. People have continuing wants. Their self-regard needs to be fed continuously. Sporadic attempts to feed the self-regard of others are not enough. Satisfactions need to be in the atmosphere, to be the spirit of the establishment or the home.

Good human relations are not something for kiss-'em-and-leave-'em treatment. People always have sensitive feelings, not just on Tuesdays and Fridays. Now you can understand why employees forget about the big Christmas bonus and desert the factory on the first day of the fishing season. What counts is not how well they are treated once in a while, but how they are treated continuously.

Charles S. Davis, who started as a newspaperman and coal miner, then went into manufacturing and worked up to chairman of Borg-Warner Corporation, said:

> Office morale should be a continuous state. It should not be turned on and off from day to day according to the boss's mood. When a mere smile and a nod from the boss causes an unaccustomed ripple of happiness to flow over an office, that's a bad sign. It's a sign that up to that moment the people there had been tense, harassed, fearful, nervous, worried.

Motives are in people and make them want to do things. You cannot put a motive in someone's head, like a coin-in-the-slot. The old incentive idea was as artificial as expecting a mule to eat excelsior by putting grass-colored goggles on him. But you can alter a situation so that brakes are released, and the previously developed inner motives have a chance to go to work. That is motivation—helping others use their motives. Prodding is not motivation. When motives are blocked, there is trouble ahead for everyone, and for a host of bystanders who cannot figure what all the trouble is about.

"It is ironic that Americans—the most advanced people technically, mechanically, and industrially—should have waited until a comparatively recent period to inquire into the most promising source of productivity, namely, the human will to work," Clarence Francis, who started as a grocery salesman, helped to organize General Foods Corporation, and worked up to become its chairman, told the fifty-second Annual Congress of American Industry.

"We need productive teamwork. We need men working willingly together toward known goals. We need, in short:

Workers who are informed
Workers who enjoy a feeling of security
Workers who are given a feeling of individual dignity
Workers who are properly and fairly paid
Workers who are given nonfinancial incentives"

Now for some close-ups and practical applications of the continuing needs that arise from human motives.

9 ■ Value of Pride in Work

Although a task may be so simplified that a trained seal could do it, the worker must be continually convinced and reconvinced of the usefulness of his job. The horse traders overlooked the need of people to feel necessary. Strategies should be planned to glamorize every job and to demonstrate its worth-whileness before it brings emptiness to workers' personal morale.

George Washington knew morale could be boosted by making people feel that their work was necessary. His soldiers faced a winter of inactivity in 1777, on the mountain above Morristown, New Jersey. Washington noticed signs of restlessness and grumbling. Grim-faced, he told the engineering officers that a fort must be built quickly. He had the sentry guard increased.

Work on the fortifications started on the double. The soldiers snapped out of their lassitude and began guessing when the attack might occur. When spring thaws came, the fort was not quite finished, but the general ordered a move.

"But will we move before the fort is finished?" the chief of engineers asked.

"It has served its purpose," Washington replied with a twinkle. "The fort was just nonsense, to keep the men busy at something they thought important."

It is still known as Fort Nonsense—though it is mighty good sense to keep people busy at something they feel is important.

There was the case of a chemical plant, where it was difficult to keep workers on the easy job of gauge tender. Employees were promoted to this from the wearisome job of wheeling cinders, but in a few weeks they would ask to be shifted back as laborers. As gauge tenders, they had nothing to do but turn a valve a few times a day; most of the time was spent looking at comic books.

Courtesy Connecticut Mutual Life Insurance Co.

The gauge-tending work was glamorized. Names of the chemicals were printed on the pipes in large letters. A few lengths of transparent plastic pipe were spliced in, so that the different-colored solutions, which blended together at this point, could be watched. Overnight the work changed into something that seemed worth while. The workers could see something happening, and the chemical terms on the pipes were impressive, even though not understood.

"A good share of our personnel problems results from the very nature of our mass-production system," said Harry A. Bullis, who started as a bookkeeper with General Mills, Inc., and gradually worked up through the ranks to become its chairman. "Under the old handicraft system, a man made an article from beginning to end. He could look at the finished product and know that his own strength and skill had made it what it was. He took pride in his work. He derived satisfaction from doing a good job.

"Today, pieceworkers often do not know the use of the part they make. Is it any wonder they become bored? The worker in a monotonous, repetitive operation must have some compensation for pride in workmanship. He wants recognition of some sort if he is to get any real satisfaction from his job. It is up to management to devise ways of giving it to him."

10 ■ Let Them Know Why

In a Massachusetts insurance company, overtime clerical work was suddenly required because of a surprise audit. The chief clerk in one department told his girls they had to stay on the job until the rush work

Courtesy Caterpillar Tractor Company, Peoria

This company tells them why, even when signs are posted in the offices.

was done, but they would be given supper money. He did not say why the overtime was required, nor why accuracy was essential. The girls were baffled about it and complained they were just wage slaves being pushed around. Those extra hours seemed 100 minutes long. The clerks reluctantly patched the work together, and it was so full of inaccuracies that the department was audited twice and severely criticized.

It was different in the policy-loans department. Here, the chief clerk treated the girls as important teammates. He told each girl why the extra rush work had to be done and suggested that they would need to try to be especially accurate, since they were fatigued. His girls worked with a will, for they knew they were doing something worth while. The auditors gave them a pat on the back.

It may take the boss a few minutes longer in the beginning to explain the why, but it saves time in the long run. It improves morale and production.

When a new employee goes to work, he should be told why his job needs to be done, before he is told how to do it.

When a task is changed in any way, even if only calling for an extra carbon copy, the employee should first be told why the slight change is needed. Don't keep employees in the dark.

11 ■ Give Them Some "Secrets"

There is more motivation to work when employees are given inside information about the business. Some companies post advance proofs of their advertisements, so that workers can learn about campaigns before others see the magazines and newspapers. The Parker Pen Company keeps its employees informed about the activities of competitors; in the employees' magazine, company affairs are reported in *unsecretive* detail, and more space is sometimes devoted to competitors' moves. Sears, Roebuck & Company posts stock-exchange quotations on the company stock several times daily. Other companies post reports on weekly sales totals, or the company's profit or loss the previous month.

Workers want to feel that they are "in the know." If not given authentic information, spurious news sometimes spreads through the gossip line.

Being given some "inside information" helped the morale of these utility workers. Both low-morale and high-morale groups had the same wage scales and working conditions, but the low-morale workers felt "included out."

Give them some "secrets"

Per cent whose supervisor told them what the company was doing

High-morale workers

Low-morale workers

Data from Survey Research Center, University of Michigan

The channels of communication for "secret information" must be kept open between the top office and the rank and file.

Morale is almost always higher among office workers than in the shop. One factor in this is that office workers are in a position to learn firsthand about so-called secrets and can understand better how their work is worth while.

12 ▪ *What the Individual Can Do*

The person who can become a bit conceited about the way he does his job gets more satisfaction from life and work and stands out from the crowd.

The trick is to handle a seemingly minor job so its importance—and the worker's promise—are evident.

That was the way George Arliss, as a boy of eighteen, handled his first minor part in a play. He did not have a single line to speak; he was just an elderly clerk who entered the office as the curtain went up. Without consulting the director, young Arliss decided to make this speechless part important. Here is what he did.

He dressed as a decrepit old man, trousers too long and wrinkled, a funny hat, and a faded coat. After taking off the old hat, he looked at it

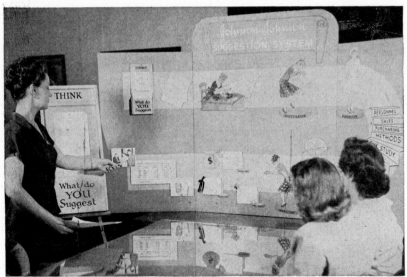

Courtesy Johnson & Johnson

Let them in on the "secrets." Suggestion systems often do not get suggestions because employees do not understand how the system works or are suspicious of it. Here a group of secretaries and clerks is being taken behind the scenes and shown, with the aid of a dramatized flow chart, how the usefulness and value of an employee's suggestion is determined.

admiringly, then polished it with his handkerchief. He slowly removed his gloves, pausing to observe the bare finger that stuck through one worn spot. From his coat-tail pocket, he produced a snuffbox and took a noisy sniff, blew his nose with a snort, put on oversized spectacles, and then pretended to work on a ledger.

When it was time for the young actor to leave the stage, he went through the same pantomime in reverse. The audience applauded, as if he were one of the leading actors. And he was destined, by his thoroughness in making a minor role worth while, to become one of the world's famous actors.

Play your part as if it were a major role, for it does have a major part in determining the roles you will be given to play later.

Charles S. Stevenson finished a business course and took his first job with a small firm that manufactured greeting cards. To fill in time, he helped a girl make invoices; he married her. To fill in more time, he went to work cleaning up basement trash—rather a comedown for a chap who could type and keep books.

He tackled this trashman's task as if it were the most important job in the company. Tons of trash and paper trimmings were collected. He was so impressed by the loss it represented that he figured ways to use the expensive paper more efficiently. From that humble assignment, he developed ideas for savings, which he passed along to the boss. It might have been a minor job, but young Stevenson made it important and started on his way to become vice-president of Hallmark, which he helped to build into the world's largest manufacturer of greeting cards.

Exercise curiosity as well as initiative to make a job worth while. Figure for yourself the why and the use of your work. Make a list of folks who would not be able to work if your work were not done, and done well. Think about the trouble the consumer would have if you were careless.

There are no small jobs, though there are people who think small about their work. "Every calling is great when greatly pursued," said Justice Oliver Wendell Holmes. Marshal Foch of France said: "Greatness does not depend on the size of your command, but on the way you exercise it."

Help your own morale by making your work worth while. Help your human relations by letting others feel their work is worth while.

The Gist of the Chapter

1. Why should a firm upgrade the social approval of its jobs?
2. Give examples of reflexes and biological needs.

3. Summarize five psychological wants in the order of their priority in motivating people.

4. Describe, and contrast, the two dynamic *urges* of depth psychology.

5. Explain, in your own words, the probable interrelationship between needs, urges, and wants.

6. Which of those parts of human nature changes the most, and what usually causes the changes?

7. What point was illustrated by the story of the girls working in an embroidery factory?

8. Why must the total situation be considered when trying "to motivate" anyone?

9. Why do people take more pride in work they think is important?

10. What was illustrated by the overtime clerical work in the insurance firm?

11. What can the individual do to motivate himself for real pride in his work?

Things to Do and Problems to Discuss

1. Make a display of advertisements clipped from a national magazine, grouping them so that they illustrate an appeal to each of the five psychological wants.

2. Collect examples of rewards and threats by which parents try to motivate their children. Classify these by the need, want, or urge appealed to.

3. Inquire of employees of several different firms about the incentive plans their firms use. Report on these, on how clear an idea the employees have of the plans, and of evidence whether or not the plans increase the will to work.

4. In the light of this chapter, discuss whether the average worker has a clear idea of why he wants to do or to get something. What problems does this make for him, and for his employer?

5. In some neighborhoods, and for some factories, vandalism becomes a real problem. Analyze how psychological needs and dynamic urges could be an important factor in causing acts of vandalism. What might a neighborhood, or firm, do to change the total situation and to lessen vandalism?

6. Oswald J.'s boss has taken credit for an idea that was really Oswald's. What might have motivated the boss to do this? Discuss the ethics involved, and what Oswald should do to get his fair recognition for the idea.

7. Effie K. is becoming careless about her personal appearance. Figure out means of motivating her to perk up her appearance. What would you want to know about her reasons for becoming careless?

8. Analyze what motives seem to be important in the results shown for the "My Job and Why I Like It" morale survey charted in Chapter 11.

9. Consider some job you know well. Analyze the total situation for frustrations that may lessen the will to work. Point out what brakes might be released to satisfy some apparently frustrated motives.

10. Review the hidden inputs given in several earlier chapters, and try to trace how psychological wants are involved in them.

11. Which of the psychological needs might cause an individual to set too high a quota or goal for himself?

12. Which of these psychological needs might make a person so self-satisfied that he has little will to work?

13. Describe some things that bosses, or teachers, or parents, have done that made you work real hard. Figure in what way you were motivated.

14. In what ways should knowledge about the wants and urges give you better empathy?

15. How could you motivate yourself for (a) accurate work, (b) getting along with others, (c) an honest day's work?

13 ■ MORALE FROM SELF-ESTEEM

WHAT THIS CHAPTER IS ABOUT

1. *Value of self-regard*
2. *What lowered self-esteem does to efficiency*
3. *Flight from injured self-regard*
4. *City danger zones for self-regard*
5. *Job prestige and morale*
6. *Little details affect job prestige*
7. *Words can build or belittle*
8. *Be careful with titles and nicknames*
9. *Varieties of misplaced humor to avoid*
10. *Authoritarians are hard on self-esteem*
11. *Respect for all others*

1 ■ Value of Self-regard

A transportation company employed a business engineer to improve office methods. He was a standoffish man, who worshiped "system." Colored pencils and a slide rule bulged from his vest pockets.

His first improvement was a system of color codes for records and correspondence. The workers liked this, for the colors brightened the desk tops, though it was a nuisance to make carbons on four different-colored papers. Fewer papers were misplaced, since pink sheets went to auditing, yellow to traffic scheduling, and so on.

The supervisor of each department was in an office partitioned off from the workers. That was bad, the systems man said, because the supervisor could not police the employees. He had large windows cut in each partition so that the supervisors could spy on every move of the workers. Now they would have to quit visiting and go to work, he said. A few employees began to look for other jobs.

Next the systems man reached into his bag of tricks to stop employees' visits to other departments for friendly chats. Employees in auditing were given and ordered to wear solid pink lapel buttons, those in traffic scheduling yellow buttons, and so on. Anyone in auditing wearing the wrong-colored button was to be shooed back to his own department and reported for visiting on company time. Messengers' buttons were of multicolored stripes; they could pass freely from department to department—but without loitering, mind you.

This wonderful button system allowed for everything—going to the rest room, for instance. When a girl in auditing went to the rest room, she was to pin on a second button, a large one with a black bull's-eye. Simple as could be. Everyone would know from the pink button to what department she belonged. The other button told why she was not in it.

The second buttons hit the wrong bull's-eye. The first buttons started a rumble of grumbling and a little joking. But there was no joking when the bull's-eye buttons were introduced. Work practically came to a standstill.

A hastily formed indignation committee of men called on the president himself. Their spokesman, trembling with fury, called the bull's-eye buttons an insult to the ladies in the office—he called them ladies, not girls. All the men were going to walk out unless those disgraceful bull's-eye buttons and the entire button scheme were discontinued. Color was all right for office forms, but workers could not be treated like office furniture. Workers had feelings.

The button rebellion was short-lived and victorious. It was a good lesson for the president, and he realized it. For years, he kept a set of buttons in his desk to remind him of the importance of preserving the other person's self-regard.

The indignation committee was as burned up over the lack of trust implied by the pink and yellow buttons as over the lack of privacy forced on the ladies by the bull's-eye. *Their own egos were involved.* While they could not talk easily about the belittled feeling the first buttons gave them, they did feel justified in complaining loudly about the rest-room buttons. Much human behavior is motivated by the wish to preserve or to increase self-esteem.

2 ■ What Lowered Self-esteem Does to Efficiency

The relation between self-esteem and morale is fairly obvious. High morale and high self-regard are almost the same thing.

But the relation between efficiency and self-esteem is not quite so direct. With manual work, injured self-esteem may not produce any significant lowering of output, except when it touches off resentful stalling on the job. Mental work, however, is almost always thrown into a nose dive when self-esteem is put under stress.

This impairment of efficiency in mental work can be due to several reactions to frustrated self-esteem. One is an emotional blocking, such as would cause the mind to "go blank" for a time. Perhaps you have had that utterly blank feeling when you have been criticized by someone whose good opinion you wanted. Words failed you because your thoughts were blank.

A loss of self-confidence or a feeling of discouragement may also be

MOST promotable bosses	LEAST promotable bosses

Workers who said: "He is quick to criticize"

18%

40%

Data from Drs. F. C. Mann and J. K. Dent at the University of Michigan

Criticism injures self-esteem. In this utility office, the supervisors who were most likely to criticize were the least likely to be promoted.

caused by frustration, which in turn causes mental efficiency to be lowered.

If we recall the priorities in the psychological wants, from the preceding chapter, we shall understand another cause. Self-regard has priority in our motivations over the work we want to do. When self-regard is under stress, we are more likely to think about that than about our work. We tend to daydream about bright comebacks, or rationalize that it isn't so, rather than keep the mind on the work. This is flight from injured self-regard, not adjustment to reality.

It is worth noting that a person himself may be the one who frustrates his self-esteem. When aspirations are too high or wishful is one example. But self-depreciating thoughts may occur even when aspirations are realistic.

The effect of self-belittling thoughts is shown by studies Dr. Arthur W. Combs made of high school graduates who were translating codes. Some of the material they were translating planted self-depreciating ideas in their minds, such as, "People do not respect my judgment." These thoughts made them 8 per cent slower in the work.

The amount of slowing down in the mental work appears to depend on how much stress is placed on self-esteem. This is shown by further studies of high school graduates who were solving problems in their heads. This is more difficult work than the code translating. The mild threat in this case was their own self-depreciation, while the strong threat came from the supervisor's suggestion that they were abnormal. The mild stress slowed them down 42 per cent. The strong stress made them take nearly twice as long as when under no threat to their self-esteem.

Other records, by Dr. Mary E. Reuder, also for high school graduates, show how aroused self-esteem makes people inefficient because they tense

First impression: do you make a hit...or miss?

How would *you* be sized up today? Do you *look* your best? You should. Because surer than anything, the day you figure nobody will notice what you wear always turns out to be the day you meet somebody important. Just a little extra time, a little extra care when you dress, and you're ready to *do* your best. You feel confident, sure of yourself. And that's the stuff success is made of. .

Dress Right —when you look your best, you do your best!

Motives of self-esteem are the spur to action in popularity appeals. This is as influential in selling as in handling people.

muscles more tightly while doing headwork. The people whose self-esteem was involved with the thought that the work was to see how good they were tensed their arm muscles much more than did those who were not bothered about their self-esteem. This indicates why mental work sometimes tires people out all over.

Research discoveries such as these help us appreciate the part self-esteem plays in mental health as well as in working efficiency.

3 ▪ Flight from Injured Self-regard

Most people have a continuing need to have their self-regard nourished. The most common form of mental breakdown seems to be caused, or made worse, by damaged self-regard.

This breakdown is known as *schizophrenia* (skiz-o-*free*-ne-ah). In it, the mental life seems to be split so that the individual has more interest in his daydreams than in the world around him. Those who have schizophrenia lose interest in things that used to be of interest, and they withdraw from contact with others. They lose their sense of humor or laugh uproariously at the wrong things. They either show no emotion or the opposite emotion of what is appropriate. Generally, they are cold and unresponsive to people. It is as if they pretended to be indifferent in order to keep their self-regard from being further undermined. Their indifference is a form of escape.

Daydreaming is sometimes used to patch up one's self-esteem.

Each year, about twenty-five thousand people in the United States are admitted to mental hospitals because of schizophrenia. About one-third of these recover. In addition, four or five times that number have mild cases, called "nervous breakdowns." After a few months, these mild cases may be able to return to work.

Many more people do not develop schizophrenia but incline that way. These are called *schizoid* (*skiz*-oid) personalities. The schizoid acts as if he had strong feelings of inferiority. He becomes close-mouthed, serious, has easily hurt feelings, and the typical shut-in personality. By shutting himself in, he avoids people who might injure his self-regard further.

This flight from reality is the core of the ailment. It is really flight from injured self-regard. Withdrawing from others, loss of initiative, and daydreaming—all aim toward flight. Daydreaming and imagination are valuable mental powers but dangerous when they become the keynote of life, thus preventing adjustment to reality.

Reality includes problems to be faced, compromises to be made, difficulties to be overcome, responsibilities to be met, irritating people to get along with. Reality is the fact of things as they are around us; it includes the bad along with the good. The bad apparently can be endured until self-regard is damaged.

The flight from reality may be shown by wandering or by the equivalent in frequent shifting of jobs or residence or friends. It may be shown by friendships with queer persons.

4 ■ City Danger Zones for Self-regard

Big cities put a strain on self-regard. Some sections of big cities are worse than other sections for schizoid breakdowns. Schizophrenia is practically nonexistent in small Pacific islands, where there is no "social pressure" as we know it. Life in a modern city, from the small county seat to the large business city, usually can be divided into zones. Birds of a feather live in these zones. (See chart on page 224.)

The downtown zone is the center where the big hotels, offices, stores, and leading theaters are located. Few people live there, except hotel transients.

A run-down transition zone surrounds the central downtown section. Here are former mansions converted into cheap rooming houses or used for small service businesses. This zone is run down because the owners are waiting for the downtown zone to expand, so that they can sell the land at a profit. Many lonely people live in these rooms. This rooming-house section and the blighted slum sections are the places where schizophrenia is most frequent. Neither his work nor way of living gives the slum dweller or solitary roomer much food for self-regard. Result in many cases: schizophrenia.

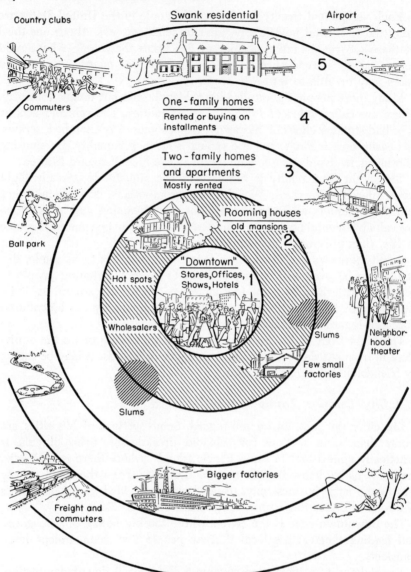

A few who live in the transition zone frequent the hot spots and take their flight from reality in alcoholic dreams or the dope habit. Whether they become argumentative or mushy in their intoxication depends on the relative strength of the death and life urges in their make-ups. Many more become introverted, turned inward, ignoring even the roomers in adjoining rooms. These introverts live with their imaginations in day-dreaming, in nearby movies, or by reading trashy fiction.

Those who take flight back into the life urges read romance and love. They listen to radio programs and attend movies on the same themes.

Those who take refuge in daydreams, centered around the death urge, read heavy doses of murder mysteries. Their favorite movies are horror pictures; their favorite radio programs deal with crime.

Schizophrenia is lowest in swank suburbs, where self-esteem is not battered down so incessantly.

Other human-relations factors exert different pressures in the various zones of the typical city, but you will come to those later. Right now let's find out more about self-esteem.

5 ■ Job Prestige and Morale

Many factory workers save and skimp so that their children can take courses to prepare for office work. Parents are motivated to make these sacrifices because office workers enjoy greater prestige than factory workers. The factory parent whose son or daughter works in an office basks in reflected glory. Parents visibly "put on airs" when a daughter becomes private secretary to the plant manager.

In the story about the janitors in the Michigan factory, you saw how the industrial-relations department solved a bad situation by raising the prestige of janitor work. As a rule, however, nothing is done to alter the prestige values of a job. As a result, many jobs sink to a low level, and they do not give a boost to self-esteem.

Surveys of the prestige ranking of various types of work have been made in many sections of the country, and they agree closely. This agreement shows that the prestige value of various jobs is about the same, whether in Boston, Massachusetts, or the Boston located in Alabama, Indiana, and Georgia, or the New Boston in Illinois, Michigan, Ohio, and Texas. Dr. Robert E. Clark has prepared this list of jobs in relation to prestige.

Prestige Ranking of Jobs

Highest:	Average:
Professional, large owner	Salesman
Teacher, clergy	Policeman, fireman
Engineer	Minor government employee
Semiprofessional	Skilled worker
Small tradesman	Barber, beautician
Subexecutive	Domestic
Major salesman	Semiskilled and unskilled
Office worker	Waiter
	Lowest:
	Peddler

How this job prestige is reflected in individual morale is shown by the records Doctor Clark studied of more than three thousand men in Chicago who were taken to mental hospitals because of schizophrenia. He found that "members of the occupations which have a relatively high income and prestige are less likely to be committed to a mental hospital for schizophrenia."

Apparently, it is good mental hygiene insurance for a person to prepare for work that enjoys prestige. It is equally apparent that there is need for industrial-relations efforts to raise the prestige status of jobs that do not cultivate self-esteem. In the following sections, you will discover ways by which a worker can help raise the self-regard of himself and other workers.

Putting on airs helps human relations—if we give the other person the chance to put them on. The office girl who wears high-style clothes and costly jewelry does not help the self-esteem of her fellow workers. As a result, she is headed for unpleasant relationships with them.

It may be safe to think big—but not to act it.

6 ▪ Little Details Affect Job Prestige

Various factors influence the prestige value of a job. White-collar jobs have higher prestige than jobs on which dirty clothes have to be worn. The amount of skill, or training, also influences job prestige—more skill, more prestige. We have already seen how modern production methods use job simplification to make jobs easy to learn. This simplification has lowered the prestige of thousands of jobs. Job enlargement puts prestige back in them.

The size of the pay check may be a factor in job prestige, but not always. Teachers and clergymen are usually paid little, if any, more than retail salesmen or policemen; but they enjoy higher job prestige. Or consider the high respect shown to nuns and monks, who work for no money. Supervisory jobs have higher prestige, although some of the people supervised may have larger pay checks. The pay envelope can't exactly take the place of real prestige.

The outward appearance of the firm's buildings, especially in smaller communities, influences the company's local prestige that the workers share. There is less prestige when one's workplace is located in the slums. Work with a widely known firm gives more prestige than the identical work with an obscure firm.

Whom you work with in the organization is also a factor. The private secretary to the vice-president has a higher prestige than the plant engineer's secretary.

Working equipment counts, too. The accountant with the new machine for tabulating is likely to have more prestige than the fellow still using the battered old hand-crank machine.

And, when your name is listed in the firm's telephone directory, your prestige takes off for the stratosphere.

A Ready Guide For Evaluating Executives or R-H-I-P

In Use by Chemists, Engineers, Trainees, and Students Throughout the General Office—HUNDREDS of SATISFIED USERS: Courtesy Monsanto Chemical Company

VISIBLE APPURTENANCES	TOP DOGS	V.I.P.s	BRASS	NO. 2s	EAGER BEAVERS	HOI POLLOI
BRIEF CASES	None—they ask the questions.	Use backs of envelopes.	Someone goes along to carry theirs.	Carry their own—empty.	Daily—carry their own—filled with work.	Too poor to own one.
DESKS, Office	Custom made (to order)	Executive Style (to order)	Type A "Director"	Type B "Manager"	Cast-offs from No. 2s.	Yellow Oak—or cast-offs from Eager Beavers.
TABLES, Office	Coffee tables.	End tables or decorative wall tables.	Matching tables Type A	Matching tables Type B	Plain work table	None—lucky to have own desk.
CARPETING	Nylon—1 inch pile.	Nylon—1 inch pile	Wool-Twist (with pad)	Wool-Twist (without pad)	Used wool pieces—sewed.	Asphalt tile.
PLANT STANDS	Several—kept filled with strange exotic plants.		Two—repotted whenever they take a trip.	One medium-sized repotted annually during vacation.	Small—repotted when plant dies.	May have one in the department or bring their own from home.
VACUUM WATER BOTTLES	Silver	Silver	Chromium	Plain painted.	Coke machine.	Water fountains.
LIBRARY	Private collection	Autographed or complimentary books and reports.	Selected references.	Impressive titles on covers.	Books everywhere.	Dictionary
SHOE SHINE SERVICE	Every morning at 10:00	Every morning at 10:15	Every day at 9:00 or 11:00	Every other day.	Once a week.	Shine their own.
PARKING SPACE	Private in front of office.	In plant garage.	In company garage—if enough seniority.	In company properties—somewhere.	On the parking lot.	Anywhere they can find a space—if they can afford a car.
LUNCHEON MENU	Cream Cheese on Whole Wheat Buttermilk and Indigestion Tablets	Cream of Celery Soup Chicken Sandwich (White Meat) Milk	Fruit Cup—Spinach Lamb Chop—Peas Ice Cream—Tea	Orange Juice Minute Steak French Fries—Salad Fruit Cup—Coffee	Tomato Juice Chicken Croquettes Mashed Potatoes Peas—Bread Chocolate Cream Pie Coffee	Clam Chowder Frankfurter and Beans Rolls and Butter Raisin Pie a la Mode Two Cups of Coffee

But the worker's feeling of prestige is also affected by the attitudes shown by others. Words count heavily. This was shown when 99 high school graduates were put to work making patterns with bricks. Each of them did exactly the same type of work, but they were led to believe that there was a difference in the prestige status of the jobs.

Before starting the work, some of them were told, "You have the best and most important job in the group."

But the remainder, although doing the same work, were told the others had the best and most important jobs—implying a low-class job left for them.

This chartoon shows how these planted ideas produced great differences in attitudes toward the identical jobs. Those who imagined their jobs to be low class expressed discontent about their jobs three times as often as the others during the first half-hour at work.

Those who thought they had low-class jobs were also more inclined to talk on the job about topics not related to the work—trying to evade thinking about what they thought was a low-class job. They also expressed more confusion about how to do the work. This confusion (blocking) may have been a result of distaste for an imagined low-class job. This confusion also made the work seem harder to do. Evasion and confusion are symptoms of schizophrenia, we recall.

Those on the low-class jobs talked more to those on the imagined high-class jobs, too. This is a typical reaction. When people try to improve their status, or self-respect, they try to get in the good graces of those they think have higher status—sometimes looked upon as "social climb-

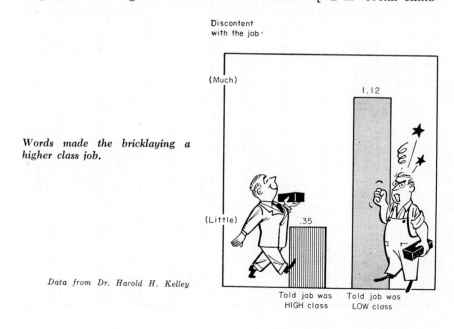

Discontent
with the job·

(Much)

1.12

Words made the bricklaying a higher class job.

(Little)   .35

Data from Dr. Harold H. Kelley

Told job was
HIGH class

Told job was
LOW class

ing." Sociologists describe this as seeking mobility upward as a means of increasing one's own self-regard.

About one-third of these bricklayers were women. The words about job status had the same effects on them as on the men. They did no more "social climbing" than the men.

These findings demonstrate the value of telling workers that their work is important and high class when they start a job. But glorifying words may not accomplish much if the workers are given battered, old hand-crank machines and have to wear dirty clothes and work for a firm in a tumble-down shack in the slums.

Words do count. Often the right words are overlooked in relations where self-esteem might be built up. Lord Chesterfield was exceptional in this respect. As he wrote his son: "For forty years I have never spoken one single word without giving at least a moment's time to consider whether it was a good one or a bad one."

If we can't say something praiseworthy about another's work, at least we can follow Calvin Coolidge, who confessed: "I have never been hurt by anything I didn't say."

7 ■ Words Can Build or Belittle

Human relations always are helped when the other person's self-regard is raised and harmed when his self-regard is belittled. People are belittled in the easiest and most unexpected ways. Big shots are as sensitive in their self-esteem as the little fellow at the bottom of the pile.

Bernard Baruch, the international financier, learned the importance of building others' self-esteem when he lost the co-operation of fabulous J. P. Morgan by so simple a thing as using the wrong word. Baruch was an up-and-coming young man who wanted keenly to have the House of Morgan take part in some of his ventures. He was making headway in the good favor of "J.P." himself until he used a word that cut their human relations.

Baruch was presenting Morgan a proposition for a partnership in a Texas sulphur dome. Geologists had reported favorably on it, but it was still an unproved venture. Morgan was interested until Baruch said, "You've taken bigger gambles than this."

Morgan glared at him. "I never gamble," he replied in an icy voice. The interview was over. The word "gamble" lost Morgan's co-operation for a while—and cost Morgan millions in profits. Investing was respectable, gambling was not, and to say that he gambled hurt his churchman's self-esteem.

Some sales organizations have lists of belittling words and phrases that should be avoided. "But people with more experience than you prefer the other model" may be true, but it injures the customer's self-regard.

Over the telephone, words may sound blunt or critical, since no pleasant facial expression can be seen.

"Do you mind waiting while I look it up for you?" is better than "Hold on." When the conversation is resumed, begin with "Thank you for waiting."

"I'll be glad to transfer you to Miss Jones, who handles that" is preferable to "You'll have to talk with Miss Jones."

"May I tell Mr. Smith who's calling?" is better than "Who is this?"

Whether over the telephone or in face-to-face conversation, jaw-splitting words may be a hazard. Try to use the other person's vocabulary, avoiding his grammatical blunders. Don't let your education show too much. One college graduate earned the dislike of the entire office force because he went out of the way to show off the big words he knew. They gave him the nickname of "The Professor."

8 ■ Be Careful with Titles and Nicknames

People give derisive nicknames because they want to protect their own self-esteem. The chap who receives an unpleasant nickname usually has earned it by belittling others. The surest way to have an unwanted nickname dropped is to build up the egos of the people who use it.

Some farsighted people protect themselves against belittling nicknames by giving themselves one in advance. Anton Rubinstein, composer and pianist, whose patron was a grand duchess, called himself "Janitor of Music in the Castle." This self-given nickname was so absurd that no one could use it in a belittling way—an important consideration in petty court jealousies. When this Janitor of Music composed his "Melody in F," he dedicated it to the Head Janitor, the grand duchess.

A person who has a good empathic index is cautious about using nicknames. He knows it is almost always unwise to use a woman's nickname. Unless she is a relative or close family friend, it is safer to use "Miss" or "Mrs."—especially if he is a married man.

Unless you know for sure that a man likes his nickname, don't use it.

Relations with older men will be helped if you call them "Mr."

Derisive nicknames for people from other lands—"Greaser," "Dago," "Chink," "Mick," "Nigger," "Wop," "Spik"—are harmful in every way. Words are important in all languages of the globe.

The title for a job may seem minor, but it affects morale. Work as custodian helps self-esteem, but the same work under the title of "janitor" lowers it. One office had difficulty keeping employees for the job of "back-door clerk." The turnover stopped when the title was changed to "receiving-platform superintendent." Words often have secondary meanings that may give them a sting. Change the word, and you may change the worker's attitude.

No task is menial when the worker's self-respect is bolstered. No worker looks up to a boss who looks down on him. As Edward Everett Hale said: "You can never lead unless you lift."

9 ▪ Varieties of Misplaced Humor to Avoid

Humor helps ease tension in ticklish situations. But it takes a clever man to use humor without overdoing it.

A precision-product firm was plagued with a rising amount of scrap semiprecious metals. To bring home the importance of reducing scrap, they started a Junk Wagon Award, which was supposed to be funny but did not strike the workers that way. For a few Mondays, the dilapidated junk wagon was hauled into the department that had the worst scrap record the preceding week. But only for a few Mondays, because, as an executive said diplomatically, "the Junk Wagon Award was not accepted in the spirit in which it was intended." The junk wagon dramatized the problem, but it also made fun of the department and its workers.

The most searing form of belittling is making fun of people. That is why ridiculous nicknames hurt so deeply. Laughing with people is safe, laughing at them is dangerous—even behind their backs, because walls often have ears.

Sarcasm is humor with a fierce sting, and intended as such.

Kidding or teasing has a friendly intention but still carries a sting. A woman should never be kidded—although she should be flattered by it, since men kid mostly the women they like; it is a clumsy way of making love.

Be pleasant and cheerful. Laugh. But let someone else dig his grave by being the office clown.

10 ▪ Authoritarians Are Hard on Self-esteem

A boss's bossing may increase the distance between him and the employees. Giving orders can easily slip toward the belittling end of the scale. Here are some everyday comments of bosses, and each has a sting that lowers self-regard.

"Effie learned this detail in only a week."

"You may not be speedy enough for this rush job."

"I hope you're accurate for a change."

"I thought of that long ago."

Any order may be inherently belittling, in which case the fewer orders, the better. Dr. Willard A. Kerr has found "a tendency for departments with most supervisors per 100 workers to have high labor turnover," which he concludes "possibly may be due, at least in part, to a characteristic American reaction—a tendency to rebel when supervision and 'regimentation' get too thick and close in the work environment."

In family relations, also, too much bossing puts distance between parents and children. A little bossing goes a long way. With good human relations, it is scarcely needed. A hint from a leader is better than an order from a boss. Consider this before giving someone an order.

Bossiness affects productivity as well as human relations. The effect on productivity is usually just the opposite of what the bossy person expects. This is shown by records from one of the country's largest home offices, which were analyzed by Dr. Daniel Katz for the Office of Naval Research. You may be astonished to learn that most of the supervisors were of the bossy sort. Three out of every four kept an "eagle eye" on the workers; only one-fourth did not breathe down the clerks' necks.

Of the supervisors of the low-producing offices, 91 per cent were of the bossy sort. The high-producing offices had the advantage of supervisors who were not usually throwing their weight around.

Close bossing makes workers suspect that the boss lacks confidence in them, a thought that bruises self-esteem. When the boss checks on work, it seems as if he were finding fault with the worker's ability; and that is a stress on self-esteem. Injured self-esteem causes jitters (confusion and evasion), which may lower production, especially in mental work. The bossiness may also touch off resentment (mortido), which results in restricted efficiency by intention rather than by accident.

Records from other occupations indicate that, when the work is not routine, or when something unusual comes up, bossiness may not cause lowered production. Workers seem to accept necessary bossing without noticeable resentment or harmed self-regard. If it is "helping" rather than bossing, fine and dandy. But bossing for the sake of bossing is something else.

That bossy person may not be your boss, of course. It may be the person working beside you or a neighborhood "buttinsky" or another guest who wants to run things at the vacation camp.

People who are inclined to be too bossy are now described as having the *authoritarian* personality make-up. About 10 per cent of people are strongly authoritarian, and another 20 per cent incline in that direction. The authoritarian "just naturally" uses autocratic methods in his (or her!) relations with others.

The authoritarians were discovered by a team of psychologists and sociologists of the University of California. This team has reported several characteristics that are usually shown by authoritarians. As you read through this list, you will understand how they do things that injure human relations. These characteristics are usually clustered together in authoritarians; that is, they have not one or two but most of the qualities clustered together.

> *Aggressive* against people who do not agree with them, or who do not do as they want them to.

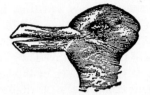

Apprehensive that others are scheming against them, or the firm, or nation.

Fatalistic in thinking it foreordained that some are born leaders; intolerant of democratic leaders.

Inflexible, believing that determination will accomplish anything if they keep at it long enough.

Practical, preferring action to thinking it over before acting.

Prejudiced against other social groups, firms, religions, nations.

Submissive in blindly following the forceful leaders of their own groups.

Those characteristics are shown by authoritarian types in many interesting ways. An example is the way ambiguous figures, such as the one that could look like either a duck or a rabbit, look to the authoritarian person. Dr. Marshall B. Jones has found that authoritarians are inflexible even in looking at ambiguous figures. The authoritarian can "see" the duck in the drawing but not the rabbit, or vice versa. This lack of flexibility in their perceptions would make it difficult for them to see new uses for materials or products or new ways of doing things. (It is sometimes called "mental rigidity.")

Authoritarians cause much damage to folks' self-esteem, including some of the 30 per cent who are authoritarian themselves.

And it is a paradox that the reason many people become authoritarian in their ways is that their own self-esteem has been injured! Instead of flight from their bruised self-regard, they overcompensate for it by dominating others.

So, the next time you feel the impulse to call someone bossy, call him "an overcompensated authoritarian" instead. It might sound like a compliment to him.

Equalitarians. Equalitarians are at the other extreme on the distribution curve. (Refresh your memory on normal distributions in Chapter 9, "Getting the Right Job.") Equalitarians incline to follow democratic methods in their relations with others.

The equalitarians feel that everybody should be accepted at his face value and not condemned because he is less gifted or of a minority group. But the authoritarians feel that group differences should be emphasized.

The equalitarians believe that others should take part in reaching decisions about things that affect them—great believers in committees and staff meetings. The authoritarians believe that a forceful leader should be the one to make all the decisions and then issue point-blank orders.

Authoritarians seldom realize that they are that way. They think that they are "just right, that's all" and do not realize that they are bossy or prejudiced. They also have poor empathy. They can't see much difference between others who are at the extremes of the authoritarian-equalitarian scale. But the equalitarians can see a great difference between these two types.

Washington, Jefferson, and Franklin were of the equalitarian make-up. Alexander Hamilton, Commodore Vanderbilt, and J. P. Morgan were authoritarian.

The authoritarians look down on people. The equalitarians build them up. A difference in the human climate results.

11 ■ Respect for All Others

It is an old truth that the best way to win a person's co-operation is to build up his self-esteem. We like people who help us like ourselves.

James McCosh, the Scotch psychologist who became president of Princeton University, observed: "The best liked people are those whose whole manner and style is a sort of a flattery to those they meet." The equalitarians can use that flattery easily, naturally. But some people have to work at it.

There are some folks who cannot take a promotion. It goes to their heads. After the promotion, they talk with lofty airs and act as if they were bestowing favors when they give attention to anyone.

Adults often adopt such a condescending attitude when they talk with children. It is a belittling attitude that children as well as adults resent.

It cost Harvard University 34 million dollars because the president looked down his aristocratic nose at a shabby couple who visited him. They asked him how much it cost to run a university. He let them feel that such poor people could not understand high finance. So, instead of giving Harvard the money, as they had planned, the Leland Stanfords returned to California and started their own university.

One automobile president says a shop superintendent's advice helped him rise to the top. The young president-to-be was being tried out as an assistant foreman. "Imagine a big sign hanging around the neck of every person with whom you talk," the superintendent told him. "That sign reads, 'I WANT TO FEEL IMPORTANT.'"

This human desire to feel important, and to be treated that way, makes some people belittle others. By whittling down the other person, they feel bigger themselves. Some criticize others to make themselves feel bigger. Some lie to give a bigger impression. A few become bothersome show-offs.

A more common trait than belittling—and more useful all-round—is to practice some of that upward social mobility we met in the bricklayers. People in all walks of life are motivated to talk to those they judge to have more prestige. This was shown interestingly by a group of highly educated professional men and women. Some had more prestige in the profession than the others. Their interactions were carefully recorded by observers for the National Institute for Mental Health, and it was found that they tended to talk to those who had a little more prestige. As someone has said, "The little shots love to talk to the big shots."

There are many other everyday examples: writing fan letters to important people, collecting autographs of current celebrities, going to meetings to hear big shots talk, going to the airport to watch celebrities arrive.

Doctor Riesman, in *The Lonely Crowd,* points out that this interest in current celebrities is stronger than in previous generations. This suggests that, somehow, we moderns are not having our wants of self-esteem properly taken care of. So, we try to brush the celebrities' elbows, hoping some of the prestige will rub off on us.

In their rush to catch some added self-esteem, people often do it backward. As a result, they actually lower their self-esteem eventually. Bragging, fishing for compliments, and showing off are examples of going about it the backward way.

The braggart and the bluffer merely pretend a feeling they don't have. The pretense is more likely to give a feeling of guilt than genuine self-regard.

Their human relations would be vastly better if they bragged about the other person rather than about themselves. Others have a continuing want to nourish their self-esteem, every day of the week and every hour of the day. There is no better nourishment for it than the feeling of exquisite satisfaction from doing any job well—raising self-esteem by works rather than by words.

— — — — — — — — — — — — — — — — — — —

The Gist of the Chapter

1. Explain ways in which injured self-esteem lowers work efficiency.

2. Tell about the most common form of mental breakdown, and how injured self-esteem plays a part in causing it.

3. Describe the zones of a city, and tell about their bearing on personal morale.

4. How do jobs differ in prestige, and what effect does this have on morale?

5. Enumerate details that affect the prestige of a job.

6. What points were illustrated by the experiment with bricklaying?

7. Give examples of how job titles and individual nicknames can affect morale.

8. What are some forms of misplaced humor?

9. Describe the authoritarian personality, and discuss its merits and demerits.

10. In what ways do people show that they want to be considered important, and what effect does it have on their efficiency and morale?

Things to Do and Problems to Discuss

1. Give an unexpected, but sincere and deserved, compliment to (a) a stranger, such as a retail salesperson, and (b) a friend or relative. Report on their reactions at the time, and also how you felt about it an hour afterward.

2. Consider some jobs you are familiar with which seem to have low prestige value. Work out plans by which (a) the company, and (b) the worker, could raise the prestige value of the job.

3. Spend some time observing and talking with people who live in the transition zone of your city. Experiment using praise with some of them, and report on the effects. Find out where they work, and try to learn their attitudes toward bosses and companies. Report your observations and deductions.

4. Think of someone you know who is a bragger or bluffer. Analyze what may have lowered his self-esteem, so that he uses those props to hold it up. Make suggestions for such a person's self-development so he may not feel like bragging or bluffing.

5. Discuss ways in which daydreaming and other varieties of flight from reality would make a person impractical.

6. In the chapter on motivation, it was said that it was the total situation from which people got their incentives. In this chapter, it was said that little details are important. Reconcile that apparent disagreement.

7. Think of some public officials who are in "hot water" much of the time. Report how you size them up as authoritarian or equalitarian, and discuss how these tendencies might keep them in "hot water."

8. Think of some companies you know that have had considerable labor trouble. Would you say the top officers in these companies tended to be authoritarian or equalitarian?

9. Dr. Alan McLean told personnel executives, "The real problem is to make a man feel as important as he really is, by making him as important as he is capable of being." Explain and discuss that statement.

10. Analyze ways in which a person might have his self-esteem injured (a) on moving from a small town to a big city, (b) on transferring from a small firm to a big firm. What should he do about it?

11. Argue whether men or women are more likely to use depreciating nicknames and to indulge in embarrassing practical jokes. How do you account for the difference?

12. Criticism is usually hard on self-esteem. What might a person do to accept criticism without having his morale lowered by it?

13. Effie K. has been given a nickname that she hates. Discuss methods (a) that Effie, and (b) that her boss could use to have the name dropped.

14. What PPI given in Chapter 9 would make a person most sensitive to little details that undermined his self-esteem?

15. Oswald J. has been promoted ahead of some older and more experienced workers, and this has set their self-esteem back a bit. How should Oswald handle himself (a) so that their feeling of hostility will not undermine his own self-esteem, and (b) so that he can help them regain their self-esteem?

14 ■ TO GET FRIENDLINESS
RATHER THAN HOSTILITY

— — — — — — — — — — — — — — — — —

WHAT THIS CHAPTER IS ABOUT

1. *Values of friendliness*
2. *Keep the individual from being lost in the crowd*
3. *Forces that mold friendly attitudes*
4. *Adults are like children*
5. *Love and the want to be wanted*
6. *The boss a surrogate*
7. *The seesaw between hostility and friendliness*
8. *When hostility becomes a disease*
9. *Make the "Howdy" rounds*
10. *Mechanical attempts to give individual notice*
11. *Learn names, and use them*
12. *Make yours a friendly place to work*

1 ■ Values of Friendliness

We recall from Chapter 12, "Motivation for Morale and the Will to Work," that the deep urges were libido (love) and mortidu (hate). Behind that polite "Pleased to meet 'cha" there is often a big dose of lurking hatred. Which feeling comes uppermost depends a great deal on how we handle our human relations with the other person. Hostility is always in the background, as the chartoon on the facing page shows.

"Why all this Pollyanna stuff? Why can't we just tend to our jobs and not bother about being friendly? After all, we're being paid to turn out production, not spread sunshine." Sounds plausible—but is it true?

Did you go back to buy again from that salesman who gave you an unfriendly brush-off? We all prefer to do business with friendly folks. Even funeral directors have to be friendly.

Production is also influenced by the friendly interactions of the members of the work group. We learned that in the story of the building contractor who used sociometric groupings of his workers. The United States Air Force has also found there is a relationship between friendliness and the productivity of aircraft mechanics. The bar on the right (page 240) shows the strong influence between crew friendliness and output. The bar on the left shows how the friendliness between crew members and their boss had an even stronger influence on their output. Not "palsy-

The mixture of feelings toward the other person when young men were introduced to each other. Almost one-third of the feelings were hostile, although there was no visible reason for hostility.

Experiment by Drs. John W. Thibaut and John Coules

walsiness" or backslapping, but attraction to the other person as a person.

We have had many examples in this book of the importance of *climate* in influencing the attitudes and productivity of workers. This climate comes from human beings, not the air conditioner.

Companies sometimes spend considerable sums to furnish and decorate offices to give an atmosphere that pleases the eye. But almost always the human climate counts for much more in the long run.

This is because the human climate shapes the *interactions* of the people to each other. Some people are *warm* and friendly. Others *cold* and aloof. Experiments have shown that warm people and warm firms have the better human relations.

Morale is tied in with friendliness. With those aircraft mechanics, for instance, the relation between mutual attraction and morale was higher than it was for production.

Absenteeism, which reflects low morale, is also tied in with the spirit of friendliness prevailing in the workplace. Managers sometimes think unnecessary absence from work is due to workers' irresponsibility. But records now show that playing hookey from work reflects lack of friendliness at work, not irresponsibility.

Labor turnover is also influenced by the friendly spirit of the establish-

Correlation
with output:

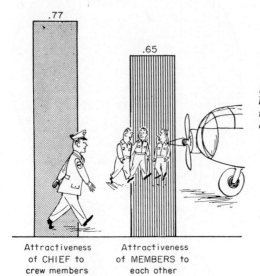

Highest production when the members of the work group were attracted to each other and to their chief.

Data from Drs. Hans H. Strupp and H. J. Hausman, Human Factors Operations Research Laboratories

.77

.65

Attractiveness
of CHIEF to
crew members

Attractiveness
of MEMBERS to
each other

ment. Recall that the average worker remains only three and a half years with the same firm. Half of them leave before that time, unconsciously hoping the next job will be in a friendlier place.

Bargaining sessions often succeed, or fail, depending on the friendliness of the atmosphere in which they are held. Records show that sessions that fail have spent their time mostly on the unfriendly interactions of aggression, defense, or negation—all expressions of the mortido urge. How the first half-hour of one unsuccessful session was spent is pictured by chartoon on page 241.

Whenever we are dealing with people in any way, it is always helpful to bear reciprocal action in mind—we get back what we hand out. This is particularly true with friendliness, which lies so close to hostility in the deep urges. The lonely crowd feels frustrated trying to find friends and, consequently, reacts strongly to any show of unfriendliness. Often the other person interprets as unfriendly something that was not intended that way. To be safe, we must let our friendly intentions show.

2 ■ Keep the Individual from Being Lost in the Crowd

Large concerns have large problems in human relations because individuals are lost in the crowd. Too many workers feel that no one cares for them individually. The bigger the business, the greater this danger.

Negation $\frac{1}{2}$ minute
"We can't accept that!"

Miscellaneous
10 minutes
"Let's open
a window."

"Our proposal
is fair!"

Questions
$\frac{1}{2}$ minute
"What is
the rate?"

Aggression
$9\frac{1}{2}$ minutes

"You'll be
sorry if
you try
that!"

Defense
8 minutes

Clarification
$1\frac{1}{2}$ minutes
"Let's say it
this way."

Data from Dr. Wesley H. Osterberg

The unsuccessful bargaining session got off to an unfriendly start.

But it is a danger even in a small business if the boss is too busy to notice individuals.

At a conference of some seventy-five supervisors of a food-manufacturing plant that was faced with labor trouble, one could sense an uneasy attitude among the men as the group was gathering. A whisper about it to the superintendent brought forth this reply: "It's because the general manager is in the room. It is the first time most of the men have seen him." He had been general manager for ten years, and conditions had been steadily going from bad to worse during that time. Some things might have been prevented if he had become acquainted with the employees during that time. But he was too authoritarian to unbend; aloof as a schizoid.

The following week, there was a meeting of about the same number of supervisors for another food manufacturer, 100 miles away. This plant had no worry about labor trouble. The meeting was a friendly get-together, part of the educational program. The general manager of this plant looked like a battered prize fighter, but that appearance was deceptive. As the group was gathering, he introduced each man by name, told about his work, and added some individual esteem-building touch, such as, "Couldn't get along without John here." An equalitarian; a warm sort, person-centered.

The supervisors in that second group did not feel lost in the crowd.

And the big boss made each feel that he was needed. *People need to feel that they are needed.* Sometimes, they like to prove by a strike that they are needed. The old horse-trader type of boss made a serious blunder when he tried to make workers feel that he could get along without them and that they were lucky he gave them jobs.

3 ■ Forces That Mold Friendly Attitudes

The human climate. The human climate of a place is all-important in molding friendly attitudes—the difference in human atmosphere between those two food firms, for example. Some companies have warm climates, where friendliness blossoms without coaxing. Others have cold climates that chill friendly interactions with people.

The effects of such climates extend to afterwork, too. The Institute of Industrial Relations at the University of California found this afterwork hangover when making studies of office and laboratory workers for the Office of Naval Research. Some of the workers had a restrictive, authoritarian boss. Other workers had a permissive, equalitarian boss. The interactions with others while at work were much more satisfying for those who had the permissive boss. In addition, those who worked with the permissive boss did more socializing with the other workers evenings and week ends.

In sizing up a prospective place to work, it might be wise to ask oneself, "Is it warm, or cold?" There will likely be more friends at work, and after, if it has a warm climate.

Propinquity. Propinquity (physical nearness) is a factor in forming most friendships. We form most of our friendships with people who live or work closest to us. The worker who is alone in a far-off corner will not have as many friends, as a rule, as the person in a work group.

Propinquity is usually accidental, causing many friendships to be formed on the basis of chance. Some people make it less accidental by joining a lodge or moving to a neighborhood where there are people with whom they want to strike up friendships. Accidental propinquity, which is the rule, shows that friendliness can bloom between almost any people. Something may be wrong if we have to go a great distance to find friends. Potential friends are right beside us, if we only look for them.

Size of work groups. The size of the work group is another factor that is largely accidental, but it is a factor to be reckoned with. When there are only three persons in a group, there is every likelihood that they will soon divide into a twosome and a leftover member—the eternal triangle. Two become very friendly with each other, while the third person is left out in the cold. In view of this, some firms are now arranging work so that three-person teams are not necessary.

Interactions seem to be at their best when there are five to seven people

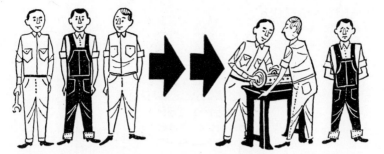

Groups composed of three persons have a tendency to break up into a twosome, with one member left outside as an isolate.

in the group. (Try to have that many when you invite the boss home for dinner.)

Similar ideals. Similar ideals are a powerful factor for drawing and holding people together, according to experiments by Dr. William R. Thompson. He found that people who have similar interests and opinions, who idealize much the same things, are most likely to become close friends without trying. Authoritarians are drawn to one another, and not to equalitarians with their different ideals. High-tariff advocates are drawn to one another and cold-shoulder the low-tariff man.

Degree the person matched the ideals:

67

6

NOT friends —ideals not matched

BEST friends — ideals matched

Experiment by Dr. Wm. R. Thompson

They chose as best friend a person who had similar ideals, or goals, or opinions.

The 3-girl teams liked working together better when they had been given a "warm" introduction.

This is another reason why it is good judgment to keep our opinions secret. You may recall Washington's advice to himself on this point.

Warmth of introduction. Warmth of introduction has also been found to make a marked difference in how people take to one another. It does not help initial friendliness in the least if a new person is introduced as an expert worker, as a rich person, as one who has traveled widely, or as an interesting person. But it does help if the newcomer is introduced as a warm person whom you will like. The effects of the kind of introduction on girls who were starting on a new job together are shown in this chartoon. These girls had not met each other until they reported for work. The way the boss introduced them made a great difference.

Personal effort to be friendly is often overlooked. Propinquity and the kind of introduction we get may be an accident, but friendliness should not be. Reciprocal action, again. Let us examine now some of the points to be considered in making this personal effort—which we hope will be no effort at all.

4 ■ Adults Are Like Children

Young children do many things to win attention. They ask questions, show off, and make nuisances of themselves unless they are given attention.

Adults, like children, want to be noticed, although adults try to conceal their craving for attention. Children are not adult enough to conceal it. The adult desire to be noticed is there, and for pleasant human relationships it is imperative to notice and to be noticed. When an adult feels ignored, he will either (1) do odd things to win attention, or (2) direct hostility toward the person who refuses to notice him.

An amusing example of the first is the 250-pounder in a chemical works, who had a lonesome job in a remote corner of the plant. The only time he saw the boss was on payday. About once a month, he took time off and came to the plant late in the forenoon, dressed in white flannel trousers, blue coat, derby hat, and swinging a cane. He strutted through the plant like a visiting director.

"He must be off his nut," the manager told the employment office. But the be-derbyed gauge tender was no more off his nut than the clerk who talks too loudly, the office girl who comes to work dressed for a princely ball, or the college man who uses words no one can understand. They are all doing something to win attention and friends.

An example of the second is the worker who makes fun of the boss behind his back or, in extreme situations, writes unsigned notes to the boss's wife or tries to organize group opposition to the boss.

Such conduct seems childish. Yet it is more common in adults than is suspected. The problem of friendly human relations is much simplified if you look on adults as oversized children. The thirty-year-old needs attention as much as the three-year-old. And the sixty-year-old may need it most, as the next section shows.

5 ▪ Love and the Want to Be Wanted

Falling in love is not all a matter of beauty, money, and sex. The desire to be noticed favorably, to feel someone needs us, is a significant part of love. Reckless early marriages are often the result of parents' failure to make a child feel needed, and the adolescent becomes overwhelmed when someone gives signs of needing his or her companionship. That is one reason why a plain girl often manages to marry the pick of the year; she makes him feel that at last someone appreciates him and needs him.

This also is pathetically shown by unwise decisions of widows when someone makes love to them—and their money. Several psychological factors affect widows when a money-seeking man starts to work on their affections. First, the widow wants to feel needed, but her grown-up children no longer need her; they give their attention to their own families. The widow, therefore, feels she has outlived her usefulness and has been shelved by her children and the world.

Some widows try to make themselves useful by interfering, as the

Nobody Needs Me Now!

Now this mother feels lonesome and frightened. Her children don't seem to need her any more. They are busy with their own private affairs. They can take care of themselves . . . or think they can. Her husband's business consumes his time and energy. What will she do with her days?

This woman can avoid many of the frustrations and anxieties of an empty middle age. In every community there are organizations in need of help. A willingness to work, to forget petty jealousies, and a sincere desire to help are the main qualifications.

Courtesy Connecticut Mutual Life Insurance Co.

in-laws call it. The mother-in-law problem arises from a restless effort to continue being useful. People need to be needed, and many mothers-in-law make nuisances of themselves pretending they need to run their married children's lives.

The spinster bookkeeper and older women who have professions or businesses are generally safe from love pirates because they have earned their money themselves. And married professional women are usually less meddlesome as mothers-in-law, since their work gives the satisfaction of being needed without having to butt in on their married children's affairs. It is said that wealthy women who have few home cares are the most meddlesome in-laws. That is understandable, as is much of the nervousness of the idle rich, since they do nothing creative to nourish the need to be needed.

Older employees who are retired on pension are often in the same psychological status as the widow and the mother-in-law. On the one hand, they feel that their usefulness is over; and, on the other, they may be a bit conscience-stricken over the pension, because they sometimes stalled on the job and did not always give their best work to the firm.

Many pensioners seem to go to pieces rapidly on retiring. They need anchorage, something to help them feel they are still useful and needed. They should take up social-welfare work or develop hobbies.

This problem of helping the retired or pensioned feel that they are not discarded is growing yearly, as the percentage of older people increases in the population.

The need to be needed continues, like all psychological wants, and always must be considered in human relations.

6 ■ The Boss a Surrogate

The child wants notice, especially from his parents. When a child starts school, the teacher shares some of the authority formerly associated

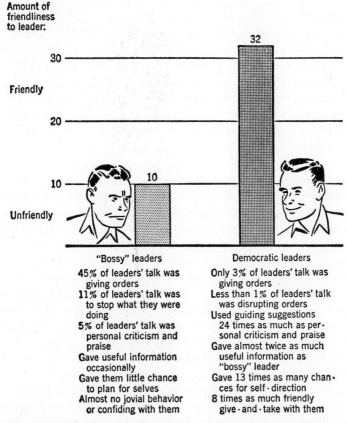

More Friendliness in and Confiding to Democratic Leaders

Amount of friendliness to leader:

	"Bossy" leaders	Democratic leaders
	45% of leaders' talk was giving orders	Only 3% of leaders' talk was giving orders
	11% of leaders' talk was to stop what they were doing	Less than 1% of leaders' talk was disrupting orders
	5% of leaders' talk was personal criticism and praise	Used guiding suggestions 24 times as much as personal criticism and praise
	Gave useful information occasionally	Gave almost twice as much useful information as "bossy" leader
	Gave them little chance to plan for selves	Gave 13 times as many chances for self-direction
	Almost no jovial behavior or confiding with them	8 times as much friendly give-and-take with them

Based on experiments with hobby clubs of 10-year-old boys who worked together in groups of five. The adult leader used "bossy" style for six weeks with one group, then switched to democratic style as he went to another group. Data reported by Drs. Ralph White and Ronald Lippitt.

with parents; so teachers also become persons from whom children especially want notice.

When the individual goes to work, the boss is the person with authority and, consequently, joins parents and teachers as one from whom attention is most wanted. Thus it goes through life. We want to be noticed, but we want most of all to be noticed by those in authority, for we were conditioned originally to the images of our parents.

The boss and teacher are parent *surrogates* (*sur*-o-gates), or substitutes for the mental images we have of our parents. Any individual is especially sensitive to lack of friendliness, or to signs of favoritism toward others, from these surrogates.

7 ■ The Seesaw Between Hostility and Friendliness

The human mind is put together much like a watch. The top layer of wheels of the watch goes around in one direction, but many of the main gears in the next layer go around in the opposite direction.

Jealousy, hostility, or hatred are due to counterclockwise spins inside the mind; but psychologists have a different word for it than spin.

Ambivalence (am-*biv*-a-lense) is the term to describe this tug of war inside the mind between opposed ideas or attitudes. Ambivalence shows up, for instance, in your everyday association of ideas.

What is the first word that comes to mind when you read the word *up?* Most people think first of *down*. Try it on another. What word pops to mind after reading *hot?* It usually is *cold*. And so on, *black* brings *white* to mind, *long* brings *short, costly* brings *cheap*.

The idea that is closest to the one you are thinking about is often the exact opposite. This is especially true of such emotional attitudes as love and hate, like and dislike, obedience and disobedience. The motives associated with the primitive life urge or death urge are often in these opposed pairs. One set of wheels is spinning love, while the set that meshes with it—hate—is spinning in the opposite direction.

Friendliness is just a hairbreadth from hostility. The one may turn into the other in a twinkling. You may like a person consciously; but, at the same time, deeper in your mind, a feeling of dislike is linked with it. You may have contradictory feelings toward a person at the same time, though you seldom are aware of the opposite feeling until something happens to bring it into the open. Then, look out!

This opposite feeling usually remains beneath the surface until the expression of the favorable feeling is blocked. If a person you like ignores or criticizes you, your favorable feeling may be blocked, bringing forth an unfavorable attitude—an ambivalent flip-flop. The criticism repulsed your friendliness; so it is kept in storage, and you will show hostility toward the critic.

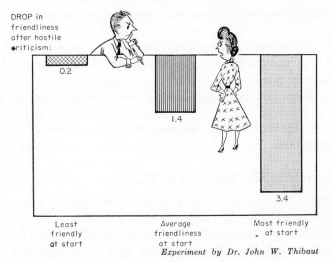

DROP in friendliness after hostile criticism:

0.2

1.4

3.4

| Least friendly at start | Average friendliness at start | Most friendly at start |

Experiment by Dr. John W. Thibaut

Hostility hit hardest on those who had felt friendliest.

Such a flip-flop is depicted in this chartoon of the quick results from unexpected criticism. The drop was most where there had a moment before been the most friendly feeling. Strong friendliness was on the surface, but the wheel going in the opposite direction was spinning just as forcefully. The stress of criticism brings the hostility to the surface in about the same proportion as the strength of friendly feelings of a moment before.

The hypocrite who feels one thing and pretends the opposite knows about his hostile feelings and conceals them. Children often are aware of these opposite feelings and, childlike, make no effort to conceal them. That is why a usually loving child bursts forth with a sincere: "Mother, I hate you." But most people do not become aware of their hidden contrary feelings, and the hostility flip-flops out in unexpected ways.

When the average person is aware of this opposite feeling peeking around the corner, he is likely to use the hypocrite's tactics and *over-correct* for it. This is why people are sometimes just "too, too sweet to be real." Their supersweetness is an effort to cure the situation by overdoing it. Suspect the salesman who pretends too great respect for your judgment. He, like the hypocrite, is probably conscious of contempt for you and considers you a sucker on whom he can unload some of his worthless stock.

Ambivalent attitudes make you dislike most the persons you hoped would like you. Belittling hurts most when it comes from parents or bosses, for they are the ones whose good esteem is wanted most. You can listen to a tirade of abuse from an intoxicated person and feel no hatred for him, only pity. But a lifted eyebrow or slight neglect from someone whose good opinion you want cuts deeply and brings up a hostile response.

That is why discarded friends make the worst enemies. But remember it works both ways, for, as former President Franklin Pierce observed: "Old foes make good friends."

Office politics and individual feuds are sometimes the result of these ambivalent feelings. The jealousy is due, not to the other person's higher salary, but to his actions. He looks down his nose at others or rebuffs their friendly advances.

8 ■ When Hostility Becomes a Disease

Hostility is likely to be strongest when it is aroused by someone of the same sex toward whom a person is attracted. This often explains the mental disorder of *paranoia* (par-ah-*noi*-ah) in which the victim shows unreasoned hatred or suspicion. Hitler may have had this ailment. Cezanne, the modernistic French painter, had paranoia and imagined he was being persecuted by his friends.

A few people without becoming mentally disordered nevertheless have a hostile, suspicious attitude so marked toward persons they want to like them that they are called *paranoid personalities* (*par*-ah-noid). These paranoid personalities are troublemakers and ruin the morale of an entire department or family or neighborhood. They are stormy petrels who imagine they are being picked on, persecuted, or cheated. They argue about line fences, add bills lest they be cheated, and think the other fellow has an easier job.

The paranoid personality thinks that he has to fight for his rights; he does not realize that he will have a fight all right, but will not get his rights that way. He goes through life in an excited, tense state, torn by the conflict of the hate that he expresses and the yearning for affection that he tries to conceal.

In an ordinary year, the President of the United States receives around two thousand threatening letters, some carrying such happy thoughts as ". . . the day will come when I will have your heart out and give it to the ants as food." Investigation of these letters by the Secret Service indicates that more than 90 per cent of the writers are mentally unbalanced, with marked paranoid streaks. These letters are merely a sample of the large number of paranoid personalities at large. Some are mad at the President, others at the bishop, others at their boss, others at their neighbors.

You will not run across many paranoid types in daily life, but there will be a few to make trouble. When a paranoid is encountered, it is wise to give him a wide berth. You can do nothing to change him after he has reached this stage. The female paranoid's pet hates are other women;

the male paranoid's, other men. So, avoid particularly the paranoids of your own sex.

The transition zones of cities—the areas of rooming houses and slums surrounding the business centers—have more than their share of paranoids. Many reformers and agitators are paranoid personalities. So are some apostles of queer religions.

Friendliness is the other side of hostility. This is the practical lesson from ambivalence, of which paranoia is the worst example. Lack of friendliness can arouse hostility. This is an illustration of that principle of reciprocal action—you smile, then he smiles. Show friendliness, and friendliness usually will be reflected in turn. But show no friendliness, and you are likely to receive hostility in return, even though you show no hostility yourself. While hostility begets hostility, the mere lack of friendliness may also produce it.

Now you can understand why parents who have "done nothing mean" to their children nevertheless may not have their children's affection. And why the manager who has done nothing unkind to his employees may have many workers who would like to wring his neck. The hostile workers cannot explain why they have this hostile attitude, and no morale survey would reveal the cause. They say they dislike him "just because" and cannot explain further. That "just because" is likely to mean that they have not been receiving friendly notice from the one person from whom they would especially appreciate such notice.

9 ■ Make the "Howdy" Rounds

The higher the position, the fewer employees an executive works with directly. Top executives seldom work through more than seven department heads. Their person-to-person acquaintances usually are more extensive outside the company than inside. This puts psychological distance between higher executives and the rank and file, an unfavorable situation for human relations inside the business.

On the other hand, supervisors and foremen work directly with anywhere from seventeen to seventy people. These immediate supervisors (surrogates) are usually so beset with duties that they seldom notice workers as individuals—until something goes wrong. Yet it has been shown time and time again that a supervisor will have fewer troubles, and fewer things will go wrong, if he continually makes a definite effort to notice individual employees as individuals.

Some twenty thousand supervisors and executives of General Motors Corporation, for instance, were given training in "Man-to-Man Relations on the Job." At more than a dozen plants, conferences and individual interviews were held to stimulate these surrogates to make the "Howdy" rounds—to visit each worker on the job for two minutes just to say,

"Howdy, how're things going?"; to give each worker individual notice systematically; to get acquainted and keep acquainted. A brief visit with *each* employee avoids signs of favoritism.

The boss who is too busy to notice individual workers when things are going smoothly is not establishing the kind of relations that will stimulate them to pull with him when there is rough going. The strong, silent man who knows the business from A to Izzard often makes the poorest boss, because he fears his dignity will suffer if he notices people. The silent treatment is a prison form of discipline.

10 ■ Mechanical Attempts to Give Individual Notice

Editors of company newspapers try to mention the names of as many workers as possible. Unless the paper is as thick as the telephone directory, most employees will be overlooked and will remain charter members of the Lost Battalion of Unnoticed Men and Women. Occasional newspaper notice is not a substitute for flesh-and-blood attention. Type is impersonal.

Company teams and parties help some, but often those who are most in need of individual notice stay in the background and do not get noticed. The boss should make an effort to contact these wallflowers who feel unwanted and in the way.

Some companies put individual name plates on each office worker's desk, no matter how humble the position. This gives a form of individual notice and helps new employees and visitors find their way around. Some firms extend this use of name plates to benchworkers; the worker's name is stenciled at his workplace and on his locker. In some cases, employees' names are painted on the machines they operate, with different colors to show their years of service. These attentions personalize the jobs.

One firm has a Who's Who display on department bulletin boards. A snapshot of a different employee is posted each day, with a friendly biographical sketch underneath. A new employee's Who's Who is posted for his first three days.

Such mechanical methods help a bit, but they are not a full solution to the problem of forgotten men and women in business. Nothing takes the place of personal regard. The boss must be all business, but a vital part of his business is getting acquainted with every last employee—and keeping acquainted.

11 ▪ Learn Names, and Use Them

"Imagine! The old grouch! I've been here for eleven months, and he still doesn't know my name." So that worker has a hostile attitude because he feels slighted when his name is "You at the third desk."

Courtesy Continental Can Company, Paterson

Friendly individual notice and a boost to self-esteem are given by this display of workers' hobbies in the main hallway. The photographs on the wall "humanize" the organization chart.

Seeing your name in print in the company magazine may be flattering, but hearing it from the lips of others touches a deeper spot.

When a new worker comes to your department, introduce yourself to him at the first opportunity. Learn his name correctly, and make an effort to remember it. Be brief, but do tell him he will find the office a good place to work after he gets acquainted. New workers usually are confused and need the encouragement of such a positive attitude and a suggestion that their jobs have prestige.

Learn the names of the bus drivers, librarians, fountain clerks, newsstand boys with whom you are in daily contact. It will help you take an interest in people as individuals, and they will give you friendlier service.

Before applying for a job, learn the employment manager's name, so that you can mention it in conversation with him. To learn his name, simply telephone the day before and ask the switchboard operator for the name without revealing your own.

The house-to-house salesman asks each housewife the names of her neighbors and uses their names when he calls on them. The inside salesman tries to learn the prospect's name early and uses it frequently. The store salesman makes regular customers of those whose names he learns, for he greets them by name.

Friendliness rather than hostility is gained by successful trial lawyers when they refer to a client in court not as "the defendant" but by name. As one veteran lawyer said: "Juries will hang an anonymous defendant, but it is harder for them to hang John Brown or Jim Smith."

Individually written letters that start with "Dear Sirs" are cold. It is better psychology to start with the mention of a person's name, even

An "introduction board" that gives new workers a friendly introduction to the entire office force. The picture with biographical sketch is usually left on the board for a week or two. When such a board is first used, it is likely to cause a traffic jam.

Courtesy B. F. Goodrich Co.

though the letter may be to an impersonal corporation. People are not indifferent, or hostile, to the sight of their own names.

12 ■ *Make Yours a Friendly Place to Work*

Big cities and big businesses are lonesome places. We may feel overlooked and ignored—but others feel the same way, if that is any comfort.

We can't expect much attention as an individual. Then what little we receive will be a pleasant bonus. We probably are being noticed, but others simply neglect to let us know they notice us.

Loud talking, a noisy laugh, flashy clothes, boisterous behavior will win notice sure enough, but not the right kind of notice. The young man who loads his automobile with useless decorations, or the girl with an overdisplay of dime-store jewelry, wins notice that would better not be won. One ring, or one brooch of good quality, if always worn, becomes a trade-mark and wins favorable notice.

Reciprocal action is the best way to gain friendly notice from others. We cannot expect friendliness unless we are friendly.

Make your greetings human, warm, not mechanical. Smile as you say "Hello." Make it sound friendly. Don't let your voice die down on the last syllable, but keep it up, like this: "Hel-*l-o!*"

At the same time, look the person in the face for a moment. Look at him, not at the gas pump or your newspaper. When at work, look up from a blueprint, typewriter, or letter, and look directly at the person. Don't keep on working, but pause and look at the person as though you are glad to see him. Give him your direct attention, not a sidelong glance.

On the job you see many familiar faces. Don't wait for them to show the first friendly gestures. Give them a friendly nod and a smile as you pass. You are surrounded by potential friends (propinquity), all waiting for a nod from you. They are more lonesome than you, many of them.

When old friends move out of town, do not let them move out of your life. Write them friendly notes from time to time, or at least post cards. Let them know that you think of them in a friendly fashion, so that they will remember you in the same way.

Keep a record of their birthdays and anniversaries, and send greeting cards or personal notes.

Exercise your skill in getting to know, and to like, more people at your lodge or union meetings, at church, at places where you are a regular customer. Learn something about them, without being nosy. Show an interest in their new clothes, in their automobiles, or in the new homes they plan to build. Show an interest in their hobbies—and keep quiet about your own, which may be difficult. And keep mum about your opinions and prejudices.

You do not need to become chummy with them. But act as if you liked them, whether you think you do or not. In most instances, acting as if you like people is the start of a real liking.

An important aside, for young men only: Be friendly with the women at your workplace, but act toward them as you do toward the men. Avoid flirting or suggestiveness—they are dynamite. You cannot be a leader of men if you follow the girls around the office or shop.

One of the country's top executives, who started as a stock-room clerk, has this little verse inside his pocket memo book:

> Like more people,
> Like them sooner,
> Tell them quicker.

It's blunt but true, that we won't be noticed much, or have many friends or much influence, unless we are friendly ourselves.

— — — — — — — — — — — — — — — — — — —

The Gist of the Chapter

1. Tell about five ways in which a friendly climate can help business efficiency.

2. What forces are important in molding friendships?

3. What problems arise from people's tendency to want attention, and to want to feel that they are needed?

4. What is the meaning and significance of the statement that the boss is a surrogate?

5. What is ambivalence in thinking, and what are some of its effects?

6. Tell about paranoia, and why business people should know about it.

7. What and why are the "howdy" rounds?

8. Compare mechanical methods and personal methods of giving individual notice.

9. How can the individual make his a friendlier place to work?

Things to Do and Problems to Discuss

1. Report on a comparison of some offices, stores, or classrooms that seem to be much different in their human climate. How much of this difference is due to the tangible furnishings? how much to friendly attitudes?

2. Describe "the friendliest person I know." Show how he exhibits friendliness, and try to explain why. How has it helped or hindered his success?

3. Keep a sheet of paper ruled in three columns beside your telephone. Head one column "Warm," the middle one "Neutral," the third one "Cold." Size up the voice and conversation on incoming calls, and tally it in the appropriate column. Which predominates at the end of a week? What made some seem

cold, others warm? How did the warmth, or its lack, affect your attitudes toward the other person? Would you talk differently over the telephone if you thought the other person was keeping a similar tally?

4. Some people make friends easily, but do not keep them long. What might be the causes, and what might be done to keep friends longer?

5. List jobs on which you think friendly attitudes on the part of the worker are least necessary. Then list jobs where friendliness would seem most necessary. Account for the difference in the length of the lists.

6. Trace the effects on friendliness of the tendency for workers to change jobs every three and a half years and residence every seven years.

7. The old-style horse-trading boss liked to lay off workers so that they would realize they were not always needed. Discuss the possible effects.

8. Review the primary interests, and point out those in which friendly personal notice would give personal satisfaction and most help to personal morale.

9. Effie K. is weak in remembering names. Refresh yourself on the chapter on memory, and prepare a plan by which she can remember names better.

10. You have recently joined the XYZ Co. While walking downtown you see a person you think—but are not positive—works in the same department. Should you smile, or speak to him on passing? stop to visit? what if it were an attractive young woman? what if a stern-appearing middle-aged man?

11. Oswald J. is a young married executive and has been friendly to his secretary. Now he realizes that she has misinterpreted his friendliness and thinks he is in love with her. What should he do now?

12. During a coffee break two people get into a political argument. One turns to you and says, "You agree with me, don't you?" What should you do?

13. The boss stops at your desk while making his "howdy" rounds. He has a smudge of soot beside his eye. Should you mention the soot? what to do?

14. How would having unfulfilled primary interests incline a person to be not friendly?

15. Analyze what is likely to happen to the friendliness of other workers when the boss is especially friendly to one or two pet workers. What business policies might also influence friendly interactions between workers?

15 ■ CREATING CONFIDENT HOPEFULNESS

WHAT THIS CHAPTER IS ABOUT

1 ■ Value of Confidence, Encouragement, Optimism

Margaret's first job was as stenographer with a firm of chemists. She had to take many strange technical terms in dictation and felt she was making a botch of it. The first few days on the job, she was tense and jittery, lost appetite, and slept poorly. She felt she was beyond her depth and a failure.

"Bet those words seem difficult," her supervisor said. "You'll find that they are easier each day. Come to see me after each dictation, and I'll go over the notes to help you with the hard ones."

The supervisor suggested that she make a list of each day's new words, date the list, and review the words in odd moments. At the end of the second week, she went over the lists with Margaret, dictating the tough words for her to write in shorthand.

Margaret had 86 per cent correct. She beamed.

"You are much better than you imagined, aren't you?" the supervisor said. "It always helps to see that you are doing better than you thought."

Discouragement is an enemy of morale. It kills faith in oneself, in the future, and in others. Yet the world seems bent on handing out criticism and discouragement. The boss frowns when work goes poorly and always seems to want it a little better and a little faster. Fellow workers also are

258 ■

likely to smirk when something is done badly and pretend not to notice when a job is done superbly.

The prevalence of what used to be called inferiority complexes is one sign of the widespread need for more encouragement. Many people only half work and half live because they are not encouraged to take pride in developing their powers.

The kind of leaders under whom people work has much to do with whether or not they have a confident hopefulness.

Reports on the leaders of 500 different groups have been analyzed by Dr. John K. Hemphill. Office groups, club groups, church groups, factory groups, athletic groups, even prisoner-of-war groups were included in this wide sampling. About one leader out of four was classed as weak or inferior as a leader. When these inferior leaders were compared with the superior leaders, it was found that nine characteristics were predominant in making the inferior ones weak leaders. These characteristics are shown in this chartoon.

You will see at once that these characteristics would undermine the confident hopefulness of those under such a leader.

Benjamin Franklin learned how to use encouragement to unlock abilities. At nineteen, he ran away from a faultfinding brother. Franklin floundered awhile before discovering that self-encouragement put him on good terms with good fortune. Others needed encouragement, too, he

Based on the 135 inferior leaders out of 500 analyzed by Dr. John K. Hemphill

The nine ways that were most influential in making them inferior leaders.

discovered; and he made a lifelong practice of giving encouragement lavishly.

James Madison's life was transformed by Franklin's encouragement. Short, timid Madison was in black despair and had lost his purpose in life. Franklin, forty-five years his senior, saw Madison's brilliant promise and recognized the signs of acute discouragement. The older man had been through it himself, years before; so he heaped big doses of encouragement and praise on the solemn young man. Madison blossomed and devoted a lifetime of service to his country, as father of the Constitution and as fourth President of the United States. Franklin showed him how to find new hopes to replace shattered hopes.

To encourage means *to inspire with courage or hope.* It does not make others self-satisfied; it gives them more nerve and confidence.

Now would be a good time to refresh ourselves on the usefulness of a confident attitude on output and efficiency. In Chapter 1 we saw how the thought of failure affected some business students in the light work of lifting weights. We also found how discouraging thoughts made it more difficult to make the mind stay put. And in the chapter on learning a new job, we found how a feeling of success speeded up mastery of it.

The right kind of encouragement is needed both for production and for good human relations. Neither is at its best when the climate breeds hopeless unconfidence.

2 ■ The New Employee, or the New Job

There are critical times when encouragement is especially needed. A new venture, for instance, has a better chance of success if it is launched with a spurt of encouragement. And when promotion comes, you have a new job and are a beginner again, with a beginner's extra need for encouragement.

The beginner needs easy tasks at the outset. New workers should be started on a "success sequence," to help them make good. Mastering the easier tasks of a job gives a feeling of confidence that carries one through the more difficult parts.

Some companies have their most skilled workers break in beginners. This often breaks the newcomer's spirit, since his lack of skill is all the more marked in contrast with the expert's skill. The expert, forgetting the years it took to make him an expert, is likely to be discouragingly impatient with learners. New workers should be judged by standards appropriate for beginners, not for experts.

The beginner should be told he is catching on well the first day. The next day, he should be told he is a little better than yesterday. Give him a positive frame of mind that will help him master the job more quickly.

Encouragement is especially needed because he has been comparing himself with others and noting his beginner's difficulties.

It is often best to let an employee of only average skill teach a new worker. He will not make the new employee seem so clumsy. In addition, the average worker will have a better understanding of his own job after trying to teach it to someone else. There is no better way to learn your work than to teach it.

The new worker needs an instructor who is patient, friendly, and helpful, and who likes people. The instructor should be person-centered, not machine-centered. The attitudes the beginner will form toward the company will be influenced by the personality of the one who breaks him in.

Great scientists and famous musicians are often the worst teachers; whereas some average performers are superb teachers who can develop

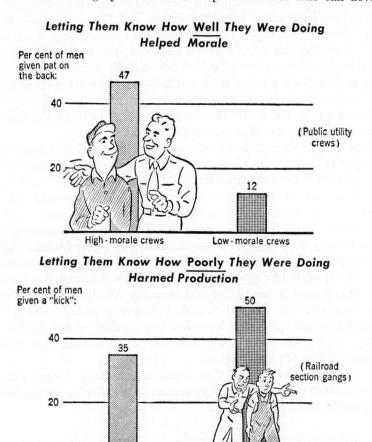

Letting Them Know How Well They Were Doing Helped Morale

Per cent of men given pat on the back:

47

40

(Public utility crews)

20

12

High-morale crews　　Low-morale crews

Letting Them Know How Poorly They Were Doing Harmed Production

Per cent of men given a "kick":

50

40

35

(Railroad section gangs)

20

High-producing gangs　　Low-producing gangs

Data from studies by the Survey Research Center of the University of Michigan

hidden talents in others. It is the same in business. The expert salesman often cannot teach others how to sell. The accountant who can add three-column figures in his head often cannot teach elementary bookkeeping. It seems so simple to the expert that he cannot imagine the difficulties of a beginner. Job skill is not so essential for a teacher as skill in bringing out the best in others. It takes encouragement to bring out the best.

3 ■ Bad Days, the Negative Streak, and the Hoodoo

Most people have bad days, when production slumps, errors increase, and accidents lurk around every corner. A keen supervisor watches for these glum days and gives lowered spirits a lift with a little encouragement.

On these depressed days, people seem hoodooed. This is because they are thinking how things might go wrong—and things naturally oblige. A machine setter in a paper-box factory, for example, had spent half a day on a setting that usually took a half-hour, and it was still not right. The superintendent stopped by and intentionally planted some encouragement to make the setter think positively and break the hoodoo. "Remember how easily you made the setting yesterday on number six," was all the boss said. But it was encouraging enough to break the jinx, and in ten minutes the machine was in production.

There is a hoodoo. It is entirely in a person's mind and starts when he begins to think, "I can't." Encouragement keeps him thinking, "I can."

Negativism is the term used for the obstinate streak that some people show from time to time. When they have a negativistic spell, they deliberately break rules or slow down or indulge in some secret vandalism or sabotage. The harder they are pushed during these obstinate periods, the more they back up. This is an illustration of the ambivalent flip-flop that brings out their mortido. An authoritarian leader may get more than his share of negativistic reactions since he is inclined to push the obstinate.

Encouragement is one of the best remedies for obstinacy. One supervisor snaps such a worker out of pigheadedness by taking a visitor to his machine and saying: "John, here, has the bowling record in the shop league." This encouraging word does not mention work, but it works wonders in winning co-operation.

To cure the vague ill will that someone may show toward you, tell him something encouraging. Skip mention of the ill will, for the encouraging words will help it vanish.

4 ■ Shifting Moods—Cyclothymia

Life has its rosy days and black days. Days when we are hopeful, days when there is discouragement. Sometimes it is not just a day, it may last a week or even longer.

These shifts in mood frighten some people into believing they are losing control of their minds. But shifting moods are so common they must be normal. An interesting thing about everyday mood shifts is that they often occur in regular cycles. Some people have short cycles, swinging from happy to sad and back again to happy in two-week periods. With others, the cycles are longer, and a swing takes about six months. With most people, however, these normal mood shifts go from happy to sad and back again to happy about every four or five weeks. The wise person anticipates his moods and works with them.

A chart of mood shifts for Gus is shown below.

These normal mood shifts are not due to the weather or good or bad news. What causes them is not yet known, though their regular rhythm in some people suggests that a physiological cycle causes the shifts.

With a few people, mood shifts are more marked. Martin Luther and Abraham Lincoln had severe moods. Extreme changes in moods are usually due to balked ambitions and shattered hopes. The lazy dolt, lacking ambition, is not likely to have marked moods. Capable and ambitious people are the ones who have marked moods.

Cyclothymia (si-klo-*thim*-e-ah) is a form of mental breakdown in which moods vary so greatly that the person is incapacitated by them. Such a person will be extremely elated, confident, happy, fast-moving, talkative, until he reaches almost a maniacal pitch. After a while, this cheerful mood is transformed into depression. It may take a week, perhaps a year, to change from the elated to the depressed period. During the depressed cycle, he is sad, weepy, pessimistic, slow moving, unable to make decisions, silent. In this phase, he is a picture of *melancholia* (mel-an-*ko*-le-ah).

Between the elated and dejected phases, there is usually a long period

Typical Mood Changes

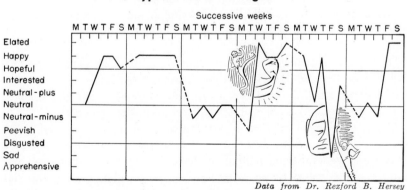

Data from Dr. Rexford B. Hersey

Gus tended toward the happy side but had his bad days. He was a 36-year-old railroad worker, married. About every six weeks he had a "sad day."

where the moods are not marked. Since the moods vary in cycles, the name of cyclothymia is appropriate.

Each year, about fifteen thousand people in the United States have such severe attacks of cyclothymia that they have to be hospitalized. About three-fourths of these recover, though some relapses are to be expected later. In addition, several times this number have lesser attacks, such as Lincoln's, which keep them from work or make them almost useless at work for a week or a month.

The most common cause of these normal mood swings seems to be the ups and downs of a person's ambitions. The swing down into gloom is brought on by the feeling that a person is balked in ambition and can do nothing; so he retreats into a melancholy mood of discouragement. The swing up into joy is due to the person's feeling that he is not balked and can do anything—overcompensating.

People who swing high and then swing low tend to be the world's doers, not the shirkers. When in the elated mood, they are "warm" and make the human climate friendly. (Schizoids, in contrast, make the climate "cold.") The cycloids usually have a sense of humor and high initiative, and may be heavy smokers. Some become heavy drinkers when they feel a sad period overtaking them. Many periodic drinkers are cycloids.

5 ▪ Handling People in Their Moods

The cycloid make-up is found in every occupation, but it predominates among salespeople. This is often the reason why a good salesman gradually slumps, and then comes back to his former standard. Bosses have an inclination to criticize a worker who is slipping, but what the depressed worker needs is encouragement. The criticism may complicate the mental condition, because it not only adds to the feeling of failure but also arouses hostility. It is silly to tell a person he has slumped; he already knows it only too well. It is better mental hygiene to remind him of a good job he recently did—as the superintendent reminded that machine setter.

During the upswing in mood, the individual may be overly optimistic and take on too much work. Too much work helps bring on the discouraged feeling, which later causes a slip into the downswing. Salesmen ask to have their quotas increased when they are in the upswing.

The psychological moment to ask the boss for a raise, or Dad for the use of the family automobile, is when they are permeated with the optimism and general good feeling of the upswing. Daniel Boone made a rough-and-ready test to see whether the girl he liked was in the right mood before asking her to marry him. He cut her dress, apparently accidentally. When she took the damage in good spirits, canny Daniel popped the question. They lived happily ever after, partly because he watched her moods and conducted himself accordingly.

During others' downswings, it is especially timely to pass out brief words of encouragement to them. When we are in a downswing, there is no better medicine than to keep busy at something that once seemed worth while and to recall some of our previous successes.

Apply for a job or a raise when in an upswing in mood. You will make a better impression then and also will be able to take a turndown with less damage to your ego.

And if we really have to call something unpleasant to another's attention, let's wait until he is in an upswing.

6 ▪ Business Decisions in the Mood Cycle

This letter came from a banker in Minnesota.

> I studied only elementary psychology at Oberlin thirty-five years ago but have observed during thirty years in a bank the up-and-down moods of customers and want to tell you about one extreme case of a businessman and personal friend who had a six months' cycle.
>
> For twenty years I noted his alternate semiannual moods and could predict their recurrence by the calendar. When I reminded him that six months would find him in another slump, he always insisted that it would never happen again.
>
> During his downswing he attended strictly to his business in every detail, watched his credits carefully, and in spite of worry slept better than during his ups, when his energy, enthusiasm, and optimism were boundless.
>
> Ill-advised financial undertakings were repeatedly made when he was in the up cycle, to be deeply regretted when down. This was not peculiar to his particular case, for frequently customers have thanked me when down for having refused their requests for loans when up.
>
> It has been my attempt as a banker to try to level out both the up and down curves for myself and others. My opinion is that both extremes should be guarded against. The business judgment of a person is at its worst at the top and next to worst at the bottom of the curve and best midway between.

It may be a poor policy to "Do it now" and carry out a business decision that was made in either the up mood or the down mood. Decisions made in the up mood may be recklessly optimistic; if acted upon, they may mean overexpansion and failure. Down-mood decisions are made timidly and with self-criticism.

Whenever an important decision is to be made, a second or a third look is wise before acting. This gives a chance for the self-revision of decisions. All too often in handling people, the first impulse is followed; and the other person's confidence is undermined or his negativism brought out.

Fortunately, in modern business organizations, the board of directors, or staff committee, acts as a check-and-balance on decisions made by one man in the wrong phase of his mood cycle. Sometimes it is the banker who tempers the hasty decision.

7 ■ Why Russia Has Few Cycloids

There are not many cycloids in the rooming-house and slum areas of cities. But the swank residential districts have more than their share. It is an ailment of successful people, who wish they were still more successful.

Interestingly enough, there are few cycloid breakdowns in Russia. This is easily understood when you recall that under communism, as under the czars, Russian culture stifles rather than stimulates individual ambition. Russians are imbued from infancy with the idea that each has the same lot in life. They have no tradition of starting at the bottom and working up.

In the United States ambition has always been stimulated. It is a tradition from the pioneer days, when people migrated here with nothing and became landowners and proprietors through their own efforts. This atmosphere of climbing up in the world gives motivation for striving to succeed but also gives causes for breakdowns when a person has too much ambition or feels that he is a failure.

Many psychologists believe that competition for grades in public schools prepares the mind for later attacks of kill-joy or excited symptoms of balked ambition. Individual competition for athletic awards and scholarship prizes, rather than team competitions, also has been blamed. But lack of encouragement and teachers who neglect to praise children can be as bad as direct personal competition in building this dread of failure.

8 ■ The A–F–D Sequence

When a person has set his level of aspiration too high or is given the feeling of failure in other ways, he may have to endure the sequence *from Aspiration through Frustration into Demoralization.* There are many famous examples to show how this sequence undermines morale and produces extreme mood shifts.

George III, King of England, had five distinct and serious attacks of cyclothymia. The first was when he was twenty-seven; he spent half a year in dejected brooding. Each succeeding attack was more severe, until at fifty he was so maniacal he had to be kept in a strait jacket. (Since modern culture frowns on cruelties linked with the death urge, strait jackets are now outlawed in most states. Quieting drugs and calming tub baths are used instead of physical restraint.) During one breakdown,

George III talked for nineteen consecutive hours. At one time, he stood up and started to talk in the middle of church services.

How could a king, the top man in his country, have balked ambition? Because, like many top executives, he wanted to be too good. George III wanted to be "a good king" and worked hard at it. He was not a clever politician; he could not evade issues or compromise his conscience. Politicians who were out and wanted to get back in harassed him, feeding his feeling of failure, which first became acute when he was twenty-seven. He tried too hard to be a perfect king and, as a result, was a pathetic failure. Mental specialists say that, if he had adopted a "come what may" attitude, and had been content to do a fair job without striving for perfection, he would not have become the victim of his balked ambition, as he did.

Success is relative, an attitude of mind. Onlookers may envy a man's accomplishments; yet he may feel a complete failure because he set his sights sky-high.

That is the James Forrestal story. He was the son of an Irish immigrant, yet made himself a powerful Wall Street banker. He served as Secretary of the Navy during World War II and finally broke while serving as the first Secretary of National Defense. Forrestal did a magnificent job, though not so good as he wanted to. It was the discouragements he encountered, as he tried to persuade the Army, Navy, and Air Force to cooperate as one national defense group, that balked his ambitions. This resulted in a mental depression, during which he jumped to his death from a window of the naval hospital. Such suicides are the result of the turning inward on oneself of the death urge. The paranoid, in contrast, is more likely to direct the death urge outward and kill someone else.

Overmotivation can be dangerous. Occasionally, some workers have been overstimulated by incentives or contests, only to have the starch taken out of them when the bonus had to be cut or someone else won the prizes.

Reasonable aspirations and heaps of encouragement are a good combination for mental health and morale.

9 ▪ Adjusting Ambitions to Reality

Modern business conditions have changed, making some ambitions that used to be instilled in young folks unrealistic. The unlimited frontier is disappearing and competition is increasing. Two consequences of these changes merit special consideration.

1. There is not so much opportunity for upward mobility as formerly. When small firms combine to form a larger one, the executive positions are reduced in number. As jobs have become simplified and methods standardized, one supervisor can handle more employees than under the old systems. This is particularly true for the large corporations but holds for middle-sized firms as well.

The situation in New Haven, Connecticut, a place of medium-sized and small firms, may be used as an illustration. Dr. August B. Hollingshead analyzed the changes in the city's firms from 1910 to 1940. He found that the "room at the top" had shrunk greatly during those thirty years.

In manufacturing firms, for instance, the number of officers per firm in 1940 had been cut to less than half the number in the same firms in 1910. Some of the functions that the officers performed in 1910 are now being done by office workers on modern business machines—more jobs for office workers, but fewer for executives.

2. More preparation is needed to advance in business than formerly. Although routine jobs have been simplified, the higher positions have become more complicated. Competition makes more demands on the higher positions today. So do government regulations and organized labor. The widened responsibilities that come with increase in firm size require special preparation; the old-fashioned business sense and diligent work of yesterday are no longer enough. More self-development is necessary to move up.

This has resulted in a paradox. Today, there is a smaller proportion of openings for executive work, but firms are hard pressed to find people who are qualified for such work. That is why firms are scrambling to hire those who do have broad training for business and why leading companies are setting up facilities for training their promising junior executives themselves. The days of messenger boys becoming presidents are not over—but now the messenger boys have to get some extra, and broadening, training. Sometimes this is a blow to the confidence of those who thought they would climb upward by just sticking to the job long enough.

How do people expect to get ahead? Dr. Nancy C. Morse found that about half the office clerks of a large firm with standardized and simplified operations thought it was merit and hard work. Those who thought that way were in general the most satisfied employees.

But one out of four claimed that knowing the right people—personal pull and favoritism—got one ahead. These were, in the majority of instances, the dissatisfied employees. Advancement in the company was on the same standards for all—why did one-fourth think it was pull? Interviews with these advocates of pull and favoritism revealed that they had keenly wanted to be promoted and had taken a cynical attitude when they weren't. Their frustrated ambitions had distorted their judgments as well as increased their dissatisfactions.

More of us need to balance our hopes with the realities the modern world offers—not to reach for the sky unless we are willing to do the work and preparation to get us there. And we need to keep others' hopes satisfied by showing them proper encouragement and appreciation.

10 ▪ Praise Can Build

There have been no systematic studies of the effects of praise in business, but many studies have been made with school children. Without exception, it has been found that praise helps learning, helps the amount of work done. Praise, in short, makes people work harder and feel more co-operative—as any salesman knows.

The lack of direct business data about the use of praise is eloquent. Its absence indicates a lack of appreciation of its importance. "You'll never see the boss until something is wrong" is all too true. The boss is like a clam when work is done well, but like a lion when done poorly.

This neglect of encouraging praise is often deliberate. The horse-trading type of boss believes a praised worker will want a raise and that fault-finding keeps the worker trying harder. This psychology is completely wrong.

The bosses of an eastern company were instructed to talk with each of the nearly eight hundred semiskilled workers and to give each one praise for some little thing. The management had expected this to bring a rash of requests for salary increases. In anticipation of such requests, a review board had been set up to handle them. But there was not a single request for a raise! Yet production increased; and rejections, absenteeism, and tardiness declined.

Praise is more effective than criticism to gain desired results. Better than criticizing an employee for tardiness is praise for twelve days of punctuality before the tardiness occurred. Thus, praise can be used to emphasize a desirable goal or quality. Desirable actions grow best in a seedbed cultivated by praise and encouragement.

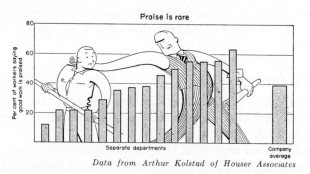

Data from Arthur Kolstad of Houser Associates

Only four out of every ten employees of this medium-sized company report they are given praise or recognition for good work. The variation from department to department indicates lack of supervisory training.

Praise should be definite, not vague. It is not effective praise just to tell a girl she is pretty. Tell her something definite, that she resembles a well-known beauty. Tell the good bookkeeper that you admire the accuracy with which he can add in his head. Tell any employee that his interest in promoting safety is appreciated, not just that you appreciate his interest—period. Put a handle on praise by making it definite.

11 ■ Praise Not a Cause of Conceit

Many parents imagine that their children will become conceited or big-headed if praised. This is absolutely incorrect. It is discouragement, belittling, and faultfinding that produce conceit.

The overconfident, big-headed braggart is trying to make up by pretense for the self-distrust he secretly feels. This pretense is a mental compensation. He compensates for a feeling of inadequacy by putting on a false front. Since no one ever told him he was good, he unconsciously tries to bluff the world—and himself—into thinking he is good.

Little Julia Ward was the redheaded baby of the richest banker in New York. Parents and older brothers and sisters made a fuss over the freckle-faced, pug-nosed mite. Enough to make her conceited, family friends said. But it did not. When four, she surveyed herself from carrot-top to toe in a long mirror. "Humph!" she said aloud to herself, "I don't see what's so wonderful about *her*." You may know her better as Julia Ward Howe, author of the stirring words of "The Battle Hymn of the Republic."

It is easy to understand how mistaken notions originate about the imagined dangers of encouragement and praise. People are so eager to have it all for themselves, to feed their own self-esteem, that they selfishly conclude it is bad for others. Some even like to pretend they are so modest that they do not want the honest praise that is due them.

Oliver Wendell Holmes, famous author, physician, and teacher, was more honest about it. When someone complimented his work, Holmes would say: "You know I am a trifle deaf. Won't you please repeat that a little louder?"

12 ■ Good-Finding

You will not find "good-finding" in the dictionary, but it should be there. Good-finding builds human relations and individual morale. Fault-finding harms both.

Good-finding is an expression of optimism that gives others optimism. The faultfinder says, "Unpleasant weather we are having." The good-finder says, "Better than no weather at all."

The good-finder overlooks weak points, gives attention to good points.

When he notices weaknesses, it is with a constructive attitude. Near-sightedness, for instance, does not strike the good-finder as a weakness; for he knows that it gives an advantage in close eye work—inspecting medicine ampules for flaws, for example. Deafness, in similar fashion, is an asset if you work in a noisy place. (Edison refused to wear a hearing aid, for he said his wife would talk his arm off if he could hear her.) Little desire to use one's intelligence becomes an asset for routine assembly work, which is monotonous to persons who want to use their brains.

One manager used an object lesson to bring home the importance of looking for folks' good sides. A small Oriental tapestry was hung face side to his office wall, with the unattractive underside showing. When a sub-

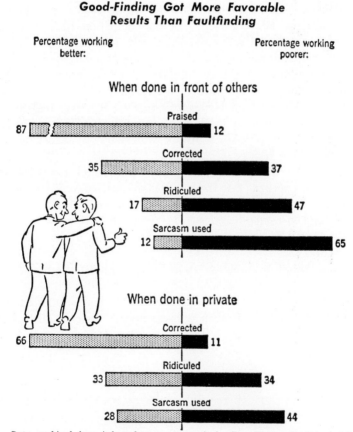

Good-Finding Got More Favorable Results Than Faultfinding

Percentage working better: Percentage working poorer:

When done in front of others

Praised — 87 / 12
Corrected — 35 / 37
Ridiculed — 17 / 47
Sarcasm used — 12 / 65

When done in private

Corrected — 66 / 11
Ridiculed — 33 / 34
Sarcasm used — 28 / 44

Data combined from independent surveys made by Drs. Thomas H. Briggs and Donald A. Laird

Good-finding in front of others was reported as almost invariably causing the person who was given a pat on the back to work harder. Notice that there is least sting when the faultfinding that has to be done is done in private.

ordinate complained about a worker, the executive would point toward the tapestry and say: "Now, let's look at the good side of the man."

It's a good habit to look for good points or for strong uses that can be made of weak points. As the chicken thief replied when the judge asked whether white or black chickens were better: "Well, the white ones are easier to find, and the black ones are easier to hide."

The successful executive does not think in terms of weak points. He thinks: "How can we make best use of what this person has?" And good use of what he has makes it no longer a weak point.

Charles V, Holy Roman Emperor and King of Spain, inherited the greatest empire of his day. Great military strategist that he was, he could not hold his empire because he failed in human relations. His mind was bent to notice annoyances and weaknesses. Little gripes upset him more than big injustices. His knowledge of human nature became lopsided, because he noticed and remembered mostly people's weaknesses. He could win battles, but not people. He could not appoint good administrators, because he knew only their limitations. So, disgusted with human nature, he abdicated and hid himself in a monastery.

In contrast, Chief of Staff General George C. Marshall had the habit of noting and remembering individual strong points. This enabled him to place the right officers in key positions to develop the victorious citizens army of World War II.

And look at this man, a baseball player who struck out 1,300 times. That is a world's record. But the same man also made 851 home runs. And that is a world's record. Babe Ruth, who made both records, remembered, and is remembered for, his home runs, not his strike-outs. He was the Home-Run King—also the strike-out king if you want to emphasize failure.

A sure way to fail in human relations is to emphasize faults.

(What answers do you want to change now, to the questions the New York Central System used in their correspondence course? The questions are on pages 162 and 163.)

— — — — — — — — — — — — — — — — — — — —

The Gist of the Chapter

1. What effects do discouraging thoughts have on personal efficiency?
2. What can be done to build self-confidence when starting a new job?
3. Tell about negativism and the conditions that bring it out.
4. Describe cyclothymia and its principal cause.

5. What are some "psychological moments"?

6. Why are there few cycloids in Russia?

7. How did James Forrestal illustrate the A–F–D sequence?

8. What are some of the realities to which ambitions have to be adjusted at the present time?

9. Discuss the use and misuse of praise.

Things to Do and Problems to Discuss

1. Review the pertinent points in this part of the book (Chapters 10 to 15) and in the first three chapters. Then write a description of "An Ideal Employer from the Human-Relations Point of View."

2. Write a description, from the same chapters, of "An Ideal Employee from the Human-Relations Point of View."

3. Keep a record of your own mood changes, using the same system as in the chart of Gus's moods. How can you account for the downswings? the upswings? How can this acquaintance with your mood cycles help you?

4. Recall some people you have known who committed acts of vandalism or took company property. Analyze how negativism or other factors motivated them to do those things.

5. You praised Effie K., then found that another worker should have received the praise. What do you do now?

6. Trace the relations between an increase in the competitive spirit in business and the feelings of friendliness. Look back in Chapter 14.

7. It is generally observed that there is an increase in negativism in most people during their early teen years. This is at a time when many of them first take up regular work. Discuss the possible causes of the flare-up in negativism at this age and its effects when starting the first job.

8. Figure out the possible relationships between the slowing down of the promotion rate and the cycle of job satisfaction described in Chapter 10.

9. Oswald J.'s boss has asked his opinion about the desirability of putting a gold star on the bulletin boards in departments that have good housekeeping and a blue star for those with poor housekeeping. Help him decide what to tell the boss about this.

10. What can a worker do to keep up his confidence when he is not given encouragement? How can he avoid fleeing from reality or becoming paranoid, which are poor ways to give himself encouragement?

11. Discuss the ethical aspects of giving praise that is not honest, even though it helps the individual's morale.

12. The boss has praised Jim's work to some other workers he does not praise. What effect is that likely to have (a) on the confidence of the other workers, (b) on their human relations with Jim?

13. Discuss reasons why some people "fish for compliments."

14. Discuss whether beginners on a job should be kept together or scattered among experienced workers. Consider Chapters 2 and 7 in justifying your decision.

15. You are starting beginners on work for which they will need six weeks' training in order to have the needed skills. Plan methods for keeping them confident and trying hard during this long period of inefficiency.

part 3

Personality and Emotional Health

PERSONALITY AND EMOTIONS make life and work interesting—or a hell on earth. The next three chapters take up emotional and personality factors in individuals. To get your thinking headed in this direction, try answering these questions from the correspondence course "Be a Better Leader!" of the New York Central System. These copyrighted questions are reproduced by special permission of the personnel department.

Place an X in front of the answer you think best for each question.

1. *What is the prime rule for self-improvement?*

    ___ Never admit a weakness in yourself.
    ___ Pass your mistakes off on your subordinates when you can get by with it.
    ___ Be conscious of the weaknesses you observe in others.
    ___ Know yourself, your faults and shortcomings—and try constantly to overcome them.

2. *What is a good test of your sense of humor?*

    ___ Reading the funnies.
    ___ Being able to tell many snappy stories.
    ___ Being willing to laugh at your own peculiarities.
    ___ Being ready to poke fun at others.

3. *If an employee has made himself a little foolish, how will you conduct the problem interview?*

    ___ Make a flat accusation, thus settling the matter.
    ___ Give him time and opportunity to talk until he finds his own responsibility.
    ___ Make an example of him by ridiculing him in front of others.
    ___ Suggest he look for another job, since you can never recommend him for promotion.

4. *What basic fact must you keep in mind when an employee brings a problem to you?*

    ___ Be on guard, for he will probably ask a favor.
    ___ Remember that most employee problems are trivial.
    ___ Remember that employees have problems because of some character weakness.
    ___ Remember that it is real and serious to the employee, and deserves your sympathetic attention.

5. *What will you do about the worried employee?*

    ___ Discover the cause of worry and try to help him eliminate it.
    ___ Tell him to quit worrying, he should have your troubles!
    ___ Don't do anything; let him solve his own worries, since everybody worries.
    ___ Buy him a good dinner, and tell him to forget what's bothering him.

6. *What will be your attitude toward first-day nervousness?*

    ___ Nervousness is a sign of a poorly adjusted personality.

—— The new employee has been smoking or drinking too heavily.

—— It is usually the result of the desire to please. Often the best workers are overanxious at first.

—— He should take something to quiet his nerves.

7. *What should be your attitude toward selfishness in an employee?*

—— It is an indication of weak character.

—— It is rare among workers and can be ignored.

—— The selfish employee thinks only of himself and cannot fit into a group.

—— It is common and can be directed to the mutual interest of the worker and the company.

8. *How are you going to develop a thorough understanding of people?*

—— Consider everybody alike, according to a pat formula.

—— Study each worker individually, according to his personality and background.

—— Simply conclude that you cannot understand people, human nature being what it is.

—— Reprimand them regularly and observe their reactions.

9. *How can you get people to discuss their problems with you?*

—— Tell them you are an authority on human nature.

—— Impress them with the reasons for your success.

—— Show a genuine interest in your people, so they will be glad to talk with you.

—— Take them to lunch and ask a lot of personal questions.

10. *How can you develop emotional stability?*

—— Pass irritating problems on to others and be nonchalant.

—— Blow off steam at every opportunity.

—— Learn to welcome the challenge of every new or difficult situation.

—— Turn aside from problems and keep busy with easy routines.

11. *When your reactions to other people are unpleasant or unfavorable, what should you do?*

—— Keep your feelings hidden; try to find better characteristics in these people.

—— Give vent to your feelings, but only to your friends.

—— Try to ignore people you do not like.

—— Conclude that all people are alike and not worth your consideration.

12. *How should you handle the employee whose complaint is not justified?*

—— Save his face and carefully explain all the facts.

—— Tell him he is wrong and should know better.

—— Tell other workers what a "dope" he is.

—— Get him out of the department before he is a disturbing influence.

16 ■ PERSONALITY
FOR BUSINESS LIFE

— — — — — — — — — — — —

WHAT THIS CHAPTER IS ABOUT

1 ■ What Personality Is and Its Value

A worker may have a "pleasing personality" and yet be fired because part of his personality is a handicap in his work. This was the case with John R., an expert accountant who could add like lightning in his head. He was handsome—and knew it—dressed like a fashion plate, was popular with everyone in the office, and had worlds of tact. The men called him "The Ambassador," and girls sighed when they looked at him. At office parties, he was their favorite master of ceremonies and was always performing new card tricks at lunch hour.

Yet John R. was let out when the accounting department was reorganized. A meek little man with thick glasses was made head accountant. John R.'s popularity had made him so satisfied with himself that he neglected to keep up in his field. He failed to study changes in tax laws that affected accounting. He went to social parties and entertained with card tricks instead of going to meetings of the accountants' society. He could figure so rapidly in his head he thought it a waste of time to learn machine accounting methods. The man everyone liked was let out because he liked himself too well.

Pleasingness is only a part of personality. John R. had plenty of pleasingness, but he neglected to cultivate other parts of his personality, such as ambition, initiative, co-operation, responsibility, diligence.

Personality is your style of life. John R. had a good-fellow and playboy style. The new head accountant's style was that of a serious businessman.

John R. had as much ability for accounting as the new head of the department, but his style of life did not make full use of his ability for the company.

Style of life has a great deal to do with holding a job and getting promotion. H. Chandler Hunt, veteran business educator, studied reasons for discharge among the office workers of seventy-six companies. Reports on 4,000 discharged workers showed that only 10 per cent were released because they were unable to do typewriting, bookkeeping, and shorthand well enough.

The remaining 90 per cent were taken off the payrolls because of wrong personality characteristics. They had such habits as carelessness, lack of co-operation, dishonesty, no initiative, discourtesy, self-satisfaction, and trouble getting along with others.

Psychologists have made more than fifty definitions of personality. Some definitions emphasize *the effect a person has on others*—his value as a stimulus for winning co-operation, friendship, confidence, and such. Other definitions emphasize the organization or balance of personal qualities to give *co-operation in one's own mental life*. This is personality hygiene, how a person's characteristics tend to pull together or fall apart. A personality is not put together well when a grown woman uses baby talk, or when a man has a world of ambition but will not apply himself

Why they were not promoted

Personality is important in promotions in the offices of these seventy-six companies.

Per cent

Because of personality   For lack of skill
and character

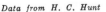

Data from H. C. Hunt

to achieve it. Later, you will learn many practical points about personality hygiene.

Training to get ahead in the world obviously should include personality training. Fortunately, personality can be improved. Charm, popularity, glamour—these are only a small part of personality. There is much more to our style of life than the impression made on others. Personality shows itself even when there are no people around to impress. But let's start the study of personality with external impressions, which are recognized easily.

2 ■ *Personality in Walking*

Each person has many characteristic little ways of doing things. Some of the characteristics may not be conspicuous; but add them all together, big and little, and you have personality.

Sometimes, it is one of the seemingly little qualities, such as a tiny chip on the shoulder, that causes job trouble, or apparently little qualities may be steppingstones to success. Such was the case with Stanley C. Allyn, twenty-two-year-old accountant with the National Cash Register Company. One day, the president heard him walking past his sanctum. "Bring that young man in here," he said to a secretary, "I want to know him. A fellow who walks like that is bound to get somewhere." Allyn did get somewhere; at forty-nine, he became president of the company.

Just about all our actions are expressions of deeper personality forces. Walk can show confidence or timidity, carelessness or preciseness, enthusiasm or laziness. The following entertaining classification has been reported by *Today's Health*, a publication of the American Medical Association.

"The Waddle," with the toes turned out
"The Mince," where the toe comes down first instead of the heel
"The Bounce," where the walker rises on his toes
"The Pound," where heels are slammed down firmly
"The Rocking Chair," where the walker rocks back and forth with each step
"The Peer," when the head is stuck ahead of the body
"The Kangaroo," when the person walks in a good position to be spanked
"The Roller Skate," with short steps and arms held close to the body
"The Jumping Jack," who raises his knees too much
"The Hip Switch," when the hips move more than the feet

The right way to walk, say physicians, is with shoulders, trunk, and hips in a straight line, head held back slightly, arms swinging slightly, and feet pointing pretty much straight ahead. High-heeled or uncomfortable shoes, or other uncomfortable clothing, may cause a person to walk in a funny fashion until it becomes a habit.

Long-legged people are likely to acquire a mincing walk, since they take short steps to keep step with average-height persons. And short people often are just the opposite, taking steps that stretch them too much. Overweight also changes a person's walk.

Style of walking is so characteristic of many people that they can be identified by the sound of their footsteps. Listen for the steps of people you know.

Experiment by walking as if you felt sure of yourself, as if you were all business, and note whether the new style of walk makes a difference in the attitudes of others and in the way you feel toward yourself.

3 ■ Clothes and Personality

Customers approach the neatly dressed salesperson, not the sloppy one. The employment manager favors the applicant who is dressed in average style, not flashy. Clothes are important in the first impression you make. First impressions are often wrong, but they are likely to be lasting and to produce permanent prejudices.

Clothes are more than a superficial part of personality, however. Personal appearance expresses the individual's wishes. The clothes a person selects usually indicate the image he has of what he would like to be. There is considerable make-believe in selecting clothes, like the small boy who dresses up to play cowboy. Grownups, too, imagine a role they would like to play and then dress for the role. The young executive, conscious of his youthfulness, selects clothes suitable for an older man of distinction. The older man, regretfully conscious of his age, may shift to snappy suits more suitable for a college boy.

In one small office, individual tastes in clothes were so marked that it served as a basis for nicknames. One man was called "Deacon," one "Tex," one "Colonel," another "Frenchy." And the 300-pounder whose clothes were so tight that the buttons popped, of course, was called "Tiny." By the nicknames, you can picture how each dressed. And each man felt flattered by his nickname, for it conveyed the impression he wanted to make.

In a large hotel office, there were the following behind-the-back nicknames, based on clothes: "Mrs. Astorbilt" for the girl who overdressed and wore too much cheap jewelry; "Merry Christmas" for the one who decorated herself with red and green bows and puckers; "Babe" for the elderly woman who dressed in girlish clothes and used too much make-up; "Squire" for the one who always wore mannish, tailored tweed suits, flat heels, and a four-in-hand tie; "Sweet Sue" for the plainly dressed girl who used practically no cosmetics (she was the most popular in the office and the first married); and "Dynamite" for the one who wore revealing clothes, and summer and winter wrapped herself in furs that reeked of heavy perfume.

Personality Qualities That Affect

the Value of College Graduates

in Business

Score
Value

94 Is exceptionally fair and square.

92 Seeks and does additional tasks beyond those required.

84 Is respected by almost everyone.

80 Can stand criticism without feeling hurt.

76 Makes people feel at ease during conversation.

74 Is usually pleasant and cheerful.

72 Mixes easily.

70 Is likable.

68 Willingly conforms with regulations

60 Seems to enjoy authority.

56 Is very outspoken.

54 Is somewhat reserved.

50 Stays in the background.

46 Expects too much from others.

40 Is frequently embarrassed and flustered.

34 Dodges responsibility

30 Is very selfish.

24 Is always discontented.

22 Is unco-operative.

14 Is a chronic slacker.

Data from Dr. Richard S. Uhrbrock

Look also at the check list on page 8.

Selection of clothes gives clues to the motives of individual personalities. People tend to dress for the roles they wish they could play in life, not always for the parts they have to play. Sometimes, they dress for a role that is not best for the job. Unusual taste in clothes may reveal what you want to be, not what you are. Unfulfilled primary interests are often a factor.

A food packager learned the importance of appearance in building attitudes among his employees. Cleanliness being important, the girls were provided daily with clean gingham allover aprons. These garments were clean, but in all stages of fading; and they were cut in a Mother Hubbard style. The girls hated those shapeless, dingy work clothes, hated the company, and sometimes acted as if they hated themselves.

A change of work garments was suggested. Five girls were selected to serve as a style committee to design a new uniform. The committee was selected one noon hour by lot; the manager of a near-by movie theater drew names from a hat. He knew more about tickets than clothes, but his presence gave a Hollywood note to the committee. A stylist from the leading department store acted as style consultant to the committee, adding more glamour to the plan.

The committee decided on a dress that was a modification of a nurse's uniform—revealing the role they would like to play. Two large concealed pockets also were suggested, something that had never occurred to the management as important. The Monday the girls first wore the new uniforms was a glorious day for them. They were changed personalities.

And there was something besides the changes in personal appearance that helped change their personalities. This was the democratic, permissive way the boss encouraged them to decide on the new uniforms themselves. The boss was an equalitarian. The girls acquired a little more self-esteem, friendliness, and confident hopefulness by participating in the decision that was important to them.

4 ▪ Facial Appearance and Personality

Facial appearance for most of us is a minor part of personality. But it becomes a major item when the appearance is either unusually attractive or unusually homely. Here is how those extremes are likely to affect personality.

The girl with a baby-doll face and the boy who looks like the collar advertisements are likely to be treated by their parents in ways that make the youngsters feel pretty well satisfied with themselves. They catch their parents' pride, become proud of their good looks, and have little motivation to use their abilities as a way of accomplishment. So, they act as if their mere presence in a company is sufficient to merit a pay check.

But with the homely youngster, who knows he is homely because others tell him so, the situation is quite different. His motives are aroused to accomplish things, for he knows he cannot coast through life on good looks. Thus, homeliness becomes an asset when it stimulates one, perhaps in desperation, to develop virtues that make others see beauty where a camera would record only plainness.

A homely eleven-year-old lad in southern Indiana became the most familiar face in America. His face is still one of the best known—and loved—in the world. Homely, yes, but attractive and good-looking for what we know about his ways.

Dr. G. Stanley Hall, the psychologist, wrote that Lincoln's "long limbs, rough exterior and frequent feeling of awkwardness made him realize early in life that he must cultivate mental or moral traits which it is so hard for a handsome man or woman to excel in. If Lincoln had been a handsome man, he would have been a very different one."

The qualities Lincoln cultivated made those who knew him think of him as good-looking. Strangers might think him a caricature; but those who knew him, never.

It is an old saying, "Handsome is as handsome does." Lincoln did handsome. He told one of his White House advisers: "Every man over forty is responsible for his face."

It was much the same situation with another famous occupant of the White House. This was the wife of a handsome President. During the Roosevelts' years in the White House, their opponents warned: "Stay away from Eleanor—she'll charm you to their side regardless of your better judgment." Her personality outshone mere beauty.

Plainness can be a steppingstone to personal magnetism. Cultivate the magnetism of always making people feel right. An attitude of bitterness or hostility makes faces ugly. Attitudes of friendliness and sweetness make homely faces attractive.

5 ▪ Judging Personality by Appearance

Appearances are often misleading. This is bound to be true, since a person's appearance may represent what he wishes he were like, not what he actually is. But, in addition, most personality characteristics are specific, not generalized.

The neat dresser will not necessarily be neat in his work. Thomas A. Edison dressed in loose clothes mostly for comfort and was oblivious to stains and wrinkles. But he was meticulously neat in his writing and experimental work. While it is natural to assume that the careless dresser also will be a careless worker, facts do not bear out this assumption. Since most people believe a neat appearance means neatness in other ways, it is still wise to be neat in appearance.

People do not have generalized personality traits of accuracy, punctuality, and so on. These traits are highly specific. A girl may be punctual on a date, but not in her work. The executive may be accurate in arithmetic, but not in spelling. The same executive may be pleasant with customers, but not with employees.

Some underlying personality trends are indicated by different styles of wearing clothes, but it takes a couple of expert psychologists to figure the significance of individual cases. People often dress sloppily, for instance, because of miserliness or regression. They may wear out-of-fashion clothes because of a stubborn streak. They may wear flashy clothes because they crave attention. But these are guesses that would have to be confirmed by further analysis in each individual case.

Personal appearance is valuable for its own sake, particularly for those who meet the public, and for those who need a little more self-confidence. The person who is conscious that his clothes are appropriate and neat will have less bother with self-consciousness. Unsuitable clothes may make a person feel like the man who dreamed that he was clad in his night-shirt and trying to hide from churchgoers on Easter Sunday.

6 ■ There Are Many "Best" Personalities

Individuals who have widely divergent personalities still are able to make good in the same work. Marshall Field and John Wanamaker are excellent examples of this. Both were self-made merchant princes, but there the resemblance almost ended. Some of the ways in which they were different are:

Marshall Field	John Wanamaker
aloof	friendly
critical	sympathetic
slow-moving	rapid-moving
stingy	generous
shy	not shy
no sense of humor	good sense of humor
hard on workers	helpful to workers

But underneath those differences, they had many characteristics in common. Both were hard workers and tended strictly to business—yes, those are part of personality. Both were careful and accurate. They emphasized quality in merchandise and work. They kept eagle eyes on expenses and insisted that goods be sold at fair prices. They made decisions promptly and kept up with their work.

Neither drank nor gambled nor "ran around" with women. Both were intensely ambitious and exerted themselves to achieve their ambitions. The characteristics in which they differed were parts of their personalities that related more to personal popularity than to business achievement.

People often accuse those whom they do not like of having "poor personalities" and praise the "good personalities" of those they like. Or someone says Hank has lots of personality but poor Herrold has little. Psychologists cannot agree with these common judgments, for personality includes so much that it is meaningless to call one good and another poor. "Good" and "poor" are judgments of value, not scientific descriptions of personality. They reveal more about the person who calls another "a weak personality" than about the one who is supposed to have the weak personality.

READ CAREFULLY FIRST: Read both sides of the description and then circle the one number which best shows where this man stands. If he leans extremely to the left, circle the "1"—if he leans extremely to the right, circle the "10," or circle any number in between which best shows this man's standing on each point. Skip an item only if you cannot fairly make a decision.

	DOES HE LEAN THIS WAY?		OR (Average)		DOES HE LEAN THIS WAY?
A	Apt to take it easy. Seems to lack physical zip and pep.	1 2 3 4	5 6	7 8 9 10	Likes vigorous physical activity. Full of zip and pep.
B	Inclined to make fast decisions. Acts on spur of the moment. May leap before he looks.	1 2 3 4	5 6	7 8 9 10	Tends to be slow on decisions. Considers all sides. Overly cautious and serious-minded.
C	Inclined to take the lead in any group. Over-anxious to boss others.	1 2 3 4	5 6	7 8 9 10	Likes to stay in the background in groups. Inclined to let others take the lead.
D	Reserved and quiet, usually prefers to be alone, or to work by himself. Tends to be shy.	1 2 3 4	5 6	7 8 9 10	Extremely sociable and friendly. Likes to have people around him constantly. Does not hold back with others.
E	Inclined to be moody—easily discouraged—excitable or "up and down."	1 2 3 4	5 6	7 8 9 10	Optimistic and cheerful outlook. Calm, unruffled disposition.
F	Tends to be touchy. Has to be handled carefully. Apt to take things personally and to resent criticism.	1 2 3 4	5 6	7 8 9 10	Faces facts. Is not touchy and can take criticism. Hard to "get his goat." Likes "call a spade a spade" attitude.

		1 2 3 4	5 6	7 8 9 10	
G	Agrees with others too easily. Gives in to them. Not apt to stand up for his own ideas.	1 2 3 4	5 6	7 8 9 10	Does not agree with others readily enough. Apt to insist on own way, and to argue for own point of view. Inclined to be bossy.
H	Critical-minded. Sees faults and defects in people and things. Apt to be hard to please.	1 2 3 4	5 6	7 8 9 10	Not at all critical. Takes people and things as they come. Seems to be easily satisfied.
I	Poised, self-confident, not easily irritated or annoyed.	1 2 3 4	5 6	7 8 9 10	Tends to worry and to have doubts about himself. Tends to be irritable and jumpy.
J	Tough-minded toward others. Not considerate and sympathetic. Tends toward hard-boiled side.	1 2 3 4	5 6	7 8 9 10	Extremely considerate and sympathetic toward others, tends to be tenderhearted.
K	Grasps new ideas quickly. Learns fast. Sees into things easily.	1 2 3 4	5 6	7 8 9 10	Slower on grasping new ideas. Gets ideas but takes longer to do so.

COMMENTS: (In this space add any remarks or comments which will give a better or more accurate picture of this man.)

STRONG POINTS

WEAK POINTS

Rating scale for personality qualities.

Courtesy Glenn E. Mitchell, Kroger Co.

Apparently, any personality is suitable for business if it includes enough of the characteristics that help an individual make good in the world—and if it does not go to extremes in some characteristics. The golden mean—the path of wisdom and safety between extremes—should guide individual personality development. There is a tendency to overdo or overcorrect when a person is trying to improve his personality. Thus, when he tries to smile more, he tries so hard that he goes around grinning like a Cheshire cat. To the psychologist and psychiatrist, the best personality is the one that avoids extremes. This is the *rule of moderation*.

Dr. G. Stanley Hall, who started the psychological laboratory at Johns Hopkins University and later was the first president of Clark University, formulated a set of *goals for personality development*, which are widely cited. Here they are.

> *Second breath*—experience mental exaltation and inspiration when tackling a job or life itself.
>
> *Mobility in emotions*—feel pleasure and sorrow, and all degrees and kinds of emotions. (Schizoids do not do this; cycloids go to extremes.)
>
> *Sympathy*—feel with others, as the person-centered individual does.
>
> *Love of nature*—learn about nature, including human nature, for a fuller understanding of life.
>
> *Sublimation*—transform animal inclinations into actions of social and religious value, as anger into righteous indignation.
>
> *Loyalty*—subordinate self to a larger cause, and keep conscience clear.

7 ■ How Personality Is Formed

The attitudes that dominate personality and the role an individual has picked to play usually are apparent before high school is completed. It does not take an expert to tell by then that some people are friendly, others are aloof; that some are ambitious, others are self-satisfied; that some enjoy people, others prefer their own company; that some are generous, others stingy; and some are stubborn, others are submissive as lambs.

Early experiences have been found to be of considerable importance in heading personality in one direction or the other. Extreme stinginess has often been found to be the result of skimpy feeding as a babe in arms or of too early weaning. Many other people are molded into the happy-go-lucky groove before they can talk.

The authoritarian personality seems to start from early experiences with a stern father who "ruled the roost" and made the children "knuckle under."

Other childhood experiences may cause the personality to shift this way or that during grade-school years. But, during the later teen years, the personality that will likely predominate in later life can usually be forecast. Two factors make this forecasting possible.

Pity Poor Pete.

Pete feels that the whole world is against him. No matter how hard he tries, he can't seem to please his mother. Unless mother changes her ways, Pete may become a weak, submissive, anxiety-ridden man. Or perhaps even worse, he may develop into an aggressive threat to society.

Courtesy Connecticut Mutual Life Insurance Co.

Factors forecasting personality. For one, each individual has most practice in his own characteristic ways of thinking and acting. The carefree person has steady practice being carefree and little practice being serious. By the time a person is twenty-five, he is usually just as he was at twenty, only a little more so. And, at thirty-five, he will be still more so. That is the way practice (which is usually accidental) makes little differences into big ones—and why it is desirable to have early practice in the more helpful qualities.

Neglect is the other factor that makes personality gel firmly. People learn trades or study for professions, but they overlook practice of personality habits to help them make good in the selected trade or profession. Most adult personalities are not the result of self-guidance. Sometimes, they seem to be bad accidents.

Personality can be an accomplishment, not an accident. Many of its ingredients can be increased by intentional practice, though some characteristics are resistant to change. Those that are hardest to change are the habits that have had too much practice or are expressions of unconscious motives.

Principles for reshaping personality. Here are some principles to follow in reshaping personality characteristics.

It is easier to add new qualities than to lose undesirable ones. The best results are obtained when you try first to form new habits or attitudes. Focus on the positive rather than on the negative; add rather than take away. As desirable new habits are emphasized, they displace old ones. This is an example of the law of use, and the law of lack of use. Using the new habit strengthens the new; not using the old habit weakens the old.

In addition, some personality habits are diametrically opposed. They are ambivalent; thus, when one is added, it crowds out its opposite. As an example, when you intentionally try to become considerate and thoughtful of others, this new habit inhibits any former blunt and outspoken impulses. It is easier to replace than to suppress.

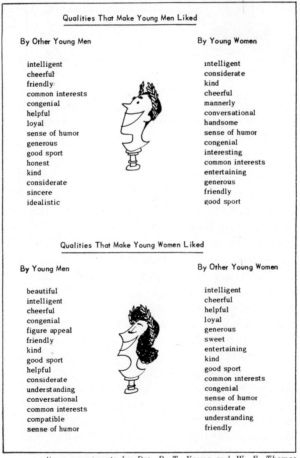

Qualities That Make Young Men Liked

By Other Young Men	By Young Women
intelligent	intelligent
cheerful	considerate
friendly	kind
common interests	cheerful
congenial	mannerly
helpful	conversational
loyal	handsome
sense of humor	sense of humor
generous	congenial
good sport	interesting
honest	common interests
kind	entertaining
considerate	generous
sincere	friendly
idealistic	good sport

Qualities That Make Young Women Liked

By Young Men	By Other Young Women
beautiful	intelligent
intelligent	cheerful
cheerful	helpful
congenial	loyal
figure appeal	generous
friendly	sweet
kind	entertaining
good sport	kind
helpful	good sport
considerate	common interests
understanding	congenial
conversational	sense of humor
common interests	considerate
compatible	understanding
sense of humor	friendly

From experiments by Drs. P. T. Young and W. F. Thomas

Some targets to aim at. The most frequently given likes are at the top of each list, the least frequent at the bottom.

A successful personality is aided if you *associate with people whose personalities are worth imitating.* Or read about great personalities, as Leroy Wilson did to help his climb to the presidency of American Telephone & Telegraph Company.

When looking for a job, especially the first job, pick a boss whose personality is worth imitating.

Find a hero to imitate—don't imagine you are a hero yourself. Admiration of someone else is good for personality development. There is inspiration from making friends with great people, if only by meeting them in books. It enhances your own personality to include great persons as part of yourself.

"Show me the man you honor, and I will know what kind of man you are, for it shows what your ideal of manhood is, and what kind of man you long to be." Those are Carlyle's words.

8 ■ Personality Adjustment on a New Job

Floundering around on your first job as you try to "find yourself" is more or less expected. Yet it is both undesirable and unnecessary.

When you leave home or school to go to work, a strange new world is entered. A changed way of life is encountered that puts a strain on personality. Many old habits have to be changed and rugged independence must be altered, since there is interdependence in this new world and less opportunity for individual whims.

It takes time to grow used to new conditions. The American Telephone & Telegraph Company reports that it takes college graduates about five years to become acclimated to modern business conditions before they start to forge ahead.

Here are some changes in personality inclinations that must be made when you take your first job.

At Home or School	On the Job
Among friends and acquaintances	Among strangers
Most associates are your own age	Associates are older
Have groups of your own friends	Have to break into new groups
Move around at will	Confined
Work intermittently	Work steadily
Changes in work from day to day	Same old routine every day
Few hours of work	Longer hours of work
Vacations frequent	Vacations rare
Tardiness overlooked	Promptness essential
Quiet environment	Noisy, bustling surroundings
Grades every week or month	Don't know where you stand
Promoted at end of term	Promotions far apart
Close touch with parents and teachers	Supervised with less personal interest

At Home or School	On the Job
Usually may plan your own work	Others do the planning
Much work done alone	Mostly work with others
Study or play with persons you like	Work with persons whether liked or not
Talking back not dangerous	Back talk must be suppressed
More or less your own boss	Much less your own boss
Familiar work	Bewildering new work
Few rules	Many rules
Not much competition	Incessant competition

9 ▪ Initiating the New Worker

The most lonesome time of life may be the first few days on a job. Some companies recognize this and train their supervisors to give special attention to new workers, encourage them, help them get acquainted with others, and break the ice generally.

Established workers seldom go out of their way to extend a welcome to the newcomer. Established workers are clannish. In companies where morale is poor, they go out of their way to make life miserable for the new man.

Old-timers concoct practical jokes and foolish errands to help "initiate" the newcomer. Cliques already exist in the department, and the new worker is left out of these circles. Some old workers may even regard the employee as a potential rival, who may be after the old-timer's job. The new man who has technical training is apt to be given the cold shoulder by self-taught workers already on the job.

Some firms try to overcome the tendency of old employees to behave like inhuman beings by asking a popular worker to act as sponsor, as big brother or big sister, to show the new worker the ropes and help him get acquainted.

The new employee himself can do much to ease his path and minimize the strain on his self-esteem the first few weeks; for example:

Be friendly, but not aggressively friendly.
Get acquainted with a few more people each day, keeping out of cliques.
Ask older workers for help and advice, and try not to excel them in any way.
Keep on guard for practical jokes, but try to enjoy any that trap you.
Expect it to be a slow process to know your fellow workers and be accepted by them.

10 ▪ Other Work Stresses on Personality

"Most occupations are social occupations, demanding skills in working with other people. Mental hygiene is not restricted to explosive emotional troubles, rather it is a normal part of the civilization we have today."

Those are the words of Dr. E. G. Williamson, of the University of Minnesota, when he spoke to counselors of the United States Veterans Administration.

Trouble shooting for personality strains is a large part of an executive's job. There is not only friction between people but also on people in modern business. New stresses arise daily. Some bosses do not notice these stresses, but the strains are there and reduce efficiency and warp personalities.

Big corporations are giving executives and supervisors special training, so that they may understand personality in action. But many medium-sized company executives, and those of one-man businesses, have to dig out this information for themselves. It is probably of more consequence in a small company, for one frustrated personality can upset, not just a department, but the entire organization. The individual worker, also, should know what may produce tension on his personality as he progresses on the job. Ignorance of tension-causing situations makes tensions worse.

Tension-causing situations. Here are some everyday tension-causing situations.

When a worker is promoted, tensions are caused all along the line. The one promoted usually is glad of the advancement, but he needs to be watched and helped, for he may (1) become overbearing, or (2) have

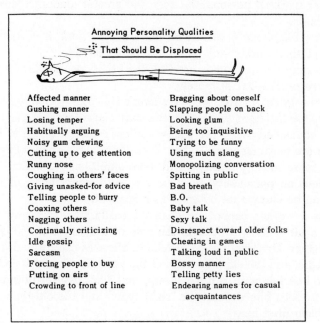

Annoying Personality Qualities That Should Be Displaced

Affected manner	Bragging about oneself
Gushing manner	Slapping people on back
Losing temper	Looking glum
Habitually arguing	Being too inquisitive
Noisy gum chewing	Trying to be funny
Cutting up to get attention	Using much slang
Runny nose	Monopolizing conversation
Coughing in others' faces	Spitting in public
Giving unasked-for advice	Bad breath
Telling people to hurry	B.O.
Coaxing others	Baby talk
Nagging others	Sexy talk
Continually criticizing	Disrespect toward older folks
Idle gossip	Cheating in games
Sarcasm	Talking loud in public
Forcing people to buy	Bossy manner
Putting on airs	Telling petty lies
Crowding to front of line	Endearing names for casual acquaintances

Taken from studies by Dr. Hulsey Cason

These characteristics annoy most people.

an attack of lack of confidence over the new responsibility. Tension also affects those who are not promoted, but think they should be. It also affects the security of those above the person promoted, for they begin to look on him as a comer who may get their jobs.

When a new model machine is given to one worker, those who continue to use the old model think that favoritism has been shown. Also, switching a worker to an older model machine strikes him as a comedown.

When an office worker is asked to help out in the shop, this seems like a demotion or punishment to him. It affects his family, too, for they are afraid that the prized white-collar status may be lost.

When a long-service employee is transferred to the night shift, he feels that he is being discriminated against, or is no longer considered the worker he used to be.

When workers are supervised too closely, when the boss seems to be breathing down their necks, they feel that they are not trusted, or even that they are slipping. Reprimands, sarcasm, pressure for production, all put tension on personality.

When a team of friends is separated, who have liked working together in the same room, they think that the change was deliberate.

When workers are changed from weekly to hourly pay rate, this too causes tension, even though the total take-home pay may be greater on the hourly basis. The prestige connected with a weekly pay rate may be better for workers' personalities than the greater amount received on an hourly basis.

When a telephone is placed on one worker's desk, it adds to the self-esteem of that worker but puts tensions on others.

When only one worker is greeted, the others are inclined to feel that they were overlooked purposely.

When a typist in the vice-president's office is promoted to private secretary for the head draftsman, this may cause tensions, for more prestige is connected with the vice-president's office. Stresses related to prestige are more frequent in the office than in the shop. Office workers may be more socially sensitive and more ambitious than shop workers.

Frictions on personality are on every hand, every hour, of every day. Many can be eliminated by good management.

When a worker cannot be changed easily, the company often can change a bit. This was done in the case of a thirty-five-year-old woman office worker, Dr. Arthur Weider relates. She was careful and painstaking in her work, and the carefree ways of the younger women irritated her. It was her first job with a large group, and her fussy criticism of others caused trouble. She was not the "right type," and the old-time supervisor would have fired her.

But the modern supervisor gave her special statistical work that required her painstaking accuracy. She was given also a secluded place to work, where the younger generation would not annoy her. By planning a way to make use of an undesirable personality quality, it became desirable and of advantage to the company.

There is much more to using personality in industry, however, than getting better output at lower cost. Said William Lyon Phelps, long-time teacher at Yale: "It is better to be an interesting personality than an efficient machine." But, if you do not adjust your personality to the stresses of life, you are neither an interesting personality nor an efficient machine.

— —

The Gist of the Chapter

1. What is personality, and how does it affect efficiency in business life?
2. How is style of walking related to personality?
3. Tell how clothes reveal a person's "secret" wishes.
4. What are the six most valued personality qualities Dr. Uhrbrock found in business life? the six at the bottom of the list?
5. Discuss facial beauty as a part of personality.
6. Explain Dr. Hall's six goals in personality development.
7. Tell how personality is usually formed and how the individual can go about changing it.
8. In what ways is one's personality under stress when starting on a new job?
9. After being on a job some time, what events may occur that put personality under strain again?

Things to Do and Problems to Discuss

1. The newspapers have columns on charm, etiquette, psychology, love advice. Follow these closely for a week and report on the points made in them that have a bearing on personality.
2. Consider some job with which you are acquainted. Figure out what personality changes, or characteristics, would be needed if the employee were promoted to the next higher job.
3. More than seventeen thousand words allude to personality qualities. List as many as you can think of in three minutes. Then count (a) those you listed that refer to pleasing qualities, and (b) those referring to unpleasant qualities. What is the significance of the one variety predominating?
4. You are hiring a receptionist. Think of two girls you know, and estimate their personality qualities from the lists in this chapter. Discuss which girl seems to have the personality more suited for this kind of work.
5. Think of someone you know who has lost a job. Analyze to what extent his personality qualities may have caused him to lose it. In what ways might

he have changed and not only kept the job but have qualified for promotion?

6. How can personality be shown over the telephone?

7. Collect some discarded business letters and judge how they differ in personality, such as "warm-cold," "friendly-hostile," etc. Try rewriting some so they have a more agreeable personality.

8. In what ways can one's style of driving an automobile indicate something about one's personality?

9. Refresh yourself on negative conditioning from earlier chapters, and show how that could be used to alter some undesirable personality qualities.

10. Effie K. and a friend came to work on a new job at the same time and have worked side by side. Now you want to promote the other girl. Discuss how you should handle this situation to prevent tensions on the emotional health of these erstwhile close friends.

11. Oswald J. is supervising a group of clerks, one of whom likes to play the role of clown and is always showing off. How could Oswald work through the clown's show-off streak to motivate him to play a more useful role?

12. What factors in your own personality may mislead you—halo effect, etc.—when estimating another person's personality qualities?

13. What points made in Chapters 13, 14, and 15 would affect personality?

14. Another employee in your department has blamed you, unjustifiably, for a poor job she did. How could you take this situation without excessive stress on your personality? If you were the boss, how would you handle it?

15. What is the difference between negativism and negative conditioning?

16. Discuss personality strains that might make people critical and fault-finding.

17 ■ A MATURE PERSONALITY
WITH LITTLE NERVOUS TENSION

― ― ― ― ― ― ― ― ― ― ― ― ― ― ― ― ―

WHAT THIS CHAPTER IS ABOUT

1. *Personality kinks in the hidden overhead*
2. *The need for personality maturity*
3. *Stages in personality development*
4. *Attitudes of maturity*
5. *Homesickness*
6. *Signs of nervous tension*
7. *Psychosomatics*
8. *The high-blood-pressure personality*
9. *The stomach-ulcer personality*
10. *The headache and heart personalities*
11. *A better personality by facing frustrations*

1 ■ Personality Kinks in the Hidden Overhead

"A major problem of our time," Dr. Franz Alexander told an audience of social-work executives, "is to produce socially minded, co-operative adults, without sacrificing individuality."

Business leaders have become deeply concerned over this problem. They have seen too much evidence of the hidden costs of personality stresses and strains in business. Some of these costs are:

The premature retirement of valued employees because of high blood pressure, stomach ulcer, or other disabilities in which personality strain was a cause—what is known popularly as "nervous tension."

The upping of accident costs by negativistic, confused, hostile workers.

Labor turnover and absenteeism that are concentrated among workers who are put under stress by business life.

The restricted efficiency that is often a symptom of hostile or immature personalities.

The "going to pieces" of workers when they are given responsibility.

Poor morale and at times labor trouble that center around employees or groups who are out of step with reality.

Vandalism, embezzlement, and similar "business crimes," which usually involve a warped personality.

Are personality kinks common in business?

Dr. V. V. Anderson, in an eastern department store of 1,200 employees, found that 19 per cent of the salespeople and 23 per cent of the office employees had kinks that were serious enough to interfere with their business usefulness.

Many later surveys in other companies have confirmed the general finding: About one worker out of five has some personality characteristics that are adding to the hidden overhead of business.

But we should emphasize another aspect of this situation: About one worker out of five would get much more out of work and life if he could make some adjustments in his personality.

Are executives immune from these kinks? The percentage is about the same. But the consequences are sometimes worse—the executive often sets the human climate for the business; and his actions affect large numbers of people, both in and out of the firm.

Such facts have led many firms to set up special programs for ironing out personality kinks wherever possible. The following chart shows the mental-hygiene program in one firm. As you study the chart, you will be impressed with the wide scope of this work.

The old-time "efficiency expert" thought in terms of such things as brighter lighting and posture chairs—tangible things. The modern leader has seen that tangible improvements bring no actual improvement if the supervisor still barks orders at the girls and keeps them on pins and needles wondering what he will fling at them next.

The tangible features can be altered quickly. But it takes time, patience,

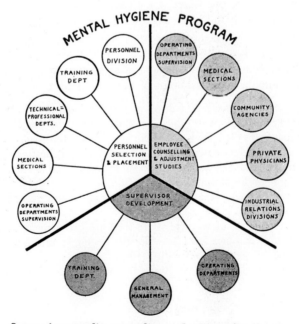

Scope of personality counseling at the Caterpillar Tractor Company.

and high strategy to change the human atmosphere that puts a ceiling on the benefits from the tangible improvements. We shall learn more about ways to improve the human climate in the chapters on leadership. To get an understanding first of what the individual can do to adjust to business, we can start with the topic of personality maturity.

2 ■ The Need for Personality Maturity

Philip has a good job. He is the best dresser in the office. He does the work expected of him, but no more. He never offers to help anyone. A few people in the office, who are of another religion, he definitely avoids, and he is choosy about his friends. The boss says Philip is a good worker, has plenty of ability for the job, but does not seem to be promotional material—for some reason.

That reason is obvious when we learn about Philip's home life. He was raised by a widowed mother, who wanted her boy to have as happy a childhood as any boy with a father. She skimped on herself so that he could have good clothes, good times, and treats. She worked so that he could go through business school and be qualified for "a high-class job."

After Philip landed that high-class job, the mother hinted that he should help pay household expenses. That made him lose his temper. For a week afterward he sulked. His money still goes for clothes and for good times with the group of young fellows with whom he spends every evening. None of his money is spent on girls, and he saves none. When a salesman tried to talk him into taking insurance, Philip just laughed at him. Sometimes he grumbles about the unfairness of things because he cannot afford an automobile.

Philip is old enough to vote, but his emotional development halted in his early teens. That is the "some reason" why he does not seem like promotional material to the boss. Philip is a man in age and size but is still boyish in his personality. Someday he may accept responsibility, plan for the future, and be less self-centered. If his emotional attitudes ever grow to man-size proportions, he will be good promotional material, since he has real ability.

If he does not become man-size in his attitudes, he will likely never advance much. Then, the now rather likable chap may become a crabby, faultfinding fellow who hates the world and himself. It takes grown-up attitudes to get along in a world of grownups. Yet many adults are all mixed up and confused, and their personalities start to fall apart, because something has kept them from growing up in their emotions.

3 ■ Stages in Personality Development

For convenience, growing up in personality, from birth to maturity, is divided here into ten stages, with thumbnail sketches of each stage.

You will recognize these stages if you look back on your own life—and if you have passed through them successfully. But you will find some adults around you who continue to linger in some of these stages.

1. Stage of dependence. Everyone starts life completely dependent on others. A few are never weaned entirely from this dependence and always have to lean on others. Philip thought his mother still owed him a living. Other grown-up persons think their parents should make major decisions for them.

2. Stage of comfort and eating. The chief interest during the first couple of years of life is bodily comfort and food. How you yelled if you were uncomfortable or hungry! A few grownups still think comfort is the most important thing in life and fret like children at slight discomforts.

3. Stage of impulsiveness. When you began to toddle around and explore your childhood world, you became bewildered. Your parents praised you when you took your first steps; but, when you tried this new walking by yourself on the street, your parents scolded. You did not understand the change from praise to punishment for walking. Many other things were puzzling and confusing in your little world. The child mind could not figure this out. Some children decide to follow their own impulses instead of the parent's warning. The child acts first and thinks later. So do adults who have not outgrown childish impulsiveness.

Courtesy Connecticut Mutual Life Insurance Co.

Petty Dictator—Stage of low boiling point.

Courtesy Connecticut Mutual Life Insurance Co.

Sitdown Strike—Stage of stubbornness.

4. Show-off stage. Shortly after you learned to walk and to pick up things and throw them around, you became enthusiastic about learning to handle your muscles and liked to get attention by showing off the things you could do. "Watch me!" you exclaimed. If no one watched, you probably made yourself obnoxious until someone did. This show-off streak is normal in childhood.

Philip has not outgrown it yet. That is why he is prouder of his clothes than of his work. Clothes are his way of making people, even strangers, notice him.

5. Stage of low boiling point. About the time you are a three-year-old show-off, your parents begin to worry about the mischief you get into. They are always stopping you just as you are doing the most interesting things, such as putting crackers end to end on the living-room floor. You don't like being interrupted, and you get your spunk up. You get mad as a hornet and stamp, scream, and try to bite.

Some people go through life with a low boiling point, sulking when told to do something, losing temper at little things, and trying always to get even with others.

6. Stage of stubbornness. You found that as a child you were too small to win by physical strength. But you could be stubborn and thus corner your parents. They won't let you do what you want—very well, you won't do what *they* want. Better yet, you'll do the exact opposite of what they want! So, you become negativistic, or contrariwise—doing it quite naturally through ambivalence. If your parents handled you wrongly during this contrary stage, it may have become a permanent habit, and you go through life feeling "won't" every time you are told to do something.

Philip did not have this habit, because his mother never forced him to do anything he did not want to do. But some adults have lost an eye because they were too stubborn to wear goggles for protection, just because the boss said "you must wear them."

7. Stage of inferiority and gullibility. Starting school is a terrifying experience to some children. There are so many new people, and getting along with some of them is unpleasant. The teacher made you do things that taxed your ability. And there was always some child who did things better than others. Some children teased you, and some may have hit you. Perhaps you began to feel insecure and to lose confidence in yourself. Teacher seemed to know so much that you believed everything she told you.

Some people never grow out of this early school stage of feeling inferior and being gullible. They lack confidence in themselves, and consult fortunetellers or allow superstitions to make their decisions.

Philip did not seem to feel inferior; in fact, he seemed very well satisfied with himself. But he was gullible in being a sucker for fads and in not thinking for himself.

8. Gang stage. Toward the end of grade school, boys begin to form boys' clubs, and the girls form girls' clubs. These mutual-admiration clubs are part of the gang stage. The individual begins to co-operate with a group. A few will not sacrifice their self-interest for the fun of the gang, unless they can be "chief." As adults, some remain lone wolves, some still want to be chief, some are still in the childhood gang stage.

Philip had not graduated from this stage. He and his friends formed a clique in the office. They admired one another and would not pull with the other employees.

9. Interest in the opposite sex. Sometime during high school years, another stage is entered. The gangs and clubs begin to break up, because many of the members develop more interest in the opposite sex than in their own sex.

Philip has not started this stage yet. Neither have some people, who married because "it was the thing to do," but get their real companionship with a small gang of the same sex in the club or tavern.

10. Mature independence. Late in high school years, or shortly after you start to work, the stage of mature independence is gradually entered. You plan ahead for a career, look forward to having your own family, provide for old age, and help your community by co-operating with large groups. You become a responsible citizen and individual. You work, co-operate, and do not go to extremes.

Courtesy Connecticut Mutual Life Insurance Co.

Stage of interest in opposite sex.

4 ▪ *Attitudes of Maturity*

Philip lacks emotional maturity because the earlier stages dominate in his life. He has not yet entered the last two. He still persists in the first stage, wanting others to take care of him. The world owes him a living, he feels. "I didn't ask to be born," he comments. Well, whoever heard of anyone who did?

Philip still prefers present comforts to future advantages. When his wishes are crossed, he sulks. He is centered in himself mostly, next in his gang, or the office clique. His co-operation with larger mixed groups and other workers is of the passive "Well, if I have to" sort.

Here are some earmarks of the mature personality.

He is *tolerant;* the immature cannot stand those who do not believe as he does, or who have different clothes or eat strange foods.

He *accepts responsibilities,* even seeks them.

He *thinks for himself;* he does not follow fads or buy on impulse. It is more difficult to sell him.

He is calm and exerts extra effort to *keep on an even keel* when necessary. If the other fellow gets mad or wants to argue, he smooths things over.

His work is *motivated by a long-range plan,* not by whims or the desires of each passing week. He saves to buy a home and does not use earnings for weekly payments on jewelry or a fur coat. He is more interested in the future than in the past.

He *does not show off* to bolster his self-confidence; he is not seeking the limelight.

He *can say "No" to himself* and make it stick.

He is understanding and *does not nurse grudges* or try to get even.

He tackles unpleasant tasks *without self-pity*, without feeling he is being picked on. If he is picked on, he does not let it bother him.

He can take orders *without becoming obstinate.*

He can *make up his mind* decisively without dillydallying, but not as an impulsive child.

He has *close friends of both sexes* and keeps his mind and talk free from vulgarity. His friendships are long-lasting.

He *admits his shortcomings,* but at the same time recognizes his strengths without being vain over them. He is not an alibi artist.

He *can take criticism* and profit from it, without sulking or hitting back.

He is weaned from dependence on his parents. He honors them, but *runs his own life.*

As we grow up, we constantly have to replace personality habits and emotional attitudes and acquire new ones. Outlook and attitudes have to be adapted to our age and place in life, or the place in life will remain childish.

Clowning is appropriate for a four-year-old who wants to gain attention, but not for a twenty-four-year-old.

Loyalty to a small gang of boys is appropriate for a thirteen-year-old, but not for the thirty-three-year-old who should be loyal to a larger and a mixed group.

The teen-ager may giggle at everything, be late, and follow fads, but not the mature person.

The body grows automatically without requiring any attention. But in the case of fully half of those who are growing up, the emotions need a little self-direction. When emotions do not grow up, the person is called infantile and maladjusted—out of step with what is appropriate for his years.

The average person can help his emotional development to a mature level by imitating mature models. Pick a hero who is about five years older, some person who is well regarded by everyone, who has a little better job than you have. Make that person a model to imitate. Don't envy the qualities he has; cultivate them for yourself. Stick to old friends, but lift yourself by raising your sights.

Some young people make the error of trying to imitate a successful person three times their age. That is too wide a gap. It is not appropriate for the twenty-year-old to take on the personality of a sixty-year-old grandfather. But it is appropriate for him to have the habits and outlook of a twenty-five-year-old married man who is going places in the world.

The sixtyish woman who dresses sweet-sixteenish and acts kittenish is fooling no one, not even herself. She has put her emotional development in reverse gear.

5 ■ Homesickness

It often is a strain on personality when one leaves home for work or school. Homesickness can be painful, not just for a fifteen-year-old away from home and friends for the first time but also for grown men who have not grown up emotionally. Big men can feel insecure and bewildered in the new city, or with the new company, and can become physically ill from homesickness. There are a few men who have had to give up good positions as branch managers because of nostalgia for the home town.

Colleges try to lessen homesickness among beginning students by having them come a week early, when the campus is not so crowded and confusing. Activities are planned so that the newcomers will be kept busy every minute, have fun, and get acquainted with others. And yet there are always 5 per cent, or so, who become so homesick that they have to make a special trip home.

New employees, especially from out of town, are likely to have similar periods of homesickness; and the razzing and practical jokes that old-timers play on beginners do not help. This slows up learning the new job and lowers morale.

It helps if the new worker is made well acquainted the first couple of hours with the small part of the plant or office where he will work. A hurried tour through a big plant will only make him more confused. It is better to show off the rest of the place to him after a couple of weeks on the job, when he is feeling at home.

A sponsor or "official best friend" also helps prevent lonesomeness in the new worker. A more mature worker—not just older, but emotionally mature and poised—is a real help in starting the new worker right. If the interviews have indicated that the new employee has been dependent on a parent, the best friend could be a fatherly sort of employee. But, if the interview revealed hostility toward the parent, as is the case in about one out of three, the sponsor should be an employee who is nearer the new worker's age.

In the case of a new woman employee, when interviews have shown hostility toward the mother, her sponsor—and her permanent supervisor—should be a man, not a woman.

The individual who plans to go away to school or to work should prepare himself for breaking home ties. A few weeks before leaving, take a few overnight trips to new places. Don't go with members of the family, and don't telephone home on arrival. Practice being friendly and getting acquainted with new people of the mature sort. Practice a little more independence and self-decision. Begin to look forward to the new location. Learn all about it from the library and chamber of commerce. Subscribe to the daily newspaper of the new location for a month or so before going there. Write the company in which you are interested and ask for copies of the employees' newspaper or magazine.

6 ■ Signs of Nervous Tension

"Nervous tension" should be put in quotation marks because it is not an exact term. Many different aspects of personality and emotional adjustment are included in it. These range from working too tensely to emotionally caused stomach ulcers or heart attacks.

There has probably always been nervous tension. But in our modern congested, competitive, interdependent, and ambitious world it is more handicapping than previously. In addition, specialists believe that modern conditions (the total situation) are such that nervous tensions have increased. Consider anxiety, or worry, as an example. Anxieties are a part of nervous tension and are often due to a strong motivation to be liked by others. We have already learned how this motivation has increased in the lonely crowd.

Frustrations of one kind or another are usually the cause of the tension. As we shall see in a moment, different kinds of frustrations precipitate different kinds of tensions. By and large, nervous tension is produced by frustrated ambitions, frustrated friendliness, frustrated self-esteem.

Tense people are sometimes described by their friends as "wound up too tightly." People who are wound up too tightly are anxious, restless, striving. Little troubles or small obstacles appear huge to them. They squander their energies by overdoing, and doing too often. They press down hard when they write and hold a pen with enough strength to lift a 10-pound weight. Their appetites are poor. They have trouble sleeping because they take their frustrations to bed with them.

They carry the germs of frustrations within them, since their desire for success is greater than their satisfaction with what success they have. Their frustrations are ever continuing.

These pent-up and continuing frustrations produce four groups of personality symptoms. Knowing these symptoms will help you understand people who are difficult to get along with, or who are centers of poor morale in a business.

Symptoms of frustration. Here are groups of personality symptoms in frustration.

Antagonism. Antagonism is a sure sign of frustrations. Attack and destructiveness are evidences of an effort to fight thwartings. Antagonism is the keynote in:

bullying	revengefulness
gossiping	rioting and mob behavior
bossiness	antisocial attitudes
sarcasm	chip-on-shoulder attitudes
nagging	

Childish responses to irritations. In these evidences of frustration, the person regresses to behavior that is more suitable for expressing a six-year-old child's emotions than those of an adult. Examples are:

tattling	weepiness
name calling	hotheadedness
horseplay	clique joining
pouting	suggestibility

Fixed habits. People with fixed habits persist in banging their heads against the same place in the wall. Rigidity rather than flexibility is their outstanding characteristic. They become set in their ways. They develop useless mannerisms and cling to strict routines. Their breakfast is always the same, eaten at just the same time, in the same old place. Any change from the breakfast routine ruins the day for them.

They seek security from frustration by trying to keep things unchanged. Though making a routine of life saves the trouble of making small decisions, it does not solve frustrations. This sort of frustrated person becomes a slave to needless details. As workers, they are steady as clockwork but are really inefficient, since they spend too much time in unproductive activities.

In the chapters on personal efficiency, we saw how systematized habits help us to remember, learn, and work. Fixed habits, however, may overdo the good accomplishments of systematized habits, for fixed habits are likely to cover little details that do not matter much—like the commuter whose day is ruined because he did not have his usual seat on the train.

People with fixed habits may be easy victims of petty criminals. The clerk who takes the money to the bank at the same minute every day, following the same path on each trip, makes it easy for a watchful crook. Break the routine, and make it difficult for the criminal who may be contemplating a robbery. Make the deposits at irregular times, and take various routes to the bank.

Break the routine, too, when you feel you are falling into fixed habits that serve no useful purpose. If you do not think you are a slave to many fixed habits already, just try ending your breakfast with fruit juice, rather than starting it with fruit juice. Or start the day with a cup of tea instead of coffee.

Giving up. This is another way some people react to their frustrations. Chronically unemployable people, who have given up hope and become resigned to living at low levels on charity, are examples. Externally, they may appear to be anything but tensed; but their withdrawing into hopelessness is an evasion that does not cure the inside tenseness. Whatever aspirations they may have had vanish, and they fail to substitute reasonable aspirations to take their places. They become careless, incompetent workers, dispirited and filled with self-pity. Trying to motivate them with offers of bonuses or by contests seldom works, for they are motivated negatively and give up in the face of frustrations.

They need to have some second-choice wishes or to make compromises with their aspirations rather than give them up.

7 ■ Psychosomatics

Psychosomatics is the study of the part the mind (psyche) plays in bodily (soma) functioning, especially bodily ailments. It is a booming new field for research by clinical psychologists and medical people. We shall give a few typical cases in which the role played by mental factors is clear-cut.

Emotional tensions start in the mind, but they have profound effects on the body.

You have noticed that when a person is angry his face flushes with blood and becomes pinkish. Anger also makes his stomach flush, and it may be the start of an ulcer. The angry person tightens his fists, and his arteries also tighten—this may be the beginning of high blood pressure.

You have also noticed that when people are frightened, their faces tend to become pale. So do their stomachs; digestion is harmed by fright. Pleasant table talk helps digestion; frightening talk makes the stomach heavy as lead.

Many vital processes are thus influenced by emotions. Blood pressure,

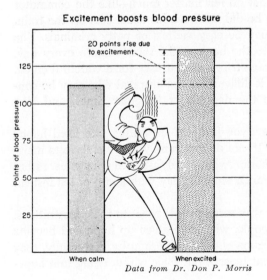

Excitement boosts blood pressure

20 points rise due to excitement

125

Points of blood pressure

100

75

50

25

When calm   When excited

Data from Dr. Don P. Morris

Average results of moderate excitement on twenty-six people.

heart rate, digestive movements, the flow of digestive juices—all are strongly affected by emotions. Everyone has noticed some of these bodily changes after an emotional outburst. Even mild emotions or moods or attitudes, when long continued, may produce serious bodily changes.

Researches in psychosomatics show that physical health may be influenced by personality health. Consider, for instance, that common ailment of businessmen—high blood pressure. It is responsible for half of all deaths of persons past fifty years of age.

8 ▪ The High-Blood-Pressure Personality

Edwin was a prosperous self-made businessman, successful as the world guesses at success. At fifty-four, he was top man in a large firm, owned by himself and three partners. They had built it from scratch. The partners did not get along smoothly with one another, but stuck together for business reasons. How they did argue with one another!

Edwin tried to be pleasant when the senior partner or a customer made suggestions to him. But inwardly he boiled. He would have trouble going to sleep that night because he was still brooding over the incident.

He began to have a buzzing noise in his ears, a few dizzy spells, and an occasional headache. His physician found it was high blood pressure and sent Edwin to an expert, who reported that it was due to emotional tensions. Edwin had started on the road to high blood pressure as a boy. He had been bossed too much by his parents and developed a hostile attitude toward being bossed.

An attitude of *resentment to authority is the keynote* of the personality that boils over and causes high blood pressure.

People who cannot stand being bossed are candidates for the high-blood-pressure squad. On the surface, they may be gentle, generous, model workers. But many calm-appearing people are seething inwardly. This misleads their friends to say, "I didn't think Edwin was the least bit nervous, isn't it awful!"

The fidgety, jumpy, high-strung, nail-biting, worrisome person shows his tenseness in outward behavior. But there are many who feel that way but conceal it. The hostile feelings suppressed for years gradually build up dangerous pressure in arteries and veins.

A domineering boss may arouse hostility in anyone and boost that person's blood pressure. But even a model boss may boost a worker's pressure if the worker has pent-up attitudes against being bossed. Such people feel intensely frustrated when told to do anything, no matter how mildly they are told. They can get along with anyone—except a boss. Some people realize that they cannot stand bossing without resentment; so they try to find work where they will not have a boss. But there are not enough boss-free jobs to go around.

People with high-blood-pressure personalities are hard workers, but hard work does not cause the trouble. The hard work is a symptom of the resentment—a sort of working off anger.

There are many physical causes of high blood pressure, which have nothing to do with emotions and personality. Kidney disease, hardening of the arteries, tumors, and other physical causes will make blood pressure shoot upward. Suppressed rage can make the disease worse when there are such physical causes. Suppressed rage also can cause the ailment when there is no physical cause.

9 ■ The Stomach-Ulcer Personality

Stomach ulcers also are common among business people. There are about a half million Americans with one of these. More men than women have ulcers. The death rate from ulcers is declining slightly, because ulcer patients now are being educated in the part that emotional flare-ups play in causing ulcers.

Resentment is a factor in causing ulcers, but a different kind of resentment than in high blood pressure. Blood-pressure resentment is toward being bossed; ulcer resentment is toward the world in general for not letting the individual be more of a success.

The ulcer personality is found in the person who craved more affection and approval than he received in childhood. The lack of affection gave him a feeling of failure. That feeling lingers on; and, as an adult, he works hard to be a success and often is successful. But the competitive spirit in modern business continually touches off his resentment toward the world in general.

He may try to increase his worldly success by playing tips on the stock market or horse races. For twenty or thirty years, he works diligently to be a success, not realizing that he is urged on by childhood lack of love and affection.

His underlying sourness against the world in general sours his stomach, just as grief or fear causes nervous indigestion in some persons. Those men—it is usually a man—live an ulcer pattern of life, which disturbs digestion. The pills they take for sour stomach do not change the sour attitudes; they can give only temporary physical relief.

After an emotional upset, the stomach may begin to digest itself in one place. That is the start of the ulcer. The ulcer grows worse or better as emotions go up or down. When stocks go up, the ulcer is better; when they go down, the ulcer flares up again. When success in any undertaking is threatened, ulcer is worse. When the man is bothered by guilty feelings about his hostile attitude toward others, ulcer is worse. But winning a golf game may help it a little.

Stomach ulcers notoriously come and go. This is because ulcer personalities have emotional ups and downs, as most of us do.

Ulcers need not be a price paid for success. But they are part of the price when a man tries to achieve success in the ulcer way.

Some ulcers start from physical causes, but many start from emotional indignation. Once an ulcer is started, medicine or surgery is needed. But, after medical care has cured an ulcer, another may be formed if the person persists in his ulcer personality.

Success does not cure the ulcer personality. The man needs the things he unconsciously hopes success will bring—affection and approval. The boss who never says a good word, who keeps employees guessing about whether or not they are approved, adds to their ulcer attitude. Competitions and contests between employees also add to the ulcer pattern of life.

10 ∎ The Headache and Heart Personalities

Headaches. Headaches are big business. Some eighty million dollars' worth of headache pills are sold in the United States each year. Some of these headaches come from eyestrain, sinus trouble, constipation, brain tumor, or other physical disorders. Some of them are merely social conveniences to get out of unwanted engagements. "Monday morning headache," when not due to an unwise week end, may be a symptom that the job is a headache.

Monday morning, social, and migraine headaches occur mostly among persons who have an inner reluctance to accept responsibility. Such persons were pampered and spoiled as children and object to leaving the family protection. This certainly was the case with Effie, the best typist in the office, who had severe headaches when she was promoted to the job of scheduling work. Headache pills did not relieve her aching head, but it was cured when she went back to typing, giving someone else the responsibility of scheduling. The headache personality is not so well understood or so clear-cut as the blood-pressure and ulcer personalities. But dreading responsibility usually is a large factor in it.

Heart trouble. Heart attacks—feeling the heart pound, or shortness of breath and wheezing—are often an anxiety or fear reaction. Some mothers develop spurious heart attacks when their children consider marrying or leaving home for other reasons. In these instances, the attack is just another way to dominate the children and is not really a heart ailment. The heart is healthy, but it is made to race and cut capers by the emotions.

Actual heart disease can be caused by emotions, since they constrict the coronary arteries, which supply the heart itself. This may produce excruciating anginal pains in the region of the heart. Many attacks of acute indigestion are in fact anginal attacks. With continued emotion, a serious blocking of the heart arteries sometimes results.

The coronary or anginal personality usually is a successful person who has striven mightily for success. He cannot bear to know that someone is better than he. This starts in childhood, when a boy makes himself competitive with his father and tries to excel him. As an adult, he keeps on trying to excel the foreman, the vice-president, or anyone above him. He takes bridge and golf lessons so that he will be the best player. This anxiety to excel cuts short many careers of brilliant promise.

Coronary deaths used to be mostly among men, but in recent decades they have been increasing among women. It is now something that the career girl, too, must watch in her personality.

Bodily health obviously depends not only on the care of the body but also on the care of a person's attitudes and personality. Mayo Clinic records show that more than half the patients who consult doctors have bodily ailments that are caused, or made worse, by their attitudes and emotions. Much lost time in business is due to emotions rather than to germs and diseased organs.

These emotionally caused disabilities actually are caused *in* the body, they are not imaginary. But they are caused *by* ideas and attitudes—the most powerful influences in your life. Always keep bodily conditions checked by a capable physician, but also keep your attitudes in check, so that you have the varieties that promote health rather than illness. And handle other people so that they, too, will have health-bringing attitudes.

11 ▪ A Better Personality by Facing Frustrations

Life and business are filled with frustrations. Being thwarted in many things we should like to do, or be, or have, is inevitable. But people who change their desires gracefully to what can be done, rather than grumble or fight over what cannot be changed, will have the least nervous tension.

Frustrations are handled more easily when you decide to tolerate them. This is an art many people have learned. Such people have good morale, come what may. They radiate poise and confidence. They inspire trust and friendship.

Dr. Daniel N. Wiener has found that frustrations are not so serious when they are recognized. He compared successful and unsuccessful salesmen as one instance. Both groups of salesmen had about the same kinds of frustrations. But the difference was this: The successful salesmen knew of their emotional problems; whereas the unsuccessful salesmen did not admit the existence of theirs. The successful salesmen, knowing and admitting their emotional problems, were better able to adjust their lives so that nervous tension did not develop.

Most frustrations can be solved easily. Lucky that it seems easy, for life is crammed with frustrations if you look for them. Frustrations caused by everyday environment are easier to eliminate than those carried inside the mind. Frustrations carried inside may be shown by hostility, suspiciousness, overweening ambition, or a striving for perfection. These are much harder to eliminate than frustrations caused by passing strains from the outside world.

The antagonisms of the gossip, the bully, and the domineering boss cause additional frustrations for these persons. When we frustrate others by attacking them, they are likely to frustrate us in return. Push them, they push back, as happens in family scraps and in arguments between capital and labor. The nagging boss is more gossiped about, and his workers are more inclined toward revengefulness.

People who are too strict with themselves expect too much from life; or their ambitions are too high and also keep winding them up. They create more frustrations for themselves daily and are their own bad enemies.

People who have good personality balance take life as it is. They may be regretful at times, but they adjust their aims and desires to reality without bitterness. On the other hand, a few people are motivated more by their frustrations than by the adjustment of their desires to reality. These have poor personality health. They fight back at frustrations and neglect to enjoy the good parts of their lives.

There should be a great deal of give-and-take in life. People who want mostly to take are easily frustrated. Most of life's frustrations can be solved by yielding a bit here and there. Antagonistic, childish, and rigid persons do not yield. Give-up persons yield too much. Strike a balance between getting and giving to help unwind any tensions you may have.

The more things we want, and the rarer they are, the more likely we are to be trapped by our wishes. Sweet wishes can turn life sour. It is good personality hygiene to have a lot of second choices and to become satisfied with them. A big step toward solving frustrations is made when you can say, as did Socrates: "How many things I can get along without!"

Dr. G. Stanley Hall's list of goals for personality development were given in Section 6 of the preceding chapter. We are now at a point where these can be supplemented by the following list, which was addressed to groups of parents and teachers by Brigadier General William C. Menninger, consultant to the Surgeon General of the United States Army.

Attributes of Emotional Health

Dealing constructively with reality—making successful compromises
Freedom from tensions and anxieties
Satisfaction from giving to others
Satisfactions from relations with others
Accepting frustrations for possible future gains
Profiting from experience
Shifting hostile feelings into creative and constructive channels—sublimation
The capacity to love

The Gist of the Chapter

1. List a half dozen examples of the way personality kinks add to the hidden overhead.

2. Outline the stages of personality development from infancy to adult maturity.

3. What are a dozen ways in which the mature personality is shown?

4. Discuss homesickness and methods of dealing with it.

5. Describe the four groups of personality symptoms resulting from frustrations.

6. What is psychosomatics?

7. Tell about the high-blood-pressure personality.

8. What are the causative attitudes of the stomach-ulcer personality?

9. Describe (a) the headache, and (b) heart personalities.

10. What is meant by facing frustrations, and how is it done?

11. List the attributes of emotional health given by Dr. William Menninger.

Things to Do and Problems to Discuss

1. What agencies are there in your locality where you could get suitable help for an employee who has nervous tension? Report on them.

2. Make some observations in the transition zone of your locality (cheap rooming-house section), and report what you note about the stage of personality development of people living there.

3. Analyze the advertisements in a popular magazine, and report on those that seem aimed at people with nervous tension or some psychosomatic complaint.

4. Compare a scandal sheet with the *New York Times,* or the *Christian Science Monitor.* (Most libraries have these papers.) Report on the indications that the scandal sheets are edited for emotionally immature readers. Report on a similar comparison of the *Atlantic Monthly* with some pulp or romance magazine.

5. List some things that frustrate you when they happen. What can you do about it to lessen the frustrated feeling?

6. Review the story of Patrick O., given in Chapter 1, and tie it in with the points in this chapter.

7. People with ulcer personalities have marked ups and downs in their moods. Review the material on cyclothymia in Chapter 15, and figure how it may have a bearing on the ulcer personality.

8. Refresh yourself on the libido and mortido urges from Chapter 12; then study the present chapter to see how those dynamic urges are shown in nervous tension.

9. Consider some person who is difficult to get along with, and report on him (or her) in the light of this chapter. Will this understanding make it easier for you to get along with him? How?

10. Effie K. wears poor color combinations in her clothes. You spoke to her tactfully about it, but she has been upset ever since. Now you have just found out that she is color-blind. What do you do about it now?

11. In what ways did Franklin, Washington, and Jefferson show personality maturity?

12. Consider some person who is generally regarded as a failure. Size him up in the light of the information in this chapter. How well does this account for his lack of success?

13. Describe in detail the personality of some person about ten years older than you whom you regard as worth imitating.

14. Personnel directors agree that "a successful executive must have a high amount of frustration-tolerance." What do they mean by frustration-tolerance, and why would executives need lots of it?

18 ■ HOW TO CONDUCT A PERSONALITY INTERVIEW

_____

WHAT THIS CHAPTER IS ABOUT

1. *How natural changes in personality come about*
2. *Methods that make the tensions worse*
3. *The dynamic psychology of changing personality*
4. *Listen, listen, listen*
5. *The method taught supervisors*
6. *Use pauses and turnbacks*
7. *Response to feeling, not with feeling*
8. *A sample interview*
9. *Results of these interviews*
10. *Grievances and stresses*
11. *When expert help may be needed*

1 ■ How Natural Changes in Personality Come About

Listen in on these conferences in two different offices.

FIRST OFFICE. "Wonder what's come over Ed? He used to be an accurate bookkeeper, but he is making errors recently. He keeps away from people, too. Maybe I'd better give him a pep talk."

Ed's personality is showing changes because he is upset about office politics and is going sour. The boss should straighten out the politics and should give Ed some encouragement, not a pep talk.

SECOND OFFICE. "Elsie may have to go. She is spending half her time daydreaming and the rest of it looking at the men. Too bad, for she was one of our most promising secretaries when she came with us."

It is too bad, for no one in the office knows that Elsie's one and only boy friend died of pneumonia, and the bottom has dropped out of her world for a while. If she is handled correctly, she may become a better secretary than ever. A too quick or superficial judgment of her personality will only make life more miserable for her and may cost the company a potentially superior employee.

These are examples of changing personalities that make life puzzling for businessmen. People are forever changing, losing interest, becoming jealous, acquiring worries, having discouragements, and developing conceit. These changes often modify their business value as well as their adjustments to life.

Surface changes in personality usually are caused by:

Relationships with other people at work, as in Ed's case

Human relationships in personal life off the job, as in Elsie's case

Inner struggles, as with the ambitious young man just out of technical school who inwardly frets when promotion does not come as rapidly as he had hoped

Glandular or other bodily changes, in a few cases, as when the thyroid gland slows down

Changes in personality do not just happen. Before the surface changes are noticed by others, there has been a period of inner struggle and turmoil. The surface change is the result of this secret, sometimes unconscious, struggle with real or imagined troubles. The changes follow an inner effort to harmonize opportunity with aspiration, to balance dread of failure with a feeling of accomplishment, to offset faultfinding with self-encouragement.

The boss must be on the lookout for early signs of personality changes in workers. Then the situation can be corrected before it reaches the stage where he can think of nothing more constructive than to give a once valuable employee a one-way ticket to nowhere. Sometimes, the boss himself is the cause of the changes. The boss must expect personality changes in situations like these:

When a worker is promoted (The promotion may go to his head or cause restlessness in other workers who had hoped for promotion.)

When there is a change in methods or machines

When a new worker is added to the group (This sometimes alters human relations in the office.)

When a worker has strong leftover interests not needed in his work

Routine office decisions may cause marked personality changes, as was shown in a small office where desks had to be rearranged to make space for extra file cabinets. In the change, one girl was given a location beside a window. Another girl, who had started work with the girl now at the window, immediately began to sulk and gossip. The boss attributed her changed attitude to a previously unsuspected "ugly disposition."

It was suggested to him that the sulking girl may have felt that the other girl was receiving special recognition when she was placed at a window. Things were evened up at once by giving the sulker a new calculating machine, as a sign that she too was favored. Her sulking vanished in a gloating smile, and the office feud was over before it had a good start. People may be funny—but still they are people, and little things can make big changes in surface personalities.

Whenever a change of any sort is made, there is a chance it will have an unexpected effect on some personalities. The executive must be on the alert every day and make immediate adjustments in the human relationships that are involved. This cannot be done by a fight talk or "selling" them on the idea that it is all for the good. Psychological methods should be used to help people help themselves in solving their personality problems.

2 ▪ Methods That Make the Tensions Worse

If your closest friend's feelings are easily hurt, causing him to go around in a mist of discouragement and self-consciousness, what could you do to help him lose his touchiness? Would you try any of the following?

Tell him to snap out of it.
Argue him out of this foolish attitude.
Tell him how sorry you feel for him.
Convince him that people are not trying to belittle him.
Tell him that most people are like him, so why worry.
Tell him to talk back to those who criticize him.
Advise him to stay away from people, so that they will not have a chance to hurt his feelings.

Each of those ways is exactly what should not be done. It would be better to do nothing. Yet those methods are what most people try.

Such homemade attempts to help another's personality are likely to cause one or more of these undesirable results:

Increase his feeling of inferiority
Cause him to develop a compensatory attitude that the rest of the world is wrong while he is right
Make him withdraw into a world of daydreams
Make him eccentrically proud of being different
Give him a dislike for the person who tried to help him

Amateur attempts almost always either fail or produce harmful results. You will recall that there is some inner unrest beneath the surface, which causes many personality quirks. The person is unaware of this inner tension that surrounds hidden motives. The tension needs to be eased, and only psychological methods will release it. The methods used by most parents, teachers, bosses, and best friends actually may add to the tension. So may some self-improvement books.

Here are some definite "don'ts" when one is trying to help a person who is in a quandary.

Don't criticize him.
Don't give advice.
Don't give sympathy.

Don't try to persuade him.
Don't tell others about his troubles.
Don't make fun of him.

3 ■ The Dynamic Psychology of Changing Personality

Insight is the key to changing personality. This is an understanding, by the person himself, of the way some previous experiences have made him feel and act. To help another make personality adjustments, one must lead him to have insight into himself, to see himself as he is—especially his motivations and frustrations. He cannot get this insight from the outside. But, as soon as he begins to have self-understanding of what is behind his own actions, he experiences an *emotional release,* and his attitudes clear up as if by magic.

You may think for certain that your best friend's feelings are tender because he was the ugly duckling of the family and the butt of his broth-

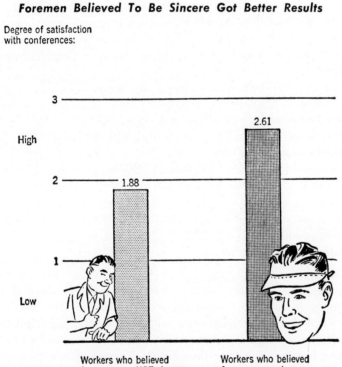

Foremen Believed To Be Sincere Got Better Results

Degree of satisfaction
with conferences:

Workers who believed
foreman was NOT sincere

Workers who believed
foreman was sincere

Data reported by Dr. Alvin Zander and John Gyr of the Research Center for Group Dynamics at the University of Michigan

Telephone linemen and installers were dissatisfied with the system used by foremen in rating the quality of their work. The foremen of 12 crews sat down to talk it over with them, iron out the difficulties, and let the men know they were fair in rating them. These conferences produced least change in attitudes in those crewmen who thought the meetings were unsatisfactory and that the boss was insincere.

ers' and sisters' jokes. Whatever you do, don't tell him what you think! That would only increase his *resistance* to releasing the pent-up emotions.

Insight into the bothersome tensions has to come from within the person himself. The best way to help him obtain this self-knowledge is by having him talk about himself, and then talk some more, until he finally puts these vague inner feelings into words. When he can at last put these *repressed feelings* into words, he can begin to tie his personality problems together.

When he is thus led to understand his emotional background, there is a feeling of profound relief. He can see himself in a new light, and a heavy load has been lifted from his mind. This is called *abreaction*—a reaction away from pestering emotions that frees the personality from their influence. The abreaction is a relieving experience that reduces the inner tension.

Putting the vague feelings from the past into words is called *verbalization*. He has to talk at length before this stage is reached, as the examples will show. He also has to talk to someone who knows how to listen and how to keep him talking about the emotional feelings that cause the inner tension.

Making his own decision is a crucial last stage. Preaching or warning or threatening is a dangerous and waste effort. Lead him to make his own decisions after he can verbalize the problem. When the right leading has been used, he will be able to say, with Socrates: "Now I know myself and can make my own decision."

You can lead him best to, and through, this stage by being sincere and earnest, not flippant or clever. Let him realize that you are thinking of his interests, not of your own. Study the chartoon on page 319 to gain a better understanding of the importance of sincerity.

4 ■ Listen, Listen, Listen

Talking, by the other person, is an indispensable ingredient in the personality interview. Not small talk that conceals, but talk about things related to the personality problem. The talk must be kept on the right track, so that the emotional aspects will be brought to light and the tensions released. Telling the person what he should do gives no help and may make him feel more lost than before. Listening the right way gives tremendous help in clearing the fog. Interrupting the person's talk is harmful.

Some skilled executives have this knack, without pointers from a psychologist to help them. Benjamin F. Fairless, who started as a schoolteacher and worked up to the chairmanship of the United States Steel Corporation, said: "When one of our vice-presidents or the head of one of our operating companies comes to me for help, I generally counter by asking questions. First thing I know, he has told me how to solve the problem himself."

Letting off steam is essential in the personality interview—but it should always be the other fellow's steam. It is difficult for an authoritarian to learn to listen.

5 ▪ The Method Taught Supervisors

A booming application of psychology in business is supervisory and executive training in the art of encouraging people to talk the right way to clear up bothersome situations. This gives the employee insight into himself, releases inner tensions, and helps him decide for himself. It is the exact opposite of the old threaten-and-fire-them method.

This method is illustrated in the supervisors' training that was given in a needle-trades firm of nearly one thousand employees by Dr. Bernard Covner. A series of lecture conferences was given the supervisors as a classroom group. Recordings of actual personality interviews were played to let the supervisors hear the methods when used by experts.

Personal conferences also were held with each supervisor. More recordings of successful interviews were listened to; and the supervisors were given actual practice, until it was certain that each had the right idea and approach.

They also were taught some points in sizing up personality qualities. They were made to realize that general impressions, such as judging one worker as a "weak sister" and another as a "world-beater," gave no help. They were taught to think about the many sides of each employee's personality.

They were given a specially prepared manual for rating people. There was no total score used to estimate personality, but a series of ratings on several characteristics considered important in a going and progressive business. The supervisors analyzed each of their workers on these char-

Recording equipment being used by Dr. Bernard Covner as an aid in teaching psychological interview methods.

acteristics at the start. Secretaries, skilled machine workers, janitors, all were sized up in this way before the interviews. Then each supervisor talked over the rating with each employee, one by one. This was the personality interview.

A psychological moment was chosen for each of these interviews—the moment when the employee seemed in a congenial frame of mind and the supervisor himself in a good mood, and at a natural breaking place in the employee's work. The personal interviews were held in private. Employees were treated with friendly sincerity. They were offered cigarettes or chewing gum to make them feel more at ease with their immediate boss.

6 ■ Use Pauses and Turnbacks

After a little small talk, the employee was told first about some of his strong points, which showed up in the analysis. This part of the interview was brief and was followed by a pause to give the employee a chance to begin talking.

When the weak points were brought up later, and briefly, another pause shifted the opportunity for talking to the employee. Pauses are essential for the person leading the interview.

The supervisors had been trained not to make suggestions themselves. Pauses gave the workers a chance to make their own suggestions. If the worker did not volunteer a suggestion for himself, the supervisor asked what ideas he had about it.

The other person commonly asks: "What can I do to improve?" The amateur tells him—but he should not. These supervisors had been trained to answer such questions with the *turnback method.* A supervisor would turn the question back to the employee by saying: "What do you think you might do?" Turning the question back keeps the other person thinking on his own problems, so that he can reach a decision himself.

The turnback is extremely important. It is a modern example of the Socratic method of leading people by asking questions. When anyone comes to you for advice, use the turnback to help him originate his own advice. That is the kind of advice he will accept and follow.

Use the turnback, also, in the employment interview, and when asking for a salary increase. This forces the interviewer or boss to make the offer. Turn back the first wage offer in an employment interview (but don't reject it) by saying, "To what could that be raised after my work pleases?" When the boss asks how much increase you want, turn it back by saying, "You are in a better position than I am to judge. What do you suggest?" A rejection closes bargaining; a turnback keeps it open and forces the other person to make the next move. If you give a definite figure in answer to the question, "How much do you want?" you are out on a limb. By turning it back, you have not committed yourself, and in many cases receive a better offer. But that is applying the turnback method in a situation different from a personality interview.

7 ▪ Response to Feeling, Not with Feeling

Those supervisors had been trained also to help release emotional tensions by using the method of *response* to *feeling*. When the worker said something that showed feelings of resentment, jealousy, worry, discouragement, embarrassment, or what not, the supervisor mirrored the attitude. By reflecting the other person's mood, he is kept on the track and may continue until the feelings of which he has been unaware are at last put into words. For instance:

"Sometimes I get awfully griped at things," one worker said in a discouraged voice.

The amateur would respond to that with, "Well, don't we all get griped at times?" or "I know and feel sorry for you," or "That is something we all have to put up with," or "Tell me what gripes you." But such comments by the interviewer would bungle the interview. Here is how those trained supervisors handled that remark.

WORKER. "Sometimes I get awfully griped at things."
SUPERVISOR. "Scmetimes there are things that gripe you." (Then a pause for the worker to go on talking. The supervisor did not change the other's mood.)

Those moods that show feeling need to be preserved until some of the repressed feelings are released. Reflecting the feeling the other person has just shown helps him on the way to relieve tensions. The mood can be reflected by repeating the other person's own words. That does not console, criticize, or agree with him—it merely gives the understanding that the interviewer catches his feelings. The fact that the other person shows feeling means the trail is getting warm on something he needs to understand.

This method of response *to* feelings should be used more in everyday life. The tendency, however, is to respond *with* feeling rather than *to* feeling. Train yourself to control your own feelings and to respond to the feelings of others in noncommittal fashion.

When a child comes crying, "I hate Susy," the wise parent reflects the child's upset mood without feeling it herself. Such a parent says, "Susy makes you hate her" and pauses for the child to say more.

The use of these strategic methods is shown in this interview between an employee, who is still learning his job, and a supervisor. Note how the supervisor leads the worker to understand himself from the inside out. Contrast it with the old-style methods that produced mostly resentment or discouragement.

8 ▪ A Sample Interview

SUPERVISOR. "Good morning, Bill. Won't you sit down?"

BILL. "Thanks."

SUPERVISOR. "Well, how's the work going by now, Bill?"

BILL. "Oh, so-so."

SUPERVISOR. "Bill, you remember the other day there was an announcement about rating all the workers in the department?"

BILL. "Yes, I wondered about it."

SUPERVISOR. "I thought you might like to know more about it."

BILL. "Um-hum." (He seems hesitant about saying anything, and acts a bit uneasy.)

SUPERVISOR. "You have been rated on several qualities we think are important for your job."

BILL. "I see." (A little curiosity, but no enthusiasm.)

SUPERVISOR. "In general, your rating was good. You are industrious—work hard without having to be prodded. And you have a good understanding of your job, considering the short time you've been on it." (The good points are given first. Let's see if the good news thaws Bill out.)

BILL. "Well, I guess there's plenty more for me to learn, isn't there?" (Will the supervisor jump at this, and tell him what he needs to learn? See how he uses the turnback to keep Bill talking.)

SUPERVISOR. "You think you still have quite a bit to learn?"

BILL. (He twists his shirt collar.) "Yes—well—er—I mean when I look at some of the guys that are really good, I think—I think 'Gee, will I ever get that good?'" (He pauses, but the supervisor is wise enough to say nothing and waits for Bill to resume.)

BILL. "Well, I—I get sort of discouraged." (Now the supervisor might rush in and tell him not to be discouraged, which would be the wrong strategy. Instead, the supervisor responds to Bill's feelings, which does not interrupt Bill's mood.)

SUPERVISOR. "You feel discouraged when you compare yourself with some of the older workers."

BILL. "Yes, I—well, I watch them work so fast; and I say to myself, 'You gotta go faster,' but nothing happens. Except maybe my rejections go up." (The supervisor continues to respond to Bill's feeling, so that the worker can find his own answer.)

SUPERVISOR. "You think you have about reached your limit in speed."

BILL. "Yeah. It's been the same now for quite a spell. I try to speed it up, but just can't seem to. It's—well, I hate to think that's the best I can ever do."

SUPERVISOR. "You want to do better, but can't seem to make progress."

BILL. "That's it. I'm not satisfied, but what more can I do?" (Pause.) "Maybe I don't use the right methods."

SUPERVISOR. "You think your trouble may be faulty methods."

BILL. "Yes! That must be it. I don't know—do you suppose—is there some way I could check up to see what I do wrong?" (Bill's face brightens. He is beginning to understand what his trouble is in production, and to put it into words. He is on one of those plateaus you learned about in the chapter on learning. Now the supervisor begins to talk more and makes good use of hero worship at this psychological moment.)

SUPERVISOR. "Most workers, even the ones you admire most, strike a snag when learning the job. Take Jack, for instance. He's one of the best we have. He had the same trouble as you when he was learning."

BILL. "He did! He's really good now. I didn't suppose he ever had any trouble." (Bill is feeling much better and is eager for help now. So the supervisor plants a suggestion—but in the form of a question, not bluntly.)

SUPERVISOR. "Do you think it would help if you worked along with Jack awhile? Let him see whether he can discover some short cuts for you?"

BILL. "Yes—that would help me. I don't want to see my rejections go up when I try to speed. Maybe he can help me with that, too."

SUPERVISOR. "You think you might need some help keeping your rejects low?"

BILL. "I—well, so far I think I've been doing all right there, haven't I?"

SUPERVISOR. "Yes. Your rejection rate is O.K."

BILL. "I guess I'm sort of proud of that one thing. I'm afraid to work too fast for fear I'll start to lose ground on rejections."

SUPERVISOR. "You feel that, if you emphasize speed, you may lose that good record on rejects?"

BILL. "That's it. I think—well, sure those other guys are good. Their production records are better than mine, but look at their rejections. At least I have lower rejections, and that makes me feel better."

SUPERVISOR. "Um-hummm-m." (He says nothing, so that Bill will keep on talking and thinking. Bill is on the verge of a great self-discovery.)

BILL. "It makes me feel better, and I think about it a lot." (Pause.) "You know—you know I just happened to think, maybe I'm too careful."

SUPERVISOR. "You have to expect some rejects. We don't expect perfection; and, if perfection is your goal, your speed may suffer."

BILL. "That's right, but I'd never figured it that way. I hope Jack can help me figure it out." (The supervisor makes a mental note that Bill has accepted the suggestion about Jack. Bill has hero worship for Jack, and they should work together well. Now that the way seems clear to solve this problem, the supervisor gives Bill an opening to bring up any other problems.)

SUPERVISOR. "What else about your work has been bothering you?"

BILL. "I guess that's the main thing." (Pause, after which he slides back in his chair.) "Oh, sometimes I get griped at little things."

SUPERVISOR. "Sometimes there are little things that bother you."

BILL. "Yes—well, I guess they aren't very important."

SUPERVISOR. "These other things seem unimportant." (Notice that the supervisor is going only as far as Bill goes. He lets Bill lead, so that he can talk about things it is difficult for him to express.)

BILL. "Yes—well, no. I mean they aren't unimportant." (Pause, and he pulls himself up in the chair.) "I guess I don't like to talk about them, because I know it's mostly my fault."

SUPERVISOR. "Um-hum."

BILL. "I get griped, but mostly I'm mad at myself. I mean, well sometimes I got a job to do that I don't like. I slam the tags down—then I'm ashamed. Or sometimes when I take it out on one of the other fellows— I feel ashamed again." (The supervisor does not mention he knew that Bill had a quick temper, which he wanted to talk about. Instead, he reflects Bill's mood to keep him talking, so that Bill can use his own incentive to improve.)

SUPERVISOR. "You feel ashamed of some of these things you do."

BILL. "Yeah—it makes me mad because—well, I know I shouldn't behave like that."

SUPERVISOR. "You find it hard to behave right sometimes."

BILL. "Yeah. Sometimes I guess I just don't stop to think of the other fellow. I think I can do better if I really try."

SUPERVISOR. "The fact that you recognize a tendency to be thoughtless is a step in the right direction." (He gives Bill encouragement, not criticism.)

BILL. "I don't know how I happened to talk so much. Guess I have sort of rated myself, haven't I?"

SUPERVISOR. "You have done a pretty good job figuring out your strong and weak points."

BILL. "I think if I work hard at it, and if Jack helps me, I can improve my production, too."

SUPERVISOR. "I think you can, and if I can help you, or if you want to talk things over again, just let me know." (The interview closes with the employee encouraged to come back.)

BILL. "I'll do that. Thanks for all the help. I was jittery when I came in, but you made me feel fine."

Bill left "feeling fine" because of the pauses, turnbacks, and responses *to* feeling that helped him clear his own small problems. The supervisor did not try to reason it out with Bill. Instead, he gave Bill the real help of leading him to dig up the answers himself.

9 ■ Results of These Interviews

The aim of these interviews was to smooth out little problems before they became big ones. Shortly after their first trial with the new-style interviews, thirty-seven of the supervisors were asked how the interviews had gone. Here is what they reported.

How did the employees take the interviews? Half a dozen thought they were school-kiddish, and that the problems discussed were none of the supervisor's business. One woman cried but was very glad to get some things off her mind.

The report that employees' responses had been favorable or enthusiastic was made by 86 per cent of the supervisors. Typical comments were:

It was just like a pleasant conversation. They weren't upset. Talked about everything, including home affairs.

Only one thought it was hooey, and she changed when we were through.
They were glad to know where they stand, even those who have been here some time.
They all liked the chance to see their strong and weak points.

With the remaining 14 per cent of the supervisors, who reported indifferent responses, the supervisor might not yet have been in the swing of conducting tension-relieving interviews. It is difficult for the bossy type of supervisor to keep from talking himself when he should merely lead the employee to talk.

Did the interviews benefit the employees? More than half the supervisors said that the single interview seemed to help the employees. The supervisors were for the interviews, although they meant extra work for them. Here are some of their comments.

> Brought out a lot of problems we didn't know about—girl being sole support of the family, for instance. Some helpful suggestions were made.
>
> Started a lot of them thinking. One went so far as to make up a couple of new products and send them to the design department.
>
> Before the interview, Mary S., cafeteria worker, was curt and acted as if she were doing customers a favor. She did the exact amount of work assigned her—no more, no less. She was just plain nasty, and I was near the point of firing her. *After the interview,* she changed. She is more pleasant with customers and fellow workers. She also helps others with their work when she finishes early.
>
> Before the interview, Lillian W., machine operator, was a top producer. But her attitude, mm-m-m! She was a steady beefer. Everything was always wrong, and naturally she didn't get along with anyone. *After the interview,* she was a different person. She's not perfect yet, but she's a lot easier to get along with and seems to enjoy her work more.

Did the interviews help the supervisors? This new-style interview method requires practice to avoid the impulse to do all the talking. It takes effort to learn to use the strategies of the pause, the turnback, and the response to feeling. Many of these supervisors were old-timers, a bit set in their ways. Yet some of them learned how to use the new methods and greatly improved their relationships with the employees.

After the ice was broken, the supervisors began to help workers talk things over more often than the prescribed twice a year. Here are some supervisor comments shortly after their first experiences in the interviews.

> I was very skeptical. I thought the company was taking a big chance. But it was an experience I wouldn't have missed. I won't be scared next time. My only complaint is the time it takes.
>
> This thing is a "must." I know now that my emphasis in the past has been too critical and not enough on the appreciative side.

Was nervous about how I'd do it. But I've learned a lot about people.
Lots of personal things come up. You learn their attitudes. I enjoyed it.
Biggest help was the turnback, after I got on to how to use it. Let them
talk it out. I didn't get led in so easily. The methods are good to know.
I have used the response to feeling before, and it really helps. That is
the best way to interview, I think.

Did the interviews help the company? Management reported there
were specific gains in production, attendance, and attitude. These gains
were significant enough to have emphasis on the interviews increased.
Here are some of the gains as department heads viewed them.

All on their toes since the interviews. I can be out of the department
several hours now; yet they all keep plugging away. When I go back
unexpectedly, I can see a difference. Miss C. used to say she could
always tell when I was out of the department; but since the interviews,
that has changed.

Before the interview, Rosa P., machine operator, was doing passable work.
She got by without making the best use of her time. She was absent five
or six days a month. *After the interview,* her output began to climb
almost immediately, and her earnings have been 10 to 25 per cent
higher. Her absences now average a day and a half a month.

10 ■ Grievances and Stresses

Most grievances are signs of stress. It is almost impossible to argue
a worker out of a pet peeve, since the gripe is often a symptom of underlying stress and strain. The gripe is psychological, not logical. It takes
psychology, not logic, to cure it.

Whether the complaint is from a customer or an employee, it is best
handled by using the principles we have just studied: (1) listen, listen,
listen, (2) turnback, and (3) respond *to* feeling.

When this method was used with a woman who complained about the
cafeteria food, it relieved her so much that a week later she dropped
around to comment on how much better the food was. There had not
been any change in the food, but there had been in her tensions.

When grievances are involved, the "listen, listen, listen" part can well
be expanded. After the worker has told his gripe once, ask him to repeat
it. Then, after this second telling, repeat it yourself, using the employee's
words.

The second telling will be much calmer than the first. And he often
will include something else in the second telling. This something added
to the second telling is usually a significant part of the complaint. In the
case of the woman who complained about the cafeteria food, for instance,
in the second telling she added this: "And the cashier seems to think she
is so high and mighty." The cashier was asked to smile when figuring

It pays to listen to complaints

Per cent whose supervisors heard complaints

The high-morale workers got rid of their grievances in this utility firm because their supervisors listened to their tales of woe. This chart does not mean that high-morale groups had more complaints, but that they could talk more of them over with the boss.

High-morale workers   Low-morale workers

Data from Survey Research Center, University of Michigan

the amount, and to count the change carefully for this woman. Presto! The food tasted better.

After listening to the employee's story twice and repeating it yourself, then ask: "And what else?" And pause for him to take it from there. This strategy often encourages the worker to tell something additional that he has been holding back, something critical, but which he is half-ashamed to mention.

Depending on the attitude shown near the end of the interview, it may be helpful to close on a positive note. Have the complainer himself give a positive comment. Ask: *"What do you like best about your work?"*

These strategies are extremely helpful, not only in personality interviews and in handling grievances, but also in handling customer complaints and in the sale itself. The underlying psychology is to lead the other person to make a decision for himself, not to push him to one, nor to give him one you have made, which he better follow—or else. That is the basis of the new psychology of leadership to which the remainder of this book is devoted.

As the famous Benjamin Jowett of Oxford advised a young graduate: "It is most important in this world to be pushing, but it is fatal to seem so."

11 ■ When Expert Help May Be Needed

Most of the natural changes that occur in personality are not likely to be serious, although they may lower individual efficiency in one way or another. There are some changes, however, that indicate that some serious inner emotional disturbance is taking place. The individual himself is seldom aware of this and, consequently, usually neglects to get the expert attention that he needs.

Dr. Louis J. Cantoni has called the following signs of serious personality disturbance to the attention of personnel executives:

1. Periods when the person is *confused* and does not seem to know what is happening, where he is, or to recognize old acquaintances; he may talk to people no one else can see. This sometimes occurs in older workers, but also occurs at all ages. In these periods, which are likely to recur, the person is "out of touch" with the world around him.

2. Having unreasonably optimistic views about his abilities and the things he can do in the future. This may become extreme flight from reality to the point where the person has *grandiose paranoid ideas*.

3. Deterioration in ability to concentrate and remember.

4. Letting personal appearance run down, especially in a person who used to be careful about clothes and appearance. This is *regressive behavior*.

5. Becoming seclusive and showing discomfort when obliged to be with, or to work with, others.

6. Becoming suspicious of some others, without reason, and possibly belligerent toward them. This may be *persecutory paranoia*.

7. Displaying inappropriate emotions, such as laughing at someone's serious blunders, or displaying no emotion at all. This may be early *schizophrenia*.

8. Having depressed spirits with a slowing down of mental and physical activity; possibly unexplained crying spells. A *mental depression*.

9. Periods of unexplainable excitement and feverish activity. A part of the *manic-depressive* cycle.

10. Having an overpowering fear or anxiety that is not warranted by events and may be a *panic state*.

There will be a few times during your business career when some associates will develop one of those symptoms of serious emotional upsets. It may mark the beginning of a breakdown, and the sooner an expert is called upon, the better.

When such a situation arises, it should be talked over at once with the personnel or health departments, so that they can call in the help of a specialist. About a dozen firms have a specialist—psychiatrist—in full-time employment for helping out in such instances. But all personnel and health departments have to deal with distraught persons from time to time and are acquainted with the local specialists whom they can call

upon for the highly skilled therapy that the near-breakdowns desperately
need.

— — — — — — — — — — — — — — — — — — — —

The Gist of the Chapter

1. What are four general classes of causes of personality changes in business
life?

2. Give six "don'ts" when trying to correct personality changes.

3. Explain emotional release, resistance, repressed feelings, abreaction,
verbalization, and insight.

4. How should pauses be used in a personality interview?

5. What is a turnback, and why is it important to use?

6. Explain and illustrate what is meant by "response to feeling."

7. How can this method be used in handling grievances?

8. Tell about ten kinds of personality changes that usually call for expert
treatment.

Things to Do and Problems to Discuss

1. Find out about the local or near-by mental hygiene society and report
on its aims and activities.

2. Find out about the local or near-by clinics and specialists in emotional
breakdowns, and report on their functions.

3. Alcoholism causes some serious business problems, and it is now considered an emotionally caused ailment. Find out about and report on organizations near you that specialize in this problem.

4. Compare the personality interview technique given in this chapter with
the employment interview technique given in Chapter 9. What are their simi-
larities? differences?

5. Why is a person likely to take a dislike to you if you try to straighten
out his personality by old-style direct methods?

6. A psychologist has found that juvenile delinquents become less of a
problem if they are paid to come in and give a talk on what they (the delinquents) think about delinquency and its causes. In the light of this chapter,
why may that help the delinquents? Could this approach be used for such
business problems as having the careless worker give a talk on the value of
accuracy?

7. Prepare a report considering the advisability of encouraging workers to
air their gripes. Draw on material from Chapter 11 also.

8. You notice that Effie K. is crying at her desk. You know nothing about
any troubles she might have. Discuss what you should do in such a situation.

9. Recall the case of Philip, who lacked emotional maturity, from the pre-

ceding chapter. How could personality interviews be used to motivate him to acquire some attitudes of maturity?

10. One of the workers Oswald J. supervises is a "chronic arguer" who keeps the department on edge. How could Oswald use a personality interview to change this characteristic?

11. Your stenographer has fallen in love with an older executive in another department. You have reasons to distrust the man's motives. How could you handle this?

12. Discuss sincerity as it applies in all aspects of life and business.

13. In what ways would leftover primary personal interests cause a stress on personality? What can a business do about this? What can the individual himself do?

14. How will talking over with others such problems as these give a business person better insight into what makes people tick including himself?

15. Discuss open-end questions in relation to pauses and turnbacks.

16. Check over the questions from the New York Central System, at the beginning of this part of the book, and see which of your previous answers you now want to change. Does this make you feel you are making progress?

part 4

Personal Leadership and Group Co-operation

PERSONAL LEADERSHIP is a goal for the individual, and group co-operation is a goal for the business organization. The remaining chapters of this book are devoted to these goals. To give you a preview, here are questions from the correspondence course taken by some seven thousand supervisors and executives of the New York Central System. The copyrighted questions are included here with the permission of the personnel department.

Place an X in front of the best answer to each question.

1. *When can you be sure people will follow you as their leader?*

   ___ When you are given a title.
   ___ When you have been supervisor long enough for them to get used to you.
   ___ When you show them you can help them win some of the basic things they want.
   ___ When you take their side whether they are right or not.

2. *What is the only real test of leadership?*

   ___ Obtaining blind obedience from the workers.
   ___ Being able to command respect and win co-operation.
   ___ Making certain your employees are afraid to question your instructions.
   ___ Satisfying the boss's self-esteem.

3. *What should be your attitude toward the worker who is different from average?*

   ___ Get rid of him because he doesn't fit into the group.
   ___ Recognize his differences and unusual traits and make them work to your advantage.
   ___ Try to force him into a mold.
   ___ Ridicule him in front of other workers.

4. *How do you become a good leader?*

   ___ By being born an executive.
   ___ By study, training, and learning by experience.
   ___ By trial and error.
   ___ By making friends with the top bosses.

5. *What must you do as a member of the management group if you and the company are to be successful?*

   ___ Work with others as a member of one big co-ordinated team.
   ___ Try to advance yourself quickly.
   ___ Do your own job and let others worry about theirs.
   ___ Be sure your favorites get all the breaks.

6. *As a supervisor, what must be your relationship with other supervisors?*

   ___ Have lunch with them often.
   ___ Co-operate with them as fully as possible in the conduct of the business.
   ___ Offer at least once a week to buy them a drink after work.
   ___ Overlook their actions which conflict with your operations.

7. **When you are about to make a change in your department, how should you proceed?**

___ Make the change suddenly so nobody can object.
___ Explain carefully to all affected employees what you plan and why.
___ Surround the change with an air of mystery to impress employees with its importance.
___ Don't bother about it. They will get used to it eventually.

8. **To what extent must you make decisions as a supervisor?**

___ Make all the decisions.
___ Make the major decisions, consulting superiors when necessary.
___ Leave it all to your superiors.
___ Talk it over with the workers involved before making a decision.

9. **How will you know when you are succeeding as a leader?**

___ When the workers are all afraid of you.
___ When you know your subordinates like to be led by you.
___ When your hat doesn't fit any longer.
___ When your workers start asking special favors.

10. **What should be the supervisor's responsibility with respect to company policy?**

___ Adhere to just the policies he approves of.
___ Criticize policies that are unpopular with the workers.
___ Write a memo to the president about policies he doesn't like.
___ Make sure all his workers understand the policies and the reason for them.

11. **What should you keep in mind when you give instructions?**

___ That they are never a command, but an effort to get people to co-ordinate their efforts with yours.
___ That every instruction you give increases your authority and prestige.
___ That the instructions you give should never be questioned.
___ That you had a boss who growled at you, so you might as well growl at your people.

12. **On what will your success as a supervisor chiefly depend?**

___ On how other people react to you.
___ On the neighborhood you live in.
___ On the school you attended.
___ On the clubs you belong to.

19 ■ THE NATURE AND BASIS
OF LEADERSHIP

— — — — — — — — — — — — — — — — —

WHAT THIS CHAPTER IS ABOUT

1. *The dollar-and-cent value of leadership*
2. *Psychological basis of leadership*
3. *Coercive leadership*
4. *Leadership by assignment*
5. *Leadership by teaching and explaining*
6. *Leadership by inspiring and molding ideals*
7. *Levels of leadership responsibilities*
8. *The supervisor*
9. *The executive*
10. *The board of directors*
11. *The president and executive vice-president*
12. *The administrator*
13. *The manager*
14. *Who bosses the bosses?*

1 ■ *The Dollar-and-Cent Value of Leadership*

Could we get along without bosses?

The Industrial Health Research Board of Great Britain discovered the importance of bosses when the board tried to compare the efficiency of different makes of typewriters. Experienced typists, who typed continuously, used one make of machine for a year and then were switched to a different make. Toward the end of the year, it seemed that the girls using typewriter C were in the lead.

Then the experimenters switched supervisors, but not typewriters. Under supervisor J.C.'s leadership, every typist improved her speed, even those using rickety, old machines. But supervisor P.H. was a nervous woman, who had the opposite influence. After the typists had worked under P.H. for a month, output went down with every last one.

The supervisors had more effect on output than the machines did.

The records of two small factories in the same small city show that the boss can cause labor turnover, too. These competing plants made the same product, paid the same wages, and were as alike as two peas, but for their general managers. The Acme plant's general manager was the leader type, and the labor turnover from quits was 15 per cent a year.

But the Apex plant, whose general manager was the sledge-hammer type —he ordered and bullied with a loud voice—had a quit rate of 55 per cent.

Absenteeism. Absenteeism from sickness may depend also on the boss, proving the truth of the popular remark, "He makes me sick." You are not surprised at this, in view of what you now know about psychosomatics. During an epidemic of colds, 80 per cent of office workers in department G of a large company were absent one Friday. But only a few were absent from the department across the hall. The supervisor of the department with the high sickness rate was a chronic nagger whose employees were glad to have an excuse to stay away from work.

Those three examples are from the files of the Industrial Health Research Board. The following is from the Industrial Relations Center of the University of Chicago.

Accidents. Accidents were studied for five years in a firm of 5,000 employees. At the outset it was found that departments having autocratic supervisors had accident rates four to five times higher than in similar departments where the supervisors used democratic methods. When the foremen who had high-accident departments were switched to previously low-accident departments, the accident rates went up under the new man.

Business used to have to buy only the kind of leadership it could find, and much of it was low grade. That has made headaches for modern business, since it inherited the labor dissatisfaction caused by old-style bosses.

This condition is changing now, since business is seriously developing new-style leadership from within its younger ranks. A survey by the American Management Association in 1946 showed that only 5 per cent of the firms had executive development programs. A similar survey in 1954 showed that more than one-third had such programs then, adding to the cash value of leadership by training.

2 ■ Psychological Basis of Leadership

The need of leadership arises from the long period of infancy and childhood, during which everyone is dependent on older persons for fifteen to twenty years before being on his own. While children may dislike adult interference with their desires, nevertheless they become trained to look toward superior persons for permission or instructions. While growing up, almost everyone has training in followership, but not in leadership.

While people may prize their independence as they strike out on their own, they are not so independent as they imagine. They have been brought up under the absolute power of parents and teachers and have what is sometimes called an "authority complex." This impulse to follow someone better than themselves is deeply ingrained from sheer habit. There may be no supermen; yet people like to imagine there are and look toward someone in authority to guide and take care of them.

This widespread followership habit makes dictators and gangster leaders possible. The gangster and dictator glamorize themselves, thus adding the power of hero worship to control over their followers.

But the followers themselves do considerable glamorizing of those they look upon as leaders. This was shown in tests that Dr. O. J. Harvey made of groups of three persons who were engaged in work that required muscular skill. The three people in each group had been carefully selected, so that they had obvious differences in prestige—a leader, a middle member, and a lowest member. The others in the group overestimated the skill the one with most prestige actually had and also underestimated the skill of the member with least prestige. This study for the Office of Naval Research confirms people's inclination to think the big shots are supermen.

While most people are made followers by early life experiences, a small number turn in the opposite direction. Resentment and stubbornness are marked in these. Tyrannical parents make some children submissive for life; whereas, with other children the tyranny produces high-blood-pressure personalities or rebels. As rebels, they choke with resentment when bossed. They can be a disrupting influence far out of proportion to their numbers. They have a lingering hatred of their parents, which is shown by hostility toward anyone in authority. Some show their hostility to authority by becoming "cop fighters" instead of having high blood pressure; their greatest joy comes from picking a fight with an officer of the law. A few would rather pick a fight with a foreman than a cop.

Sometimes, the rebels battle authority from under cover rather than openly. They hold down production, are intentionally wasteful of materials, and make the boss's life as miserable as possible.

3 ▪ Coercive Leadership

Leadership methods may be divided conveniently into four grades, although there is no sharp line separating one grade from another.

Relatively unskilled workers in a factory in a small industrial city were paid high wages; yet they were restless and went on strike about every eighteen months. One cause of this restlessness was visible. On a wall of each workroom was a sheet of cardboard as big as a desk top, on which shop rules were displayed in type the size of newspaper headlines. The number of days layoff and other punishments for breaking each rule were underlined. (Hitting the foreman called for immediate discharge of the rebel.) This firm was trying to lead by shouting in big type, "Do as we tell you or take the consequences."

On the eastern side of the same city is a plant that employs skilled workers. These skilled workers are paid no more than the unskilled in the other factory; yet they have never threatened a strike, nor have they formed a union.

The skilled workers are not faced daily with a list of rules and penalties printed in oversized type. Instead, on employment they are given pamphlets that list rewards they can win. They are given two and one-half days' vacation with pay if they are not tardy for six months, and a full week's vacation if they are not tardy for a year.

The unskilled workers are bossed by threats. The skilled workers are led by rewards. Little differences of this sort make big differences in folks' reactions.

Coercive leadership uses fear and intimidation to enforce blind obedience. Those king-sized shop rules listing penalties were a variety of coercive leadership. This is the lowest grade. It produces fear and hatred, keeps efficiency low, and causes unrest. It is frustrating to self-esteem.

Consequences. This style of leadership makes workers hate their bosses and the system the boss represents. Workers vote against political candidates that the coercing boss favors, just because the boss is for the candidates.

Leadership by rules and regulations always tends in the direction of mental coercion. This is an inherent danger in a company so large that it feels the need of a rule book. Leadership in socialistic countries becomes coercive as regulations extend to more and more phases of life and are enforced by bureaucrats who have police powers.

Coercing is parents' favorite method of leading. A famous example is the mother who said: "Go see what Ralph is doing, and tell him to stop it at once, or I'll come out and spank him."

Psychoanalysts report that the tendency to use coercive methods as adults is a hang-over from the emotional immaturity of childhood.

Leadership by coercing tends to be self-perpetuating. Some workers become so hardened to rough handling that nothing short of an earthquake will stir them. The coercive leader has to become more of a bully as workers acquire protective immunity to ordinary coercion. Coercion feeds on itself. This vicious cycle cannot be broken abruptly. A year or more of democratic leadership is usually required before workers adjust from their old habits of waiting until they are given stiff pushes.

Leadership methods are seldom the outwardly mentioned reason for a strike. But how resentment toward the bosses' methods may be a "background cause" is shown in a West Coast strike. The workers of one organization had been on strike over wages and seniority. A comparable organization in the same locality was not on strike. These two groups of workers were interviewed individually, to learn their attitudes toward their bosses. As the chartoon on page 340 shows, a much larger share of the strikers were dissatisfied with their type of leadership at work.

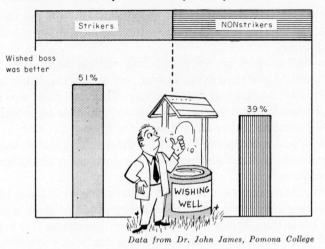

Data from Dr. John James, Pomona College

More of the strikers wished their bosses were better.

Both groups of workers were uncertain about their bosses getting any better, although the nonstrikers were more hopeful. Both groups thought that it would be at least four years before their bosses showed any improvement. Both groups also felt quite strongly about their bosses.

4 ■ Leadership by Assignment

Leadership by assignment is a bit higher grade than coercing. In its simplest form, it merely allots the work to different members of the group. The order giver is an example, although he may lean toward the coercive grade. If he gives orders in a blunt, coercive manner, it is not leadership by assignment. But if he gives assignments as explanations and instructions, it is a higher grade.

Leadership by assignment is an advance over coercion, because it wins a bit of co-operation and not much resentment. Although it does not build teamwork, at least it is not likely to disrupt teamwork. At the present time, most foremen, supervisors, overseers, section heads, and lead-men use methods of assignment and little more.

The young or inexperienced boss inclines toward the order-giving or even coercing stage. As he gains experience and confidence—and if he really tries to become a leader—he advances from these lower grades and becomes adept in methods of the third or even fourth grade.

5 ■ Leadership by Teaching and Explaining

This grade of leadership is on the upbuilding side. Coercing tears down the individual and group spirit. Assigning is rather neutral, usually neither tearing down nor building up. Those two lower methods depend on the authority of the leader's position and job title or on his physical strength in some instances.

Leadership by teaching and explaining depends on the worker's respect for the leader as an individual. It produces some loyalty to the leader, cements the workers to him, and increases their skills and efforts. Coercive leadership may call forth signs of feverish activity when the boss is present, but leadership by teaching and explaining produces results when his back is turned.

People who have technical training usually lead by teaching and explaining, although some impatient ones relapse to order giving, and a few domineering ones slip all the way back to coercion.

6 ■ Leadership by Inspiring and Molding Ideals

Leadership by inspiring is the highest and most upbuilding. It is creative. It uses the head and heart, not lungs and hands.

The creative leader builds a group spirit of teamwork; so it is seldom necessary to give orders. When orders are needed, they are given as instructions and explanations. The creative leader does not confuse interference with influence. He has less detailed planning to do himself, since he has stimulated the individuals to plan for themselves.

People willingly give him authority to lead them. They are loyal to him, because he is considerate and personally helpful. They are loyal to

Leadership Practices

Coercing Boss	Inspiring Leader
Threatens	Rewards
Finds fault	Encourages
Talks	Listens
Keeps them guessing	Keeps them informed
Wants to do all the thinking	Stimulates others to think
Tells others what to do	Tells *why* and *how* to do it
Ignores others' problems	Helps others solve problems
Wants prompt obedience	Wants long-run loyalty
Blunt	Considerate
Flaunts his authority	Tries persuasion
Production-centered	Employee-centered
Assumes worst in people	Assumes best in others
Takes advantage of others	Gives a square deal
Vulgar-minded	High-minded
Impulsive	Considers before acting
Thankless	Appreciative

the cause or business he represents, because hero worship makes them want to imitate him. He does not have to argue or persuade to make them follow his ideals. They feel that he has faith in them, and they return that faith in the man and his ideals.

There has always been a shortage of inspiring leaders. They may be on the increase, however, as a result of the leadership training courses now under way in large companies.

Eli Lilly, founder of the giant pharmaceutical company bearing his name, told his foremen: "The days of the dictatorial, blustering boss are numbered; and that is a blessing. Your modern supervisor serves as a co-ordinator, an encourager, a smoother-outer of difficulties. Above all, he sees to it that all persons get a fair deal and that all questions from those working with him are viewed from a sympathetic standpoint. The first responsibilities of our supervisors are to build men and women, then medicine."

To the alumni of the Harvard School of Business Administration, Clarence Francis gave this Hippocratic oath for business leaders: "I believe that a business's greatest assets are its human assets, and that the improvement of their value is both a matter of material advantage and moral obligation; I believe that employees must be treated as honorable individuals, justly rewarded, encouraged in their progress, fully informed, and properly assigned, and that their lives and work must be given meaning and dignity, on and off the job. . . . If I have the supervision of so much as one other person, I will strive to honor these principles in practice."

7 ■ Levels of Leadership Responsibilities

There are about five million persons in the United States who have executive positions or other business leadership posts. Of this number, about one hundred thousand have major executive responsibilities. There is, in other words, one leader for about every ten or twelve employees.

These five million or so who are leaders in title, if not always in performance, are responsible for the work of others. Their responsibilities cover these three broad functions:

1. Getting things done
2. Keeping costs reasonable
3. Building group spirit

Business leaders of all levels, from straw boss to chairman of the board, have those inclusive responsibilities. In practice, most of them emphasize the first two and neglect the building of group spirit. When group spirit becomes so negative as to cause concern, they blithely blame the condition on politicians or labor leaders.

Ability to meet those responsibilities requires:

Knowledge of technical details
Knack with people
Planning and judgment

The leader at the supervisory level needs a good supply of the first two and some of the third. At the higher executive levels, the last two are more critical. Advancement to higher responsibility comes, not from increased technical knowledge, but from improved business judgment and ability to handle people.

Let's follow through and consider the responsibilities of the various ranks of executives, starting with the bottom of the ladder.

8 ■ The Supervisor

The supervisor is at the bottom of the ladder; yet in many ways he has greater responsibilities than the chairman of the board. He is the immediate boss of one to a hundred workers. To these workers, the supervisor is Mr. Company.

In the contest on "My Job and Why I Like It," 47 per cent of the General Motors employees who participated wrote "the ability and con-

Professional Foreman Functions Chart

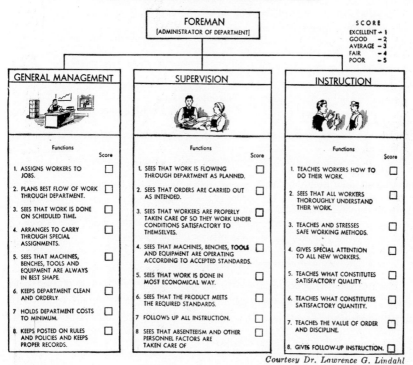

Courtesy Dr. Lawrence G. Lindahl

RATING SCALE FOR SUPERVISORS *

	Yes	?	No
Does he habitually anticipate and act on special conditions, which if not recognized would seriously interfere with the job?	2		
Does it take him unusually long to learn new work or methods?			3
Is he inclined to report or take action in production or personnel situations without first getting all the facts?			1
Does he resent adverse criticism of any of his employees regardless of its justification or source?	1		1
Does he generally check employees to find whether or not they are in fit condition to perform their assigned duties?	2		
Is he exceptionally well informed about personnel problems of the employees who report to him?	2		
Does he often neglect to consider the relation between the work of his group and the work of other groups or departments affected by it?	1		2
Would you select him to handle a difficult job that involved co-ordinating the work of a number of employees?	5	2	
Does he stick to his plans as a rule, but modify them when special conditions indicate the need for a change?	3		1
Is he inclined to duck making decisions on difficult problems within his range of responsibility?			2
Do the employees in his group run into difficulty because instructions have not been complete or understood?			2
Is the volume of work done by the employees in his group more than satisfactory?	2		
Is the work of the employees in his group outstanding in quality?	1		
Does he handle serious and unusual problems exceptionally well?	4		
Does he embarrass unnecessarily the employee affected when he handles disciplinary problems?			1
Does he carefully review errors with employees and instruct them so as to prevent future errors of the same kind?	2		
Does he resent personal criticism from his superiors?			1
Is he so familiar with the operations and figures of his group that he can discuss its work without referring to records?	2		
Does he habitually pass along all necessary information to the supervisor who takes over when he leaves off or finishes?	2		
Are his reports of job progress and completion habitually sufficient in all details (including time, accuracy, and other essentials)?	2		
Is he generally inclined to shift the blame when the work of his group goes sour?			1
Does he often fail to inform his superiors about personnel conditions in his group?			1
In his contacts with his superiors does he generally neglect to present the employee's point of view?			1
Does he manage his regular work in such a way that he can handle special assignments?	3		
Can you use him for a wide variety of tough jobs?	4	1	
Do you believe he could handle the next higher job reasonably well?	4	2	
Does he take the initiative in handling new or difficult problems?	4	1	
Is he inclined to duck new or additional responsibilities or work?			1
Is he generally resourceful in meeting difficulties?	3		

The items on this scale show the responsibilities expected of the supervisor. The numbers on the right show the weight attached to each desirable response. The total of these scores classifies a supervisor as follows:

0—15 fair or unsatisfactory	32—47 very good
16—31 average	48—63 exceptional

* Courtesy Dr. F. H. Achard, Drahca Personnel and Training Services, Boston.

sideration of my immediate boss" as a reason for liking their jobs. Only 2½ per cent mentioned the pension plan provided by the board of directors.

The supervisor—sometimes still called foreman or overseer—has a face-to-face relationship with the workers. Where a supervisor has a department of a hundred workers, these personal contacts are brief and rare—which is a good thing if he is a coercive supervisor. Surveys have shown that supervisors who have oversized departments are kept so busy that they cannot interfere and needlessly boss individuals. The supervisor with only a few employees may do too much bossing. Thomas Jefferson had this in mind when he said: "That government governs best that governs least."

The supervisor's decisions usually concern day-to-day problems and minor emergencies, such as rearranging work because an employee is ill, settling a complaint about poor tools, or devising some strategy to lessen horseplay. The supervisor does not set policies that affect other

Data from Survey Research Center, University of Michigan

The bosses of high-output offices spent more time supervising than helping out with the work.

departments, although some of his ideas may be adopted by other supervisors. He is cautious about getting tangled up with another department, although his work may be affected by other departments.

The supervisor carries out company policies but does not originate them. He may not like a policy but is responsible for seeing that it is followed. Knowing the policies is part of the preparation for supervisory work. So is knowing the people who are affected by the policies.

The supervisor usually has a high amount of know-how for the operations in his department. Some supervisors persist in putting a hand in and helping out on the work. Others spend more of their time supervising: making sure that supplies will be there when needed, training workers, keeping in touch with related departments, taking a personal interest in the workers, building group spirit. Which do you think is the better policy?

When the production records of 600 office workers were analyzed, it was found that the supervisors who lent a hand to help out on the work were mostly in the low-output offices. The supervisors of the high-output offices were much more likely to spend their work time co-ordinating the group activities—keeping the organization going as an organization. (See chartoon on page 345.)

Come to think of it, the football coach doesn't carry the ball himself.

9 ■ *The Executive*

There is a wide range included under the class of executive, and some executives are paid ten times the salary of others. Sometimes, the title is given to a staff specialist who really does no executive work.

The executive supervises workers indirectly through the supervisors. The supervisor knows the department; whereas the executive is in charge of several departments and should know the business. The supervisor's job is to keep his department or section going smoothly; the executive's job is to keep the business going as an organization.

The executive usually leads by remote control. Most of his person-to-person contacts are with other executives and with supervisors. This makes many workers feel that the company is not interested in them personally. Although the executive may have personal contacts with only six supervisors, he can control several hundred employees through these supervisors. The executive talks with fewer employees but influences more of them than supervisors do.

The executive's decisions are concerned with long-range policies that affect a large portion of the employees, such as a change from hand-operated to motor-powered machines, an increase in safety activities, or a longer lunch period.

The decisions made by the executive must be in harmony with the policies adopted by the president or board of directors. He also must be acquainted with the policies of other divisional executives, so that there is no conflict.

The executive may do some routine work and some carrying out of policies himself. But, if the business really needs him as an executive, he is worth more if he plans, organizes, and stimulates, while others do the production.

The higher the executive climbs, the farther ahead he must see and plan. As he climbs into a bigger office with more bookshelves and over-stuffed furniture, his face-to-face contacts with the rest of the organization diminish. His personal leadership may slump until he becomes just a name on the letterhead to most employees—a forgotten man. His lack of contact with the mass of workers may lead him to overlook the human side in his decision making, thus diminishing his stature as a leader—low empathy.

The executive should spend a definite time each day maintaining his contacts in shop and office, else he may lose his leadership over them. Executives can work as well with shoe leather as with the seats of their trousers. Shoe leather helps human relations and morale.

10 ■ The Board of Directors

Now we will jump over the heads of the president and executive vice-president for a moment to look at the board of directors. But in business life, never go over the head of your immediate boss to talk with his boss, unless you want to put yourself under suspicion of politics or disloyalty to your boss.

The decisions of the directors concern questions of general business policy: whether to move to a new location, to discontinue one line of business, to lower wages or keep wages up and skip a dividend. The directors are trustees for the owners, or stockholders, and they are usually knee-deep in financial questions.

Directors seldom have face-to-face relationships with workers, but they should have. The directors set the general tone of the business, which in turn sets the quality of leadership given the rank and file. Many of their decisions affecting workers are based on theory, unless they have visited remote corners of the business and have an acquaintance with employees and processes. Too many try to direct from a bank or club downtown. The directors tend to be a conservative force, tempering executives' enthusiasms and bright ideas.

11 ■ The President and Executive Vice-President

In theory, these top officers, the president and executive vice-president, administer the policies determined by the directors. In practice, they may

‖‖

EXECUTIVE RATING SCALE

Instructions: Place a check mark in the square opposite the appropriate description. Include comments, both
favorable and unfavorable, which may be helpful in further clarifying your rating.

ABILITY TO MAKE DECISIONS
Slow, vacillating, and unreliable... ☐
Often unable to weigh factors involved and slow in reaching a decision............... ☐
Cautious and hesitant, but sound decisions eventually reached........................ ☐
Usually prompt and accurate in reaching decisions................................... ☐
Objective, accurate decisions rapidly reached....................................... ☐
Comment:...

ABILITY TO ASSUME RESPONSIBILITY WITHOUT UNDUE STRAIN
Nervous, fussy, and often appears over-burdened....................................... ☐
Anticipates troubles and frequently worries over possible consequences of acts or decisions... ☐
Usually free from worry and meets problems as they arise............................. ☐
Knows what he is supposed to do and is rarely concerned about consequences of decisions....... ☐
Faces responsibilities calmly, faces facts squarely, and accepts consequences of decisions............. ☐
Comment:...

SENSITIVENESS TO HUMAN TRAITS AND REACTIONS
Inconsiderate and often arouses antagonism.. ☐
Indulges in bluffing, bullying, and boisterous argument............................. ☐
Understands desires of others and responsive to feelings of others.................. ☐
Good judge of people, sympathetic, and encourages co-operation...................... ☐
Keenly alert to human nature, persuasive, and self-controlled....................... ☐
Comment:...

PERSONAL HABITS, APPEARANCE, AND MANNER THAT
BUILD AND MAINTAIN CONFIDENCE
Slovenly, hesitant, evasive... ☐
Accepted but not respected, often ill-mannered.................................... ☐
Conventional in habits, attitude, and manner....................................... ☐
Neat, straightforward, and confident.. ☐
Clean-cut, assured, and dynamic.. ☐
Comment:...

TECHNICAL KNOWLEDGE, EXPERIENCE, AND TRAINING
Lacking in all three or seriously weak in one..................................... ☐
Marked weakness in one or two of these factors................................... ☐
Any weakness in one fairly well compensated for by strength in other factors.............. ☐
Adequate knowledge, experience, and training for the usual demands of the job................. ☐
Thorough training which has resulted in mastery of facts backed by experience.................... ☐
Comment:...

INTEGRITY, FAIRNESS, AND SINCERITY
Tricky and not to be trusted... ☐
Frequently suspected of sharp dealing by others................................... ☐
Honest according to his own judgment, tries to be fair but is not always sincere.............. ☐
Honest and sincere but not always able to convince others of his fairness...................... ☐
Makes everyone feel that he is honest, fair, and sincere...................................... ☐
Comment:...

FORCEFULNESS, ENERGY, AND PERSEVERANCE

Indifferent, weak, and gives up easily...☐
Efficiency hampered by deficiency in one or more of the three characteristics.............☐
Consistent worker and carries task to completion, but not forceful.........................☐
Energetic and persistent, usually forceful...☐
Positive, persistent, and vital to an exceptional degree.....................................☐
Comment:...

ABILITY TO INSPIRE, TEACH, AND DEVELOP MEN

Unable to transmit knowledge or encourage others in self-improvement.............☐
Able to teach but uninspiring...☐
Successful in teaching but does not motivate...☐
Presents material clearly, interestingly, and encourages further study.........................☐
Gifted in the power to stimulate and direct the development of others...........................☐
Comment:...

POWER OF ANALYSIS, DISCRIMINATION OF RELATIVE VALUES

Hazy and confused in his thinking...☐
Slow and erratic in analyzing a situation...☐
Usually sees problem clearly, assigns correct values, but over-deliberate in analyzing details...☐
Can pick out important points in a problem, and arrive at correct conclusion....................☐
Keenly analytic and capable of weighing accurately all factors in the problem.....................☐
Comment:...

OPEN-MINDEDNESS

Prejudiced and opinionated, unwilling to change mind in the face of new elements....☐
Frequently biased by former opinions...☐
Usually free from prejudice and willing to revise opinion.....................................☐
Receptive and never lets old judgment blind him to new facts...................................☐
Alert in seeking new facts and revises opinions when evidence warrants...........................☐
Comment:...

TACT AND SELF-CONTROL

Blunt in statement and frequently becomes angry or excited.......................☐
Often irritates others by speech or manner...☐
Rarely loses control of temper and seeks to avoid conflict.................................☐
Considers others' attitudes, is restrained and diplomatic in trying to overcome differences.........☐
Self-controlled, considerate, courteous, calm, and extremely tactful...............................☐
Comment:...

HEALTH

Ill health and nervous indisposition often interfere with work........................☐
Frequent periods of illness, lacks vigor and vitality.....................................☐
Loses little time because of illness but uses more energy than the job requires...............☐
Has reserve energy to devote to problems beyond those required in the day's work.............☐
Display of health and vigor stimulating to others...☐
Comment:...

Lines may be drawn connecting the check marks for the various traits in order to provide a graphic picture of trait relations.

|||||||||||||||||||||||||||||||||||||||||||||||||||||||||||||||||||||||||||||||||||||||||||||||||||||||||||||||||||||||||||||||||

From Executive Ability, Its Discovery and Development, by Dr. Glen U. Cleeton

The responsibilities expected of the executive. Compare with the preceding rating scale for supervisors.

be the real policy makers, while the board members are rubber stamps. In other instances, they are office boys for the board.

As a president's work increases, or when he wishes semiretirement, some of his responsibilities are laid on the shoulders of an executive vice-president. In such instances, the title "and general manager" is added.

Larger companies may have several executive vice-presidents, each in charge of several vice-presidents. In many smaller companies, the title of executive vice-president is given a man to keep him from resigning, without any change in his duties or responsibilities. In others, the title is used to give prestige and make it easier to contact customers who are flattered when called on by such a high officer.

12 ■ The Administrator

The administrator is the executive who interprets general policies and laws to keep the organization in line. This type of leadership is represented by most government executives, though some commercial executives are mostly administrators. The operation of government bureaus and sections is fenced in by laws and tied up in red tape. The bureau chief or section head has to be half lawyer, half executive, with a dash of politician added. Major decisions already have been made for them by Congress, state legislature, or city council. Any major decision they want to make requires a new law.

In city and state operations, the administrator is often a political appointee or elected official, who may be out of a job after the next election. His leadership is likely to be tinged with efforts to keep his party in power.

At the federal level, most administrators are career men and women, under civil service. The top administrator is an appointee, a political officeholder; but the bulk of supervisory and executive positions are held by permanent employees who administer the department. These administrators have to be slaves to duty and regulations that prevent much show of originality. Their ideas usually have to be approved by Congress before becoming effective, a factor that lowers governmental efficiency.

The administrator works in a glass house, subject to the floodlight of an investigation if a taxpayer becomes disgruntled. The career administrator is usually a capable person whose leadership is restrained by the cautiousness his public position demands. Since his employees usually are supplied from the civil-service pool, and may be transferred to other offices or cities, the government administrator has little encouragement to rise above the order-giving and rule-enforcing level. And, since the ceiling on his promotions is rather low by business standards, there is not much motivation for him to become an inspiring leader. Yet these administrators are the backbone of government, keeping federal services running, despite political struggles between the ins and the outs. The administrators of post offices, public-health service, the Federal Bureau of Investigation, and the Bureau of Standards are examples of this level of leadership responsibility.

Some business executives make their decisions largely on the basis of precedent—what has been done before. These lean in the direction of administrators. This is particularly true with the conservative executive, or one who is uncertain of his own judgment, or one who is coerced by a higher executive of the ramrod variety.

Executives of larger companies may be forced to a semiadministrative level, because of the company book of rules and procedures and government regulations on business. The railroads are an example of this situation. In other instances, the working agreement with a labor union may change supervisors into administrators rather than executives.

13 ■ The Manager

The manager occupies a variable position in leadership responsibilities. Strictly speaking, the manager's responsibility covers pennies and not people. His leadership of people is indirect, through the budget. The homemaker who is "a good manager" keeps expenses within the family income and has some money left over for savings and insurance. The business manager keeps an eagle eye on expenses, income, and what is left over for profits and expansion.

The controller comes closest to the strict meaning of manager in business. But the term has come to be used for any sort of boss. There is justification for this, since at all levels of leadership income and outgo must be watched. Managing of expenses is an essential function in all leadership, but it should not cause neglect of teamwork and morale.

The executive who concentrates on a daily operations sheet that shows profit and loss is like the farmer who is proud of his big crop, but overlooks the fertility it has taken from the soil, which must be replaced. Some department managers, and some proprietors of small businesses, are so eager to have a good profit-and-loss statement that they deplete the human soil and, consequently, cannot get teamwork when times or competition become tough. When an executive studies an operations report, he should keep in mind the people behind the figures. Profits and losses do not make themselves; they come from the co-operation—or lack of it—of people in the organization.

Profits in some periods are not an index of leadership. When patents or trade secrets or inventory speculation are factors in producing profits, the profits reveal little about leadership. When demand is rising and competition is low, as in wartime, profits indicate nothing about leadership. Some executives, who imagined it was their leadership that made profits, have been shocked to see those profits vanish when patents expired or hostilities ceased.

"Big business must be human if it is going to succeed," said Alfred P. Sloan, "because what makes the wheels go round will always be human beings." The basic responsibility in all levels of leadership is those human beings; they are the organization that must be maintained.

14 ■ Who Bosses the Bosses?

So you would like to be a boss and get away from being bossed? Sorry, but it cannot be done.

Up through the levels of responsibility, each little boss is bossed by a slightly bigger boss. Every lord has an overlord. Bosses are as inevitable as death and taxes, and you might as well try to get along with them. The leader has to be a good follower of his boss.

Each bigger boss has a larger desk, more salary, and more responsibility. Yet big bosses are not always better personal leaders than the little bosses. Big bosses often make life miserable for little bosses. In some companies, the most boss-picked-on employees are the vice-presidents. A critical, demanding president is in their hair most of the time. The vice-presidents, in turn, get in the hair of the executives who are responsible to them. It is a rare company or government bureau that does not have at least one high-bracket executive who demoralizes the leadership of many others.

Bosses are people, too, and need to be bossed with care. The executive whose face-to-face leadership is principally of executives and supervisors has more need to upgrade the quality of his leadership. He has more need because his own grade of leadership is reflected in the way his subordinates handle their subordinates. Many workers are bawled out needlessly because their boss has just been put on the carpet by his boss. Work under the right kind of bigger boss is good leadership training; the wrong kind can ruin leadership training programs.

Each boss who has a slightly bigger (though not necessarily better) boss is inclined to exert himself more to get along with his boss than with his workers. This pressure from above leads many supervisors and executives to study their boss more than the workers they supervise. They are quick to take a hint from their boss, but may not sense that anything is wrong with the morale of their workers until conditions are in a sorry state.

The paths that rumors take through an organization give an illustration of the way workers, and bosses, are inclined to make an impression on someone above them. In one white-collar organization rumors were deliberately started, and the paths they took were reported by undercover observers in each department. Dr. Kurt W. Back found that the bulk of the passing was done in an upward direction.

The big bosses are usually out of touch with the workers and get news of them secondhand through intermediate executives, who relay only the favorable news, since the unfavorable might reflect on them.

Here is some testimony on that point, given by Joseph Schaffner, late president of Hart, Schaffner & Marx, to the United States Industrial Relations Commission: "I was so badly informed about the conditions that I called the attention of a friend to the satisfactory state of the employees. It was only a few days before the great strike of garment workers broke out. When I found out later of the conditions that had prevailed, I concluded that the strike should have occurred much sooner."

The Gist of the Chapter

1. How does the style of leadership influence output, turnover, absenteeism, accidents?

2. Explain how people get the habit of feeling they should be led.

3. Tell about coercive leadership.

4. Contrast leadership by assignment with leadership by teaching and explaining.

5. Describe the highest form of leadership outlined in this chapter.

6. What duties loom large in the supervisor's job as supervisor?

7. In what ways does an executive's functions differ from those of a supervisor?

8. Contrast the functions of the board of directors, the president, and the executive vice-president.

9. What are the functions and limitations of an administrator?

10. Where do managers come in?

11. Who bosses the bosses?

Things to Do and Problems to Discuss

1. Get organization charts from some local firms; also from a school, library, hospital. Report on them in the light of this chapter.

2. Observe some young children playing together. Note the kind of leadership methods they try to use on each other, and report on them.

3. Size up some public officials, such as the mayor or governor, who are much in the newspapers. From the news accounts, try to classify their leadership methods as coercive, assigning, teaching, inspiring.

4. Discuss the usefulness of patience to a leader.

5. It has been said that people want to follow some leader. Discuss how fashions, slang, recreations may illustrate this.

6. Discuss what is meant by the statement that the chief function of the executive is to maintain the organization as an organization.

7. Refresh yourself on the characteristics of the immature personality. Discuss what influence these would likely have on leadership methods and success.

8. Rate some boss you have worked for, perhaps part-time, on Dr. Achard's rating scale for supervisors. Discuss examples from his conduct which made you rate him as you did. Skip any questions you cannot answer. What do the skips indicate about your own observation?

9. Oswald J.'s club has asked him to give a talk on the company. Discuss whether he should get permission from his boss, and if he should ask the boss for some points he should make to his club about the company.

10. Leaders are said to be more interested in efficiency than their followers are. Explain how such a difference could be accounted for. Chapters 1 and 2 may help you.

11. Which type of leadership method (coercive to inspiring) is more likely to be successful when using the personality interview described in the preceding chapter? Why?

12. Discuss the authoritarian and equalitarian personalities in the light of this chapter.

13. How do the social and community responsibilities increase with each step up the ladder? Do these also include the wife? What should the ambitious person do to prepare himself for these outside responsibilities?

14. Analyze Dr. Cleeton's Executive Rating Scale. Discuss the extent to which personality characteristics, motivation, and technical training would be needed for a high rating in each category.

15. Consider some person in a position of leadership, who appears to be moderately successful. What could he do to become more successful as a leader?

16. Two crews were thrown together for a rush job. The work was botched because each supervisor had assumed the other would do the checking. What was wrong? How could it have been avoided?

20 ■ DEVELOPING PERSONAL LEADERSHIP

_ _ _ _ _ _ _ _ _ _ _ _ _ _ _ _ _ _

WHAT THIS CHAPTER IS ABOUT

1. *The power of position*
2. *The consent to be led*
3. *The power of knowledge*
4. *The power of understanding others*
5. *Six cardinal skills to develop*
6. *Special requirements for higher executives*
7. *Requirements vary with the group to be led*

1 ■ The Power of Position

"What helped you most in your climb to the top?" The president of one of the largest banks in the South replied: "It is easy for me to tell what helped me most. I fell in love with a beautiful girl, and it happened that she was the only child of the founder of this bank." He was being unduly modest, but his frankness illustrates one way some achieve leadership of a sort.

The power of position is the most common source of a leader's power and is likely to fall in the low grades of coercing or order giving. Parents, teachers, policemen, and most minor executives have power over others chiefly from the authority of their positions.

When the position of authority is reached somewhat accidentally, leadership is often uninspiring and weak. An example is the owner's son who inherits the job. This is especially true when the son would prefer to be in another line of work.

The authority of position usually is sought, not thrust on people. While not everyone wants the responsibility of being the boss, many who seek the authority want desperately to become bosses. The aggressive person often tries to boss even when he does not have the authority. Those who want too much to become bosses may become the worst bosses. They do not realize that a little bossing goes a long way.

An example of how those who seek the authority are likely to be on the bossy side was shown by some committees of high school graduates. Their person-to-person interactions were observed through a one-way mirror. In half the groups one member was definitely appointed chairman. In the other groups no leader was designated; but after a few minutes of committee work it was obvious that some members thought they were "natural" leaders, and they tried to run the others. This cartoon shows how these "natural" leaders tried to "wear the pants."

Regalia and trappings of office are used to make the authority of position visible. The chief clerk wins more regard when his desk is larger than the other clerks' desks. Each higher level of supervision is given a little more expensive setting, as the chart on page 227 shows.

Uniforms also make authority visible. The doorman or elevator starter has no legal authority over the public, but the uniform makes the public follow his say-so as if he were a marshal. The uniforming of minor officials has been a tactic used for generations in European countries.

The badge of authority can be shown also by ordinary clothes. Factory workers, for instance, wear blue shirts and no neckties. But their supervisor wears a necktie and dresses a shade better than those he is to lead. The superintendent, in turn, wears a white shirt and changes it more often than the supervisors; his suits cost more than those of the supervisors and fit better. The vice-president in charge of manufacture dresses

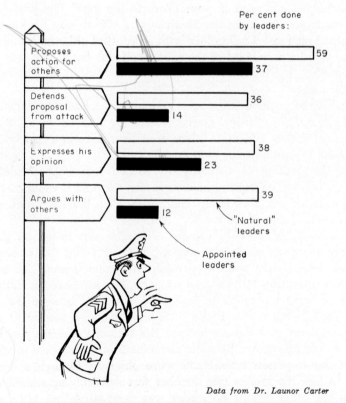

Per cent done by leaders:

	Per cent
Proposes action for others	59
	37
Defends proposal from attack	36
	14
Expresses his opinion	38
	23
Argues with others	39
	12

"Natural" leaders

Appointed leaders

Data from Dr. Launor Carter

The "natural" leaders used bossier methods.

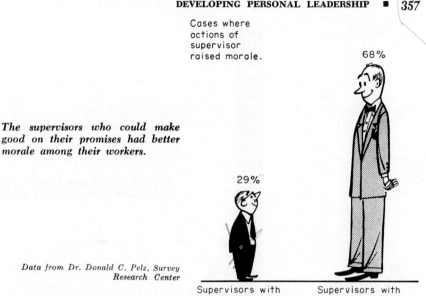

Cases where
actions of
supervisor
raised morale.

68%

The supervisors who could make good on their promises had better morale among their workers.

29%

Data from Dr. Donald C. Pelz, Survey Research Center

Supervisors with
LOW power

Supervisors with
HIGH power

like a man of distinction, unless he has other extraordinary qualities of leadership; so he does not need the help of a badge of authority.

Such badges of authority are needed especially in the lower ranks of leadership. The slight superiority in clothes or uniform does more than give the appearance of authority. It also gives the wearer the feeling of having authority. Clothes affect the wearer as well as the onlooker.

Sometimes a person is given a high-sounding title, but no authority to go with it. Will the title alone give him enough power? What happens was found in a survey of some eight thousand employees of a metropolitan electric-power firm. Some of the supervisors who made promises of better conditions, of pay increases, and such, had high-morale workers. But other supervisors who made as many promises had low-morale workers. Further analysis showed that it was not the promises, but the power to make good on the promises, that counted. This chartoon shows how the supervisors who could get results with the higher-ups were generally the ones with high-morale workers.

In the case of the white-collar workers, the output was significantly higher for those bosses who had influence with the higher-ups.

2 ■ The Consent to Be Led

The authority of position (or of appearance and manner that indicate it) is not inherent in the position. After all, the authority lies in the consent of people to be led. Consent to be led is often overlooked; yet it is the real source of the power of position. Most people want to be led and

Productivity in
bosses' departments:

They turned out more work for the boss who they thought was good.

Data from Dr. C. H. Lawshe, Occupational Research Center, Purdue University

Workers LEAST
favorable to bosses

Workers MOST
favorable to bosses

give their consent willingly. They may, however, withdraw their consent if they lose confidence in, and respect for, those in authority and feel that this authority has been overused.

Teen-age boys withdraw consent to their parents' leadership by running away from home or taking jobs in distant cities. Workers withdraw their consent by:

Quitting jobs; absenteeism
More or less ignoring the boss
Setting up their own leader, as a steward
Going into open revolt; stalling

Citizens withdraw their consent by voting politicians out or by ignoring unpopular laws.

Much recent research in group dynamics and social psychology has shown beyond doubt that the final power of authority comes from the group that is being led. Each work group has certain *expectations* of what its leader should be like, and especially of how he should lead the group. It gives most power to—that is, follows most enthusiastically—the one who comes up to these expectations.

These expectations are usually constructive and reasonable. For instance, workers seldom expect their leader to work beside them at the same kind of work they are doing themselves. They expect him to perform leadership functions, such as taking care of their complaints, helping solve their work problems, making good on promises to them.

Seemingly slight differences between supervisors may cause a partial withdrawal of the consent to be led and result in a noticeable reduction in output. This was shown by the study of 208 office workers in a Kentucky factory. The productivity of workers who felt most favorably toward their bosses was contrasted with those feeling least favorably toward their bosses. The chartoon on the facing page depicts the differences.

Here are some of the human-relations points on which these workers had sized up their bosses:

Being easy to see when you have a problem to talk over
Not criticizing you for things that couldn't be helped
Being prompt to take care of your complaints
Making good on his promises to you
Showing an interest in your ideas and suggestions
Giving good explanations of how to avoid errors
Giving sincere answers and no run-around
Discussing why work changes may be necessary

Having the power of position and a fancy title or uniform or a luxurious office is no assurance of leadership. The power of position must be granted to the individual by those he is supposed to lead. The power of position is usually a help, but no guarantee.

Data from Dr. John K. Hemphill

Most of the people did not lean heavily on their leaders.

As an example, consider what was found when 500 adult groups were analyzed. Some were small groups, others large; the average group had 30 members under one nominal leader. But most of the people in these established groups did not lean heavily on their leaders. More than half of the presumed followers acted and thought on their own individual responsibility. As the chartoon on page 359 visualizes, only about one out of ten felt they should be in close step with the leader.

3 ▪ The Power of Knowledge

The power of knowledge gives force to leadership, since it wins consent better than mere position. People tend to follow those who obviously know what should be done, regardless of the leader's rank. In a medium-sized Pennsylvania bank, the employees virtually ignore the cashier, who is supposed to be headman. They look to a quiet woman, who is a superb accountant, as their real leader. There are many such instances, where the person who has the position does not have the leadership because he lacks the knowledge.

There is the weak executive, whose intelligent secretary or assistant is the one in whom actual leadership resides—the power behind the throne. The boss who is weak in knowledge or impulsive in judgment often has his leadership short-circuited to levelheaded people with more background for the job. Those he is supposed to be leading catch on to his inadequacies and follow some unofficial leader in whom they have greater confidence.

Some apprehensive executives weaken an organization by getting rid of the unofficial leaders, to preserve their own positions. Others try to maintain their prestige artificially, by not hiring anyone who has special technical or business training, thus further weakening the organization. Such tactics are varieties of peasant cunning, comparable to the horse trader's tricks.

The leader who is going places is glad to be surrounded by a few people who are more capable than he is. Half-qualified "yes men" can add to nothing but an executive's conceit. As Andrew Carnegie said: "The able executive is the man who can train assistants more capable than himself." If he has not trained them, he should be doubly thankful to have them.

Lammot du Pont said: "There's one trick about management that I learned early. It is to surround yourself with men who know more than you do, and listen to them."

Capable assistants can push a leader up the ladder if he works with and through them. Two heads are better than one, especially when the second head has more knowledge or higher intelligence.

The smart assistant pushes his boss up and follows him up. The shortsighted assistant tries to push the boss out and is likely to find himself outside, too.

4 ■ The Power of Understanding Others

We recall that empathy is the ability to understand how the other person feels. Researches are accumulating that indicate that this is one of the essential ways the leader gets power over others. The successful leader seems to be able to read the minds of his followers. By knowing what they want, he can co-ordinate their activities toward the goals in which they are interested. Fuller consent to follow him is a result.

This is illustrated by some groups that voted for the members they would like to follow as leaders. One member out of five received no votes, not even his own—ignored by the group. Those who were voted leaders greatly excelled the average members in their ability to read the minds of the others about what they wanted from the group activity, as shown by the bar on the left of this chartoon. When compared with those who received no votes, the leaders' superiority for taking the "pulse of the people" was even greater.

One purpose of morale surveys is to provide information about how the group feels. Public-opinion surveys are also being used by many po-

Superiority of
leaders in judging
group opinion:

Those who were voted leaders excelled in reading the members' minds on topics they took seriously.

9.0

6.1

How did you know what I wanted?

Data from Drs. Kamla Chowdry and Theodore M. Newcomb

Compared with
Nonleaders

Compared with
those ignored
by group

litical leaders, and by some federal departments, so that they can act more in line with what the public (their followers) wants.

To a large extent, the successful leader follows the group's aims rather than imposes his own aims bluntly on them. It sometimes happens that a labor official understands workers' aims better than management does and, as a result, has much greater power over the labor force than the nominal bosses have. In view of this, some companies like to promote union stewards to supervisory positions.

The power of knowledge can be used to understand what is on others' minds when one gains a deeper knowledge of industrial psychology and industrial sociology.

5 ■ Six Cardinal Skills to Develop

One of the landmarks in the modern study of leadership was made by Dr. John K. Hemphill. He got information about 500 ongoing groups from many parts of the country. Some were large social groups; some, small work groups. Both men and women were included; the average age was thirty years. There were 500 leaders and some 15,000 followers included in the groups.

How many of the leaders were considered successful? About three out of four were doing a good enough job to be considered successful. (This does not mean, of course, that they were doing the best job of leading that might have been done.)

Next Dr. Hemphill compared the successful leaders with those who were failures. By contrasting the successes and failures, it was possible to spotlight the skills that were significant in making a difference in leadership.

Making quick decisions, for instance, was not found to be a significant element. In the past, however, many people who have set out to make themselves leaders imagined that they should be able to think faster than their followers.

The skills that were found to be significant in making a leader a success could be catalogued into six groups or functions. Each of these functions puts a spotlight on one of the objectives the leader should keep in mind in his day-to-day methods. These six groups of spotlighted skills are all focused on mobilizing the mental and social forces in the group, so that the followers are motivated to work together toward goals they understand and accept. The next chartoon pictures the six cardinal skills needed. Skill A was found to be the most significant of the batch. Skill B was next most significant, and so on, with skill F, "Human-ness," at the bottom of the list, though still significant.

A close-up look at each of these cardinal skills will reveal what the would-be leader should aim for. We will give some operational examples

Based on researches of Dr. John K. Hemphill

The six most essential functions of successful leaders.

of methods which show how easily the targets can be hit when the person has enough flexibility to qualify as a leader.

A. Set group goals WITH the members

"Our boss asks our opinions frequently."

"He talks over changes with us."

"The boss uses some of our suggestions."

"He tells us about things that may be coming up."

"We have frequent group confabs on work problems."

B. Help them REACH the group goals

"My boss gives me help when I need it."

"He shows he is proud when we do a good job."

"He can help us on the technical details of the work."

"He listens to complaints, and takes care of them promptly."

"He sees that we have good equipment and materials on hand when we need them."

C. CO-ORDINATE the members

"Our boss delegates authority wisely."

"He lets us help each other."

"He gives us all a chance at choice jobs—no favorites."

"He lets us know how each of our jobs is important."

"He helps us work out things together."

Courtesy "Man to Man" course of General Motors Corp.

D. Help members FIT INTO THE GROUP

"Our boss understands the way we feel about things."
"He is good at seeing that the right people work together."
"He made me feel at home with the crew."
"Our leader takes a personal interest in us."
"He gives me a chance to do the work I am best at."

E. INTEREST IN THE GROUP, not self

"Our leader is usually pulling for us."
"My boss does not stand between me and the company."
"He is good at getting us overtime, transfers, and changes."
"He gives us sincere answers, and no run-around."
"Our leader will stick his neck out for us."

F. "HUMAN-NESS"

"Our boss is easy to see and talk to."
"He is reasonable in what he asks, and in enforcing rules."
"I feel free to talk over my personal problems with him."
"He gives us a pat on the back when we do a good job."
"I feel that I know him well."

6 ■ Special Requirements for Higher Executives

Our previous study of the levels of leadership responsibility indicates that an executive vice-president might need different personality qualities from a supervisor. Chris Argyris, of the Labor and Management Center at Yale University, after studying many higher executives, believes that they rate high in ten characteristics. This is his description of high executives, from a talk at the Graduate School of Business at Columbia University.

1. High frustration tolerance. Do not "blow up"—or sulk—when things don't go as hoped. Can hold feelings in check without interfering with ability to work. Able to work enthusiastically for some long-range goal that they realize may be a gamble.

2. Encourage participation by others. In reaching decisions, they welcome participation by others rather than insisting on the acceptance of their own ideas. This demands the ability to consider seriously ideas that they might not like at first and also to take some implied criticism of their own ideas. "A man of decision" is coming to mean a man who leads others to reach a decision.

3. Continually question themselves. Look for mistakes in their own methods or thinking, but do not become upset over any blunders. Try to understand their own prejudices better than most people.

4. Cleanly competitive. Realize that other firms and executives are out to beat them, and enter into the competition without a feeling of hostility. Can take hostility shown them without indulging in self-pity.

5. Impulses to "get even" under control. Can take hostility from others without trying to get even with the instigator. Let the other person know that they realize what he is up to, but do it without showing personal hatred.

6. Win without exulting. Never excited when they reach a goal or victory. Feel good about it, but are not carried away in a spirit of triumph.

7. Lose without moping. They are good losers as well as considerate winners. A setback on one goal does not cause them to give up on other goals.

8. Recognize legal restrictions. Recognize restrictions imposed by laws and agreements, which make it more difficult to reach some of their goals; but they do not feel that these limitations mean that someone is out to get them; not paranoid about it.

9. Conscious of group loyalties. Aware of their group loyalties, such as lodge, club, technical society, management group, church, and close personal friends. Anchored to these groups to which they feel they belong, and which give them comfort when they make decisions that are unpopular with other groups.

10. Realistic goals. Realistic goals, high enough aspirations so that they have to "make a fight" to achieve them, but sensible enough to be achievable.

Looking back over that list will show you that the number of characteristics that revolve around competition is impressive. In this competitive world, the successful higher executive apparently needs to be a person who enjoys competing, one who can also "rise and fight again" after a loss—and fight hard and fair.

Remember Philip, whom we met in the section on personality immaturity? Wonder how he would rate on these ten characteristics.

Dr. Robert N. McMurry has observed that not more than one or two persons out of 10,000 "have what it takes" to become top executives. Experience in middle management positions seldom gives practice in the policy-making, risk-taking decisions that the top man has to make without going through an attack of "nervous tension."

7 ■ Requirements Vary with the Group to Be Led

No "one best personality for leadership" has yet been found. Studies show that many differing sorts of personalities can have good leadership. Recall John Wanamaker and Marshall Field. Also consider the keymen who built a great steel empire. Andrew Carnegie was a pint-sized "smoothie," a tactful diplomat, and a gentleman in all his relations with others. Charles Schwab, his million-dollar-a-year right-hand man, was a physical giant, a hail fellow well met. Bill Jones, the left bower of the empire, who asked for a big salary and got it, was a diamond in the rough and as serious as an undertaker.

A wide variety of personalities can become leaders because there is a wide variety of people to be led. The people with whom the leader works vary more than do tools or materials. Remember that leadership requires the consent of the people who are supposed to become followers. Office workers will give that consent to a smoothie, but not to a diamond in the rough. A road-construction crew will give their consent to the rough diamond and be indifferent to the smoothie.

Different types of work may call for different leadership methods. This is shown by observations of naval officer cadets who were given two different kinds of work—mechanical assembly and committee work. Both jobs were similar in requiring problem-solving, but the assembly work dealt with tangible things, the committee work with ideas and attitudes. The interactions of the men were observed while doing both types of work. The same men did both jobs, but the person-to-person interactions of the men were much different for each job, as the chartoon on page 367 shows.

Not much spontaneous leadership was shown at either task. Disagreeing and arguing, included in Miscellaneous, accounted for nearly 10 per cent of the interactions in Committee work, but only 2 per cent while Assembling. Apparently the leader of a committee has greater need of the ability to "pour oil on troubled waters."

The special demands for committee leadership need to be underlined, since that type of work is on the increase in all levels of leadership. More use is being made of *executive teams*. This policy is one symptom of the

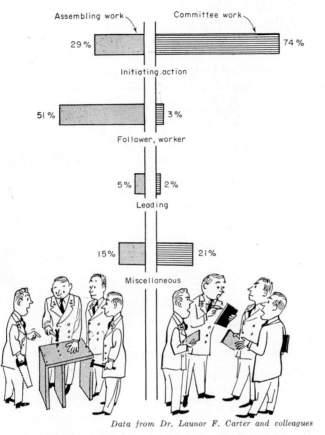

Assembling work

Committee work

29%   74%

Initiating action

51%   3%

Follower, worker

5%   2%

Leading

15%   21%

Miscellaneous

Data from Dr. Launor F. Carter and colleagues

Their interactions with one another were different when doing assembling work than when doing committee work.

swing into a more democratic organization of business. It also becomes necessary with the increases of size and interdependence of business departments. One executive may or may not have all the information that is needed in reaching the decisions. And a team is good insurance when one executive is lost—fewer indispensable executives and more co-operating teams of executives and specialists. Some firms call this "a group think."

Chris Argyris listed encouragement of participation by others, which is related to this ability to do teamwork. This teamwork will likely increase in significance as business continues to grow and develop new procedures. Skill at conducting small group discussions is something the ambitious young executive needs to acquire.

The size of the group as well as the nature of its work also requires

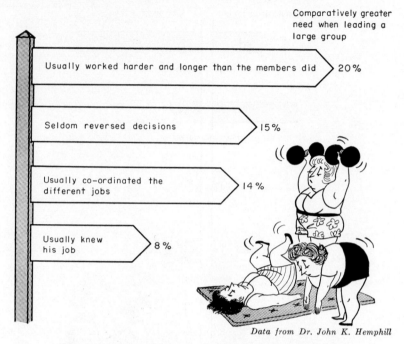

Comparatively greater
need when leading a
large group

Usually worked harder and longer than the members did 20%

Seldom reversed decisions 15%

Usually co-ordinated the
different jobs 14%

Usually knew
his job 8%

Data from Dr. John K. Hemphill

More was expected from the leaders of the larger groups.

changes in leadership methods. This is shown by a comparison of successful leaders of different-sized groups. The chartoon compares leaders of 184 groups that had more than 30 members in each and 181 groups that had less than 30 members to be led.

The Gist of the Chapter

1. What is meant by the power of position?
2. How do clothes and job titles help the power of position?
3. Discuss consent to be led.
4. What are things workers expect from their bosses?
5. Explain how the power of knowledge can help leadership.
6. Give examples of the power of understanding others.
7. Describe the six cardinal skills Dr. Hemphill found essential for successful leadership.
8. Outline ten special requirements desirable for higher executives.
9. Explain why a person may be a successful leader with one group but a failure with another group.

Things to Do and Problems to Discuss

1. Observe some firm or office, and report on how the level of leadership responsibility is shown by the regalia of office or position. Review earlier material in this book on job prestige.

2. Engage in casual conversation with different workers, and try to find what they think are some of the "good things" their bosses do. Relate these "good things" to the six cardinal skills given by Dr. Hemphill.

3. Refresh yourself on empathy from earlier in the book, and report how this could be improved to give the leader more power from understanding others.

4. When the general manager promoted Oswald J. to section chief, the manager told him, "You can't be their boss just because I say you are." What did the general manager mean?

5. Supervisor A. was walking through Supervisor B.'s department, when A. saw some employees wasting time. He called them down, but they just laughed at him and one commented, "Run along and tend to your own knitting." Did A. make a mistake? What would you guess about A.'s notions of leadership? Would it have been a mistake if a serious safety infraction were involved?

6. Should new supervisors, during their period of leadership training, be given a great deal of authority at the outset, so that the power of authority will help them? Argue both sides, then reach a conclusion.

7. Compare the skills given on Dr. Hemphill's list with those given in Chapter 16 on personality for business.

8. The crew you supervise worked extra hard to get out a rush job before quitting time. Should you take the responsibility of rewarding them by letting them go home early?

9. In a thoughtless moment you told a neighbor that your boss was only a fair executive, and that you would do his job much differently. Now you learn that the grapevine has told him about your remarks. What do you do next?

10. Some firms ask fellow workers whether or not they would like a certain worker as boss. This is done to be more certain they will give consent to the new supervisor's leadership. What can you say for and against that procedure?

11. Describe some work groups of widely differing kinds, such as day laborers and accountants. Analyze ways in which they might call for different kinds of leadership methods.

12. Discuss the special requirements for higher executives, especially to determine (a) why the requirements are needed, and (b) how an individual might develop the qualities listed.

13. Some men work hard to be elected to some public office, while a few have to be drafted for public office. In the light of this chapter, discuss which kind is likely to be the better leader.

14. Your high school alumni association has appointed you chairman for

next year's reunion. How could you apply Dr. Hemphill's six cardinal skills in that activity?

15. When her firm started a leadership training course along the lines of this chapter, Effie K. said she did not want to take it because she did not intend to become an executive. But she decided to take it anyway, after the training director told her it would help her lead her husband when she got one. Review the chapter to decide what Effie might use later for that domestic purpose.

21 ■ THE STRATEGIES
OF IMPELLING LEADERSHIP

WHAT THIS CHAPTER IS ABOUT

1 ■ Impelling vs. Compelling Leadership

Compelling leadership relies on authority, power, rules, threats. The forces come from outside the follower, or employee. High-pressure salesmen, some traffic policemen, domineering parents, officious public servants, and aggressive bosses tend to use mostly compelling methods. They give little heed to the other person's desires and goals.

Impelling leadership makes use of forces within the followers themselves. He leads his followers to want to do things. As you review some of the results of these contrasting methods, you may be astounded how much better results the impelling leadership produces, both immediately and in the long run.

But it seems that compelling methods are much more widely used than the impelling strategies, so don't expect too much of your boss. You will recall from the chapter on motivation, for instance, that half the time office supervisors do not explain why work changes are made. The clerks are compelled to follow the procedures, willy-nilly.

You will also remember that the building contractor got every twenty-ninth house free when the workers worked with the men they wanted to.

Sometimes you will hear executives complain that workers don't have initiative. But three-fourths of the clerks in one large modern office wanted to use their initiative to make decisions about their work.

Leadership methods may have much to do with the presumed disappearance of initiative. Workers' initiative has also been put in cold storage by "efficiency engineers" and central time and planning departments that assume that workers will cheerfully fall in line with the new procedures. Such centralized methods departments are more compelling than impelling.

The above examples have been mostly from white-collar groups. Yet it is generally recognized that office supervisors do not make so much use of compelling methods as factory supervisors do.

The differences between compelling and impelling methods are of significance in all walks of life. They help determine the kind of human relations that prevail in a family, a neighborhood, a church, or any other organization, as well as in the workplace. The results of coercive, or compelling, methods are pretty much the same, whether used with one's girl friend or on employees.

We shall start our comparison of these methods with some experiments on housewives' use of foods, which have become classic in the field of group dynamics.

2 ■ The Leader's Basic Strategy

People follow their own decisions best. An experiment with midwest homemakers shows this. Health authorities wanted more milk used. They tried two different ways to increase milk consumption. First, they tried a logical method. Skilled lectures were given to homemakers, explaining reasons why they should use more milk. A month afterward only 15 per cent of these women were using more milk.

Then they tried a psychological method. Groups of half a dozen women were brought together to talk over among themselves the benefits of using more milk. The leader of the discussions did little talking himself. He just got the discussion started, answered any questions they asked, and kept the conversation on the subject of milk. These small groups of women decided that they should use more milk. No outsider told them; it was their own decision. A month later, 50 per cent of these women were using more milk in their homes.

These two experiments demonstrate a leader's basic strategy: *the leader should lead people to decide for themselves.* Telling people what they should do seldom makes them want to do it. But, when they decide for themselves, they feel impelled to do it. You obey an order meekly if you have to, but you follow enthusiastically when you are led to your own decision.

The force of leadership depends on followers' decisions to follow, not on the good sense or loudness of the leader's commands.

This is interestingly confirmed in sales experiences. The Ace Company

More Housewives Followed Their Own Decision Than the Expert's Advice

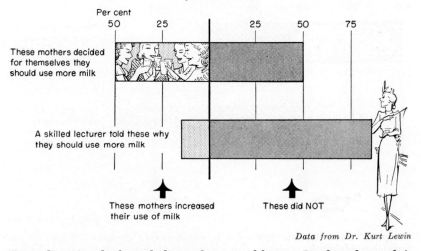

Per cent

50   25   25   50   75

These mothers decided for themselves they should use more milk

A skilled lecturer told these why they should use more milk

These mothers increased their use of milk   These did NOT

Data from Dr. Kurt Lewin

Group discussions lead people better than a good lecture. People make up their minds better when they talk things over than when they are merely told.

tried to provide year-round employment by making cheap electric toasters during slack seasons. The company planned to supply merchants with these toasters on consignment; payment was not required until the toasters were sold. The plan kept the plant going through the first slack season, for merchants were glad to have toasters without having to pay for them until sold.

But the Ace Company was soon in a tight financial position. The stores had not sent any money for the toasters. Men went out to collect but found little to collect. The merchants were making no effort to sell the toasters. They were putting their effort into merchandise they had chosen and in which their own money was involved.

When the Ace people planned this undertaking, it had seemed like good logic. They were virtually giving the stores something for nothing. They thought that merchants would give full co-operation, since they had a chance to make a profit without risking any of their own cash. But Ace had to learn the hard way that people co-operate best when they are actively involved. The merchant feels impelled to sell goods he has picked and paid for, not only to get his money back but also to vindicate his judgment in deciding to buy them in the first place.

Whether buying milk, selling goods, handling office workers or children, a person's own decisions impel more than the advice of an expert or the voice of a boss.

The experiments on increasing milk consumption show that people

Easier to Lead When Emotions Are Involved

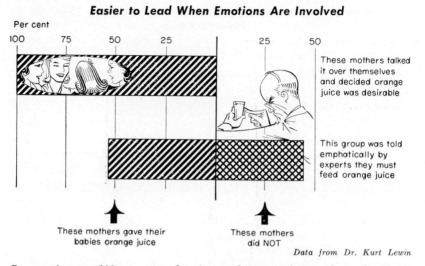

Data from Dr. Kurt Lewin

Co-operation was 100 per cent when it was their own decision but only 55 per cent when advised by an expert. The followership is higher than in the preceding chart, since the mothers are more emotionally concerned with young babies.

follow better when their heads are in it. Here are two that show that *people follow still better when their hearts also are in it.*

Most mothers are wrapped up heart and soul in their babies. When a nutrition expert told mothers about the importance of orange juice for their babies, 55 per cent were following his advice a month later. This is more than three times as many as used milk because an expert told them they should.

And when groups of half a dozen mothers talked over for themselves and decided to give their babies orange juice, 100 per cent of them did. This is twice as many as increased the use of milk after talking it over among themselves.

The milk and orange-juice experiments suggest two cardinal conclusions for increasing the power of leadership.

1. Two or three times as many people follow when it is their own decision than when told by an expert.
2. And many more follow when their emotions are involved in their decision.

3 ■ Destructive and Constructive Emotions to Impel

The rabble rouser uses the *destructive emotions* that are linked with the primitive mortido, or death urges, of human nature. Fear, hatred, jealousy, despair, and rage are examples. They are latent in everyone.

Well-intended bosses sometimes touch off these destructive emotions, also, and produce results the complete opposite of what was expected. The speediest worker, for instance, is set up as an example because the supervisor thinks rivalry will act as an incentive to improve the sluggards. The opposite usually results. The sluggards lie down all the more and gang up to make life miserable for the boss and his pet. Instead of one big family, the shop resembles the feuding of mountaineer clans.

In contrast, there are *constructive emotions*—joy, laughter, pity, wonder, cheerfulness, affection, hope—which are linked with the primitive libido of human nature. They foster co-operation and preserve the race. These are the emotions that impelled 100 per cent of those mothers to give their babies orange juice.

Constructive emotions are usually pleasant; destructive emotions, unpleasant.

Constructive emotions are likely to be signs of inner peace of mind, but destructive emotions are signs of inner tensions and distress.

Constructive emotions tend to make people help one another; destructive emotions destroy life, property, and reputation.

In the long run, destructive emotions tend to destroy the individual who has them, by stomach ulcer, high blood pressure, mental disorder. Constructive emotions are almost invariably beneficial to the mental and physical health of the individual and those with whom he works.

Tender emotions are powerful impellers. That is why people who have only fair abilities, but are likable, are better leaders and salesmen than are brilliant pickle-dispositions.

Salesmanship gives many examples of impelling leadership through constructive emotions. Selling is leadership on a person-to-person basis. The prospect must be led to think favorably of the salesman as well as of his product. Consumers cannot be annoyed into buying. The skilled salesman leads the prospect to talk himself into buying, as the homemakers talked themselves into using more milk. If the salesman argues, the chances of a sale are weakened. The salesman uses constructive emotions as he guides the prospect to picture the satisfaction, prestige, comfort, value he will have by making the purchase.

The salesman helps prospects make up their own minds. There is no sale until the prospect decides. The central task for all leaders is to help people make up their minds. It is their own decision that motivates their action.

4 ■ Compelling Leadership in a Jewelry Factory

"Who says so?" The answer often foretells success or failure of leadership.

The girls who soldered earrings in a novelty-jewelry factory were up in arms because someone had sawed six inches off the ends of their worktables during the night. They claimed that this made the tables too small for their work. All forenoon they sputtered. Some girls became so angry they cried. Output went way down.

"Whatsa matter with those women?" the foreman exclaimed. "I watched yesterday. Those tables were a couple feet longer than any of them needed. Not enough room between the tables for the trucks; so I had the carpenter make more room by taking six inches off one end. The girls don't have anything to bellyache about. Women sure are funny."

Those girls were no funnier than anyone else. Logically, they had nothing to complain about. Psychologically, they did have a complaint. For one thing, the prestige value of their jobs had been cut when the size of their work area was cut. More critical than that, however, was the fact that human nature makes people rebel when anything happens that affects their work—unless they have had a part in planning the change. The good sense of a plan does not count so much as whose plan it is. When you feel the plan is yours, you have more will to follow it.

The foreman probably thought he was saving time by having the change made at once, without taking time to talk it over with the girls. But the direct way he did it actually lost many hours and put him in bad. Perhaps he thought he was paid to do the thinking for the department. He may not have known that the real leader is paid to get others to think, so that they will follow him enthusiastically.

5 ▪ Impelling Leadership in a Textile Plant

In one textile mill, productive efficiency was too low to be healthy. The equipment could not be changed, and the only thing to do was improve the leadership. The employees were on piece rate and should have had a selfish interest in turning out all the work possible. Psychologists were called in to see what could be done. They chose two groups of workers for an experiment in impelling leadership.

The bosses told one group that time studies showed they should be turning out more production. More production would mean more money for the workers. Then the bosses put on pressure to make the girls work faster. This was compelling. The workers could have made more money for themselves, but scarcely one did. In fact, during the next few months, their average output dropped, as shown by the bottom curve in the chart, "Impelling Leadership Increases Output." Some workers went to pieces, as the bosses put on more pressure. This old-style "production drive" was self-defeating.

Now let's see what happened to the other group of employees. They were brought together in small groups to talk over what might be wrong with production. The workers did the talking, not the bosses. A psychologist served as discussion leader, to keep the talk going and on the topic. He did not tell them how to turn out more work; he left it up to

Impelling Leadership Increases Output

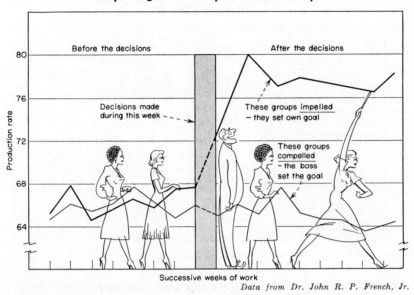

Before the decisions

After the decisions

Decisions made during this week

These groups impelled — they set own goal

These groups compelled – the boss set the goal

Production rate

80

76

72

68

64

Successive weeks of work

Data from Dr. John R. P. French, Jr.

Output increased 18 per cent when the girls in a sewing factory made their own decisions to increase output. All workers were on piece rate. No changes were made in working conditions.

the girls to decide whether it might be possible, and how. After several discussion meetings, these groups decided that they could increase their output and set a goal toward which to try.

The next week, their output jumped to a new high. And during the next few months, it averaged 18 per cent higher than before this impelling leadership was used. No one told these girls to move faster or waste less time. It was their own decision. They were impelled from inside themselves. They had no motive to slump on the job, to prove that the boss was wrong. These groups were impelled to increase production, not to resent being compelled.

Since they had agreed in front of others that they could do more, they had an added motive to make that decision come true. Just as a telephone message is more likely to be delivered if you ask the name of the unseen person with whom you leave it.

6 ▪ Impelling Leadership When Changes Are Introduced

Another test of the merit of impelling leadership came later when a change in work methods was needed. People who are used to working a certain way usually resist any change in method. Companies have found it easier to break in green workers than to try to force experienced em-

The Girls Took to the Changed Work Method Better When They Helped Plan It

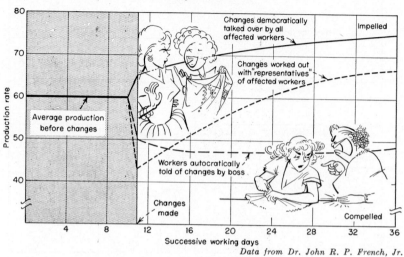

Autocratic, "representative," and democratic leadership produce three distinct
results when changed methods are introduced to power sewing-machine operators.
All three groups were on the same piece rates, and work conditions and methods
were the same.

ployees to learn new ways. When this textile plant was faced with changed
methods in some departments, the psychologists tested three ways for
leading workers to adapt to the changes.

Compelling leadership. One group was bluntly told, in the old-fashioned
way, that changes were to be made, and they might as well make the best
of it. Their production went down about 20 per cent and stayed down.
This was compelling leadership that did not lead. See the bottom curve
in the chartoon on this page.

Representatives. Another group of workers was told about the proposed
changes by "representatives," not by the bosses. Engineers explained the
whys and wherefores of the changes to these representatives. Then the
representative workers returned to their departments to explain to other
workers what was going to happen. When the changes were made, these
departments slumped at first but gradually improved until they were
slightly better than with the former method. They are shown on the middle curve in the chart.

Impelling leadership. Impelling methods were used with the third
group. Small groups of these workers were brought together under a
discussion leader, and the workers themselves talked over the problem
and changes that might solve it. The workers, not the boss, did the talking in this "group think." The changes they finally decided to make were,

of course, the changes that were used for all workers. This group, however, decided on the changes for themselves. They had a steadily increasing output after the changes were made, as shown in the top curve of
the chart. This impelled group reached a level 20 per cent higher than
they had before the changes; the compelled group fell 20 per cent below
their former output.

You may want to look again at the chartoon in Chapter 2 that outlines
the steps that are followed when changes are made by the democratic
method.

7 ■ The Development of Impelling Leadership

Few companies operate at an efficiency as high as 85 per cent. Most
are nearer 50 per cent efficiency. Companies continually drive to raise
efficiency. Yet these very drives are a cause of lowered efficiency, as you
now can understand.

Most bosses use compelling methods when they want to increase efficiency. They take the direct route, as the foreman did when he had the
tables sawed off. Compelling produces only halfhearted obedience at
best and more often arouses lasting lethargy.

*When any action is contemplated that directly touches the worker's
life, the strategy of impelling is essential.* Company finances, expansion,
and other top-level decisions may be made autocratically without much
harm. But, when individuals are concerned, look out! if the decisions are
made solely by the brass hats. Henry Ford II says: "Whenever possible,
the men below should be given a chance to participate in making those
decisions."

Impelling leadership demands patience. The peppery manager who
wants things done the instant he thinks of them lacks the patience to
lead employees to take part in decisions. In an emergency, a forceful direct order may be appropriate and cause no harm. But, in all other situations affecting workers, the best way to lead is to take time to make them
want to follow. Trying to "do it now" has lowered many executives' leadership and has reduced workers' efficiency.

Impelling leadership requires ability to keep in the background. Some
aggressive supervisors cannot do this. They are inclined to dominate in
a conference, when it would be more effective if they merely presented
the problem and then gave any technical information the others needed
to reach their decision. Philip D. Armour summed it up by saying: "Most
of my success has been due to keeping my mouth shut." The impeller
listens.

Impelling leadership treats people as seedbeds for ideas. The impellers
plant ideas in others' minds. They share problems with employees. They
inspire others to think. And, although the leaders may know the answers,

they keep mum and wait for others to discover the same answers. Making others admit that your idea is the right one does not make it impelling. It has to be their idea.

That autocratic foreman who sawed off the tables to surprise the girls should have followed this impelling procedure:

Called attention to the trouble of pushing trucks through the narrow aisle
Asked for ideas for making more room for the trucks
Kept the girls thinking and talking about possibilities until *they* offered a
    solution
Made the change immediately as they recommended

It looks easy when outlined that way. But it is not easy. It takes about two years of self-discipline and practice before the superior supervisor can acquire the knack of leading workers to decisions. Some of them can never get the necessary patience and control of a domineering streak for impelling leadership.

It is not impelling for people merely to talk things over. The talk must lead to a decision—their decision.

People need to be led. Most people want to be led. But they consent wholeheartedly only to the impelling leader who (1) arouses constructive emotions, (2) has patience, (3) keeps in the background, (4) plants ideas, and (5) leads them to a decision.

8 ▪ Accident Reduction by Impelling Leadership

The leader should be all business. But giving orders is not his business. It is leading others to decisions to follow him.

An Ohio factory, for example, had a high accident rate. Insurance companies charged them an extra premium. As a result, the management decided to hire a consulting safety engineer. He studied each machine and submitted a long list of safety recommendations.

His recommendations were installed at considerable expense. But the accident rate did not come down. The workers "did not believe in" the silly safety devices and rules and ignored them. The company tried to compel workers to use the safety equipment; but they did not feel impelled to follow, even though their own fingers and eyes were at stake.

One department supervisor used a different approach. He told his men the new safety gadgets needed to be changed. "You fellows could make something better yourselves," he told them, to plant an idea. In a few days, a young worker came to him with a new idea for a better safety device.

"Now that sketch looks sensible," the supervisor told him. "Let's see what Steve thinks about it; he's the oldest man in the shop." Steve had a minor change to suggest. That lunch hour, Steve, the Kid, and several workers huddled around a machine, talking over better ways of protection. By quitting time, they had plans between them for a device they were sure was better than the expert's.

The supervisor let them explain their idea to the machine shop, where a model was made. It was put on the Kid's machine first, and he was proud as Punch of it. The rest of the department liked the device, and soon all wanted one. This new protection was faithfully used, too, since it was their idea, not something an outsider tried to force on them.

The office manager heard about this experience, and it set him thinking. He soon got his workers into huddles to see what accident hazards they could find and eliminate. In a few days, they provided him with a long list.

Hands were pinched while closing disappearing-typewriter desks. (This hazard was eliminated by attaching a handle for closing.)

Desk and file drawers were left open to stumble over. (Without any ruling, the office workers began to close drawers of their own volition.)

Loose razor blades in desk drawers. (Solved by fastening them to small cardboard with adhesive tape.)

Collisions at blind corner. (Hazard was eliminated by installing a mirror to give view around corner.)

Pencil sharpeners projected where people bumped into them. (The sharpeners were relocated.)

Weak springs in swivel chairs caused loss of balance. (The janitor tightened the springs.)

Waste paper on floor caused slipping. (More of it lands in wastebaskets now.)

An all-glass door caused people to try to walk through it. (Hazard eliminated by lettering on glass.)

Loose linoleum squares caused tripping. (The squares were cemented down.)

Wire edges on filing-cabinet drawers caused cuts. (The rough places were covered with adhesive tape.)

Running to time clock caused collisions.

Heavy parcels were stacked dangerously in the storage room.

For years, the office manager had been trying to improve office housekeeping and break up the commuters' crush at the time clock. Now these and many other little danger zones were cleared up because the employees themselves developed the ideas.

Getting workers to talk things over is the start; but to reach a decision, the discussion must be brought to a head by the leader.

Make haste slowly is a requisite for impelling others. The leader himself may be quick to see what needs to be done, but he does not expect others to be equally quick on the trigger. Human nature has too much inertia to make up its mind speedily. We live in an age of speed, but are slowpokes about giving consent to follow another's ideas. This slowness tempts some would-be leaders to make the decisions themselves and to give direct orders. But the impelling leader knows the superior value of biding his time until the other person has the idea for himself—that is a psychological moment. You will learn about other psychological moments shortly.

9 ■ Six Steps in Impelling Leadership

Making haste slowly does not mean just sitting by and waiting for something to happen. The impelling leader makes things happen by these six steps.

1. Plan far ahead. Plan for followers to reach their own decisions before an emergency arises. The impelling leader needs more foresight than the compeller. Weak leadership results unless there have been long-range plans and strategies. Short-range plans cause emergencies. Emergencies call for blunt orders, and blunt orders weaken the leader's power over others.

2. Subtly arrange events. Assist followers in reaching their decisions. Do not leave decisions to chance or to outside influences. Plant ideas to start followers thinking. Florence Nightingale, the founder of modern nursing training, relied on this method. "I propose in private to Mr. A.

Courtesy Chesapeake and Ohio Railway Company

During lunch hours, and after work, repair-shop employees planned and made this model for remodeling the railway shop to work on diesel locomotives. These men from the job found "bugs" galore in the plans of the consulting engineers who did not work in a shop. The railroad directors approved the men's plan and put two and a half million dollars behind it as a starter.

the resolution I think he is most capable of carrying in committee and then leave it to them," she confessed.

3. Keep followers thinking about the problem. The impelling leader does not nag by harping about the problem. But he does keep the problem in the fore by demonstrations and planting more ideas.

4. Keep the leader's plans or ideas a secret. The impeller needs a poker player's caution about revealing his own feelings. He does not spout his opinions and ideas; he asks for the other person's. This leaves the "yes man" in the dark and keeps others from feeling they are just rubber stamps for the boss.

5. Be thankful if followers develop a good decision not thought of by the leader. As the impeller stimulates others to reach decisions, he is multiplying abilities and getting other points of view. He may get two ideas to grow where only one grew before. He should not be embarrassed if "the little people" sometimes think better than he does. He should feel flattered that his impelling strategies are helping develop little people into bigger ones. He will not be embarrassed, anyway, if he kept his own ideas a secret—then it cannot be said, "The boss was wrong."

6. Make haste to carry out what followers have decided. Go slowly until followers have decided; then become a man of action in carrying out their decision. If the leader carries out a decision as soon as he hits on it himself, the effect is like pulling a trigger on an empty gun. Load the gun by sharing the power of decision in problems that involve followers. By giving up a little, the leader gains a great deal.

Instead of "doing it now," plan first, so that it will be done eagerly by others. Slow at the start, until it is their idea; then hasten to put it into action.

10 ■ Give Them Responsibility and Credit

Most of the daily developments in an office or factory can be handled in impelling ways without having formal discussion meetings. The human climate, usually set by the leader, can make things impelling without any conscious attempt to do so.

When the leader has the habit, for example, of delegating responsibility to his employees, the workers are much more likely to feel impelled from the inside rather than coerced by the boss. Here are several illustrations.

Rugby School was upside down when Thomas Arnold was put in charge. The older students had long been out of hand; they made the lives of the younger students miserable and drove the teachers to distraction. To change the situation, Arnold asked the older students to help him make Rugby a better school. As they began to share the responsibility with him, their conduct was transformed.

A businessman applied the same psychology of leadership when a gang of young neighborhood boys broke into his office and turned it topsy-turvy for fun. He hired some of the boys to guard his office against depredations by other boys.

Did you ever have a boss ask: "Will you take charge of this for me?" You worked like a beaver, didn't you, when he shared even that little responsibility with you?

Business Week magazine has advised executives to give their secretaries more of the responsible work for which the girls have been trained. The secretary who is not given some projects for which she is responsible may find an excuse for taking a job with another executive.

Giving credit is closely related to sharing responsibility. Both make others feel actively involved. They are no longer bystanders but have become active participants.

Cordell Hull, the Tennessee hillbilly who became Secretary of State, accomplished much of his diplomatic work by seeing that the other person received credit. The foreign minister of Argentina, for instance, was strongly anti-United States. Secretary Hull won him over before a Pan-American conference by a combination of flattery and giving him a chance to get the credit. Hull explained to the Argentine the program the United States wanted adopted.

"Now, Mr. Minister," he continued, "we want the best man down here to put that program forward, so that we can give it our support. We hope you will do it; but, if you won't, we will get the next best man to do it." The irascible Argentine diplomat was won to our side by that simple strategy.

People are zealous for credit. The astute leader gives others the credit, even when they do not deserve it. For when they are credited with an idea, they are much more likely to follow it willingly. Sometimes the credit is made to seem incidental, as by saying: "A couple of weeks ago you thought it might be helpful if we worked out a new way of keeping inventory records."

An old Jesuit educator has said: "It is surprising how much good a man can do in the world if he allows others to take the credit for it."

The impelling leader has to be big enough to control his own wishes for receiving the credit. "It marks a big step in a man's development," Andrew Carnegie observed, "when he comes to realize that other men can be called in to help him do a better job than he can do alone."

11 ■ The Strong and Weak Executives of One Firm

The 96 top executives of one corporation were studied by Dr. Earl Brooks at the New York State School of Industrial Relations at Cornell University. The executives were reported on not only by their superiors but also by their own employees. When averages were struck, about the same number of executives came out "Excellent" as came out "Below-average." Then Dr. Brooks went to work looking for details that made a difference between being "Excellent" and "Below-average." The differences he discovered illustrate many of the points of this chapter.

Consider delegating responsibility to subordinates, which we were just discussing. The superiors reported that 73 per cent of the "Excellent" executives delegated effectively, but that none of the "Below-average" did.

The following gives a quick rundown of other pertinent facts that apparently made a difference between being "Excellent" or "Below-average." The items toward the top of the list had most bearing on successful leadership in this corporation.

	"Excellent" Executives Per Cent	"Below-average" Executives Per Cent
They always, or almost always:		
1. Had workers share in making decisions	100	10
2. Co-ordinated the activities of workers	100	10
3. Made full use of skills and abilities of workers	100	10
4. Let workers know how they were doing	83	zero
5. Saw that authority of each worker was clearly understood	83	10
6. Kept workers informed of activities in other departments	83	10
7. Kept workers informed about things affecting their work	92	20
8. Encouraged workers to exchange information	92	20
9. Knew how well workers were doing	100	30
10. Encouraged workers to express their ideas and opinions	100	30
11. Selected the right person for the job	100	30

12 ■ Effects on Output and Morale

We have learned earlier how restrictive leaders are likely to create a human climate that prompts workers to restrict their efficiency. Records show, in addition, that output may be lowered, even though the climate is not frigid enough to produce intentional stalling. A slight chilliness can lessen the will to work, although there is no deliberate stretching the work out. This comparison of large offices, where identical operations were performed, shows what a chilly climate can do. (Chartoon on page 386.) The supervisors of all the high-output offices were of the impelling style; whereas only one-third of those in the low-producing offices were. All the compelling bosses supervised low-producing work groups.

Such records should be taken seriously by the person who wants keenly to lead others. This is worth repeating because it has been found that the

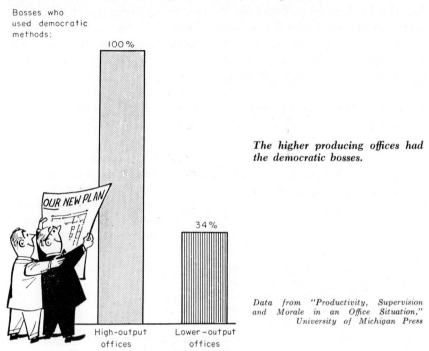

Bosses who used democratic methods:

100%

34%

High-output offices

Lower-output offices

The higher producing offices had the democratic bosses.

Data from "Productivity, Supervision and Morale in an Office Situation," University of Michigan Press

person who "just naturally" bosses others is usually one who inclines to be compelling in his methods of handling people.

An inclination to be compelling is shown in everyday life by: Telling others how to do things, although not their boss. Taking charge of something without being asked to. Pointing out to others how they are wrong.

In short, aggressive people, and those with "lots of initiative," may have chilling-sized doses of bossiness.

In the part of this book that dealt with morale, we learned about the need for building self-esteem, confident hopefulness, and friendliness rather than hostility. The chilly climate that restrictive methods set up would not be expected to help worker morale. This expectation is confirmed by many studies.

People need to be led. And usually they want to be led—if led properly. Leaving them alone is not leadership. Young executives sometimes assume that democratic methods mean leaving the workers to their own devices and impulses. That is usually disastrous. People's efforts need to be co-ordinated. Group spirit needs to be built, and group conflicts need to be lessened. Individuals need to be trained for better job performance, encouraged so that they use their full will to work, and helped through personal difficulties. The leader cannot do those essential things by ignoring his followers or leaving them alone. In a way of speaking, the leader should be the great co-ordinator and stimulator.

— — — — — — — — — — — — — — — — — — —

The Gist of the Chapter

1. What effects do leadership methods have upon the initiative of those being led?

2. Tell about the experiment to increase milk consumption and its significance.

3. What additional points were illustrated by the orange-juice study?

4. Give examples of destructive emotions. of constructive emotions.

5. What blunders were made by the foreman in the jewelry factory?

6. Explain how output was increased in the textile plant.

7. What was the most successful way of changing work methods in the same plant?

8. List five things to watch in developing compelling leadership.

9. What are the six steps in using compelling leadership methods?

10. What is the point in giving unskilled workers responsibility and credit?

Things to Do and Problems to Discuss

1. Study the advertisements of some courses on "Leadership." In the light of this and the preceding chapter, how helpful would it be for the leader to take courses in public speaking, winning arguments, and remembering names and faces?

2. Interview a few workers to get examples of (a) situations where their boss has himself taken the credit for things the worker has done or for ideas the worker has offered, (b) where the boss has given the worker credit. Report on how the workers felt about each instance, and how their will to work was affected.

3. Discuss situations in which "Do it now" would be a good way, and other situations when it would be harmful.

4. What effect would high levels of personal aspirations have on making a person lean toward the compelling or impelling side?

5. A contractor is building a new house for Oswald J. As Oswald watches the men at work, he wants to make some suggestions to them. Should he give orders directly to the workmen, talk it over with them, with the contractor, or what?

6. Occasionally a boss thinks he is "applying psychology" when he (a) gives a worker credit that is not deserved, or (b) pretends that the worker suggested doing something that the worker has never thought of. Discuss the possible effects, and ethical points involved.

7. When a supervisor arouses a competitive spirit between workers in the same department, is he likely to arouse constructive or destructive emotions? when a company arouses a competitive spirit toward rival firms?

8. Phyllis M. is a private secretary who could handle more details for her boss than he gives her to do. How could she get him to delegate more responsibility to her?

9. Describe some situations in which compelling methods would seem to be called for.

10. Effie K. wants her boss to buy a new office machine for her work. Explain to her how she could apply the strategies in this chapter to lead the boss to conclude that it was necessary to get a new machine.

11. You have planted ideas, and now the workers have reached a solution that will mean more work for you. Discuss what you should do in this case. Should you share the responsibility in some way to lessen the burden on you?

12. One of your young engineers is continually writing memos to the higher-ups and going over your head in doing this. You suspect that it is because he wants to get the credit. Discuss possible ways to handle this situation.

13. One of your supervisors, who apparently wants to stand in well with his workers, criticizes company policies that are not liked by the workers. He believes he is being democratic by this open faultfinding. Discuss the pros and cons and how to handle this situation.

14. Make a comparison of likenesses and differences between impelling leadership methods and the personality-interview method given in Chapter 18.

15. Discuss the differences between the Soviet methods in government and industry and the United States methods, in terms of impelling or compelling leadership.

22 ■ IMITATION, SUGGESTIBILITY, AND ROLE PLAYING IN LEADERSHIP

WHAT THIS CHAPTER IS ABOUT

1. *Imitation—the power of example*
2. *Suggestions and indirect orders more impelling*
3. *Suggestions most impelling from those who are liked*
4. *Role playing to find what should be done*
5. *Working through soft spots*
6. *Waiting for the other fellow to make the first move*
7. *"Psychological moments"*
8. *An impelling voice*
9. *Practice in personal leadership*

1 ■ Imitation—the Power of Example

Have you ever noticed how many people cough in church after one person has coughed? Imitation prompts people to do as others do, without pausing to wonder why. Secret-service operatives took advantage of imitative conduct during Franklin D. Roosevelt's hush-hush conference at Casablanca. A jeepload of secret-service men preceded the armored car in which the President rode. To draw the attention of the street crowds away from the President, all men in the jeep looked upward at the same point in the sky. Everyone on the street did the same and were so busy looking at the sky they did not see the President.

Children are called "little monkeys" because of their imitation; yet adults, too, are amazingly imitative. An elderly man at a movie, for example, imitated the screen hero's courtly bows and bumped his head on the seat in front of him.

Big shots are as imitative as the next person. One president's unpredictable moods made most of his vice-presidents avoid him—but not the one in charge of research and development. This vice-president made it a rule to speak before the president did, smiling and saying something cheering before the president could show a grouchy streak. The power of imitation impelled the president to be more agreeable.

The impelling leader needs to be somewhat of an actor. He should originate, by acting if necessary, the attitude for the others to imitate.

A customer may be irritating, but the skilled salesman acts as if the purchaser were the most delightful person in the world. As a spokesman for Selfridge & Company, Ltd., says: "In this store, we do not, when considering promotion, look for the young man or young woman who wears a look of portentous solemnity. More likely the choice will fall on one who can smile, one who is not only cheerful but is also likely to be the cause of cheerfulness in other people."

By the clever use of imitation, the impeller can get things done without saying a word. While walking through an office with the manager, one supervisor stooped to pick up a piece of paper that had missed the wastebasket. During the next minute, half a dozen workers inspected to see whether they had missed their baskets. His example was imitated cheerfully and without thinking; an order, on the other hand, might have caused grumbling.

The leader's example should help inspire the desired conduct. John Wanamaker did not have to enforce rules about punctuality, since he was always the first at the store. In contrast, another store tried to obtain punctuality by removing the steps leading to the employees' entrance five minutes before opening time.

The "whispering strategy" quiets noisy children by imitation. Instead of telling the children to be quiet, the parent speaks in a whisper. Almost invariably, children imitate the whisper; and quiet is won without a struggle. This whispering strategy is useful also with an adult who is inclined to raise his voice in an argument. Just keep your voice lower than usual, and imitation may take the argument out of him. It is hard to argue in whispers.

An example of how little bosses imitate bigger bosses comes from a big city electric-power company. Some of the first-line supervisors were not cost-conscious; others were very cost-conscious. Analysis revealed that the supervisors who were most cost-conscious were under bosses who were also most cost-conscious. The attitudes of the big bosses are "caught" by the bosses under them.

Dr. Douglas McGregor told a session of the National Office Management Association: "The most effective training for a potential executive will be the day-to-day treatment that he receives from his own boss. Every time a man deals with a subordinate, he is in effect training him."

2 ■ Suggestions and Indirect Orders More Impelling

Suggestibility is the imitation of ideas and attitudes. People tend to think as the leader thinks—but not when he tries to compel them to think his way, and not unless they like and admire him. If your employees do not think the way you wish they would, don't blame *them*. Plant more suggestions. Argue and order and plead less.

Disputing
points made
by others:

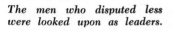

The men who disputed less were looked upon as leaders.

10.4%

6.2%

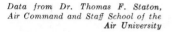

Data from Dr. Thomas F. Staton,
Air Command and Staff School of the
Air University

Rated as leaders
by the others

Not rated
as leaders
by others

Would-be leaders often try too obviously to lead. They issue direct, blunt orders when they should plant suggestions. It takes longer to plant ideas, but it gets better results in the long run. The followers are then following their own decisions.

Ideas have to be planted indirectly to have impelling power. There is no suggestibility in a direct order, such as "Open the window." But to say, "It is getting stuffy in here" is an indirect way to suggest that a window be opened. The indirect is more likely to be followed without resistance or criticism.

Impelling leaders often use questions to plant ideas. Owen D. Young, the farm boy who became chairman of General Electric Company, tried not to give orders. He asked questions. "How long will it take to get these credit reports?" was his indirect way of saying "Get the reports at once."

The skilled salesman uses an indirect suggestion when he asks: "What color hat do you think would look best with your new suit?" The bungling salesman would have said: "You need a new hat."

Questions that can be answered "yes" or "no" are not effective for planting ideas. They are closed-end questions; when they are answered, the subject is closed.

The impelling leader uses *open-end questions* and keeps the other person thinking. Had that salesman asked, "Do you want a gray hat?" it would have been a closed-end question. And a "no" answer would have stopped the sale. An open-end question keeps the other person talking and stimulates his thinking. Stimulate people; don't quiz them.

Demonstrations and reading. Demonstrations and reading can be used to stimulate people and to plant ideas indirectly. The new general manager of a Michigan chemical factory was an engineer in his early thirties, a comer. His subordinates were old enough to be his father, men who had grown careless and overconfident from long experience. They would have sputtered at direct orders from a youngster. To wake them up and to plant ideas for modernizing their work, Bill arranged excursions to other chemical works. He did not find open fault with the men. He acted as amazed as they at the methods and housekeeping of other companies. "I don't see how that company does it," he would say, "but if they can do it, I know that you fellows can do it better."

Before his fortieth birthday, Bill was vice-president in charge of half a dozen plants. His skill in planting ideas indirectly, without belittling the other person, pushed him to the top.

When you feel like giving blunt orders, it is wise to:

> Stop
> Look
> Figure an indirect way

"Mr. Jones cannot see you now" is negative.

"Mr. Jones can see you at 1:30" is positive. The negative statement will cause grumbling. The positive will win co-operation, even if it means waiting a half day.

"No smoking here" is negative and invites violation of the rule.

"Smoking area around the corner" is positive and more likely to be obeyed cheerfully.

The impelling leader thinks positively—about what can be done. He gets others thinking positively, by imitation. Opportunities rather than restrictions, merits rather than demerits, are kept in the forefront. The positive outlook generates an optimism that knocks the *im* out of impossible.

3 ▪ Suggestions Most Impelling from Those Who Are Liked

Suggestions have greater force when they come from persons who are liked and respected. The pleasant, likable salesman makes more sales than the pickle-faced one. Leaders who are liked, even idolized, have most success planting ideas. Popularity is not the impelling leader's goal, but popularity helps achieve his goals.

It is difficult to take suggestions from a person who finds fault, for faultfinders are disliked. Criticism puts people on the defensive and stiffens resistance. The impelling leader learns how to make corrections without faultfinding. He helps, rather than criticizes. When H. J. Heinz saw

MOST promotable bosses	LEAST promotable bosses

Workers saying: "My boss is likable"

56%

32%

Data from Drs. Floyd C. Mann and James K. Dent

Supervisors who were considered likable by their workers were more likely to be considered promotable by the company.

poor workmanship, he never mentioned it. Instead, he pitched in and worked with poor workers a few minutes to show them the better way. This was one of the strategies by which he built the peddling of his mother's horse-radish into the famous 57 varieties of prepared foods.

In all personal leadership, it is wise to try to have people like you before you try to lead them. In selling, try to have them like you, before trying to sell directly.

Where there is liking, there is imitation and suggestibility. Where there is disliking, there is resistance and avoidance. Along with being indirect, try being likable. And put the accent on the positive.

People also are impelled strongly by their own interests. The impelling leader has to put himself in the other fellow's shoes and figure what will make the other fellow want to do something. This requires empathy, which you first met in the chapters on human relations and morale.

One factory was plagued by accidental falls as women workers rushed downstairs at quitting time. Big signs were posted telling them to walk, but the signs did not halt the stampede. Finally, a full-length mirror was installed one-third of the way down the stairs and another two-thirds of the way down. These halted the quitting-time rush, for the girls paused to primp a moment in front of the mirrors.

4 ▪ Role Playing to Find What Should Be Done

Many puzzling problems in leading people become as simple as ABC when the leader takes the other person's point of view. In studying personality, we found that most people dress and act and talk to play a role in life that intrigues them. But that role playing is unintentional.

Another kind of role playing is done intentionally to help get another person's point of view. This kind of role playing is part of the procedure

Courtesy Allen H. Taylor, Daystrom Incorporated

Role playing in supervisory training. The two foremen at the end of the table are acting out a situation in which a worker has a complaint. One foreman takes the role of the complaining worker. A recording of the spontaneous skit is played back later, so that the foremen can criticize their handling of the situation.

known as the *psychodrama.* In a psychodrama, you act out another person's part. The acting is spontaneous; there are no written lines to read or memorize.

Salesmen used to be trained by having them memorize a sales demonstration. Sales training now includes role playing. Salesmen switch roles and play the parts of customers. Pretending to be a customer makes a salesman feel from the inside how a customer reacts when a salesman does all the talking or belittles his good taste.

Foremen also are trained by having them take the role of workers who are being criticized, or who have complaints to make.

One autocratic old river-boat skipper was hired as barge captain by an oil transport company. The old tyrant soon had mutiny on his hands. To change the captain's ways, the skipper was asked to play the role of deck hand, while the industrial-relations man played the role of browbeating skipper. In the skit, the pretended deck hand was "laid out in lavender"—just as the skipper laid out his men.

"By Jerusha! No man should talk that way to me," the skipper ejaculated after a few minutes.

"All right, then let's shift roles. I'll be deck hand, and you be captain. Show me how it should be done." And the captain, having played the role of the other fellow, gave the industrial-relations man a demonstration of more human treatment after realizing how the other fellow feels.

A few "natural leaders" take the other fellow's point of view as a matter of course before planning any action. "I liked to get the other man's point of view," Owen D. Young said, "so that I could restate it better than he could." But most people need to discipline themselves to study what will interest or stimulate the other person. Role playing is one of the best aids to gain an understanding of others' yearnings and tender spots.

5 ■ Working Through Soft Spots

James Gordon Bennett's soft spot was dogs. He usually had several in his office. Scheming reporters would win the great editor's favor by concealing bones in their pockets when they went to his office. The aroma of bones would draw the dogs to the visitor, and Bennett could not help favoring a person his dogs liked.

J. P. Morgan's weakness was his grandchildren. He had refused to allow anyone to write his biography, until one prospective biographer said:

"Mr. Morgan, what would you give to have a biography of your grandfather?"

"I'd give a great deal."

"That may be just the way your grandchildren will feel in a few years."

That hit his soft spot, and he agreed to make information available for writing his life story.

Everyone has a soft spot or a blind side. The impelling leader finds these favored feelings and works through them to make people want to follow him. He does not take people for granted but continually studies them as unique individuals.

6 ■ *Waiting for the Other Fellow to Make the First Move*

Waiting for the other fellow to make the first move is often the surest way to win his consent to follow.

Donald Smith, a redheaded Scotch immigrant, was agent for the Hudson's Bay Company, in Canada's wilderness. Word came to his post that a half-breed trapper had some rare black foxskins, which he would not sell to the company because of complaints over previous trades. Young Smith tramped twenty miles across the snow to the half-breed's cabin, arriving at sunset. The reception was as chilly as the weather. Smith asked to spend the night, since it was five more miles to the next cabin.

In his coat pocket, there were a few pieces of candy and some colored pictures for the children. Smith addressed the trapper's squaw as "Madame" and helped her with the fire and meal. Not a word was said about furs.

The next morning, as Smith was leaving, the sulky trapper exclaimed, "Aren't you going to look at my furs?" He rushed out some breath-taking black fox, set his own price, and Smith gladly paid.

Donald Smith, who knew the value of waiting for the other fellow to make the first move, became the first Baron Strathcona and Mount Royal. He built the Canadian Pacific Railway and became governor of the oldest company in the world, the Hudson's Bay Company.

Patience to wait for the other person to make the first move always helps a leader. That first move shows a willingness to follow or to do business. It is more impelling, since the other person originated it himself. It is a "psychological moment."

From the account of Doctor Covner's work, remember the importance of the pause, as you wait for the other person to resume talking. That is an example of waiting for the other person to make the first move.

And from earlier in the present chapter recall the usefulness of setting the right attitude for the other person to imitate. Set the right attitude; then wait for him to make the first move.

7 ■ *"Psychological Moments"*

A psychological moment is a time when the other person is in a mood to follow a leader. There are many psychological moments, not just one. The impelling leader waits for one of these favorable moments

—or creates one. Donald Smith created one when he started to leave, after a visit of several hours in which furs were not mentioned.

The psychological moment is often a matter of proper timing. When enthusiasm is rising, almost any moment is a psychological moment. After the peak of enthusiasm is past, and the other person is cooling off, the moment is gone. The time to ask for decisions, or a sale, is when enthusiasm is on the rise. Watch the other person for signs of interest. Leave him while his interest is high and after one of your own remarks.

Talk should be timed so that it does not intrude on the other person. If a man is in the middle of figuring his income tax, it is no time to interrupt him. Interruptions always make the mood unfavorable. Wait until the person has completed his task or reached a stopping point.

Busy men do not have many stopping points. In such cases, a leader plans for psychological moments. An invitation to lunch, golf, or a ball game can create a psychological moment. When Harvey Firestone was trying to start his rubber company, he needed help from the busiest banker in Akron. Firestone was watching for an opportunity when the banker was not busy. When he learned that the banker was going to be in Chicago one week end, Firestone went there, too, and "just happened" to run into the banker in a hotel lobby. It seemed to be a casual meeting. The banker had no business on his mind and took a fancy to the young fellow who had not intruded.

The expert tests the readiness, or psychological willingness, of the other person with small talk. If the conversation shows the other person had a poor night's sleep or is in a bad mood, it is foolhardy to expect co-operation at that time. In such a situation, simply make some pleasant, short conversation and come back another time when the mood may be more favorable.

Always test receptiveness before trying to lead people. If a person is argumentative, suspicious, restless, or if he changes the subject, he is not in a mood to co-operate. Put yourself in his shoes, play his role in your imagination, and ask yourself whether you would co-operate if you were acting and talking as he is at that moment. The leader has to be good at taking a hint as well as good at giving one.

8 ■ An Impelling Voice

Voice training can help personal leadership. Some voices annoy, and other voices bellow frighteningly. Strangely enough, many would-be leaders think that the voice that counts is one that sounds like thunder. It is not.

A commanding voice that shakes the rafters may be desirable for an auctioneer. It obviously is not essential for personal leadership. A booming voice may be a handicap if it commands rather than leads.

A voice that makes people sit up and take notice does demand attention—so does a blaring radio. The radio noise can be lowered by turning a knob, but it is not so easy to tune down the other fellow's insistent voice. A loud voice is too insistent; it intrudes. It yells orders, instead of giving instructions or asking co-operation.

The person who has a booming voice should weigh every word before he utters it, for loud words sound more commanding than may have been intended. A shouting voice sounds compelling—but the leader should impel. Shouts grab involuntary attention—but the leader should win voluntary attention.

The leader's voice should be loud enough to be heard and no louder.

Leadership sometimes is helped by a soft voice, so soft that the other person has to listen closely to hear. This is the "whispering strategy." Skilled salesmen use this, lowering their voices and talking confidentially. The other person has to exert himself to hear and becomes actively involved. This whisper strategy draws people closer together; whereas shouting puts distance between them. Did you ever hear people shouting to make love?

Wonders can be accomplished by voice training. Caruso and Melchior, world-famous tenors, both started as baritones. They raised their voices to the higher pitch through training. Sarah Bernhardt changed her thin, high-pitched voice to one with resonant, deep quality. Brahms, the short, squat musician, was a timid youth, self-conscious about his squeaky voice. He deliberately talked in a gruff manner to change the quality of his voice. He succeeded but ruined his good singing voice forever, and his speaking voice became rough and unpleasant.

The following qualities need to be watched in leadership voice training.

Helpful	*Harmful*
pleasant tone	annoying tone
enthusiasm	spiritless expression
clear pronunciation	mumbling
inflection	monotone
confidence	hesitance
earnestness	languidness
moderate tone	loudness
rhythm and phrasing	wordsruntogether

Voice instructors train some businessmen in those helpful voice and speech qualities. Eleanor Roosevelt took such training after she was in the White House. Here are some of the rules these instructors teach.

1. Move the lips more when speaking, to improve enunciation.
2. Talk from the front of the mouth and with the tip of the tongue. This relaxes vocal cords and gives the voice a more pleasant quality.
3. Talk at the same time from the stomach, not from the throat. This gives a deeper tone. (Brahms made the mistake of talking from the throat and ruined his voice box.)

4. Practice humming "mmmm-mm-m" and "nnnn-nn-n" through the nose, to develop resonance.

5. Practice saying "yes" with as many meanings as possible. This improves expressiveness. You can make "yes" mean approval, scorn, doubt, irritation, and even "no."

6. Emphasize *key phrases*, as Lincoln did, to help *win attention* and make instructions *clear*. (Read that sentence aloud, emphasizing the words in italics. You will be astounded at the difference it makes.)

7. Give emphasis occasionally by making the voice softer. That is a method public speakers and salesmen use to make listeners sit on the edge of their chairs. It is a form of the whisper strategy.

8. Talk in phrases – as this illustrates – with a brief pause – after each phrase. Phrasing makes it easier – for others to follow you – and helps you – think ahead. It also makes it easier – for a stenographer – to make accurate notes – of your dictation.

9. Raise the voice on the last few words before you stop speaking. This has an electrical effect on listeners, whether they number one hundred or one.

10. Keep cigars, chewing gum, tobacco, pencils, hairpins, and what-not out of the mouth when talking. Besides causing mumbling, things in the mouth force the talking back into the throat, where it should not be.

Give up the idea of a booming, commanding voice. A pleasant, clear, enthusiastic voice helps leadership.

Lasting leadership comes from impelling people to want to follow. The impelling leader:

Arouses constructive emotions in others
Guides others to decide for themselves
Shares his responsibilities with others
Gives others credit and encouragement
Sets a model for others to imitate
Plants ideas for others to develop
Uses few "don'ts"
Keeps himself likable
Takes co-operation for granted
Considers what the other person wants
Lets others make the first move
Can take a hint as well as give one

9 ▪ Practice in Personal Leadership

Most people apparently do not improve their leadership after they are five years old. It is a teaching of psychoanalysis that a person's ways of handling others is "set" by the time he is five.

Childish methods of leading (coercing and order giving) predominate among adults because they take those ways for granted and have not tried to learn better ones. A few people, whose parents had exceptional wisdom in handling children, learn the mature ways of leading (teaching or inspiring). But adult leadership as a rule is just "obeying the impulse"—and the impulse is usually a childish one. At age thirty-five, you handle people as you did at five and may boss like a child instead of leading like a man.

Leadership has to be learned. There is no innate idea of the best way to lead people.

Some people seem to be "born leaders" because they were lucky as youngsters and were started leading others in a way that makes others want to follow. These young leaders have more practice month by month in leading—while others have more practice as followers.

Charles H. Percy, who became president of Bell & Howell Company at the age of twenty-nine, is a good example of practice in leadership. He started his career at the age of five, selling magazines. This was not for boyish fun; it was a necessity. He had other boys working for him when he was eight, thus gaining practice handling others. Through most of his years in grade school, he captained his grade baseball team—more practice leading others. In high school, he supervised distribution of a newspaper in his suburb and ran a parking lot nights. He started college with savings of $50; yet went through and actually made money by using his experience in leadership to organize a purchasing agency for fraternity supplies.

When he became company president, though only twenty-nine, he had some twenty-four years' experience in business and in leading others—more leadership experience than many of his executives, whose average age was almost twice his.

People learn to lead by leading intelligently. Bossy people have practice in bossing, not in leading. Practice is essential to develop leadership, but the practice should be in the qualities and strategies that really help leadership. If you merely follow your natural impulses, you may be leading like a five-year-old.

The leadership practices in which many young executives have most experience are often wrong. Patrick C. Farbro made a study of the *mis-conceptions* about methods of leading that were held by 224 supervisors and engineers in one manufacturing plant, which is better than most plants. Most of these men were college graduates, in their early thirties, with only a few years of supervisory experience. They had no special training in leadership. They had picked up their own ideas about how to handle people—probably before they were five. Many of these ideas were in favor of methods that cause trouble for both leader and business. This list shows the percentages of these technical men who held the following *wrong ideas of handling people*.

55 per cent thought it undesirable to put plates on each important piece of equipment to show its value and cost of operation.

48 per cent thought it undesirable to ask employees to recommend acquaintances for positions.

43 per cent believed gripes about other workers are more likely to be true than gripes about working conditions.

37 per cent thought it desirable to fine workers for violating rules.

33 per cent did not believe that the way a worker is treated by fellow workers will probably determine whether he likes his work or not.

33 per cent did not believe it was a sign of poor leadership on their part if a worker went over their heads with a complaint.

32 per cent thought it undesirable to assume responsibility for employees' health.

31 per cent believed no honest worker would go on strike against a company that pays a good wage.

28 per cent thought it desirable to make an example of one worker to prevent trouble with others.

27 per cent believed that the best way to have rules obeyed is to put plenty of teeth in them.

26 per cent did not believe that knowing about an employee's home life is a great help in selecting the right person for a responsible job.

26 per cent thought it undesirable to arrange monthly cost reports so as to give recognition to a department with a good record.

25 per cent believed that if a man is capable of doing a good job he will be interested in it without stimulation from his supervisor.

24 per cent thought it undesirable to explain the duties and responsibilities of their jobs to the workers under them.

23 per cent thought it undesirable to ask workers to comment about the way the company treats them.

22 per cent believed that the usefulness of the product he makes is of little concern to the average employee.

21 per cent believed that the kind of job a person holds has little effect on his social standing.

21 per cent believed that sympathizing with workers' difficulties only encourages complaints.

20 per cent thought it desirable to tell inefficient workers to get busy or get out.

18 per cent thought it desirable to prohibit conversation between workers on routine jobs.

17 per cent thought it undesirable to transfer a dissatisfied but capable worker to another job.

14 per cent did not believe a supervisor is a misfit unless he has the confidence and loyalty of his workers.

14 per cent thought it undesirable to make efforts to smooth out personal dislikes among their workers.

13 per cent thought it undesirable to ask workers for suggestions before setting up an important project.

11 per cent thought it undesirable to teach some responsible worker how to handle the supervisor's job.

Each of the notions in that list is incorrect. The percentage of misinformation in their "innate ideas" about leading employees is dangerously high in some items. These men's technical training in the stresses and strains of materials had not enlightened them on the stresses and strains in human nature. Their empathic index was low.

What a person thinks shows what he will do or will be used to justify what he has done. That is why ideas of handling people are significant. In building personal leadership, it is vital to learn by reading about methods of creative leadership and then to practice the right methods. Many try to lead, but few succeed because they follow wrong hunches in handling others. It is not safe to assume leadership without first studying about it.

— —

The Gist of the Chapter

1. Why does it help if the leader sets an example?
2. Compare imitation and suggestibility.
3. When are indirect orders most useful? Why?
4. Describe role playing and its uses.
5. What are the advantages of waiting for the other person to make the first move?
6. Discuss "psychological moments."
7. Outline qualities the leader should watch in his voice.
8. What rules do voice instructors usually emphasize?
9. Who says that most people do not improve their leadership after they are five years old, and what significance does it have for the ambitious individual?

Things to Do and Problems to Discuss

1. Report instances you have observed where leaders got results by setting an example that was imitated.
2. Recall ten different direct orders you have been given, and write them in a column on the left side of a sheet of paper. Then write beside each order how it could have been given indirectly, or by suggestion, or as a question.
3. Consider five people you know only fairly well, and report what you have noticed as their soft spots. Point out how they might be led through these.
4. Consider some supervisor or executive you have known. Check through the list of misconceptions about handling people given at the close of this chapter, and estimate which of these misconceptions this leader had.
5. You see signs that another worker may be taking company materials home for his own use. What should you do about it? How could you apply the

points in this and the preceding chapter in such a case? What difference would it make if you were an executive?

6. Review the Primary Personal Interests from Chapter 9, and discuss how they would give keys to discover another person's soft spots.

7. Take up again the problems of Phyllis M. and Effie K., from the close of the preceding chapter, and work them out in the light of the present chapter.

8. It is World Series week, and you have important work to do. One of the employees near you has brought a portable radio to the office and is listening to the game. How could you handle this distracting situation?

9. You are chief of the invoice section. Some employees in shipping are by-passing their chief to talk over problems directly with you. Discuss ways in which you could use the points in this chapter to get them to go through the correct organization channels.

10. Look back over the projects and problems given earlier in the book. Report which ones called for role playing. Also pick out some that could have been answered by role playing, and try them that way.

11. At last Effie K. is beginning to show signs of promise, and you feel it would help her to read a certain business book. What impelling strategies could you use to get her really to want to read the book?

12. New tax laws force you as chief accountant to ask for overtime work in setting up new records. What impelling strategies could you use with your workers?

13. When Oswald J. left for his vacation, he said to his workers: "Now don't turn out more work than while I am here, or they'll think I'm no good as a supervisor." Production hit a new record while he was gone. Discuss.

14. In view of imitation and suggestibility, discuss why it is valuable for a young person to start with a boss who is a good teacher and leader. How would you determine whether or not it would be wise to copy his methods and strategies?

15. "When I want to be sure people remember something, I say it in a whisper so they will think it is gossip." Discuss.

23 ■ GROUP CO-OPERATION
IN BUSINESS LIFE

_ _ _ _ _ _ _ _ _ _ _ _ _ _ _ _ _

WHAT THIS CHAPTER IS ABOUT

1. *Co-operative motives can be induced*
2. *The feeling of belonging to a group*
3. *Group feeling helps production*
4. *Why people link with certain groups*
5. *The power of groups over individuals*
6. *The problem of crushes and chums*
7. *Cliques in communities and in business*
8. *Geography, occupation, and social status in forming cliques*
9. *Group folkways in business*
10. *Mores put teeth in folkways*
11. *The power of group taboos*

1 ■ Co-operative Motives Can Be Induced

Some executives like to describe their departments as "just one big family," or as "a team." Sometimes the description is correct, and it could be correct in many more instances.

An example of one way a leader can make the situation favorable for teamwork was demonstrated by Dr. Martin Grossack. He had ninety young women, all high school graduates, working in teams of five persons.

These teams shared a common goal: To find a useful answer to a human-relations problem, similar to many of the problems at the close of the chapters of this book. They worked out the problem by writing memos and suggestions to each other. Production was measured by the quality of their final solution.

But Dr. Grossack had motivated some of the girls to be *individually competitive* by secretly telling them they would be rewarded for the quality of their own individual solutions. Other girls were secretly told their reward would be based on the decision reached by the team—*co-operative motivation*.

Could these secret instructions influence their co-operativeness? Definitely yes, as the chartoon on page 405 shows.

There was also a difference in the way the girls worked. The memos written by those with the induced co-operative motivation were more

Offered GROUP incentive	Offered INDIVIDUAL incentive

Started with a
co-operative
attitude

82%

23%

Experiment by Dr. Martin M. Grossack

When merely told that group work counted, more of them were co-operative.

relevant to the problem and offered more real solutions. The memos of these girls invited more interactions toward themselves. Their work was definitely more co-operative—not every girl for herself.

It is worth noting, in addition, that the girls with the induced co-operative attitudes received more co-operation from the other girls, even from those who had been motivated to be individually competitive. This illustrates our old acquaintance, the Principle of Reciprocal Action.

Results have been found to be much the same when the work was mostly a muscular activity. This is illustrated by an ingenious "bottleneck experiment" devised by Dr. Alexander Mintz. When the experimenters worked selfishly they caused traffic jams in the experiment.

Each person held a string which had a cone tied to the other end. The cones were dropped into a large glass bottle. Then water was slowly let into the bottom of the bottle. The participants, who stood around the bottle in a circle, tried to fish their cones out before the rising water touched the cones.

Quick action was needed, co-operation, too, because only one cone could be pulled through the bottleneck at a time. If several tried to pull their cones out regardless of the others, there was a cone jam—as happens when three automobiles try to get through a stop intersection at the same time.

In one set of trials, the people were offered individual rewards if they got their cones out dry. What resulted is shown in the column on the left of this chartoon—they produced traffic jams in three-fourths of their trials. When motivated to look out for No. 1, they pulled strings foolishly—"Me first" behavior.

But other groups were told at the start that it was a test of co-operation; there were no individual rewards. As the missing column on the right indicates, there was not a single traffic jam when a co-operative attitude had been induced.

Dr. Mintz tried to cause traffic jams in the co-operatively motivated groups by having accomplices shout and swear excitedly. But this distraction did not cause any jams.

Such findings give grounds for believing that the co-operativeness of a group depends to a large extent upon the cues they have picked up, especially from their leaders. The cues may be given intentionally, by planting the idea of a big, co-operative family and teamwork. They are also often given without an individual realizing it—and in the wrong

Experiment by Dr. Alexander Mintz

Not a single "traffic jam" at the bottleneck when they were motivated for group teamwork.

direction—if the boss himself is not a co-operative person, if he does not delegate, if he does not let the workers plan, and if he does not give credit.

We can get a more practical understanding of how co-operativeness can be induced by reviewing some of the characteristics of groups, and the forces that groups exert on individuals.

2 ■ The Feeling of Belonging to a Group

"Where do you work?" is a favorite question when one is making conversation with strangers. They don't ask about the kind of work—just where.

One person will answer, "Over on the southwest side." That answer shows no pride in job, nor spirit for the company. The person may have some group spirit about where he works, but it is not strong enough to mention in casual talk.

"I work in the accounting department," another says without mentioning the name of the company. That answer indicates some pride in the accountant's vocation, but it makes one suspect that his loyalty is stronger toward the department than the company.

"I work with the XYZ Corporation," a few others answer. That shows more group spirit, since it suggests that they feel themselves part of the entire company, not just a cog in one department.

Of all the persons who were asked, "Where do you work?" not one has yet said, "For the best company in the country." The first time that answer is received, the man's boss will be sent an orchid or a box of cigars.

People need to feel accepted, to feel that they belong to a congenial group of which they are proud. This feeling of kinship is encouraged from earliest memories of home, and people want it to continue through life. They want to be accepted uncritically, for what they are, by those around them.

Some six hundred years ago, Petrarch (*pee*-trark), the poet laureate of Rome, wrote: "An absolute solitude is contrary to human nature." The loneliness of housework and of one-worker offices reflects the need for congenial companionship. Those few people who deliberately become hermits are presumed to be slightly queer.

When a person is not accepted by a group, it is a severe blow to his self-esteem and mental health. The person who is kept on the outside looking in almost always reverts to childish behavior. His efficiency suffers, and he becomes un-co-operative or downright troublemaking.

In the General Motors Corporation contest, "My Job and Why I Like It," 48 per cent of the employees said: "Because of the co-operation and team spirit of my fellow workers." Only 8 per cent mentioned the opportunity to enjoy the benefits of the free-enterprise system; only 2½ per cent mentioned the recognition given seniority. Group feeling is highly valued by the individual.

You belong to many groups but perhaps do not realize it. You feel that you belong to the state in which you live or the one where you were born. But you also feel that you belong to a region, such as New England, the Deep South, or the West Coast. You also feel that you are part of the country, a very large group.

But usually you feel more keenly that you belong to a smaller group, close at hand. Thus you may feel more a part of your suburb or ward than you do of the state or region. The feeling of being a part of a group is still stronger toward your immediate neighborhood or card club or perhaps work group—unless you unfortunately have been repulsed by some of these close-at-hand groups.

A group does not need to be organized with dues, officers, membership cards, and such trappings. Most small groups are not organized. They are just a collection of like-minded people who gravitate toward one another and who become more like-minded every week. Chums, pals, and buddies are examples of such unorganized groups.

You say "we" when speaking of groups to which you feel you belong, such as family, lodge, or pals. Of other lodges or churches, you say "they," for you feel an outsider with them. To some people, the company where they work is "we"; to others it is "they." Whether workers say "we" or "they" depends partly on the individual's group spirit, partly on the company's organization and policies.

3 ▪ Group Feeling Helps Production

Giving an individual a reward, or bonus, for meritorious work does not inspire group feeling. When the reward goes to the group, however, the reward is an incentive for co-operative work toward a group goal. Slight as this difference may seem, it makes great differences in the results. Dr. Morton Deutsch made a series of measurements of these differences.

Teams were made up of men of about equal ability and preparation. They were put to work on problems in mathematics and in human relations. Records were kept on the quality of their work, their work methods, and their work spirit for a five-week period. Here is a summary of the findings—the figures are index numbers, not percentages.

	Amounts Co-operative Groups Excelled
Working methods	
Following each other	319
Co-ordinating their efforts	259
Working systematically and in an orderly way	197
Being aware of where they are headed	181
Accepting each other's ideas	135

	Amounts Co-operative Groups Excelled
Working spirit	
Working together	255
Feeling obligation to others	217
Desiring to win respect of others	195
Being attentive to each other	127
Having friendly attitude	107
Work results	
Better quality of work	188
Understanding of work	148
Increase in effectiveness in 5 weeks	132

The teams that had not been inspired for group activity did excel in two characteristics. (You are welcome to these, if you want them.)

Difficulty in getting ideas across to others	166
Desire to excel other members	225

Many jobs require teamwork. A team of three girls ironed sheets on a power mangle. The team on one mangle was slow, and the girls complained of fatigue—because one girl on their team was a "sore thumb" who did not fit in with the other two. She was transferred to hand ironing, and a more acceptable girl put in her place on the mangle team. Fatigue disappeared at once, and output jumped. The shifted girl had the aptitude for the mangle, but she did not fit in with that particular team. Result: friction rather than teamwork.

Even when teamwork is not required, the presence of a congenial group is stimulating. Individuals may work independently and in comparative silence; yet they receive a lift from the mere presence of "their kind of people." This is the power of social facilitation.

New workers should be placed with bench mates or office mates who seem congenial. The supervisor should check closely the first few days to see whether the newcomer is fitting in with the immediate group around him. It often helps to ask the ringleader of the group to take the new employee under his wing and see that he gets started right.

Every small group has a spokesman or ringleader, and the executive should work through these unofficial leaders. There is better teamwork for the bigger cause when the spokesman feels that he has a part in decisions that involve his group. The spokesman may not be the type the executive would choose, but he is the one the group chooses to follow.

People work better in a congenial group partly because they want to make a good impression on this spokesman. But, if these spokesmen think that workers should restrict their output, the workers will do so, even at the loss of piece-rate earnings.

The presence of a group normally increases working spirit and effort. When it does not, something is wrong with the spokesman and the attitude he has set for the group to imitate. The executive must spot all these informal groups and their spokesmen. The leverage for changing group attitudes comes from changing the clique leader's outlook. We shall hear more about this shortly.

4 ■ Why People Link with Certain Groups

Mutual admiration. All workers are organized, whether they belong to unions or not. Mutual admiration and the craving for congenial companionship draws them to many others to form spontaneous groups. Admiration is the dominant factor in forming lodges, card clubs, women's societies, and such. Groups organized around mutual admiration touch off libido yearnings. Members of these groups experience an expansion of feelings that are associated with the preservation of the race. They may become as fluttery as young lovers at their meetings.

Mutual resentment. Other groups are formed because of mutual resentment. This is a dominant factor in forming gripe sessions, reform societies, anti-this-and-that clubs. These groups are drawn together from rebellion at stern parents, unappreciative bosses, or the difficulties of making a go of life. The mutual-resentment groups touch off the mortido or death impulses of the members. These groups form, not from liking each other, but from hating something together. Hate, destructiveness, criticism are increased—even toward their own members, as shown in the rapid turnover of their spokesmen.

The strife within resentment groups adds to the members' frustrations and thereby increases the need to act violently. That is why resentment groups produce trouble for everyone and make few real gains for anyone. They feed on their own mortido.

5 ■ The Power of Groups over Individuals

Whether an admiration or a resentment group, all groups have some common powers over individual members. Many workers turn down promotions because that would remove them from their group circles. Speedy workers hold back so that a less proficient member of the circle will not be shown up as a poor worker. Affiliation with groups alters the course of an individual's life in many ways.

Members of the same groups have a willingness to co-operate with others in the same group. They hold together. Their slogan might be that of the Three Musketeers: "One for all and all for one." The workers' all-spirit is likely to be for only the three who work together west of the drinking fountain, or the four who play cards together during lunch hour, or the two who graduated from the same business college. It is often just three or four against the company—unless the company has fostered wider group spirit that includes all the company.

Dispersed and assembled groups. A midwestern physician was in an automobile accident in New England. No one was injured, but there was considerable property damage. The local constable held the doctor. To make the situation more serious, the physician did not have his driver's license and car-ownership certificate. Did he ask to see a lawyer? Not at all.

He asked to be taken to the village physician. Although the two doctors were total strangers, they belonged to the same craft group. They found that they both belonged to the same ritualistic lodge, too, and so did the justice of the peace. The Midwesterner was let go, without bond, on his own recognizance. Groups, like blood, are thicker than water.

The physicians belonged to the same *dispersed groups.* Although widely separated geographically, they felt kinship in their profession and lodge. This gave them a willingness to co-operate, even when it was necessary to bend a few laws to co-operate. Dispersed groups may have a stronger influence on the individual than *assembled groups* in the same room. Diemakers from two competing firms, for instance, often co-operate better than they co-operate with bookkeepers in their own companies.

The Power of a Group To Keep People from Trusting Their Own Eyes

Per cent of times persons adopted the wrong estimate the group had made:

Original research by Dr. S. E. Asch, while a fellow of the Guggenheim Memorial Foundation

The figures below the vertical bars in this graph indicate the number of persons in the groups. All deliberately gave incorrect answers to see whether they would mislead the newcomer. The data show that people can resist the influence of a group of one or two others. The opinions, however, of a group of three were as overpowering as those of the larger group of sixteen people.

Whether individuals belong to a dispersed group or to a clique from adjacent benches, the feeling of belonging inclines them to think like their group. Members are more likely to be influenced by their group than by company policies. They imitate the clique leader, whom they like, and pick up ideas from him by imitation; whereas the boss's pronouncements and lectures pass in one ear and out the other.

While members within a group think alike, and co-operate eagerly with one another, groups are slow to co-operate with other groups. They live a sort of cat-and-dog existence. They put up with each other but do not pull together. High school clubs and cliques are examples of this careful disregard of other groups. "I like Imogene well enough," a high school girl told her mother, "but I couldn't go to the movie with her because she belongs to another club." Among groups of older people, it is the same. The Rotary service club works to help the city, so does the Kiwanis—but they seldom work together on the same projects. Groups and their members live under a polite truce, not with active co-operation. There is plenty of group spirit, but it is for small groups.

6 ▪ The Problem of Crushes and Chums

How small groups operate to cut across company spirit is well shown by those small and ever-present groups called "crushes," "chums," and "cliques." Let's get acquainted with crushes first.

Crushes. A crush is an infatuation for a person of the same sex. It is usually sudden and shown by a younger person. A crush is more intense and more emotional than mere friendship or admiration or hero worship.

Crushes are most likely to develop when the sexes are separated, as in some boarding schools and offices. Mixed working groups are a preventive. Crushes indicate emotional immaturity and a great need to feel appreciated. They harm group spirit because they set up smaller groups and cause jealousies and gossip that interfere with teamwork. Many spats between women workers are due to jealousy that originated in a crush. Unsigned telltale notes about other workers often are the ambivalent result of an unreciprocated crush.

Where there are younger workers, crushes are to be expected. They usually mean that the persons need fathering or mothering. The supervisor should try to provide that need himself in an unobtrusive way but should not be disappointed if it fails to work. It will not work for the compeller but likely will for the impelling leader. The supervisor needs to be on the watch for crushes and should transfer the person making the advances to a work location where there will be contacts with both sexes.

Crushes usually do not last very long—but they can disrupt group spirit in that brief time.

Chums. Chums are close friends of the same sex. They are intimate friends with whom hopes and secrets are shared. Chumminess develops gradually, while crushes are sudden. A group of chums can be expanded to include three or four people, without jealousy raising its ugly head. Chums may stick together for life, while crushes usually dissolve within a few months. Chums play together, and want to do things together, while crushes want to possess and admire each other exclusively.

Constant companions, buddies, and pals are varieties of chums. The teen years and early twenties are the periods when chumminess is most marked. Chumminess serves a good purpose in individual mental hygiene, for it is a recognition of individuality and personality. Chumminess keeps one from feeling lost in the crowd.

Chumminess can be considered the building block on which the larger mutual-admiration groups are founded. Chumminess can cut across social barriers, and create larger groups that have greater tolerance.

7 ■ Cliques in Communities and in Business

Cliques. Cliques (pronounce it "kleeks") are enlarged groups of chums. There is no intimate sharing of secrets as between chums, but otherwise a clique is just a big group of chums. A clique is seldom bigger, however, than a dozen people.

Crushes, chums, and cliques are all mutual-admiration groups, and often are of the same sex. All are closed corporations; their membership is limited and exclusive. Once cliques have formed, it is difficult to combine them because of this exclusive feeling.

These cliques make it lonesome for people who move to new localities. Since existing cliques are closed corporations, there is no place for a newcomer. The stranger may feel that others are snobbish and take a dislike to everything associated with them. It takes a couple of years for the ice to thaw. If the newcomer belongs to a lodge or church group, the barriers will break down sooner. When a company imports key employees from other localities, special effort should be made to get the new employee and his family into the local swim as early as possible.

Every community is shot through with cliques. The society editor of a newspaper in a city of 10,000 has a card index of more than 300 cliques she has to consider when reporting news of card clubs, cooking societies, and other group activities. Such cliques lessen co-operation for the larger community good, as Dr. Edward L. Thorndike's findings show. He found that the worst records for juvenile delinquency, infant mortality, deaths from typhoid fever, leaving school before graduation, illegitimate births, and such came from cities where there were most organizations of the clique variety. Cliques watch the interests of their cliques and spurn the larger welfare.

Business, too, is loaded with cliques. There are cliques among the most humble workers, and sometimes cliques on the board of directors fight with each other. Dr. H. H. Jennings has found that the sterner the boss, the stronger cliques become in an organization. When employees are not permitted to move around or visit during work hours, more and stronger cliques appear. Thus, rules that are sometimes adopted to break up cliques actually make them more powerful.

Cliques just naturally form even under the best of conditions. Consider a workroom in an electrical-instrument factory, for instance, where twelve operators and two inspectors worked. The operators worked at adjacent benches, four men to a bench, as shown in the accompanying chart.

There were two definite cliques in this small workroom. The three operators on the far side of each bench had different work and different wage rates than Francis, Arthur, and Jeff on the near side of the benches. The inspectors had different work status, too.

Clique A, the larger, included four wiremen on the far side, one inspector, and one solderman. This clique occupied the front of the room and acted as if they felt much superior to the other clique. Clique A gambled together during lunch period. They bought expensive candy, which they shared with one another but did not share with the other clique. Most of the talk was with members of their own clique, and they tried to talk about things superior to the other clique.

Clique B was smaller, and at the back of the room. They stuck together during lunch hour but did not gamble. Occasionally, they would go out after work for an evening together; the other clique refrained from doing this, for they wanted to bolster their attitude of superiority. The men in clique B swapped jobs with one another from time to time, to break the monotony. The other clique did not swap jobs, for they wanted to be different from the boys in the back of the room. The men

Data from Dr. F. J. Roethlisberger

Cliques in one workshop. Explanation in text.

in B bought lots of cheap candy, which was shared only in their clique. Jim ate so much one day it made him sick—of course, no one in the other clique felt sorry for him.

Al was not completely in clique B. He fooled around with Joe continually but was somewhat aloof with the others, who were also reluctant to accept him. Perhaps his relationship was more that of Joe's chum; but, in the chart, the clique circle has been jogged to show that he gravitated toward B.

Arthur, Henry, and inspector William were on the outside looking in on these cliques. They had not formed one of their own. They were apparently lone wolves, not interested in chumminess or clannishness. Inspector William may have felt that the dignity of his position should isolate him from the others. Or geography may have kept these three out of the cliques.

8 ■ Geography, Occupation, and Social Status in Forming Cliques

Geography starts many groups. "A gentleman from Louisiana, suh!" and "A Texan, by gosh!" identify geographic groups. Geography helps start cliques in the office, too. People in the front row of desks feel a kinship that they do not feel toward people in the back row. Geography is an accidental but potent factor in forming loyalties. People who live midway between two large cities have divided loyalties, though they usually identify themselves with the better-known city. The same applies in business geography, as Arthur's and Henry's predicaments show.

Arthur and Henry were at the middle bench. Clique A took in the front bench and spread over to include one man from the middle. Clique B covered the back bench and almost spread to include Al from the middle. Arthur and Henry were left out geographically. Perhaps, instead of being voluntary lone wolves, they were social isolates, who felt hurt because the others did not count them in. Such being the case, it would be easier to build company spirit in Arthur and Henry than in the close members of the closed cliques.

Occupation is sometimes a factor in starting cliques. It can cut across mere geography, as it did in the case of the midwestern physician in the highway accident in New England. Thus the Gregg shorthand writers from various departments may eat lunch together and high-hat the Pitman writers.

Social status within the firm may be a determining factor also. The private secretaries who write Gregg may have lunch together but not with the general stenographers, although they write Gregg, too.

Some outstanding personality may determine the formation of a clique. One group likes to gather around peppy Vivian from the central file room. Or the group of serious young workers look up to Emil, because he has a helpful attitude in showing them new technical developments.

Belonging to a clique makes the individual feel happier and probably helps his mental health. But it is likely to be a handicap for his future advancement. The clique limits his range of acquaintance and sources of information. The clique mind is a single-track mind. The clique causes overconfidence and too quick self-satisfaction. Today's fun may come with the clique, but future advancements involve larger groups.

9 ▪ Group Folkways in Business

An American clock manufacturer sent one of his best branch managers to open up business in China. Since the big market for clocks in the United States came from gift sales, he tried in China to promote their sale as wedding gifts. Chinese merchants were horrified, since it is considered an insult to present someone with a clock in China. The Chinese word for clock sounds very similar to the word for death, and a gift of a clock is looked on as a subtle way of wishing the recipient were dead.

When an American company opened a soda-pop bottling plant in Siam, they had Buddhist priests conduct the opening ceremony and bless the plant. Otherwise, they could not have sold their product.

Strange oriental customs? Not so strange, nor so oriental. Try selling coffee that contains chicory in Chicago. Or try selling coffee without chicory in New Orleans. Might as well try opening church services with "Hail, hail, the gang's all here!"

Some things are "appropriate," and other things are "not appropriate."

Folkways. Folkways is the term used for the routine habits of life that are considered appropriate. They are folks' ways of doing things, which are passed on by groups. An oriental folkway, many thousand years old, makes Chinese eat with chopsticks; whereas our folkway calls for knives and forks. Yet our folkway of using a fork is relatively new. George Washington used a two-tined fork to hold meat while cutting it, but not to raise food to his mouth. Coffee for breakfast in the United States and tea for breakfast in England are folkways. The export manager has to be in step with folkways in many lands; but even inside a country folkways vary, as chicory in coffee varies in different sections of the United States.

Manners, customs, and fashions are folkways. Folkways make people in the same group dress alike. "When in Rome, do as the Romans do" simply means that the wise person follows the folkways of the group he is associating with. People who dress differently or have different manners from one group are on the outside looking in. They strike the group as eccentric if they do not conform; on the other hand, the customs of the group seem senseless to these outsiders. There often is no sense in folkway customs anyway, but they have great power over people.

Many seeming racial differences are nothing more than different folkways.

It is an army folkway to salute officers. In some firms, it is a folkway to call the boss by his first name; in other firms, "Mr." is the folkway.

A folkway among some groups causes them to sneer at the man who follows safety precautions as a fraidy-cat. It is a folkway in other groups to taper off work half an hour before quitting time. In the early days of the steel industry, it was a folkway to take pride in having been employed in many different mills. Folkways cannot be changed by posting notices or listing penalties. Group ways have to be changed gradually and usually through the unofficial clique leader.

10 ■ *Mores Put Teeth in Folkways*

Mores (*mo*-rez) are folkways that have become moral customs. Going to church on Sunday is a moral custom for some, but other groups think that Friday or Saturday is the day to go to church.

Not giving clocks as gifts is a folkway in China; no mores are involved. But having priests open the soda-pop plant in Siam involved mores.

Even within one city, mores vary widely among different groups. In one company, workers feel that they are doing a good deed when they punch the time clock for tardy or absent friends. In another firm, workers think it right to appropriate company tools and materials for their own use at home. Exaggerated claims are considered proper in some sales organizations. Until Wanamaker and Macy stores were started, the mores allowed businesses to charge all they could get, prices varying from one customer to the next.

Like manners, mores change from generation to generation, reflecting changed group attitudes and evaluations. Recall the shifts you have observed toward divorce, lipstick, and women's smoking in public. Shifts in mores usually are made slowly, unless speeded up by some emotional reformer. Dueling took several generations to become obsolete. It took a couple of hundred years for women's smoking to become approved, and it is still under taboo by many groups.

11 ■ *The Power of Group Taboos*

A *taboo* (ta-*boo*) is a restriction on conduct, imposed by group membership. Taboos are prohibitions. They are closely related to mores, though not always. There are millions who will not eat beef because the cow is their sacred animal. Some groups are vegetarians for religious reasons, others for esthetic reasons.

Many taboos have concerned women. Elizabeth Blackwell was the first woman to attend medical school, and the men students objected. Women drew their skirts to one side as they passed her on the street.

No boardinghouse would serve her meals. Was that back in the Middle Ages? She received her medical degree in 1848. Blackwell Hall at Hobart College is named in her honor now. Taboos do change.

But taboos, or "the times," change slowly. Dr. Bertha Van Hoosen was appointed professor at the University of Illinois medical school in 1894. She was thirty-one, a woman, and redheaded. The students expressed the taboo they felt for women medicos by refusing to attend her clinic. But Doctor Bertha was a practical psychologist as well as a skilled surgeon. From North Dakota she imported a rare case, the like of which had never been seen in Chicago. She paid the expenses of the pathetic patient herself. Word of this rare case spread through the hospital like a prairie fire. Students left other classes, deserted laboratories and gray-bearded male professors, to see the demonstration of this rare condition. For three hours, her clinic was the liveliest place in town. The redhead had buried their taboo against "hen medics" in the avalanche of their curiosity.

Taboos kept women out of office work until 1862, when a central New York State banker, General Francis E. Spinner, was United States Treasurer. His office staff trimmed paper money by hand. About twenty men were employed in this work, but the man-power shortage during the Civil War produced a labor shortage. General Spinner obtained Lincoln's permission to hire Jennie Douglas to cut paper money. She became the first woman government office employee. In October of the same year, seven other women went to work cutting and counting money. The taboo was disappearing because of the crisis.

Taboos that are imposed by groups are deeply impelling in their influence over conduct. The prohibition a company tries to impose against smoking lacks the force of a taboo, because it comes from outside the group. Don'ts from the boss are about as effective as laws against mountaineer moonshiners. But a don't from the group has the force of a command direct from heaven. A don't posted on the bulletin board is not a taboo—it is an irritation to be evaded.

Some of the bloodiest labor strife has been the result of bulletin-board attempts to impose taboos. Pullman's industrial city was a model for its day; yet soon after completion it was the scene of a frightful strike. Taboos in the use of buildings, which Pullman tried to impose autocratically, were the cause of the trouble and changed the workers in the model homes into a resentment group.

Many company policies amount to artificial taboos. Unwritten taboos, not in the book of rules, usually are accepted better. For example, a man with an agency that advertises one make of automobile, like everyone else in the agency, may not dream of owning a competing make.

The introduction of new products often is slowed down by public taboos. It took Gillette five years to sell the first seven safety razors.

The safety razor was under taboo because it was considered sissy. Enormous expenditures for advertising are necessary to change taboos. Many good products died a-borning because the company did not have funds for enough advertising to change the taboo against change.

Taboos related to business practices often are crystallized through trade or professional associations. Codes of ethics are examples. Taboos that originate in such associations usually have more power over individual behavior and thinking than government laws. This is because the trade-association taboos come from one's own group; whereas laws are imposed autocratically by others.

Folkways, mores, and taboos are accepted uncritically by group members as "fitting and proper." These customs of doing and thinking often are harmless among mutual-admiration groups but may be loaded with danger in mutual-resentment groups.

In the next chapter we shall examine the bearing of such group forces on understanding group conflicts and building spirit for a larger group.

———————————————————————————

The Gist of the Chapter

1. Describe what Dr. Grossack and Dr. Mintz found about the effects of induced co-operativeness.

2. What are the groups to which a person is likely to feel a kinship?

3. Tell what Dr. Deutsch found about the effects of group feeling on production.

4. What are the differences between admiration and resentment groups?

5. Discuss the findings and significance of Dr. Asch's experiments on judging the length of lines.

6. Give an account of chums and crushes.

7. What are cliques, and what was their influence in the electrical-instrument factory?

8. Describe the factors that are influential in forming cliques.

9. Give illustrations of folkways.

10. How are mores related to folkways?

11. Discuss taboos.

Things to Do and Problems to Discuss

1. List, and briefly describe, the groups with which you are identified, whether by choice or by accident.

2. Describe some mutual-admiration group you have been able to observe, and compare it with some mutual-resentment group. Look for ways in

which they are alike and the ways in which they are different. Compare their influences over their members.

3. Think of some group with which you are well acquainted, and report on the folkways and taboos the group sanctions.

4. Report on some differences in folkways in various regions of the United States that should be considered when (a) setting up branch plants, and (b) in national advertising campaigns.

5. Geography (propinquity) is an accidental factor in determining some group affiliations. Discuss this in relation to the forces that mold friendly attitudes, given in Chapter 14.

6. The former custodian in your department was a hail-fellow. The employment office has sent you a quiet, dignified applicant for the job. Discuss whether the applicant might fit the group's idea of what the custodian should be like.

7. A delegation of workers comes to you, the personnel director. They ask that several of them who belong to the same church be shifted so that they can work together in the same department. Discuss what you think of the plan, and also leadership methods you could use in handling such a touchy situation.

8. A clique in the receiving room is starting to cause trouble. At an executive conference, it is suggested that a couple of unpopular workers be put into this department to break up the clique. Discuss the possible effects and other methods that could be used.

9. Oswald J. has been promoted again. Most of his evening friends have been people he will now supervise. Should he spend evenings with them as he did before the promotion? What else should he do now with his evening time in view of his new responsibilities?

10. What effect will it likely have on group co-operativeness in case the boss has one or two "pets" in the group?

11. Recall from an earlier chapter that a three-person group is likely to break up into a twosome plus an outsider. With that in mind, discuss the three-girl teams operating the mangle.

12. Effie K. says the new supervisor is uncouth and not a gentleman, because he never says "God bless you" when someone in the office sneezes. She is really worked up over this. How can you explain her feelings in terms of the folkways she has picked up?

13. Your firm is being sued. You have information which you picked up from a fellow club member which would win the lawsuit for your employer. Would you tell your employer and risk having the fellow club member being called to the witness stand? Would it make any difference whether you were an executive or an assembly worker?

14. How could the information in this chapter be used to cut down the use of company telephone lines for personal calls?

15. A question or two in most of the earlier chapters present situations in which group forces should be considered. Check back and pick out a few of these questions, then reconsider them in the light of the present chapter.

24 ■ GROUP SPIRIT
AND GROUP CONFLICTS

_ _ _ _ _ _ _ _ _ _ _ _ _ _ _ _ _

WHAT THIS CHAPTER IS ABOUT

1 ■ The Leader Should Create Larger Groups

Richard Weil, Jr., former president of Macy's, New York, said: "We are a nation of joiners, and our identifications with special groups within the total community are as much evils as they are blessings."

Business has a big stake in these group feelings, because business is group activity. In addition, the individual worker and his motives can be understood only in his relationship to the group of which he feels a part. The world is not the same for any two people. The cliques and groups with which they associate are an influential part of their worlds. Since people associate with different groups, they as good as live in different worlds.

These groups may be spontaneous cliques of workers inside the company, or they may be organized groups on the outside. Whatever the group, its members tend to think alike and to have similar loyalties.

Company spirit requires executives who can weld the loyalties of small groups into a feeling of membership in one large company group. It is a central task for every executive, from the greenest lead-man to chairman of the board. Remember, the central task of the executive is to maintain the organization. Loyalties divided into small groups produce no more company spirit than a person would have for the tourist camp in which he spent a night.

Building the cohesion of a large group is no easy assignment. Modern business specialization of work inclines workers to form small groups. The accountants consider themselves apart from the secretaries, and so on with other differences in occupations. Labor turnover and temporary employees cut down spirit for the larger group. Migrant laborers and vagabond craftsmen seldom have any company spirit. They are not with any firm long enough to be assimilated into the larger group. There is seldom company spirit if a firm has high labor turnover or seasonal operations.

Population shifts also have increased the difficulty of welding large groups. Workers used to live under the shadow of the company building and could walk leisurely to work. Today, they come from many different home towns. The five who ride in together from Pulaski township do not look on the carful from Pleasant township as "our kind of people." These many wheels within wheels give rise to company politics, for each small geographical group tries to increase its prestige and belittle other groups.

2 ■ The Rise of Prejudices

Trouble comes when one group rubs elbows with a group that has different folkways. As soon as people notice that other groups are different, they begin to feel a bit insecure about their own group. To protect their "rightness," they assume that other groups are wrong or inferior or are cheats. The louder the condemnation of others, the "righter" they feel about the traditions they have unthinkingly adopted.

Prejudices are unwarranted dislikes or distrust of the folkways, mores, and taboos of other groups. Prejudices are group-protecting opinions, and prejudices are likely to cause trouble. People have an affinity for those who have the same prejudices.

Groups organized around mutual resentment have the most marked prejudices. But prejudices are found also in mutual-admiration groups. One card club talks disparagingly about the playing abilities of another card club, and so on.

Gossip and intolerance are caused by prejudices and are worse when conditions give rise to resentment groups. The gossip and intolerance are directed both against the harshness and the ideals and folkways of the other group. Groups are attacked, not by physical force, but by attempts to destroy their ideals and prevent them from reaching their goals.

3 ■ Smear Words in Group Conflict

Smear words are unpleasant expressions used to disparage the ideals or individuals of other groups. Examples are "double-crosser," "four-flusher," "mugwump," "high-brow," "low-brow," "squealer," "monopolist," "slacker," "hen medic," "scab," "bureaucrat." They are strong words that reveal the prejudices of groups. By pinning a repulsive label on others, prejudices are made to seem tangible. Smear words, of course, increase intolerance and produce group friction rather than co-operation. They also produce a feeling of guilt within some people who use them in the heat of conflict. Sometimes, they are called "snarl" words, in contrast to "purring" or "tail-wagging" words. They are not the kind of words you would use with a customer.

Group thinking and the resulting prejudices tend to emphasize the weakness of people in other groups. Calling the other group names is an expression of this prejudice. Even ladies call names when group rivalries are aroused.

4 ■ "Scapegoating" in Group Thinking

"Scapegoating" is blaming other groups when the going gets rough. The responsibility is pinned on others. The idea of letting someone else take the punishment is very old. In ancient times, despotic rulers kept a whipping boy to take the abuse their subjects heaped upon rulers. When citizens were displeased with something the monarch had done, the whipping boy would be lashed to let the people feel their complaints had been heeded. Everyone felt better, except the boy who got the whipping—and things continued just as they had been.

Scapegoating makes labor blame capital and capital blame the politicians. The political party that is out blames the party that is in—using some choice smear words in the campaign of blame. As with the whipping boy, nothing is solved.

Groups that are envied or feared are natural scapegoats for other groups. The thickheaded school bully tells teacher that the bright little boy put the mouse in her desk. Shop workers make scapegoats of office workers who are paid by the week rather than by the hour. Time-study men often are made scapegoats. The owner's son, who has advantages the rank and file do not have, is in a good position to become a whipping boy, or scapegoat. Minority groups are natural targets for scapegoating. The Nazis used the Jewish people as scapegoats. Communists use Wall Street as a scapegoat. Wall Street uses federal regulations as a scapegoat.

Politicians are past masters with smear words and scapegoating. So are rabble rousers. The impelling leader, in contrast, strives to handle every situation so that there is no call for smearing or scapegoating. There is a lack of spirit for the larger group when smearing and scapegoating occur.

When it is said that a group thinks alike, what is meant actually is that they feel alike toward people and events, for there is not much real thinking in it. As Sir Joseph Porter sings in his hilarious song in *H.M.S. Pinafore:*

> I always voted at my party's call,
> And I never thought of thinking for myself at all.
> I thought so little, they rewarded me,
> By making me the Ruler of the Queen's Navee.

Group feeling often takes the place of individual thinking. Group pressure on thinking—or believing without bothering to think—cramps individual originality. Resentment groups particularly put their stamp ón an individual's thinking.

5 ▪ Redirecting Group Thinking

Redirecting group thinking is really redirecting feeling and imitation.

What a person thinks is "right" or "wrong" is determined largely by the groups to which he belongs, or by which he hopes to be accepted. You can analyze this influence easily in the following chartoon.

To understand why people think as they do, it is necessary to size up the groups of which they are members. They may not be groups that issue membership cards or collect dues, but they are like-minded people who hold together for mutual admiration or mutual resentment. The groups may not have formal meetings on Wednesday evenings, but they feel drawn to each other to share enjoyment or hostility. Being accepted

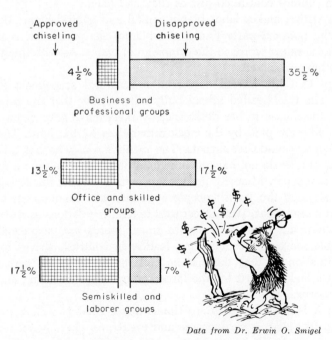

Data from Dr. Erwin O. Smigel

The groups to which they belonged had much to do with how they felt about chiseling on unemployment compensation.

by such a group of "one's kind" gives an expanded feeling and may also expand a person's intolerance and lack of co-operation with other groups.

Taboos, prejudices, and other group thinking cannot be altered by logic or arguments. Criticisms or direct attack on prejudices only harden the cement in them. An individual picks up the thinking of his groups by imitation and suggestibility—uncritically. And only imitation and suggestibility will change him. Since he imitates the clique leader, *the clique leader's thinking has to be changed first.*

The experienced lobbyist, for example, seldom tries to outargue individual legislators. Instead, he gets in the good graces of the party leaders in the state capitol and slowly makes them want to think his way. The others follow the beck and call of the party steersman—like Sir Joseph Porter.

Work through the clique leader, even of the street gang. One Sunday evening, William Lyon Phelps and Ernest Caldwell, two Yale students, walked past a gang of young toughs. One of the toughs hurled an insult at the college dudes. The dudes could not tell which tough made the remark. Caldwell, the stroke of the Yale crew, stopped in his tracks, looked over the gang in a quick glance, picked the biggest fellow, and hit him squarely in the face. Not a word was spoken. Only one blow was struck. The action was so quick and unexpected that the leader was taken by surprise. The clique leader lost his status as a leader in the surprise attack.

That brief street brawl illustrates the principles of handling a gang— or group or committee. *Work on the biggest or most influential member.*

With the more militant groups—those that were started by resentment— still more is required. *The source of the frustration has to be found and cured if possible.* The resentment may be due to unfair treatment, broken promises, financial insecurity, criticism—real or imaginary. It is easier to find the frustrations than to cure them. Often the hostility started against a harsh parent, or a self-seeking boss, twenty years ago. It has now become free-floating hostility. They just have to be hostile toward something or burst. The only thing the executive can hope for in such a situation is to *shift the hostility to some harmless object,* such as the tyranny of men's fashions or the illogical spelling of some words; get them to take part in some crusade against something where hostile attitudes will not affect their daily working attitudes.

The world is jam-packed with group spirit—too much of it, since it is mostly for smaller groups that work at cross-purposes. The executive has to work magic to blend the spirit of many small groups into a bigger company or industry spirit. Diverse religions, races, lodges, trades, neighborhoods, ages, hobbies, departments, and cliques—all put their stamp on the individual. All cause conflicting loyalties.

Executive intolerance or favoritism, criticism or belittling, harshness or arguments, make the divided loyalties stronger. People want to be led.

If the executive fails to impel, then the clique leader keeps the individual's allegiances.

The clique leader of the mutual-admiration group is likely to be the impelling sort. But the clique leader of the resentment group is more likely to be a compeller. The executive has to be a more impelling leader than either to weld the small groups into the spirit of a larger group.

The leader must be sensitive to groups. He must know what groups there are in his organization. He needs to know their folkways, mores, taboos, and prejudices. David Lloyd George, a poverty-stricken lawyer of twenty-five, had ambitions for political leadership. In two years, this obscure Welshman was in Parliament. He won his seat there because he had spent those two years attending more meetings of those groups that were opposed to him than in attending his own party meetings. From a back seat he would study the leaders of opposition groups and analyze their thinking. At fifty-three, he was wartime prime minister. And he married his bewildering blonde secretary.

6 ▪ People Caught Between Group Pressures

A few people are caught between the devil and the deep blue sea, in conflicting group loyalties. The children of foreign-born parents have one set of folkways at home, a different set at school or work. They want to honor their parents' customs, yet want to be accepted by the majority. It is an unsettling experience.

Mixed marriages often grind people between opposing social forces. When people of differing religions, race, nationality, even differing politics or social status are married, the path of true love is made rough by conflicting folkways and mores. One marries not only an individual but also that person's group ideas. It does not always work out so smoothly as with Jack Sprat and his wife.

The farm youth who goes to work in the big city is in a similar conflict. The manners and ideals of farm life are different; so the young person is befuddled to know which set of folkways and taboos is "right." Assimilating the foreign-born is not much more of a problem than absorbing the hillbilly or farm youth who moves to the city. And at present, cities are receiving more farm folk than foreign-born. Their absorption depends largely on the leadership they are given in their new groups—and which group wins their allegiance soonest.

It is always a critical time for the individual when he is displaced from his former groups. Leaving home to go to school, or even moving from one side of the city to another, makes him a displaced person. In his new location, he is on the outside looking in. It will be months before he is accepted by or feels a part of the new groups. This is a strategic time to build his loyalties to the ideals and goals of a larger group. New employees almost always have been uprooted from some of their groups. If company spirit cannot be built in them during the first few months, something is basically wrong.

Remember that group spirit, if left to itself, is likely to be for a small group. Spirit for larger groups has to be built.

7 ■ Get Workers All Together

The sales manager of the CDE Corporation wanted to pep up the sales force and distributors. He decided to have a big jamboree to celebrate the 250,000th widget the company would be making in a few weeks.

News of the celebration leaked through the grapevine to some production supervisors, who liked the idea. When the sales manager learned of their interest, he asked the shop to join the affair. The idea gained momentum for a company-wide celebration, including the workers' fami ies. The personnel manager was all for it and helped get the president's reluctant O.K.

Exhibits were prepared: the first patent, the little shop in which the first widget was made, the early crude widgets, a replica of the 100,000th, enlarged photographs of widgets used during the war, famous buildings equipped with the product, a big map of the world showing the location of foreign distributors. Even the president was amazed at the interesting material from the firm's history.

All employees and families were invited to the display on Saturday during the sales meetings. At eleven o'clock, 800 gathered in a big tent on the parking lot. The mayor and a distributor from Australia spoke briefly. The president unveiled the new model widget. He actually showed some enthusiasm, too. It was the first time most of the employees had heard his voice. Many of them had never seen him before and thought he looked very impressive.

At noon, carts of food and paper plates were wheeled in, and everyone helped himself. The personnel director noticed that the payroll clerks were eating together; so he moved some young engineers from the test room over to eat with them. That was the start of a couple of romances.

"It's hard to understand," the plant superintendent said a week later, "but there has been almost no tardiness since that big shebang Saturday."

"Yeah, and the men are using their protective goggles more," the safety director added. "Guess that exhibit on eye protection made the wives get after their men."

"Why didn't we think of doing something like this before?" the president remarked. He had enjoyed speaking his piece Saturday morning. The personnel director had to pinch himself to be sure that he was not dreaming.

There is nothing like a group rally to rally group spirit. The bigger the group, and the more they are jammed together, the better. An auditorium is not necessary. One Missouri company corrals its total force of some 450 for the last working hour about once a month. They crowd into a corner of the warehouse, on temporary benches, to listen to some celebrity who happens to be in the neighborhood. The talks are not about work or company business. They tried one, by a big banker, on the free-enterprise system; and the workers froze up, because they thought it was just propaganda. Now anything suggesting propaganda is avoided. Sometimes, they have a magician or hillbilly entertainers. The idea is to crowd everybody together for an hour's good time together. As a worker sees the other 449 jammed around him, clique A or clique B fades into the background, and he feels he is part of a larger group.

Many firms have an annual employees' variety show or a Christmas party. A small merchant takes his employees and their families on a picnic in the fall when autumn colorings are at their peak. A small-town banker takes his entire outfit to the city to see the ice show and eat at a ritzy club as a group.

Such assembled groups build group feeling, but once a year is not enough. Four times is the minimum to prevent group awareness from wearing thin between meetings. Anything they enjoy is good for such a meeting. But beware of anything suggesting propaganda.

8 ■ Let Them Participate When They Get Together

The CDE Corporation just gathered them together, to look and eat together at the first meeting. At the next general meeting, honoring ten long-service employees, they had some mimeographed song sheets, company parodies of popular songs. Group singing—like senseless school yells—helps build spirit as people take part in the same group activity.

The group activity may be nothing more than showing hands in answer to a question or laughing together at a joke; yet it does give group spirit a definite lift. Applause, or a seventh-inning stretch, gives all a chance to take part in a small way. A lifeless group meeting is better than none, but it is wiser to have activity in which all can take some part. Encourage them to take part right from the opening bell. One wizard at conducting group meetings does this by asking everyone present to shout "Hello" to him. Seems silly, but it works wonders.

Too often, meetings are called to preach to workers. That puts a cake of ice on group spirit. Letting them take part, by singing, shouting, raising hands, or putting on group stunts thaws them out. Then it is *their* meeting, their group. The individual feels more a part of the group when he moves or acts in unison with the crowd. It is one secret of military drill and the congregation's responses during religious services.

9 ∎ Give Them Some Group Heroes

Business can get further pointers in group spirit from school spirit. Schools have their heroes. It may be a football star of years ago, a scientist who made a discovery in the school, a graduate who became a big shot, or the founders of the school. Groups gravitate toward heroes. Cliques form around small-scale heroes.

The company should supply heroes who represent the entire organization, heroes who will add to the spirit for the entire group. Clique spirit can be replaced by company spirit if a better hero than the clique leader is provided. You cannot replace somebody with nobody.

Steinmetz, the electrical wizard, was a failure as a face-to-face leader. Yet he was worth his 95-pound weight in gold to General Electric Company as a company-spirit-inspiring hero. While Steinmetz was living, many employees said that they worked for Steinmetz' company, not for G.E.

GEORGE M. VERITY
1865 ——— 1942
FOUNDER
THE AMERICAN ROLLING MILL
COMPANY
1899

"ARMCO SPIRIT IS A COMPREHENSIVE
VITAL FORCE WHICH FINDS EXPRESSION
IN THE PRACTICAL APPLICATION OF
POLICIES BUILDED ON A PLATFORM
OF CHRISTIAN PRINCIPLES, IN WHICH
SELFISH PURPOSE HAS NO PLACE"

Courtesy Armco Steel Corp.

A company hero and a philosophy for all employees to see. A statue of the founder, who built a little steel roofing company into a firm with 30,000 employees.

Armco Steel Corporation has erected a statue of George Verity, its founder, where employees can see it and are reminded of the struggles and ideals behind their company. Most firms have pictures of the founders, but these are displayed in front offices where they do little to give the general employees company spirit. The sudden appearance of a few oil paintings complete with bronze plates will not produce an instant spurt in company spirit. Some group gathering, company-wide, should accompany the unveiling. Inspiring stories about these old leaders make their leadership go on and continue to build the company. Sometimes, a dead leader can do more for company spirit than a live one.

The surest way to reduce the influence of smalltime misleaders of group spirit is to build up some big-time heroes in the organization. If no heroes can be resurrected from the past, make some current ones. It may be no more than a company athletic team or singing club, but it will help build spirit for the company, as other employees will enjoy the reflected glory.

10 ■ Let Them See and Know the Brass Hats

College students see the president often, the chairman of the trustees occasionally, and the dean too often sometimes. These brass hats symbolize the organization as a whole, not a department or a fraternity. The mere sight of a top leader reminds the individual that he is part of a larger group.

A long-established military practice calls for the top brass to visit scattered camps and outposts. These are sometimes called inspection trips. Their better purpose is for stimulating spirit for the entire group, which the high-ranking officer symbolizes.

Not enough company presidents and board members walk through plants and offices. This is a primary function of their position, which they cannot delegate to others. The worker sees his clique leader almost continuously. He should see the top men of the company many times a year, not just when something goes wrong. Top officers who stick close to their offices do not build group spirit. They should have adequate secretaries and assistants, so that a couple of hours a day is enough to clear up their office duties.

When Robert W. Johnson, former chairman of Johnson & Johnson, wanted to talk with a man, he did not call him to his penthouse office. The chairman went to the man and talked with him in his own bailiwick. The other fellow felt more at ease in his own department, and more employees got to know the chairman as a fellow worker rather than as an absent figurehead.

It also helps if department heads visit other departments. Bosses of all ranks should get around and get acquainted around.

The president has a dispersed group to lead; whereas the clique leader has an assembled group, the members of which are always within sight of one another. It is easier to build small-group spirit in an assembled group. Seeing the president's name in the newspaper is not a substitute for seeing him in one's own workplace from time to time. Reading what he says on the "President's Page" of the employees' magazine is not so effective for company spirit as hearing his voice right on the job. Meet the clique leader right in his own territory. Win him, and you win his followers.

11 ■ Give Them Some Group Goals and Ideals

Goals and ideals give people something to strive for. They keep workers looking ahead, impelling them to strive ahead. As a group becomes imbued with the same goals and ideals, they are impelled to strive together—that's teamwork.

A young firm may not have many old traditions to talk about, but it should have ideals and goals to describe to each new employee. An old company, on the other hand, may have some traditions it would be better to bury. New employees usually are told how to find their way around the buildings. To build group spirit, the most important part of the workplace to explain is the company's goals and ideals. They are shown the time clock and lockers; they should also be shown the founder's picture and told about the spirit of the family with which they will be spending most of their waking hours during workdays.

Every business has a philosophy of some sort. It may never have been expressed in words, but it has a philosophy that permeates its activities and employees. Goals and ideals express that philosophy. If it has not been put into words, it should be. A few words can express a big ideal. Rotary clubs express their philosophy in just three words: "Service above self."

The 18,000 employees of the Endicott-Johnson Shoe Company expressed their firm's philosophy in a granite archway, which the employees themselves erected. Carved on this archway is: "Home of the Square Deal."

Goals are usually tangible—cutting accidents in half, reducing scrap and wastage, reducing absenteeism, increasing quality. Ideals, however, exist only in the minds of men and women, setting up standards of perfection in virtues and character. Goals can be reached, and new ones created to be reached. Ideals are models that may never be reached.

A five-year plan of expansion is a goal. The company's old heroes may furnish ideals—inspiring thrift, application, perserverance against obstacles. Most companies have goals. A few have ideals.

Ideals are more impelling than goals. The things a company stands for count more in building group loyalty than the things a company does for its employees.

A company's philosophy is engraved on this arch, which was erected by employees on the main highway in the firm's home town.

Cliques seldom supply either goals or ideals. These small groups are held together by mutual admiration of each other or by mutual resentment of other groups. When cliques are given goals, which they accept, the spirit becomes bigger than the clique. When they are given ideals in addition, the widest group spirit is started. Lodges get much of their force from the ideals conveyed by their rituals. The strongest group spirit is shown by religious groups, where ideals predominate.

The people who rub elbows on city streets have no group spirit, because they do not have common goals or ideals. A firm's employees will have little more group spirit than street strangers, unless they are given common goals and ideals. Group co-operation requires a knowledge of, and a belief in, the organization's purposes. *The goals and ideals must not only be known but also believed in.* If the ideals are not acceptable to the rank and file, do not expect much group spirit.

Most leaders who have built up big businesses singlehanded were impelled by ideals and were able to convey their ideals to impel others. William Danforth, for instance, was a sickly boy from Missouri swamps who guided his own life by a four-pronged philosophy. He stood tall (health), thought tall (mental), smiled tall (social), and lived tall (religious).

He took those four ideals into the founding of Ralston Purina Company and into the checkerboard pattern on its packages, buildings, and trucks. The squares of the checkerboard symbolize that foursquare way of living and thinking and dealing. As he was building up the company, he talked personally with each new employee, explaining his and the firm's ideals. He dared the new man to stand tall, think tall, smile tall, and live tall. Each new worker knew the president, and each caught some of the "I dare you" ideals.

Danforth converted $12,000 of borrowed capital, and ideals, into a firm which 65 years later had net current assets worth $120,000,000. Ideals are not just for ministers and do-gooders. Every business needs ideals. People have done more for ideals they believed in than for money they needed desperately.

12 ■ Give Them a Common Enemy

Group spirit is often diluted because groups under the same roof are hostile toward each other. Probably a third of the people in the world have strong hostile streaks (mortido) that narrow their co-operation to a few close friends. Harmless outlets need to be provided for their aggressions.

The drafted soldier has an outlet for them in the enemy—or his sergeant. If his sergeant is a good leader, the aggressions will be directed toward the enemy only. The student has an outlet for his aggressions in athletic contests and other rivalries with other schools.

The members of the clique in the front row may look on the clique in the back as their enemies. Both cliques may consider the chief clerk their common enemy. Average workers may look on speedy workers as enemies who will upset the pay scale. None of these conditions helps spirit for the larger group.

Providing some harmless outlet for individual and group aggressions is essential to build spirit for the larger group. An employee athletic league, properly handled, may drain some of this hostility through aggressive play. Wide-open channels for airing grievances also can help. Competing firms or industries are practical targets, for hostility can be shifted toward them. Parker Pen Company solidifies the spirit of its employees by keeping them posted on the moves of competing companies.

Be thankful for competitors. Keep employees aware of company competition as a solidifying agent for company spirit. Opposition builds spirit. If the opposition is another department, it may build department spirit at the sacrifice of company spirit. But, when the opposition is outside the company, departmental spirit is broadened to become company spirit.

13 ■ What You Can Do

Perhaps you are not yet in a position where you can initiate policies that build company spirit. Perhaps your company does nothing to build spirit. Perhaps your spirit for the company is lukewarm or chilly. But good company spirit will make your work more enjoyable and hasten promotion.

You can apply these principles anyway and increase your own individual spirit for the larger group.

1. Have a wide acquaintance in the company. Get acquainted with employees in other departments and crafts. Perhaps the company does not get everyone together, but you can expand yourself by expanding your acquaintances. Watch lest you get trapped in a narrow clique.

2. Take part in employee activities. Join hobby groups, athletic events, the suggestion system, etc.

3. Find some heroes. Learn the company history and traditions. Find some living heroes among outstanding workmen and inspiring executives. Imitate them.

4. Get to know some of the brass hats, if only from a distance. Follow their doings in the newspapers and trade news. Get to know some of them personally. They are usually flattered by such attention if you do not take much of their time and do not ask favors. It never hurts your chances if they, in turn, know who you are.

5. Learn the company goals and ideals, even though they may not be written. Work for ideals of your own that are in harmony with the best of the company philosophy. Work for ideals as well as for tangible things. Write these ideals out, perhaps as a personal slogan.

6. Keep an eye on competition, not a rival clique but outside competition. Widen your horizon to include more than the company. Take in the business, and the world.

Take down any fence that separates you from others—and keep on reading and using psychology to be a better employee and a better boss.

— — — — — — — — — — — — — — — — —

The Gist of the Chapter

1. What is the significance of the statement that business is group activity?

2. Contrast, and show likenesses, between prejudices, smear words, and "scapegoating."

3. Give three essentials to keep in mind when trying to change group thinking.

4. What is meant by being caught between group pressures, and what is the effect on people caught that way?

5. Tell about the advantages of getting the entire work force together.

6. In what ways does it build spirit if the people themselves participate in joint activities when they get together?

7. How does having some group heroes help group spirit?

8. What is the difference between dispersed and assembled groups, and what difference does it make in handling people?

9. What is the difference between goals and ideals, and how do they compare in value for building group spirit?

10. What can the individual do to keep his group spirit where it should be?

Things to Do and Problems to Discuss

1. Attend some political meeting or trade convention, and report happenings you observed which would help group spirit; also which would harm it.

2. Describe some jobs that illustrate the statement that business is group activity.

3. Eavesdrop on conversations on the bus, in a hotel lobby, or elsewhere. Report on the remarks you heard that expressed smearing, prejudice, or scapegoating.

4. Follow the letters to the editor in a newspaper, and report examples that show (a) group affiliation, (b) scapegoating, (c) smear words.

5. Apply the section on people caught between group pressures to the situation of an employee who wants to do an honest day's work but is under group pressure to stall on the job. What can he do?

6. Apply the material in this chapter to a discussion of gangs of juvenile troublemakers that roam the streets and parks at night.

7. People are influenced not only by the groups with which they are already affiliated, but also by those which they would like to get into. What are some of the groups by whom you would like to be accepted, and in what ways have you changed your behavior and thinking so that it might be possible to be accepted by them?

8. Analyze some rumors you have heard, trying to determine how they show prejudice, smear words, and scapegoating.

9. You have noticed that a member of your office clique pads his expense accounts. Discuss what you should do and the ethics of loyalty to a clique, to the firm, or to your conscience.

10. Consider some company or organization that you know. Analyze what they seem to be striving for, and write a slogan or expression of their philosophy in brief and inspiring form.

11. Executives of a chain-store company are debating whether or not to shift store managers to different locations about every two years. Discuss the pros and cons.

12. An aggressive and hostile labor union has started using a slogan that makes fun of the philosophy and aims of your company. Discuss steps that could be taken to change this situation.

13. Discuss whether workers should praise the company and their boss around the town.

14. Think of some worker whom you know who is extremely lacking in company spirit. Analyze his situation fully, and try to explain why he lacks spirit.

15. A fellow worker is laid up with an illness that will keep him from work

for a long time. The company sickness insurance will take care of him. He has been an isolate in the company. Discuss whether or not you should go out of your way to visit him during his illness.

16. Check back over your answers to the questions from the New York Central System, which were at the start of each part of this book. Change any of your earlier answers. In what ways do these changes indicate that you will be a more efficient worker and a more effective leader for having studied this book?

Index